Praise for
Building a Win-Win World

"Hazel Henderson's lucid and vigorous analysis points to a creative and hopeful future, in which cooperation becomes the most dynamic force in the world economy."
—Harlan Cleveland, President, The World Academy of Art and Science

"At a time when conventional economics is tottering into senility, a handful of thinkers are forging imaginative alternatives. Hazel Henderson is among the most eloquent, original—and readable—of the econo-clasts."
—Alvin and Heidi Toffler, authors of *The Third Wave*

"For 25 years, Hazel Henderson has been opening the doors and windows of the stifling incense-filled cathedrals of orthodox economics, letting in fresh air and light from the real world. If the priests of received doctrine would stop canting their liturgy to each other long enough to read this book, it would indeed be a 'win-win' move for all of us."
—Herman E. Daly, coauthor of *For the Common Good*

"Hazel Henderson has given us a road map for traversing the new global economy of the Information Age. She has effectively blended together a lifetime of keen insights into the relationships between science, technology, economy, and the environment in a provocative and timely book that is likely to be widely read and discussed."
—Jeremy Rifkin, author of *The End of Work*

"The most precious commodity in the world is hope, and Hazel Henderson's *Building a Win-Win World* is a motherlode. She finds paths from competition to cooperation, from hierarchy to diversity, from global abuse to grassroots solutions—and thus from isolated despair to communal action."
—Gloria Steinem, author of *Moving Beyond Words*

"By far the most lucid and practical handbook for a better world that I have seen. With her usual brilliance, Hazel Henderson cuts through today's confusion to take us step-by-step from her clear-sighted view of how things are to practical programs for a just and healthy world."
> —Elisabet Sahtouris, author of *EarthDance*

"The message of *Building a Win-Win World* is urgent. I urge politicians, industrialists, bankers, and environmentalists to read it. Full of common sense and deep wisdom, it shows the way to political sanity and planetary survival."
> —Satish Kumar, Editor, *Resurgence*, and Director of Programme, Schumacher College, Devon, U.K.

"A 'fair exchange' is the common underlying value of most cultures' mores throughout history, and Hazel Henderson cites chapter and verse, showing how to bring this to pass within our current economy."
> —Susan Davis, Chairman and CEO, Capital Missions Company

"In *Building a Win-Win World* Hazel Henderson brings together key issues about globalization, technology, and local communities in a direct and inspiring way. We all *can* build a 'win-win world'—and with this book, Hazel helps us do it."
> —Steve Waddell, Director, Leadership for the Common Good

"This book provides fascinating insights into our world. It is thought provoking as we forge new international agreements to create a win-win world for the 21st century, and it is a must-read for anyone who leads or aspires to leadership."
> —Doris Wan Cheng, Chairman and CEO, Sino Global Capital, Inc.

BUILDING A

WIN-WIN

WORLD

BUILDING A

WIN-WIN

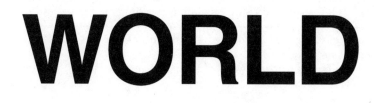

WORLD

LIFE BEYOND
GLOBAL ECONOMIC WARFARE

HAZEL HENDERSON

Berrett-Koehler Publishers
San Francisco

Berrett-Koehler Publishers, Inc.
450 Sansome Street, Suite 1200
San Francisco, CA 94111-3320
Tel: (415) 288-0260   Fax: (415) 362-2512

Ordering Information

Individual sales. Berrett-Koehler publications are available through most book-stores. They can also be ordered direct from Berrett-Koehler at the address above.

Quantity sales. Special discounts are available on quantity purchases by corporations, associations, and others. For details, contact the "Special Sales Department" at the Berrett-Koehler address above.

Orders for college textbook/course adoption use. Please contact Berrett-Koehler Publishers at the address above.

Orders by U.S. trade bookstores and wholesalers. Please contact Publishers Group West, 4065 Hollis Street, Box 8843, Emeryville, California 94662. Tel: (510) 658-3453; 1-800-788-3123. Fax: (510) 658-1834

Printed in the United States of America

Printed on acid-free and recycled paper that is composed of 85% recovered fiber, including 15% postconsumer waste.

Library of Congress Cataloging-in-Publication Data
Henderson, Hazel, 1933–
    Building a win–win world : life beyond global economic warfare / by Hazel Henderson.
        p. cm.
    Includes bibliographical references and index.
    ISBN 1-881052-90-7 (hc: alk. paper)
    ISBN 1-57675-027-2 (paperback: alk. paper)
        1. Economic development–Environmental aspects.
    2. Sustainable development. 3. Human ecology. 4. Cooperation.
    I. Title.
    HD75.6.H458   1996
    363.7–dc20   96-12250
                                             CIP

First hardcover printing: May 1996
First paperback printing: September 1997
99 98 97   10 9 8 7 6 5 4 3 2 1
This paperback edition contains the complete text of the original hardcover edition.

Editing: Mary Lou Sumberg
Indexing: Judith McLane
Proofreading: PeopleSpeak
Interior Design and Production: Joel Friedlander Publishing Services
Cover Design: Charles Rue Woods

To Barbara Ward and

E. F. "Fritz" Schumacher,

dear friends whose brilliant minds,

caring hearts, and profound wisdom

live on and inspire me still.

CONTENTS

ILLUSTRATIONS

ACKNOWLEDGMENTS

I acknowledge with gratitude all the thinkers and visionaries, past and present, who have contributed to my understanding over the years. My thanks, too, to Steven Piersanti, president of Berrett-Koehler Publishers, Inc., for restoring my faith in the U.S. publishing industry and for encouraging me to write this book; to Margaret Helen, who helped me edit the manuscript; and to Mary Lou Sumberg for her superb final editing. Lastly, my deep gratitude to my partner, Alan F. Kay, for his nurturing role, and to my mother, Dorothy Jesseman Mustard—always my wisest teacher—who departed this life in 1995, her ninetieth year.

To an Unsung Hero

Let us salute Dorothy for her heroism
For a life devoted to the loving care of others
In an often unloving world.
A rare example to others
Whatever the religions they profess,
Dorothy was the most truly saintly person I have ever known.
Acts of daily kindness–small and large
She warmed so many lives
Bringing meals on wheels, weighing babies,
Volunteering, opening her heart and home to so many.
A mother supreme
Strong and resilient, making the best of whatever each day
  brought,
Always there for her family
With open lap and enfolding arms.
Dear Dorothy–mediating conflicts, instilling ethics
By her actions more than her words.

What fortunate people
We who grew up under her wing!
This is true courage:
To toil each day for others.
This is true valor:
To keep faith with the future,
Without compensation or recognition.
Caring and sharing, honoring Nature
Are de-valued in narrow economics,
While guns, tanks and robots are paraded.
Yet the "love economies" of all the world's Dorothys
Foster life and reign supreme in the cosmic accounts.
The world will progress as it recognizes its Dorothys
Until, one day, we shall all see more clearly
The real heroes,
And follow their leadership into a brighter future.

HAZEL HENDERSON, loving daughter — in gratitude
Barley, Hertfordshire, England
October 9, 1995

INTRODUCTION

Building a Win-Win World: Life Beyond Global Economic Warfare is an effort to continue deconstruction of the economism/competition/conflict paradigm and construction of new platforms for action. We are all constructing new "quality-of-life" language together. The dysfunctional economism paradigm still controls the debate, however, and we must never forget it for an instant. The economists are still the "thought police," and we are enmeshed every day in the old structures in hundreds of ways. There has been tremendous progress. It is slow-motion good news, but that is what I am out to communicate.

The war system in human societies is at least six thousand years old, but according to much new archeological and paleoanthropological evidence, humans lived in generally peaceful, small egalitarian groups in prehistory. Most of what we are taught as the history of human civilization chronicles the rise of human ego-centeredness, technological ingenuity, and territoriality (as populations and agriculture spread), and the inevitable rise of competition, conflict, and violence in general. This kind of history of the evolution of human societies is a biased account. The conventional history of conquests, military leaders, and the lives of the powerful has been largely indifferent to the experiences of the great majority of ordinary human beings. The work of broader historians, such as Fernand Braudel (1980, 1984) and Emmanuel Wallerstein (1991), the challenge of feminist historians, and new interpretations of archaeological records have enriched our understanding of our past. This is a vital prelude to changing our view of our potential and our future.

In the twentieth century, humans have clearly demonstrated the limits of their six-thousand-year experimentation with competition,

1

territoriality, expansionism, and military conflict. More scholars are at last studying humanity's ancient war system and the roots of human violence — all the bad but important news in our biochemistry, brains, evolution, social conditioning, and hierarchical, patriarchal institutions. Increasing technological virtuosity linked to this war system has brought us to the brink of many annihilation scenarios — from nuclear and biological holocausts to slower, more insidious threats like toxic wastes, urban decay, desertification, and climate change. This book, however, will not dwell on this now-dysfunctional system and its post–Cold War expressions in civil and ethnic conflicts, as well as violence in city streets, in the media, and in our families. Instead, we will trace the emerging death rattles of this violent, competition/conflict paradigm and its dominance-submission, win-lose games. I will identify the flash points and crises that illustrate the dysfunctionality of the paradigm and force us — for our very survival — toward new approaches. As we examine these signs of human potential for personal and social learning, we see how break*downs* are often precursors and even necessary for break*throughs*.

THE GOOD NEWS IN THE BAD NEWS

This book will focus on finding the good news in the bad news: where humans are encountering the endgames of the competition/conflict paradigm, where there are signs of transition and transmutation. The very globalization of the war system, of technology, and of industrialization brought the Cold War to a dead end. Since then, the global warfare paradigm has given ground to global economic warfare, which many economists, politicians, and business leaders have hailed as a victory of capitalism and competitive free markets. Yet this global economic warfare has proved little better than the military warfare it was advertised to replace. By the mid-1990s global economic warfare had already reached crisis points of its own.

Part I of this book, "Pathological Paradigms," examines the nature of recent crises. Chapter 1, "Global Economic Warfare versus Sustainable Human Development," zeros in on flash points from global to local levels. Chapter 2, "Juggernaut Globalism and the Bankruptcy of Economics," surveys the global economy, financial markets, and the unleashed forces of free trade. Chapter 3, "The Technology Trap," examines our love affair with technology and its perverse impacts on our lives and environment. Chapter 4, "The

Jobless Productivity Trap," looks at how the noxious new brew of free-market technological innovation driven by global economic warfare has led to jobless economic growth and further global commercial exploitation of the planet's peoples and natural resources. Chapter 5, "Government by Mediocracy and the Attention Economy," examines the rise of global mass media as a new form of governance now driving our politics and private lives — and its birthing of hybrid Attention Economies.

Part II, "Slow-Motion Good News: Road Maps and Resources for Rebirth," examines our human resources and potentials for rebalancing ourselves and our societies on new paths to more cooperative, equitable forms of ecologically sustainable development. Chapter 6 describes a new force in the world, "Grassroots Globalism," as it shows itself in the emerging civil society and the traditionally cooperative, unpaid Love Economies bubbling up to challenge juggernaut globalism and competitive economism rooted in the old war system. Chapter 7, "Rethinking Human Development and the Time of Our Lives," refocuses our attention on the importance of the time of our lives — our only real asset. Chapter 8, "Cultural DNA Codes and Biodiversity: The Real Wealth of Nations," shows that the encoding of our collective experience, as it has coevolved with the biodiversity of all species, is our real source of wealth. Human resourcefulness, choices, and aspiration for personal development can create new societies. Our minds and spirits are powerful beyond our full awareness.

Part III, "Building a Win-Win World: Breakthroughs and Social Innovations," examines how our human potentials are finding expression in new forms of enterprise, institutions, partnerships, and cooperative agreements that can lead to the building of a win-win world. Chapter 9, "Information: The World's Real Currency Isn't Scarce," describes how money became mistaken for wealth and was cartelized in the global casino, and how the new, pure information currencies (which have always been the world's real currency) are now emerging at the global and local levels. Chapter 10, "Redefining Wealth and Progress: The New Indicators," takes a look behind the statistical veils of economics. It describes how old indicators of economic growth — for example, the gross national product (GNP) — are being overhauled, and how new indicators of quality of life are slowly replacing economic indicators as new scorecards of human development. Chapter 11, "Perfecting Democracy's Tools," describes the importance of the spread of democracies around the world and the urgent need to perfect this still imperfect system of collective decision making and governance, including social and technological innovations waiting in the wings. Chapter 12, "New Markets and New Commons: The Cooperative Advantage," compares and contrasts the strategies of cooperation and competition, of markets and rules/agreements, of public, private, and civil sectors, and how they can all be rebalanced to build a win-win future. Chapter 13, "Agreeing on Rules and Social Innovations for Our Common Future," reviews efforts during the 1990s to forge new international agreements and institutions to create a social architecture suitable for a truly human twenty-first century.

THE ROLE OF OUR MENTAL TOOL BOXES

This book, like my earlier ones, is also about the mental tool boxes we carry in our heads: our belief systems, cultural conditioning, assumptions, worldviews, concepts, and habits of thought. On the societal level, I have termed these collective mental tool boxes *paradigms*—extending the scope of the term originally coined by Thomas Kuhn to describe such mental processes in *The Structure of Scientific Revolutions* (1962). Our mental tool boxes are lenses or spectacles by which we humans view and construct our responses to the world around us.

Each of us, whether we acknowledge these powerful mental tools or not, shapes our world through the use of such paradigms, which evolve in response to our experience, as I elaborated in *Paradigms in Progress* (1991, 1995). For me, two of the most useful of these mental tools are (1) my "zoom lens," which I use to zero in on something that interests me and to keep going deeper with increasing magnification of the details until I have a more complete picture; and (2) my "wide shot," which allows me to pull back and see the phenomenon as successively smaller and smaller pieces of a much larger jigsaw puzzle. All of us have this mental equipment, which can be honed and perfected as a high-quality camera for viewing our world. This can help us see the flow of events and understand the paradigms we and others are using to shape our perceptions.

Developing mental paradigm-spotting equipment is also a spiritual pursuit. Such mental exercises make us deeply aware of our essence—in fact, *our souls*—since when we look at our own mental functioning we see that it emerges from our brains but cannot be placed neatly in some set of neurons. We are brought to the oldest puzzle of our species: Who is the "I" that is studying and judging all this? Every great religious and spiritual tradition has posed this question—through meditation, as in Buddhism and Hinduism; through prayer, as in Christianity, Islam, and Judaism; through contemplation, as in many indigenous traditions; as well as through rituals, ceremonies, holy days, festivals, celebrations, music, dance, and art.

Many traditions have sought to explain the marvelous paradoxes of human existence: that we possess this mental equipment and ever-expanding awareness on a shrinking planet, in an unremarkable solar system, somewhere in the arm of an equally undistinguished spiral galaxy. Simultaneously, we inhabit for a brief time a delicate and miraculous physical body, which will decompose into a few dollars worth of chemical elements and disperse again into the earth that gave us birth. This profoundly beautiful mystery evokes our questions, our imagination, and our many images of this great creation and its divinity—whether in the grand sweep of the known universe or within ourselves.

This book is my most recent album of the "snapshots" I have collected of this great unfolding human drama as I have traveled the world since I wrote *Paradigms in Progress*. How do we humans face new challenges resulting from the effects of our mental and technological ingenuity? I scan for signs of increasing levels of global awareness, responsibility, and wisdom that must emerge for our survival and development.

Indeed, I believe we humans are coming up to "graduation" time on this planet. We must now learn a great deal and grow in moral stature very rapidly. The ubiquitous goal of growth as measured by GNP must soon be redirected. We must *grow up!* Since I took up my pen to record this process thirty years ago, the global debate has been getting clearer. New paradigms are competing with dysfunctional belief systems and clarifying our situation and our future goals and choices. Since World War II we have been slowly leaving the industrial era behind. I summarized this process in the 1970s in *Creating Alternative Futures* (1978, 1996) and in the 1980s in *The Politics of the Solar Age* (1981, 1988).

Even so, these vast historical change processes are uneven. I view these uneven shifts in the industrialism paradigm in terms similar to those of many of my fellow futurists. I have been a card-carrying futurist for the past quarter century—belonging to many of the same professional societies as U.S. Speaker of the House Newt Gingrich (with whom I now often disagree) and our mutual friends Alvin and Heidi Toffler. Most futurists associate in professional societies. These include the World Futures Studies Federation, a global group with a moving base currently in Australia; the U.S.-based World Future Society, which publishes *The Futurist, Futures Research Quarterly*, and *Future Survey*; Futuribles, based in Paris, France; the Futures Library in Salzburg, Austria; the World Association for Social Prospects, in Geneva and Benin, Africa; The African Future Society; the Chinese Futures Society, in Beijing; and many similar associations in Latin and Central America, Japan, Asia, Africa, and Europe.

Futurists have almost been an underground in the academic world—often vilified by their colleagues in more established, traditional disciplines. Academe had no place for visionary futurist Buckminster Fuller, who became an author and entrepreneur in planetary design and was only fully recognized after his death. In 1995 he would have celebrated his hundredth birthday. Today's universities still operate within the defined disciplinary boundaries and paradigms inherited from the underlying ideologies of the Industrial Revolution and the European Age of Enlightenment. I described these paradigms based on the reductionism engendered by René Descartes and the mechanistic "clockwork universe" of Isaac Newton in *Creating Alternative Futures* and *The Politics of the Solar Age*. Seamless reality was partitioned into separate disciplinary boxes housed in separate buildings on campuses, while fledgling interdisciplinary programs were deemed "not rigorous" and subject to the first budget cuts. Future studies became established largely outside traditional academia—with notable exceptions, including departments at the University of Hawaii at Manoa and the University of Houston at Clear Lake City, Texas. The business sector embraced futures research as an integral part of its need to plan, to invest in research and development, and to innovate new products and services. Such corporate futures research includes the Trend Analysis Program of the U.S. insurance industry, the futures scenario building of Shell Oil in Europe, and the longer-term futures studies conducted by Mitsubishi Research Institute in Japan.

THE NARROW FRAMEWORK OF ECONOMICS

Often, the most resistant traditional discipline has been economics— for many good reasons. Economics became the primary discipline of industrial development, which became synonymous with *economic development*, i.e., GNP-measured economic growth and what I term "economism." The economism paradigm sees economics as the primary focus of public policy as well as of individual and public choices. Thus economics became the most powerful discipline—even outranking physics and mathematics—bestriding the policy process since World War II in every country in the world. I researched the genesis of this in depth for my friend Fritjof Capra's *The Turning Point* (1981) and my own *The Politics of the Solar Age*. I found independent-minded economists—a few in every generation—who had questioned the ever-narrowing framework of economics. I saw how its assumptions were concealed in a language of false universalism and specious mathematics as well as a simplistic view of human nature.

What I had stumbled on, as had those before me and others who came later, such as my friend Marilyn Waring in *If Women Counted* (1988), is that economics, far from a science, *is simply politics in disguise*. No wonder I defined myself as a futurist and was sometimes called an "anti-economist"—which is true. I want to dethrone economics as the predominant policy analysis tool of the global economic warfare system. Our global future is multidisciplinary, cooperative, and rainbow hued. Futures research is still pooh-poohed by economists, academics, and policymakers. The extended space/time horizons of futures research, its scope—global and covering decades and centuries—is an art not a science. Often futurists are proved wrong. Yet often they blindside more myopic political scientists, sociologists, and economists, who sometimes fail to get even their *hindsight* right.

Thus, futurist Daniel Bell of Harvard, who began as a sociologist, was one of the first in the 1960s to describe the passing of the *economic* era. In *The Coming of Post-Industrial Society* (1973) he described, in the broader tradition of earlier political economists such as Schumpeter, the passing of the industrial paradigm and the consequent change in the social structures it had created. Many futurists seized this image, even though it was one derived from "backing into the future looking through the rearview mirror." In *The Politics of the Solar Age*, I envisioned the coming of a new era of enlightenment, a Solar Age based on light-wave and solar-energy technologies. In this Solar Age, we humans would engage in a bottom-to-top design revolution. The centralization of industrialism would give way to a new devolution: we would reshape our production, agriculture, architecture, academic disciplines, governments, and companies to align them with nature's productive processes in a new search for equitable, humane, and ecologically sustainable societies.

The Tofflers, in *The Third Wave* (1980), also saw the end of industrialism, which they termed the "Second Wave" succeeding the "First Wave" of agricultural societies. The Tofflers' Third Wave is driven by knowledge and information technology. We agree on a coming devolution, which they described as de-massification and I described as decentralization. We have often debated, however, the relative importance of planetary ecosystems in human societies and technologies. While the Tofflers see ecosystems as malleable and continuing to respond to human criteria and goals, I see ecosystems as having inviolable principles and the biosphere as our basic life support. I believe that humans adapt and have the potential to grow and learn.

This debate runs through every conference of futurists: between the "technological optimists," who think nature will keep adapting to human demands, and the "human-nature optimists," who, like myself, think that human beings have the ability to continually learn and adapt to challenging environments. Both groups share common concerns for reshaping societies but see human progress in different terms. The former, technologically focused, are pessimistic about human nature. The latter join me in optimism about the possibilities of human learning and adaptation to reshape human nature, values, and lifestyles.

Building a Win-Win World scans the scenery and maps the collision between the externally focused, technologically driven economic growth paradigm, which has culminated in unsustainable global economic warfare, and the rise of grassroots global concerns in the emerging paradigm and movements for sustainable human development. In "mediocracies," our new form of governance based on entertainment and event-driven media, longer-term processes are often unseen "slow-motion bad news" and "slow-motion good news." My columns are unseen in the United States but are distributed from Rome by InterPress Service to some four hundred newspapers worldwide in twenty-seven languages. Hopefully, this overview will provide a more visible "wide shot" of the global paradigm clashes now creating tomorrow's realities, and expand our capacities to respond creatively.

PART I

PATHOLOGICAL PARADIGMS

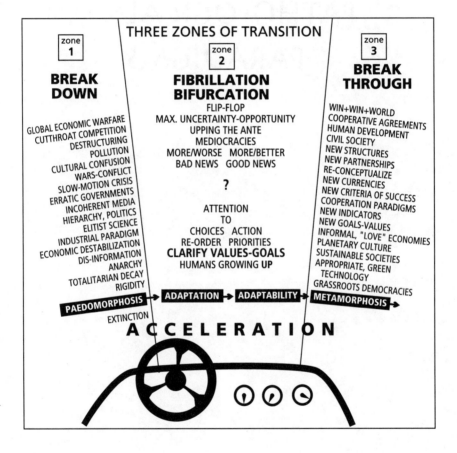

Fig. 1.   Three Zones of Transition

© 1986 Hazel Henderson   Source: *Paradigms in Progress*

GLOBAL ECONOMIC WARFARE VERSUS SUSTAINABLE HUMAN DEVELOPMENT: FLASH POINTS, TRENDS, AND TRANSITIONS

After the Cold War, the six-thousand-year-old competition/ conflict paradigm transmuted into the spread of market capitalism, global corporations, and competitive economic warfare. Management theorists and journals such as *Fortune* began to describe the global economy as a jungle or a new military theater for all-out economic warfare. The global economic warfare system collided with trends leading toward more sustainable forms of development. The common definition of sustainable development is "development which meets the needs of the present without compromising the ability of future generations to meet their own needs."[1]

While early writings on the need for a transition to sustainability were widely ignored or rejected, a considerable body of expert political and government opinion now exists that such a transition is urgent and necessary. In *Paradigms in Progress* (1991, 1995), I diagrammed three zones of transition. (See Fig. 1. Three Zones of Transition.) Influencing the emerging consensus on the need for a shift to sustainable development are at least six great globalization processes that are increasingly interactive at all levels and accelerating trends toward global interdependence. These include the globalizations of (1) industrialism and technology, (2) work and migration, (3) finance, (4) human effects on the biosphere, (5) militarism and arms trafficking, and (6) communications and planetary culture.

The effects of these globalizations, including the erosion of the sovereignty of nation-states, are driving paradigm shifts in many countries toward reintegration of fragmented, reductionist academic disciplines; emerging studies of dynamic interactive systems; and a new focus on the life sciences and futures research. A set of post-Cartesian scientific principles based on a global life-sciences view includes the following: (1) interconnectedness, (2) redistribution, (3) heterarchy, (4) complimentarity, (5) uncertainty, and (6) change. Today's post–Cold War landscape, with increasing uncertainty, cultural pluralism, and interpenetration, is producing much cognitive dissonance. Yet the new confusion also leads to the possibility of rapid paradigm shifts, social innovation, and learning. Ethnic, religious, and cultural conflict and negative scenarios, some tinged with nihilism and others bordering on paranoia, are increasing.[2]

I will not attempt to assign probabilities to any of these trends and scenarios since today's global system is so highly interactive and accelerating toward further interdependence. Seeking certainties can be comfortable but may not be the most realistic course. In a changing world, policymakers will need to scan broadly, make rapid course corrections, and sometimes resort to skillful improvisation. A useful review of recent global modeling finds many academic, business, and government models retrogressing toward competitive and economic paradigms, while grassroots movements are shifting toward sustainability.[3] Easily the best global model of sustainability is *Global 2000 Revisited: What Shall We Do?* (Barney, Blewett, and Barney 1993).[4]

A systemic shift from the paradigm of maximizing global economic competition and gross national product (GNP) growth to a paradigm of more cooperative, sustainable development—which in earlier times might have taken hundreds of years—is at least possible in today's interdependent, rapidly evolving world system. Since these are complex, synergistic pathways of interpenetration, we will examine these trends from a cybernetic perspective, identifying key positive and negative feedbacks. As I elaborated in *Paradigms in Progress*, systems theory and dynamic change models are overtaking macroeconomics, which is based on the idea that economies are in a general state of equilibrium.

The basic models of change and growth come from nature. Nonliving and some living systems can be (1) homeostatic and kept in a steady state and structure (morphostatic), like the temperature in a house governed by a thermostat; or (2) living systems that can grow and change shape (morphogenesis), like children or human cities. These two processes are governed by feedback loops, which in the case of number one are *negative* feedback loops damping the effects of change and maintaining stability, and in the case of number two are *positive* feedback loops amplifying themselves and their cross-impacts and pushing the system into new structural forms. (See Fig. 2. Two Cybernetic Systems.) In 1995 the United Nations University Millennium Project was launched to provide a global capacity for early warning on long-range issues. Two hundred futurists and scholars from fifty countries, including myself, participated in the project's feasibility phase.[5]

I will examine the collisions between the historic, global, competition/warfare system and trends toward sustainable development at seven levels of the world system:

1. Global population and the biosphere
2. International and global governance structures
3. The global civil society and cultures
4. Nation-states, domestic policies, and democratic processes
5. Global markets, corporations, trade, and finance
6. Provincial, urban, and local governance
7. Family/community/individual values, ethics, and behaviors

LEVEL 1: GLOBAL POPULATION AND THE BIOSPHERE

Over the next thirty years, global population is projected to grow by nearly two-thirds, from 5.5 to 8.5 billion people. Though this is a projection, substantial growth is inevitable because of the relatively large percentage of young people in today's population. This provides built-in momentum for further population growth, even as the number of children per family declines. Of the 8.5 billion people, about 7.1 billion will live in developing countries, primarily in urban areas. Population in industrialized countries, now 1.2 billion, is projected to rise to only 1.4 billion by the year 2025, with virtually all of that growth occurring in the United States.[6] The exponential growth of human populations is an example of positive feedback loops at work—people

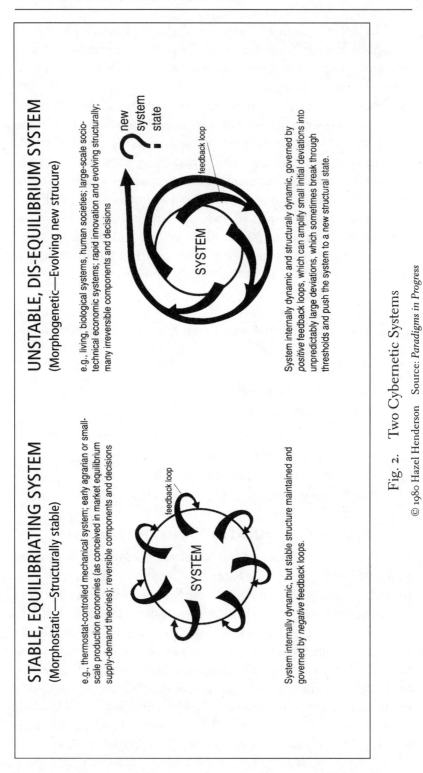

STABLE, EQUILIBRIATING SYSTEM
(Morphostatic—Structurally stable)

e.g., thermostat-controlled mechanical system; early agrarian or small-scale production economies (as conceived in market equilibrium supply-demand theories); reversible components and decisions

feedback loop

SYSTEM

System internally dynamic, but stable structure maintained and governed by *negative* feedback loops.

UNSTABLE, DIS-EQUILIBRIUM SYSTEM
(Morphogenetic—Evolving new strucure)

e.g., living, biological systems; human societies; large-scale socio-technical economic systems; rapid innovation and evolving structurally; many irreversible components and decisions

new system state

feedback loop

SYSTEM

System internally dynamic and structurally dynamic, governed by *positive* feedback loops, which can amplify small initial deviations into unpredictably large deviations, which sometimes break through thresholds and push the system to a new structural state.

Fig. 2. Two Cybernetic Systems Source: *Paradigms in Progress*

© 1980 Hazel Henderson

have more children who then have more children—and other complex factors, including declining death rates. Thus growth of sheer human numbers has become a flash point for confrontations over policy and paradigm changes.[7]

Longer-term population growth depends on the course of fertility decline in developing countries, which in turn depends on the effectiveness of family planning programs, progress in reducing poverty and elevating the status of women, and many other factors. A reasonable estimate is that global population will continue to grow, reaching ten billion in the year 2050.[8] Population growth has a significant impact on the environment, but the relationship is not straightforward. Many other factors—government policies, legal systems, access to capital and technology, the efficiency of industrial production, inequity in the distribution of land and resources, poverty in the South, and conspicuous consumption in the North—interact to modify or amplify humankind's impact on the environment.

In *Paradigms in Progress* I described how population policies of the late 1980s were slowly refocusing beyond contraception to concerns for education and pre- and postnatal health care to prevent early childhood diseases and unnecessary infant mortality. This twenty-year evolution of population policies includes the shift in focus to the Indian Equivalents formula: I=PAT. In this formula, I (Impact) is the product of P (Population size) times A (per capita Affluence) times T (damage done by the Technology used to supply each unit of consumption). While the population hawks and doves in the North and South have reached some common ground, such as the IPAT approach, there is a long way to go. Women and children are still pawns in most policies. Raising the level of industrial countries' aid programs in health, family planning, education, and sanitation is a key priority. These programs clash with old paradigms, including those of patriarchy, elite decision making, militant nationalism, free trade, global corporate commercialism, and consumerism.

The cutting edge of population policy will also need to include assessment of the past decade's successes and failures. For example, in China, the greatest demographic experiment in human history has been under way for over a decade: the one-child policy. During the 1980s, as the policy took hold, China was the darling of population hawks. The more serious consequences of this huge, unprecedentedly swift demographic transition are still underreported. How will

The world's population is urbanizing much faster than it is growing. There are several reasons: declining resource availability per capita; shrinking economic opportunities in rural areas; and hopes of jobs, opportunities, and services in urban areas. In virtually every country, per capita consumption of goods and services is higher in urban areas than in rural communities, although gaps are wide between rich and immigrating poor in burgeoning squatter settlements, often without basic municipal services. Urban populations exhibit consumption patterns that are unlike those of rural populations and have a different kind of environmental impact. City residents, particularly in industrial countries, tend to consume more industrial goods and energy-intensive services. Urban populations everywhere create concentrated air and water pollution and solid waste, which can reach crisis proportions in cities experiencing both rapid GNP growth and immigration, such as Bangkok, Thailand; Mexico City, Mexico; and São Paulo, Brazil.

Cities have been experiencing multiple crises of unsustainability. The $1.2 billion budget gap in Los Angeles caused massive cuts in health and social services to its nine million residents.[13] Murder rates in Washington, D.C., and Rio de Janeiro, Brazil, reached 60 per 100,000. New York City's tribulations led to a downgrading of its bonds by Standard and Poor's in 1995. City employment fell by nine thousand jobs in the first quarter, and the city's budget of $31.5 billion required $3.1 billion to balance. One-shot sales of city assets included a $2.3 billion "sale" of its water and sewerage systems—a fiscal gimmick of shuffling debt between city agencies.[14]

Populations in the industrialized world in 1995 were about three-fourths urban, compared with about one-third in the developing world. Newly industrialized Latin America is already as urbanized as Europe. By the year 2005, half of the world's people will live in urban areas; by the year 2025, that number will be about two out of three.[15] The rate of urbanization is a product of migration and the birth rate among the urban population. In the industrialized world, migration was a gradual process: from 1875 to 1900, the annual rate of urban growth was 2.8 percent.[16] In the developing world, urban populations have grown at an annual rate of about 4 percent from 1975 to 1990. Such rapid urbanization places enormous strain on developing countries to provide the infrastructure necessary to support their populations. By 2025, four billion people in developing countries will be classified as urban—equivalent to the world's total population in 1975.[17] The UN Habitat II Conference in Istanbul, 1996, is drawing much needed attention to urbanization.

Global collision of the two paradigms continues on additional key issues around population: (1) per capita consumption and waste in industrial societies, the environmental impacts of which are multiplied manyfold over those of populations in developing countries, even though they are growing faster; and (2) the growing consensus that population growth can best be stabilized by educating and empowering women, coupled with the further evidence that empowering women as educators, food producers, and family providers is a key factor in development. For example, one-third of all households worldwide are headed by women. The *Human Development Report, 1995* found that $16 trillion is missing from the global economy each year—$5 trillion represents the unpaid work performed by women and men, and $11 trillion is the additional unpaid work of women.[18] This crucial role of women in development has been obscured for decades by the competitive GNP-growth paradigm, which deems unpaid production for use-value "noneconomic." Empowerment of women is opposed by fundamentalists in many patriarchal religious traditions, such as Islam and Roman Catholicism, as well as by many of the world's predominantly male decision makers.

By 1995, other flash points included issues of how to tame the economic warfare in the global casino—fiercely opposed by most bankers, finance ministers, and global, corporate free-trade interests. Women at the 1995 UN Conference on Women and Development in Beijing demanded taxes on currency speculation, arms sales, and global pollution, including my own statement declaring that taming the global casino is a women's issue. In the sustainable development paradigm, economic issues are recontexted holistically as population/environment issues. These clashes are explosive because they involve not only paradigm and behavioral shifts but also a significant rearrangement of social influence and economic/political power.

Growing human populations expanded croplands and reduced forested areas worldwide by 20 percent between 1700 and 1980. In North America, some seventy-two million hectares of forest were cleared. Globally, the pace has accelerated, with more cropland expansion occurring between 1950 and 1980 than in the previous 150 years. Soil degradation has followed; agricultural activity has reduced the world supply of organic carbon in soil humus by about 15 percent of its original preagricultural stock. Carbon loss occurred at a rate of roughly 300 million metric tons per year over the past 300 years, but within the past 50 years the rate rose to as much as 760 million metric tons per year.[19]

It is estimated that since World War II, 1.2 billion hectares, or about 10.5 percent of the world's vegetated land, has suffered at least moderate soil degradation as a result of human activity. This is a vast area, roughly the size of China and India combined. If lightly degraded soil is included, the total affected area rises to about 17 percent of global vegetated land. The most widespread degradation has occurred in Asia, where about 450 million hectares are at least moderately degraded; and Africa, where moderate or worse degradation affects 320 million hectares. For the world as a whole, the principal causes of soil degradation since World War II have been overgrazing, deforestation, and agricultural activities.[20]

In 1995, the dominant economic growth paradigm calling for more industrialization of agriculture, bigger farms, and increasing fertilizer and pesticide applications (in the name of efficiency) ran into fresh evidence of diminishing returns. World grain stocks fell precipitously in 1995 as measured by the Worldwatch Institute, and by year's end the UN Food and Agricultural Organization corroborated that they were at a twenty-year low, "below the minimum necessary to safeguard world security."[21] Free trade in agriculture touched off bitter wrangling between the United States and Europe over protecting their respective farm sectors, while their farmers rioted and destroyed their crops for TV cameras. Environmentalists jumped into the debate on cutting farm subsidies in both the United States and Europe. U.S. environmentalists formed a coalition with the National Taxpayers Union Foundation demanding cuts in corporate welfare of $33 billion—from the $1 billion annual giveaway to the mining industry via the Mining Act of 1872 and the $500 million given to timber companies to subsidize "bargain basement sales" of timber from U.S. national forests, to the $425 million export-marketing subsidies to agribusiness and $460 million for another dam in Colorado.[22]

The disposal of human waste directly affects the quality of freshwater resources. Contaminated drinking water, in turn, transmits diseases such as diarrhea, typhoid, and cholera. These diseases were widespread during the late nineteenth and early twentieth centuries in Europe and North America, where they ranked among the leading causes of death and illness.[23] In the 1990s, water wars were predicted for many arid countries. The "Green Revolution" was reassessed in *The Economist* as using too much water and too many fertilizers, thereby creating salinated soils.[24] Air pollution in growing cities is reaching levels critical to public health, not only in Mexico City but also in all major cities experiencing rapid GNP growth, particularly in Latin America and Asia.

From 1850 to 1990, the consumption of commercial energy (from coal, oil, gas, nuclear power, and hydropower) increased more than one hundredfold, while use of biomass energy (fuel wood, crop waste, and dung) roughly tripled. The combustion of fossil fuels (coal, oil, and gas) emits carbon dioxide (CO_2) into the atmosphere. CO_2 constitutes the largest source of greenhouse gases, which trap infrared radiation that would otherwise escape into the stratosphere. Since the Industrial Revolution, atmospheric concentrations of CO_2 have increased by about 25 percent. Worldwide consumption of fossil fuel from 1860 to 1949 resulted in the release of an estimated 187 billion metric tons of CO_2. Over the past four decades, fossil fuel use has accelerated, creating an additional 559 billion metric tons of CO_2. Emissions from fossil fuel use have increased 3.6 times since 1950. From 1950 to 1989, the United States was the largest emitter, followed by the European Community and the former Soviet Union. Land use change, including deforestation for agricultural purposes, is responsible for an additional estimated 220 billion metric tons of CO_2 since 1860.[25]

This flash point had, by 1990, influenced the creation of the Montreal Protocol on chlorofluorocarbons (CFCs) and the *Agenda 21* treaties on climate change and forests. In July 1995, *Scientific American* published satellite photographs of Antarctica's melting ice packs and data showing that the continent's temperature had increased 2.5 degrees Celsius in the past fifty years. In its August 3, 1995, edition, *The New York Times* reported data on the depletion of ozone—now less than 40 percent of that measured in the 1960s. The bad news was the national backsliding on implementing and strengthening environmental treaties after multiple backlashes from corporations and state governments and their consultants and scientists.

Clearly, global economic growth is colliding with population and environmental trends, including desertification, ozone depletion,

analysis, and game theory: "Do as you would be done by." Honesty, reciprocity, tolerance, cooperation, sharing, and even altruism seem to be enduring values for the long-term governance of human societies. The proactive version of the Golden Rule is pure systems theory: "What would happen if everyone acted this way?" Perhaps we humans already know how to build a win-win world where we share the earth equitably and peacefully with each other and all species.[28] Competition is also a useful survival strategy found in most ecosystems, interacting with cooperation as species coevolve. In human societies, competition can evolve from fighting to negotiating. Economic competition can be benign and competition between ideas is vital. Faulty assumptions and hypotheses can be vanquished by the advance of science. A win-win world combines these two strategies, competition and cooperation, with human ethics and creativity.

The contemporary pressures of population growth and eroding environmental quality are, perforce, accelerating human learning via direct negative feedback from nature, such as acid rain and ozone depletion. Since its founding in 1945, the UN, for all its shortcomings, has focused on the great issues before the human family (peacekeeping, education, culture, health, and human rights) while struggling with older doctrines of militarism, economic warfare, and national sovereignty (even when upheld to protect repressive regimes). Since the UN's first Conference on the Human Environment in 1972 through successive conferences on population, food, habitat, renewable energy, and resources, including the Earth Summit in Rio in 1992 and the Conference on Human Rights in Vienna in 1993, new global patterns have emerged:

1. UN conferences have helped place fundamental global issues firmly on the political agendas of member nation-states.

2. These fundamental global issues have been advanced by the UN in concert (if not always collaboration) with the burgeoning group of civil and nongovernmental organizations (NGOs), both national and global.

3. The mass media, predominantly television and radio, has also advanced these global issues—albeit often inadvertently. Since the issues reflect broad human interests, the images of famine-stricken children dying unnecessarily, burning rain forests, dying fish, and fired oil wells in Kuwait began competing with

more familiar images of military violence and criminal mayhem.

These three interactive processes involving UN actors, NGOs, and mass media are culminating in a slowly developing world public opinion—i.e., another global level of "process governance" is emerging. The proposed expansion of the World Court to include an International Criminal Court (which one day might be televised) is gaining support.[29] For decades, UN agencies worked quietly, convening member-states to develop protocols and prototype global governance structures in specific functional areas, such as the International Postal Union (IPU), the International Air Traffic Association (IATA), the World Meteorological Organization (WMO), and the International Atomic Energy Agency (IAEA). These have brought order and much desirable regulation to postal services, airline schedules, air traffic control and safety, weather prediction, and monitoring of nuclear proliferation. None of these global agencies have oppressed people politically since their jurisdictions are so narrow and clearly circumscribed. They have, however, reduced some of the sovereignty of the nations who agreed to them, or to use Harlan Cleveland's phrase, the nations "pooled some of their sovereignty" voluntarily (Cleveland 1993). *Agenda 21*, signed by 178 governments at the UN Earth Summit in Rio in 1992, involved hundreds of such global agreements, most prominently on use of the world's forests, on protecting biodiversity, and on climate change. All these agreements address the need to shift human industrial and economic activities into a new, more efficient course, toward sustainable development, and are examined further in Chapters 12 and 13.

Agenda 21 spawned scores of national action plans promoting a shift toward sustainable development. By 1994, presidential-level commissions on sustainable development existed in over forty countries.[30] In these national activities, diverse constituencies interacted and learned from each other how to align their efforts toward this more comprehensive national goal. In the familiar tug of war between new paradigms and entrenched interests, implementation of *Agenda 21* by the UN Commission on Sustainable Development was checked by member-nations' backsliding and unwillingness to pay their share to finance it. In truth, implementation does not require new funds but simply a paradigm shift. Nations merely need to stop financing unsustainable activities, to cease subsidizing waste and pollution. In the United States, for example, two NGOs, the National Taxpayers Union and Friends of the Earth, proposed a "Green Scissors" budget-cutting campaign setting forth $33 billion of needed cuts in federal subsidies to corporations. State-level subsidies in the United States, as well as subsidies hidden in unaccounted for social and environmental costs, are also huge—but few researchers are paid to assess them. Shifting the focus of budget priorities challenges entrenched interests and demands much political skill, will, and marshaling of media and public opinion.

The interactions between UN actors, NGOs, the media, and public opinion are driving the sustainable development agenda forward, however. Sustainable development is an integrative paradigm providing a framework that allows the many disparate actors to reframe their issues in a larger context, and unexpected opportunities for synergy and win-win policies often emerge. Backlashes from the dominant paradigm have ranged from the "eco-realism" of economists armed with studies showing that environmental improvements have been made, to new organizations arising in the United States to protect economic freedoms and property rights, to corporations suing environmental activists.[31] Environmentalists have responded with detailed critiques of their critics. The U.S. Congress has shredded environmental protection legislation on budget and cost-cutting grounds, while the President's Council on Sustainable Development has proposed win-win strategies.

Just as the Earth Summit in 1992 showed that ecology and economics were two disciplines that needed integration, and participants at its Global Forum of NGOs produced the coalition strategies to push for ecologically sustainable economic development, both the UN's Fiftieth Anniversary and the Social Summit in Copenhagen in 1995 produced cross-cutting analyses that showed interfaces between all the issues. New policy options were revealed and helped to identify the coalitions that must be built to promote them. Haltingly, the world community is learning systems thinking: how to differentiate between issues that can best be handled by policies at the local and national level and issues that cross national borders. A critical mass of grassroots globalists, socially responsible investors, public officials, and business leaders has yet to form the needed coalitions to face down entrenched interests and institutions. A survey by the Americans Talk Issues Foundation indicates that the American people, at least, understand the need for regulation of some global activities. Symbolically, 1995 also marked the fiftieth anniversary of the dropping of atomic bombs on Hiroshima and Nagasaki—the most devastating flash point of the twentieth century.

As democracy continues to sweep the world, nations are more skittish about putting their young soldiers in harm's way in televised trouble spots around the world. Many member-states prefer to delegate problems to the UN's blue-helmeted peacekeepers. In 1994 and 1995, surveys showed that a majority of the U.S. public wanted the UN to "take the lead" in dealing with international conflicts. This requires more dependable funding for the UN because many member-states are in arrears; for example, in 1995 the United States owed over $1 billion. Some world leaders are also receiving more television coverage and general approval for making peace than war and coming to understand that peace treaties are the ultimate in photo opportunities.

At the same time, traditional military definitions of security have been gradually giving way to new definitions of environmental security and human security (from safe streets to secure jobs). This new human security paradigm may allow some further restructuring in UN member-states, and of the UN itself, consolidating focus on preventive peacemaking and sustainable development. Dr. Oscar Arias Sánchez, Nobel Peace Prize winner and founder of the Foundation for Peace in Costa Rica, is a pioneer in persuading countries to demilitarize. Sixteen countries have followed Costa Rica's lead in abolishing its military in 1949. Although these are some of the world's smallest nations, they include Panama and Haiti, which under the leadership of President Aristide began the process of demilitarizing in 1995. Teams from the Foundation for Peace demonstrate the development advantages of retraining armies for police work and civilian and infrastructure projects.[32] Guatemala, with its bloated army and human rights and judicial abuses,[33] as well as other Central American countries, cannot fail to notice Costa Rica's progress: a 94 percent literacy rate, universal health care, an exemplary criminal justice system, and increasingly ecological resource management have earned Costa Rica "First World" ranking in the Human Development Index.[34]

Global military budgets have continued their average 3 percent annual decline since 1985, resulting in a peace dividend of $935 billion, although most nations used the funds for deficit reduction, i.e.,

paying interest on their past debts. Dr. Arias has proposed a Global
Demilitarization Fund to channel future peace dividends, from further projected declines in military spending, into retraining military
personnel and converting arms facilities to civilian production.[35]
Ironically, the five permanent members of the UN Security Council
are still the main arms merchants to the world, with the United States
shamefully in the lead. About thirty million people are still employed
in the world's armed forces, and vast arsenals of nuclear and conventional weapons still remain. The global conflict paradigm is still very
much in evidence. Peacekeeping, however, and ways to fund the
UN's role in *preventing* conflict (i.e., sustainable development) are
rising on the agenda of many member-states and UN agencies.[36] (See
Fig. 3. Military Spending and the Peace Dividend.)

The UN needs restructuring to recognize its maturation beyond
a largely charitable organization to which member-states voluntarily
give alms. The UN is now an indispensable global institution that
must be strengthened and reshaped to meet global situations
undreamed of in 1945: from peacemaking and keeping, to caring for
refugees, to cleaning up global pollution and refocusing industrial
growth toward sustainable development. The UN must now be
placed on a solid financial foundation by making dues from member-
states mandatory, with interest accruing on arrears and continued
delinquency leading to loss of voting rights, as U.K. Prime Minister
John Major observed at the UN's fiftieth anniversary ceremony in
New York on October 22, 1995, and the European Union emphasized
in 1996.

In addition, several reports and commissions point to the need for
the UN to possess the authority to impose taxes, at least on global arms
trading and currency speculation, and to impose fees for use of the
global commons, such as space, the oceans, Antarctica, and the electromagnetic spectrum.[37] The UN could administer tax treaties for
international pollution, such as carbon dioxide emissions, and for the
repayment of the industrial Organization for Economic Cooperation
and Development (OECD) countries' "pollution debt" to the developing countries. This debt is estimated in the tens of trillions of dollars—far outweighing the total debt currently owed by countries of
the South to Northern banks. Another imperative is restructuring the
UN's Bretton Woods institutions to make their operations democratic, accountable, and transparent.

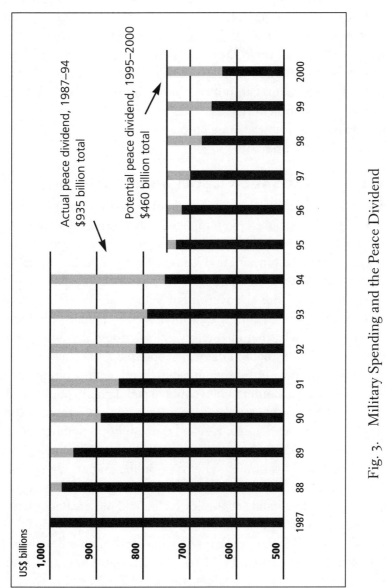

Fig. 3.   Military Spending and the Peace Dividend

Source: *Human Development Report, 1994*, United Nations Development Programme

Neglecting the UN and international agreements could be as dangerous for the world in the 1990s as was the refusal of the United States to join the League of Nations after World War I, leading to that organization's demise and later to World War II. We humans do not have to replay that historical drama yet again. The last years of the millennium, with all their flash points and wake-up calls, will be a good time to advance increasingly necessary forms of global cooperation. Such cooperation can not only move human societies toward sustainable development but also integrate fragmented policies and eliminate programs now at cross purposes, at the same time respecting diversity and subsidiarity.

LEVEL 3: THE GLOBAL CIVIL SOCIETY AND CULTURES

As I discuss in Chapter 6, social innovation in many societies comes from the grassroots, not from entrenched elites who tend to be comfortable with the status quo. Therefore, social innovation creates friction with existing institutions and leads to flash points, i.e., opportunities for human learning. The new alliances between NGOs and certain UN and national government actors, together with mass media coverage, are creating a new force in world affairs, the independent civil society, that challenges both nation-states and global corporations. Few textbooks in global geopolitics and economics yet reflect the rise of this "independent sector," both within and increasingly across national borders. Conventional paradigms in political science, international relations, and economics do not embrace this emergent property of democracies and even authoritarian regimes.

The global civil society does not fit within conventional economic theory, with its limited schema of public and private sectors. Thus, the emergence of this powerful sector, along with the informal, unpaid sectors of national economies, has caught most economists by surprise. A recent report, "International Networks for Addressing Issues of Global Change," calls for a global array of nested networks to "cross-pollinate information between business, government, academia, and NGOs."[38] The general reaction of decision-making elites to the rising global civil society has been one of alarm, because citizen groups see the issues differently from the official and mainstream interpretations of reality. In "Citizen Movements for Greater Global Equity," in 1976, I described many such citizen groups already working for greater government and corporate accountability, democratic participation, human rights, social justice, consumer and employee safety, and environmental protection.[39]

By 1995, the global independent sector had grown by several orders of magnitude (particularly in the United States and Canada, where by 1977 there were over one million such groups in the environmental field alone).[40] Much of this growth in the 1980s was in response to the laissez-faire policies of the Reagan and Bush administrations. Today, many governmental and business leaders acknowledge that they can't lead or govern without consultation with a wide spectrum of civic groups, as well as the more familiar labor unions and other interest groups. Responses range from advertising, lobbying, and public relations efforts, to educating or engineering the consent of such groups and their legislative allies, to inviting them into executive board rooms and administrative deliberations. The conceptual distance between current leaders and elites and NGO harbingers of democracy is still vast. For example, the 1994 U.S. Institute of Peace conference, "Managing Chaos," was billed as "a national conference on the roles of NGOs, governments, and international organizations in coping with international conflict in the twenty-first century." Its brochure noted "NGOs will replace nation-states in the twenty-first century as the principal actors in managing international conflict."

The UNDP and the World Bank began in 1995 to restructure their approaches and their lending as "partnerships" with civil society groups. James Gustave Speth, administrator of UNDP, in a speech before the "We the Peoples" NGO Conference celebrating the UN's fiftieth anniversary, proudly acknowledged his twenty-year civic activist background. (I had collaborated with him in those days on nuclear proliferation concerns.) Speth coined a new acronym—CSO, for civil society organization—and announced that UNDP would henceforth focus on poverty eradication: i.e., sustainable development to UNDP would mean "development that is pro-poor, pro-jobs, pro-women, and pro-nature." Speth added that most past development had not supported sustainable human development. At the UNDP, the paradigm has officially shifted.[41]

Particularly on issues of sustainable development, "first nations" (indigenous peoples) have allied with other civil society groups to do more than put pressure on governments to live up to treaties. Aboriginal land claims, such as those now being adjudicated in Canada, Australia, and New Zealand, are also based on the legitimate claim that indigenous peoples have been stewards and wise custodians of these ancestral lands—maintaining and enhancing their biodiversity. Court battles for return of these lands are buttressed by the need for more sustainable development. Thus the claims are supported by many other civil society groups, as in the case of eighty-seven thousand people representing forty-four aboriginal nations in land claim settlements in British Columbia, Canada.[42] In addition, the world has seen citizen organizations as parties to international treaties. In coalition with small businesses and farmers in Denmark, citizen groups helped derail the implementation of the Maastricht Treaty and forced leaders to confront its "democracy deficits." This triggered popular referenda in France, Norway, and other European countries over democracy, human rights, and social and environmental issues of subsidiarity. Another paradigm had shifted.

The global civil society is driving new intellectual approaches to the fundamental issues facing human societies. These groups are free of mainstream institutional blinders and are often able to envision alternative solutions and demonstrate the effectiveness of their social innovations in their own communities. Such grassroots models include micro-lending to village entrepreneurs; small-scale technologies that are labor and skills intensive, inexpensively raising the productivity of small farmers; and agricultural processes such as those offered by the Post-Graduate College in Chapingo, Mexico. Many local initiatives are networked and supported by Appropriate Technology International,[43] on whose advisory council I serve. Fifty exemplary, innovative community models were showcased by the Friends of the UN in 1995. All prove that citizens working together in the informal and independent sectors can solve many problems better than distant government and business leaders. Often what leaders can do is get out of the way by repealing bureaucratic red tape that hampers grassroots self-help. Beneath the headlines of the Mexican peso crisis are such good news stories from Chapingo as well as satellite-fed courses and programs of the Instituto Technologia in Monterrey. Mass media could, if refocused, rapidly spread the news about all the pragmatic social and technological innovations to inspire hope and replication. The African continent's good news in South Africa and Botswana was overshadowed by the massacres in Rwanda, war-lordism in Somalia, and capricious military rule in Nigeria, where General Sani Abacha jailed the democratically

elected president Abiola and the former president Obasanjo, executed civilian protesters, and ran the oil-rich economy into a $37 bil-
lion external debt.[44]

Other flash points include citizen campaigns over the past decade
to protest the insensitive, often unjust, and environmentally unsustainable project lending by the World Bank, as well as its loans for structural adjustment. This culminated in the 1994 coalition, "Fifty Years Is
Enough," and their campaign to shut down the World Bank if it and
the other Bretton Woods institution, the International Monetary Fund
(IMF), could not be radically restructured and their lending refocused
for sustainable development. Surprisingly, this campaign coincided
with laissez-faire views in the United States,[45] as well as more middle-
of-the-road views from *The Economist*, which advocates downsizing the
World Bank and the IMF and possibly merging them. The World
Bank, as a result of being ostracized at the Earth Summit, hired a few
noneconomists and brought in some of its harshest critics to teach its
staff about the local impacts of bank loans and policies. One result of
this change of direction is the Global Environment Facility (GEF),
jointly managed by the World Bank, UNDP, and the UN Environment
Program (UNEP). The GEF, under this tripartite management,
loaned $918 million for environmental projects in Mexico alone in
1994. If freed from World Bank control, however, the GEF could shift
toward sustainable development and environmental enhancement.

Restructuring the Bretton Woods institutions caught academics
and mainstream institutions by surprise. Hundreds of university seminars and conferences were scheduled in 1995 on these issues and the
subject of sustainable development. Here again, many corporate and
government futurists ignored the early stirrings of citizen movements
for perfecting democracy, social justice, and sustainable development. Women form the backbone of grassroots citizen organizations,
and their role in global production and development is now being recognized by UN agencies, governments, and businesses.[46] Current
leaders can lighten their burdens by learning to delegate some control to many such responsible and resourceful groups.

LEVEL 4: NATION-STATES, DOMESTIC POLICIES, AND DEMOCRATIC PROCESSES

Nations have become too small to solve the big global problems and
too big for their local problems. Rallying cries and flash points have

been around democracy, self-determination, and devolution. These slogans have unwound into an array of Pandora's boxes—offering new learning experiences—from rebellions against Moscow in the Caucasus and Black Sea regions to the drive by U.S. conservatives and Republicans in 1995 to reclaim states' rights from the national government. The confused rhetoric of budget battles has included arguments over unfunded mandates, block grants, and repeal of "onerous national standards," i.e., affirmative action, civil rights, environmental rules, and so on, and their federal enforcement. All this was in search of traditional American Dream goals of individual liberty, property rights, and the pursuit of happiness. These goals, however, had become intransitive in the complexities of technologically mature, urbanized, industrial societies.

In *Creating Alternative Futures* (1978, 156–58), I noted that Alexis de Tocqueville had foreseen all this as far back as 1835 in *Democracy in America*. He noted, along with his praise and enthusiasm for the American experiment, its tendencies that might lead to *economic* totalitarianism. More persuasive than Karl Marx, de Tocqueville, a systems thinker, reasoned that equality of political condition would lead to increasing incomes, which would lead to greater demand for manufactured goods, which would require greater division of labor. This specialization (which Adam Smith hailed for its efficiency) would increase the relative differences in income and "mental alertness" between workers and owners, which would result in a "manufacturing aristocracy." As the U.S. "restoration" of 1995 proceeded, others re-sounded this alarm, including Kevin Phillips in *Arrogant Capital* (1994), Michael Lind of *The New Republic* in *The Next American Nation* (1995), following Christopher Lasch's *The Revolt of the Elite* (1995). All predicted that an entrenched, white, elite overclass would continue to prosper while every other U.S. group would shrink to comparative "third world" levels of deprivation.

Second thoughts about devolution and states' rights came not only from advocates of the poor, underprivileged, disabled, children, and the environment, however, but also from business. Nothing is worse for national corporations than complying with crazy quilts of different state laws, taxes, and enforcements. I discovered this while chairing Citizens for Clean Air in New York. Once New York and California were pressured into enacting smog controls on cars, the Detroit auto industry went to Washington demanding that these standards be set nationwide—as they were in 1968. As then, so in the 1990s. In August 1995, *Business Week* editorialized against devolution as "political hype generating suspicions that the entire effort is a shell game by national politicians to shift the burden of cutting the federal budget to the states." The lead article, "Power to the States," traced the history since 1789 of the American tug-of-war between Washington, D.C., and the states over slavery, tariffs, and racial segregation, through the Civil War to the New Deal, when Franklin Roosevelt exercised federal power over labor relations and Social Security was enacted, to Richard Nixon and federal environmental standard-setting.[47]

As most U.S. citizens know, state and local governments in the United States are often the *most* corrupt, dominated by financial and corporate special interests. Local politicians almost routinely line their pockets, thanks to inside information on where airports, roads, and other projects are to be sited, allowing profits for politicians and their friends from real estate and construction deals. As the Republican Congress members dished out federal taxpayers' dollars to states in block grants for welfare, transportation, Medicaid, job training, and the environment, many observers pointed to the problems of state and local corruption. Worse, there was the inevitable problem of "free riders": states might compete to shut out the poor and needy while offering their natural resources and "pollution havens" to industry—just as was occurring at the global level. Would this lead to a similar "race to the bottom," as in the lowest-common-denominator economic playing field and global financial casino, or would it lead to more train wrecks as the two parties collided on the budget?

An earlier flash point during the late 1980s had led to the end of the Soviet Union. Mikhail Gorbachev initiated a new international debate about governance and the state of the world.[48] His speeches and actions advocating perestroika and glasnost electrified the world, accelerating the inevitable breakup of the Soviet Union and the revolutions in Eastern Europe. It has been a triumph of common sense that so many politicians, regardless of ideology and tradition, have begun moving toward democratization and markets—with the aid of newly free mass media, which has accelerated the inevitable restructuring.

But the new democrats still must avoid several potential dangers. They must not simply equate democracy with other forms of decentralization, privatization, and markets; and they must avoid being caught up in the widening confusion about the two key individual signals from people to their decision makers in government and business—*votes* and *prices*. Today, these two vital forms of feedback are failing to deliver enough timely information on the effects of policies to guide and correct decisions, both in the United States and Russia as well as every country in the world. Votes every two or four years are too slow and cannot refine voters' feedback on multiple issues, while prices that do not incorporate the full spectrum of social and environmental costs can guide markets into unsustainable paths, as discussed further under Level 5.

Democracy has emerged as a necessary process to manage the complexities of reorganizing human societies for this next quantum leap, as discussed in Chapter 11. Group decision making must now embrace

1. how to control our own population,
2. how to redesign our production and distribution systems to operate within ecological tolerances so as to be sustainable over the long term,
3. how to clean up the backlog of toxic and hazardous conditions created by our unsustainable forms of industrialization, and
4. how to do all this as equitably and therefore as peacefully as possible.

Ironically, the search for the will of the people to guide social change stalled in the United States itself—as in the 1992 and 1994 elections when polls found frustration and mistrust of government run by special interests at an all-time high.[49] Just as other countries were looking to the United States, Washington, D.C., seemed to be having a nervous breakdown. National policies, old and new paradigms, are clashing before baffled voters, but are not yet seen as part of a systemic shift to more sustainable development.

The same policy flash points around devolution, budgets, joblessness, poverty gaps, and environmental degradation are evident in most OECD countries. Only new sustainable human development paradigms and new systems of national accounts can address these issues. Taxes should be redesigned to discourage unhealthy behavior and encourage healthy, productive activities. For example, governments can reduce today's widespread subsidies to business for often

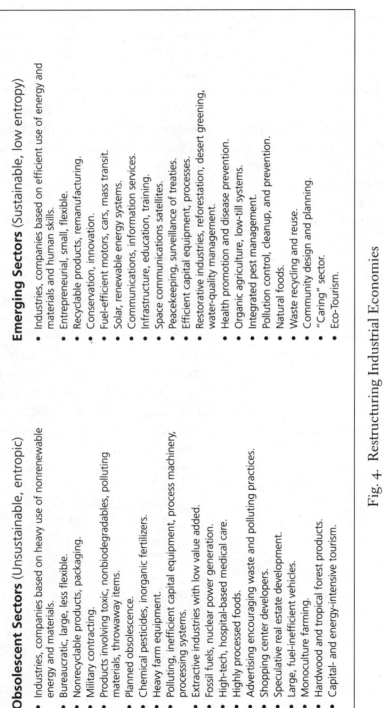

Obsolescent Sectors (Unsustainable, entropic)

- Industries, companies based on heavy use of nonrenewable energy and materials.
- Bureaucratic, large, less flexible.
- Nonrecyclable products, packaging.
- Military contracting.
- Products involving toxic, nonbiodegradables, polluting materials, throwaway items.
- Planned obsolescence.
- Chemical pesticides, inorganic fertilizers.
- Heavy farm equipment.
- Polluting, inefficient capital equipment, process machinery, processing systems.
- Extractive industries with low value added.
- Fossil fuels, nuclear power generation.
- High-tech, hospital-based medical care.
- Highly processed foods.
- Advertising encouraging waste and polluting practices.
- Shopping center developers.
- Speculative real estate development.
- Large, fuel-inefficient vehicles.
- Monoculture farming.
- Hardwood and tropical forest products.
- Capital- and energy-intensive tourism.

Emerging Sectors (Sustainable, low entropy)

- Industries, companies based on efficient use of energy and materials and human skills.
- Entrepreneurial, small, flexible.
- Recyclable products, remanufacturing.
- Conservation, innovation.
- Fuel-efficient motors, cars, mass transit.
- Solar, renewable energy systems.
- Communications, information services.
- Infrastructure, education, training.
- Space communications satellites.
- Peacekeeping, surveillance of treaties.
- Efficient capital equipment, processes.
- Restorative industries, reforestation, desert greening, water-quality management.
- Health promotion and disease prevention.
- Organic agriculture, low-till systems.
- Integrated pest management.
- Pollution control, cleanup, and prevention.
- Natural foods.
- Waste recycling and reuse.
- Community design and planning.
- "Caring" sector.
- Eco-Tourism.

Fig. 4. Restructuring Industrial Economies   Source: *Paradigms in Progress*

© 1989/91 Hazel Henderson

irrational capital investments, which promote automation and down-sizing, and at the same time offer employment tax credits to encourage full employment, or reduce some of the heavy penalties levied on employment. Nations must focus on restructuring wasteful sectors, on redirecting and changing the rules of this global economic warfare game in order to move toward sustainable development. However, forces of globalization, not national governments, are driving these industrial restructuring processes. (See Fig. 4. Restructuring Industrial Economies.) National governments must restructure *themselves*, rethink their roles vis-à-vis local levels, realign priorities, and reconnect with their electorates in new ways if they are to govern effectively. This paradigm shift will take decades.

LEVEL 5: GLOBAL MARKETS, CORPORATIONS, TRADE, AND FINANCE

All countries face the global economic warfare scenario of cutthroat competition, creeping budget deficits, and jobless growth, as well as the other vicious circles described throughout Part I. (See Fig. 5. Vicious Circle Economies.) Yet these vicious circles are now serving as flash points for transition—all the crises in the global casino have provided the needed if painful feedback. Just as feedback from individuals is vital if we are to enhance democracy and improve decision-making processes at all levels, so feedback from consumers is vital to correct prices and guide business decisions and capital markets. By 1995 it was widely acknowledged that the price system does not reflect many social and environmental costs or longer-term impacts of production on future generations. Most economic textbooks advocate discount rates in cost-benefit analyses that systematically lower time horizons by calculations of "present value" that deem worthless any benefits not realized within ten years. This narrow-gauge, short-term maximization formula still underlies most economic decision making, not only in the private-sector markets but also in government projects, bond issues, etc. This formula also pervades macroeconomic management.

The new economics of sustainable development (of less-than-perfect markets and often-irrational actors) is filtering into textbooks, corporate board rooms, and government agencies as well as the business media (for example, *The Economist*, a bastion of economic orthodoxy, via its environmental editor, Frances Cairncross and her book

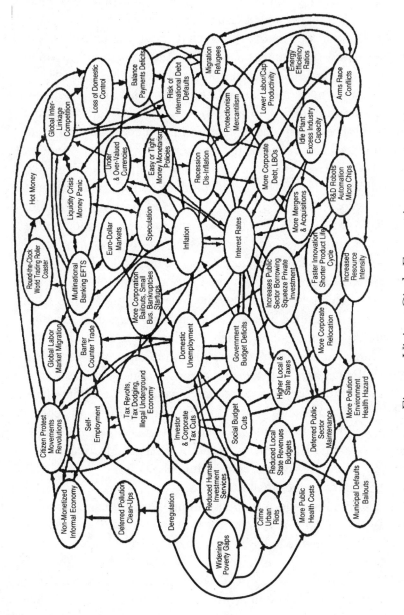

Fig. 5. Vicious Circle Economies

© 1980 Hazel Henderson   Source: *Paradigms in Progress*

Costing the Earth). The key theoretical consensus now emerging is that prices, if they are to function as sound feedbacks to markets, governments, and consumer decision making, must accurately reflect, to the greatest degree possible, social and environmental costs. Eco-labeling in Germany, France, Canada, the United States, and other OECD countries now helps consumers choose eco-efficient products. Social and environmental audits are becoming more common in corporate annual reports, as summarized in *Coming Clean*.[50]

Social and environmental treasures that are deemed priceless — national monuments, natural wonders, aesthetic and spiritual values — must be determined by democratic processes, i.e., voting and other enhanced forms of participation discussed in Chapters 10 and 11. A working consensus on the necessity of correcting the pricing system, codified in the OECD's 1970 "Polluter Pays Principle," is shared by the International Chamber of Commerce, the World Business Council for Sustainable Development, the Business Council for the Social Summit, the World Business Academy, and the Social Investment Forums in the United States and the United Kingdom, as well as the Minnesota Center on Corporate Responsibility, the Council on Economic Priorities, the Social Venture Networks in Europe and the United States, and countless professional societies, including the International Society for Ecological Economics, the Society for the Advancement of Social Economics, Economists Allied for Arms Reduction, the International Association of Architects, and various accounting groups and insurance agencies. Such groups have produced new statements of principles embodying these concepts of accountability including, for example, the Caux Principles and the CERES (Coalition for Environmentally Responsible Economies) Principles, with fifty signatories including General Motors and other major corporations and small businesses.[51]

This consensus reflects the 1970 Polluter Pays Principle, promulgated by the OECD. However, just as it took twenty years for the Polluter Pays Principle to be incorporated into today's consensus on correcting the price system, implementing the correction of prices at all system levels has just begun. The growth since the early 1980s of socially responsible investment funds is now helping to capitalize emerging sectors of more sustainable economies. Approaches to moving economic decisions toward sustainable development are still fragmented, however.

The World Business Council for Sustainable Development, for example, supports shifting tax codes toward capital, energy, and resource use, with a range of levies and fees on depletion of virgin resources, waste (such as in energy use and packaging), planned obsolescence (throwaway products), and polluting emissions. This would have the instant effect of underpinning major markets for recycling and reusing materials. In its first book, *Changing Course* (1992), the World Business Council for Sustainable Development advanced the environmental and resource depletion arguments for these taxes. They ran into opposition from polluting sunset industries and mainstream businesses concerned that such new taxes will make them uncompetitive and price their products out of world markets. Meanwhile, global markets for pollution control and environmental management are burgeoning. In the United States up to $400 billion will be contracted by the Department of Energy and Department of Defense to clean toxic military sites, Malaysia spent $432 million in 1994, Thailand will spend $1.5 billion by the year 2000, and Taiwan will spend $126 million between 1995 and 1997. Ironically, it is mostly companies based in OECD countries that stand to benefit from these markets, such as BFI, Waste Management, and Bechtel.[52]

While it is true that green taxes will penalize wasteful sunset industries, causing them to oppose sustainable development policies, a wider, systemic analysis produces a solution. In 1995, the Business Council for the Social Summit focused on the problem of jobless economic growth using rather traditional approaches: i.e., more public-works projects and training programs, making labor markets "more efficient," plus some of the job sharing, shorter workweek ideas now being resuscitated in France and Germany. Later in 1995 both the World Business Council for Sustainable Development and the Business Council for the Social Summit saw that they were actually approaching the same goal: rebalancing national tax codes toward neutrality between labor and capital. Now, both support many similar proposals: taxes on capital, energy, resource waste, and pollution rather than "flat tax" gimmicks. To achieve the desired neutrality, both business councils support either reductions in employee taxes or employment tax credits until neutrality is achieved in various countries. Such win-win policies become visible only with systems analysis. Hopefully business groups will eventually support reductions in value added taxes (VAT) and income taxes. If neutrality is still not achieved in some circumstances, business groups may also support guaranteed annual incomes—if for no other reason than to substitute for dozens of government income-support and other costly social programs. These "negative income tax" and guaranteed income proposals, made in the 1960s by conservative U.S. economist Milton Friedman, Robert Theobald, myself, and others, may be viewed at last as *socially* efficient.

The role of technological innovation in achieving greater energy efficiency, miniaturization, and material conservation is a key factor in reducing the impact of human activities on planetary ecosystems. An overall shift from hardware to software and from mechanistic to organic, biological models is primary, as described in Chapter 3. When confronted with a problem of production, we humans need to think harder and more systemically rather than rush to conjure up visions of machinery, factories, or human-built infrastructure. For example, in *Creating Alternative Futures*, I cited the case of mining metals: surprisingly, plants are infinitely more efficient than humans. Plants mine more tons of metals and other minerals each year (through their roots in various mineral-rich soils) than all the world-wide human mining operations combined.[53] Similarly, sanitary engineers taught to build pipelines and tank-based sewage treatment plants are now learning which plant species can purify water and soil by removing substances that human systems cannot—a major paradigm shift. These water-purification systems can be inspected: for example, those designed by U.S. biologist John Todd and his Canadian partner Nancy Jack Todd of the New Alchemy Institute in Falmouth, Massachusetts; or those of ecologists Howard T. Odum and Mark Brown at the Center for Wetlands at the University of Florida in Gainesville, Florida.

In energy conservation, demand-side management, now broadly adopted in the electric utility industry worldwide, is part of the innovative consultancy of the Rocky Mountain Institute of Snowmass, Colorado. While not overtly "green," demand-side management does reduce environmental damage. In 1995, solar-collecting cells cost one-third what they cost in 1980. Utilities no longer oppose solar electricity. The New York Power Authority and others are now installing solar roofs and systems integrated into buildings—where excess electricity generated can be fed back into utility grids—as I had predicted in 1974.[54] *Business Week* sees a global boom in photovoltaics.

Although the U.S. market is small, it is growing at 30 percent annually and may reach $7 billion by the end of the century.[55] Chemical manufacturing processes are being refined so as to conserve energy by 30 percent or more, leading to increased profitability for newly designed facilities in such chemical firms as ICI and BASF. For example, using "pinch analysis" to model new manufacturing processes, British-based chemist Bodo Linnhoff's fifty-person consulting group is increasing revenues by 50 percent annually.

The good news in sustainable development is that in today's global economy, in spite of some corporate and government laggards, innovations travel rapidly. For example, China has new regulations calling for installation of both compact fluorescent lighting (which saves 50 percent of electricity loads) and state-of-the-art energy efficiency, such as cogeneration in new power plants. Such technological innovation can be monitored by watching or investing in portfolios of environmentally oriented mutual funds and venture capital partnerships in OECD and emerging capital markets. Today, for less than the price of a full-size U.S. car, homeowners can buy a roof that can take care of their home's energy needs for twenty-five to thirty years.[56]

Just as environmentally sound energy production equates with reducing waste and higher profitability, so industrial processes that are environmentally benign also save energy and raw materials, and therefore reduce costs and increase profits. New consultancies, for example Sweden's Natural Step and New York–based GreenAudit, Inc., identify these systemic energy and cost savings for client companies. Imperfect markets have prevented industrial processes from being designed eco-efficiently. An industry leader, 3M Company, which operates in more than twenty countries, has begun to redesign all its chemical processes to reduce all hazardous and nonhazardous emissions by 90 percent by the year 2000. Over the past decade 3M's "Pollution Prevention Pays" program has already saved the company millions of dollars.[57]

Even though cleaning up past pollution still is necessary, and often driven by insurance liabilities, the real payoff for companies, national economies, and the environment is in the industrial design revolution now under way—not only involving "greener" technologies but also reinventing management. For example, when a group of industries in an area pool their efforts, they can reuse more of each other's waste as inputs. This has been achieved in the town of

Kalundborg, Denmark, which thinks big and in systems terms. Here, industrial waste and waste-process heat are exchanged between a power plant, an oil refinery, a pharmaceutical manufacturer, a plaster-board factory, a cement producer, farmers, and the district supplier of home heating. These win-win-win approaches show the future potential of organizing common systems through cooperation—to complement the competitive market place. This paradigm shift is occurring rapidly.

LEVEL 6: PROVINCIAL, URBAN, AND LOCAL GOVERNANCE

Many sustainable development policies are best initiated and managed at the provincial, urban, and local levels. Transportation is often a flash point, as cars compete for agricultural land and road space, and also compete with more efficient public transit and bicycles. Urban and local governments can best design sustainable transportation systems: from bus and commuter rail services to road pricing in order to rationalize automobile road travel and modify rush-hour use. Even while national governments argue over standards and block grants, local governments can act. Lanes can be dedicated to private vehicles with many passengers as well as corporate and government carpool vans; bicycle lanes can be established; and car-free zones and pedestrian shopping streets can be provided in downtowns. Numerous examples of these urban initiatives in OECD countries can be seen in Amsterdam, Bonn, Stockholm, London, Madrid, Brussels, Paris, Washington, D.C., Seattle, and many other cities. In China, Shanghai and Beijing are models of transportation efficiency, built with wide lanes separated from cars, trucks, and buses for safe bicycling, and with good subway systems as well.

However, the increase in private cars and motorcycles in China and worldwide has led to greater congestion and pollution. The first automobile company to offer the world market a low- or zero-emission vehicle (whether electric, hydrogen fuel cell, or other hybrid) will serve the requirements of Los Angeles and many other OECD cities—an enormous market. Other initiatives in the areas of recycling, water treatment, and local taxation of waste disposal are best implemented at the city level, such as the innovative policies of Mayor Jaime Lerner of Curitiba, Brazil, discussed further in Chapter 9. Also, Bangkok's deteriorating environment is now creating markets for G-7–based companies such as Britain's North West Water Company, which signed a $256 million contract in 1995 to build a water treatment plant there.

City, state, and local governments usually have jurisdiction over zoning and land use. Zoning changes can lead to more efficient use of the sprawling urban bedroom communities surrounding U.S. cities by allowing multiple zoning, so that people can work at home or closer to home and larger, unrelated "intentional families" can occupy large houses zoned for single-family use. Such efficient use of urban space could save an average family $5,000 per year, according to architects Duany, Plater, Zyberk of Miami, Florida.[58] Additionally, city and local governments can best implement ordinances on residential construction for energy efficiency, solar heating and cooling, as well as tree planting and more urban parks. Trees can substitute for air conditioning in residential neighborhoods, reducing ambient air temperatures by as much as ten degrees Fahrenheit—saving both electricity costs for consumers and new power plant investments for utility companies.

In Detroit, Michigan, gutted inner city blocks are being converted into parks and neighborhood gardens. Local and city authorities can also license farmers' produce markets, which allow access to small producers in the area. In many U.S. cities, local farms have found competitive advantage by selling higher-priced, organic produce to upscale urban dwellers who reject pesticide-laden farm products. U.S. farmers are switching to organic production in record numbers, due to the high prices of fuel, fertilizer, and pesticide inputs; competition for conventional crops; and the higher profit margins in pesticide-free produce.

Local taxation can also be a tool to achieve sustainable development goals, for example, full-cost pricing of public services such as electricity, water, and waste disposal. In the United States such groups as the National Association of State, County, and Municipal Governments and the League of Elected Officials share information on innovative programs. The fastest growing initiatives are those developing "Sustainable Communities" plans, such as Sustainable Seattle. These programs are linking up and promoting local versions of Agenda 21, as proclaimed recently by the Governor of the State of Iowa.[59] The World Health Organization has, for a decade, networked its "Healthy Cities" initiative, such as Healthier Toronto. Some two thousand representatives of such programs convened in San Francisco in 1993 for the International Healthy Cities Conference. Another set of important local initiatives are the local currencies and barter exchanges described in Chapter 9 and the new urban quality-of-life indicators, such as those pioneered by the city of Jacksonville, Florida, since 1983.[60] All of these local networks and initiatives communicate with each other, with national governments, and at international levels and provide test beds for replication.

LEVEL 7: FAMILY/COMMUNITY/INDIVIDUAL VALUES, ETHICS, AND BEHAVIORS

All of the multiple, interacting levels of sustainable development activities discussed so far are generated by changes in perceptions, values, and lifestyles of individuals and families. Naturally these changes create conflicts and flash points of their own. Indeed, conflicts about ideas and values are healthy—they maintain cultural diversity. Only conflicts that are not channeled constructively lead to alienation, further conflict, and eventually violence. Psychology plays a key role in helping people understand how to channel conflict constructively and how to meet their needs for belonging, approval, self-esteem, work, and family and social roles, as well as how to assert their individual creativity and search for meaning, purpose, and self-actualization at their highest potential.[61] Industrialism, like all other cultures, offers individuals a menu of ways of being and behaving that provide internal consistency along with social roles, jobs, income, political participation, and a sense of larger national purpose.

This national purpose of industrial and military competitiveness with other nations is becoming ever more counterproductive, however. Industrialism's cultural menu is encountering contradictions as it enters maturity and transitions into post-industrial stages. Post-industrialism is characterized by predominantly nonmaterial service sectors, information richness, high technology, and affluence, often coexisting in most OECD countries with widening poverty gaps, joblessness, urban decay, drugs, suicide, crime, fragmented families and communities, loneliness, and loss of meaning. (See Fig. 6. Profile of Human Distress in the Industrial Countries.) These conditions, the results of maximizing growth combined with rising levels of pollution, have produced widespread cognitive dissonance. There is a greater questioning of industrialism's value system, which is based on efficiency,

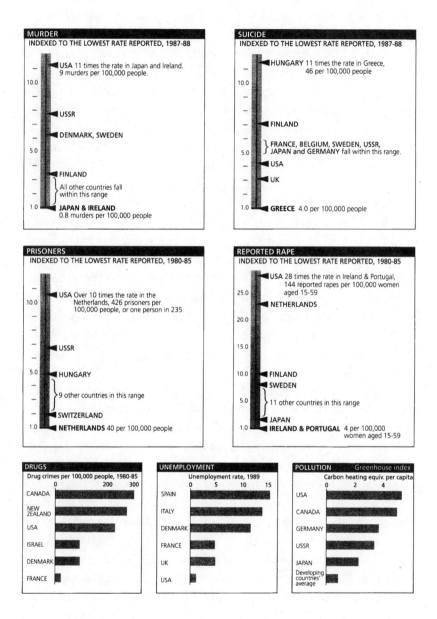

Fig. 6.   Profile of Human Distress in the Industrial Countries

Source: *Human Development Report, 1994*, United Nations Development Programme

materialism, and secular economism. In addition, these material values of industrialism and consumerism now seriously conflict with its other values of democracy, freedom, equality, and opportunities for upward mobility—let alone the higher values of social justice and human and cultural development, as discussed in Chapter 7.

The reasons for the new value conflicts are not only to save the earth, but more importantly to get back to basic values: family; community; sharing, loving relationships; and simplicity, now seen by many as *preferable* to life in the fast lane competing in the rat race for more money and consumer goods. In May 1993, I held a press briefing at the National Press Club in Washington, D.C., on the subject of "Redefining Wealth and Progress" and ways of overhauling GNP, attended by some fifty journalists and editors and televised nationally on C-Span.[62] All of this searching for new meaning *beyond* industrialism's promise of more in material terms is evident in other G-7 countries, in the rise of Green parties, recycling, and more responsible consumption and investing. Change at the psychological level has also driven the innovation of green technologies and the growth of socially responsible investing, ethical and environmental mutual funds whose market research follows these public and consumer trends closely.

This brief overview cannot do justice to the interacting trends driving sustainable development at all levels. Most editors and producers, under constant news deadlines, do not take the time to understand the sustainable development paradigm. More expansive, systemic frameworks can help reconceptualize today's great globalizations and the restructuring processes they engender. There is widely shared understanding that social safety nets, which have evolved over the past fifty years, are necessary in every society to tame markets. We cannot go on asking whose end of the boat is sinking. The clash of the global economic warfare paradigm and the sustainable development paradigm enables policymakers, business leaders, academics, and grassroots globalists to see a more comprehensive picture of the global change processes now in motion.

CHAPTER 2

JUGGERNAUT GLOBALISM AND THE BANKRUPTCY OF ECONOMICS

By the mid-1990s, nations had begun disintegrating—balkanized by pressures from within and by the forces of globalization from without. As E. F. Schumacher (1973) had predicted, nation-states were proving too big for smaller, local problems and too small for big, global ones. National leaders were complaining about losing their domestic policy options to "global competition." Enslaved by the ideas of their defunct economic advisors, they had no one to blame but themselves. National sovereignty had been ceded by conceptual blindness to trillion dollar daily capital flows that even inside players conceded were unstable, as well as "cruel," "Darwinian," and "in need of regulation."[1] Former U.S. President George Bush keynoted *Business Week's* 1995 Presidents Forum of 150 corporate CEOs on "Twenty-first Century Capitalism." His title was "New Rules for the Global Economy." Free-for-all global competition was sliding perilously toward global economic warfare.

GLOBAL RESTRUCTURING

Today's economic and technological globalism, based on nineteenth-century capitalism and the expansionist nationalism of the industrial era—culminating in the Cold War—has been driven by age-old territorialism and patriarchal structures of competition. New structures of cooperation must provide needed balance. Today's Information Age markets, driven by galloping competition, have spun off into

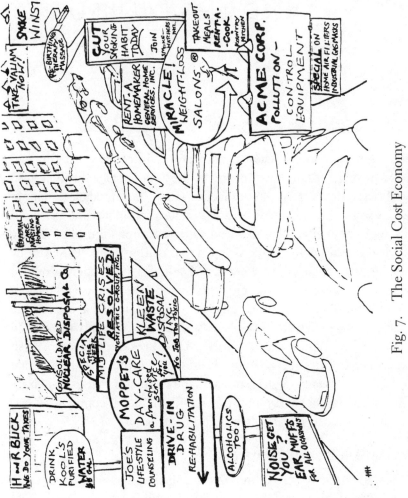

Fig. 7. The Social Cost Economy   Source: *The Politics of the Solar Age*

financial cyberspace, divorced from the realities of Main Street, human needs, and nature's ecosystems. The first casualties: welfare safety nets, as even the Nordic countries and Canada downsized their proud public services. Britain's Lord Robert Skidelsky noted in *The World after Communism* (1995) that welfare states serve the essential purpose of underpinning social cohesion, which permits capitalism to get on with its business. Paul Pierson studied the process of downsizing public services, and in *Dismantling the Welfare State* (1995) he describes how politicians learn to make frequent small cuts — rendering the process imperceptible over time. Alarmed citizens worldwide responded by organizing to protect themselves, their livelihoods, neighborhoods, and local environments from the destabilizing effects of global competition.

Even the long-awaited post–Cold War peace dividends of some $935 billion had not been redeployed to civilian sectors. Citizen groups worldwide had long since shifted their attention from military to human security (i.e., safe streets, sustainable livelihoods and development, peacemaking, and the environment), but few generals and politicians had gotten the message. Worse, of the eighty-two conflicts in the world between 1989 and 1992, all but three had been *within* nations — as destructuring released old rivalries and some nations, including Yugoslavia, Somalia, and Rwanda, simply fell apart.[2] In these domestic wars, civilians were 90 percent of the casualties. By 1993, there were 18.2 million refugees and 24 million internally displaced people. By October 1994, these figures had increased to 23 million and 26 million, respectively. Meanwhile, the world's debt trap persisted in most heavily indebted poor countries, which still owed $230.2 billion at the end of 1993.[3] Budget deficits in industrial countries grew; only one OECD member-country, Norway, had a surplus in 1995.[4]

Global restructuring continues to accelerate, driven by all these forces and in lockstep with global financial flows, over 90 percent of which are speculative. Ever more complex derivatives and "risk-management" instruments, designed to protect individual players in the financial market, add to systemic instabilities and risks. Over 50 percent of the firms using such derivatives do not fully understand them, according to Professor Richard C. Marsden of the University of Pennsylvania's Wharton School of Business.[5] In December 1994, *Business Week*, in a Special Report titled "Twenty-first Century Capitalism," predicted that "market players will become a new class of stateless legislators checking governments' ability to tax, spend, borrow, or depreciate their debts through inflation." At last, financial actors and their press organs began echoing what I and other researchers had pointed out for over a decade: the new forces of globalization had *already* undermined national sovereignty, not only in domestic macroeconomic management of fiscal and monetary policy, but also in the loss of social policy options in the areas of health, education, safety nets, employment, environment, and even the values and culture of their citizens.

The inability of national governments to even address the mounting risks to all actors is a classic example of advancing technology and globalization rendering economic textbooks obsolete. The new global "electronic commons" now engulfing national sovereignty requires a global legal framework to manage volatility and bring order to its global casino. As game theory and dynamic chaos models supersede economics, they show that rules of interaction are as fundamental as markets in human societies. The invisible hand is—and always was—our own.

Economic theory overlooks many issues of the global commons, including rules of access and allocation. Most of the issues perplexing human societies involve the global commons: the oceans, the atmosphere, biodiversity, Antarctica, the planet's electromagnetic spectrum, and space. Today's now-integrated, twenty-four-hour global casino is transforming from a classic free marketplace of win-lose competition into a new form of "electronic commons." Economic textbooks still do not teach how to recognize when markets evolve into commons (i.e., as all the niches in the market get filled up, as described further in Chapter 12), or how to spot a new "invisible foot" emerging, as each "rational" actor's self-interested behavior can endanger the whole system—unless rapid collective action is taken (i.e., establishing win-win rules). Markets work best with win-lose rules, while commons work only with win-win rules. If such win-win rules are not adopted when markets transform into commons, the result is lose-lose—the dilemma all actors face in today's global casino. An example of paradigm confusion: when U.S. Treasury Secretary Robert Rubin urged Asian countries to reform their financial sectors, he was talking more about deregulation and opening their markets than the vitally needed *regulation* of their stock and bond markets, particularly in China and India.[6]

Regulators and central bankers were forced into collective action on a crisis basis after the 1994–95 Mexican peso crisis, since none could defend their currencies, even in concert. Central bankers' policies are defeated each day by the collective action of currency traders staging "bear raids" on weak currencies at will. (For a thrilling contemporary account read *The Vandals' Crown: How the World's Currency Traders Beat the Central Banks* [Millman 1995].) U.S. Treasury Secretary Robert Rubin and Federal Reserve Board Chairman Alan Greenspan's efforts to coordinate thirteen countries' central banks to boost the dollar prior to the June 1995 G-7 meeting and later efforts gave only short-lived warning to currency traders—at a cost to their respective taxpayers of over $2 billion. Increasingly, central banks will have to shift from managing domestic money supply to focusing on global aggregates. No longer is it only developing countries that are swamped by waves of hot money washing across their borders. McKinsey Global Institute estimates that the total stock of financial assets traded in global capital markets will increase from $35 trillion in 1992 to $83 trillion in 2000.[7] Emerging markets may grow from 15 percent of world capitalization in 1995 to 44 percent by 2010. Privatizations in 1995 accounted for almost $1 trillion worldwide. Yet investors in emerging global markets took a bath in 1995 as Mexico dragged down stock markets worldwide, with only a few registering any gains over their 1993 level.[8]

Will high-tech "rocket science" stay ahead of regulators, possibly causing markets to spin out of control? Technological innovations such as computers, which have created today's global electronic commons, always outpace the social innovations they eventually call forth—often only after crises. The innovation of "circuit breakers" after the 1987 Wall Street crash now dampens the effects of program trading (where computerized buy and sell orders simultaneously executed often amplify market movements). National legislation is ineffective since only global agreements on the use of global commons can address today's paradoxes. Even high-rolling financier George Soros (1995) called for global regulation, because "financial markets are inherently unstable and liable to break down unless stability is introduced as an explicit objective of government policy." This new regulatory framework must be as global and "real time" as the markets. The many studies occasioned by the fiftieth anniversary of the UN[9] are outlined in Chapters 12 and 13.

The member-states of the UN must face up to this hurricane of global change. The UN is no longer merely a "trade association" of nations, where member-states can control its agenda by withholding dues. Nations continue to "use" the UN to either justify national foreign policy actions or to send peacekeeping forces into impossible situations they would rather avoid, such as Bosnia, Somalia, or Rwanda. The UN now has other de facto constituents, "We the peoples," as its Charter states: the global civil society composed of private, voluntary, nongovernmental organizations and enterprises, which are powerful constituencies within member countries as well. If member governments try to "starve" the UN, such groups will see that the UN's functions in the areas of human rights, global standard-setting, health, education, environmental monitoring, and human development are funded in alternative ways. The great globalization forces unleashed by industrialism—including those of the "electronic commons"—ushered in the Information Age, but not yet a Knowledge Age or an Age of Wisdom. Governments cannot control the activities of the emerging civil society, just as they cannot control transnational corporations—unless they reinvent the UN itself and their own collective responses to global change. Another round of UN-bashing in the U.S., not seen since the Reagan years, began with the Republican Congress in 1994. As U.S. politics became more divisive, the UN was caught in the cross fire. By 1995, political alienation in the United States was at an all-time high.[10] The UN was often scapegoated by domestic fringe groups such as the armed militias in many states and made the subject of their often paranoid delusions.

The UN is the only institution truly positioned to convene, foster, and broker all the actors and institutions in government, business, finance, academia, and the global civil society. From the viewpoint of national governments and the nation-state based institutions of the receding Industrial Age, the UN seems to be losing power—even as it is being asked to perform more onerous tasks with dwindling funds. Yet from the perspective of the emerging Information Age now engulfing nation-states, the UN is actually well positioned to serve the new needs being pressed upon it by the global civil society. Just as large corporations such as IBM and sclerotic central governments are reinventing and restructuring themselves—cutting layers of bureaucracy and downsizing and decentralizing to meet the "distributed information" criteria of today's organizations—so the UN can redeploy its assets to emphasize its strengths. The UN is ideally suited to foster global agenda-setting, research, and agreements to manage the global common-heritage resources of the planet. To accomplish these tasks, the UN should be compensated; these are vital services that enable markets to function and human social aspirations for sustainable development to be addressed. In many cases, the UN can and should enter into new public-private partnerships to address functions similar to INTELSAT, the International Telecommunications Satellite, or the Bretton Woods institutions created in 1945.

Meanwhile, grassroots and civil society groups in most countries, North and South, are demanding new codes of conduct for global corporations and new agreements to tame global capital markets and their traditional evaluation tools: GNP (gross national product) and CAPM (capital asset pricing models), which fail to take account of social and environmental costs of production. These demands are ad hoc responses to paralyzed national governments and their politicians, who blame global competition for structural unemployment, the shredding of safety nets, and lower investments in education and health. Other pragmatic local responses include computerized barter systems, radio "garage sales," time dollars, service credits, and other local, scrip-based currencies that employ people and clear local markets by enabling local people to purchase local goods and services when they have been starved for credit by central banks and national policies, as described in Chapter 9. Indeed, if the global casino's stranglehold on local communities continues, local information currencies, regional payments unions, virtual banks and E-cash on the Internet, global barter, and countertrade, already estimated as 25 percent of all world trade, may simply break the global money cartel by end-running it.[11] Such recently revealed "Catch-22s" force a painful new reality check: national sovereignty is fast becoming a nostalgic slogan—now ebbing away from all governments since the widespread deregulation of capital markets in the 1980s and the establishment of the World Trade Organization (WTO) in 1995.

FROM BALANCE SHEETS TO CIRCULAR PROCESSES

These new vicious circles and double binds signal the bankruptcy of macroeconomics and its limited tool kits for managing domestic national affairs. Economics textbooks no longer help us clarify *what is valuable*, or what is a *cost* and what is a *benefit*. Old economic theories have been blown away by the hurricane of change and the turbulent globalization processes I described in *Paradigms in Progress* (1991, 1995): the globalizing of technology, production, information, financial flows and stock markets, migrating jobs and workers, arms trafficking, and pollution. Most economic models, with their static, linear balance sheets and simple, linear cause-effect notions, assume that economies are national and tend toward general equilibrium; that competitive markets can allocate resources between guns, education, public transit, and investments in research and development; that relative distribution of income, wealth, power, and information between people is irrelevant; that nature's capital (clean air, water, and the environment) is still essentially free and inexhaustible; that scarce resources can always be substituted; and that the planet can continue absorbing human and industrial wastes, which economists have downplayed as "externalities." By the mid-1990s, some of the smartest economists were learning systems dynamics, nonlinear change modeling, futures research, ecology, and chaos theory in order to address the new global realities. (See Fig. 9. Differing Models of Economists and Futurists.) Even U.S. foundations, usually a conservative force, began to address *causes* in the perverse workings of economic theories, a change from their traditional focus on economic *effects*.

As markets and privatizations spread around the world, the macroeconomic management paradigm itself created much havoc — even in the G-7 countries, the world's "richest" societies: the United States, Britain, Japan, Germany, France, Italy, and Canada. As these changes, along with spreading democracy, opened new possibilities for human development, economics textbooks continued narrowing the policy options and debates, particularly in the former Soviet-bloc countries and the aspiring nations of the Southern Hemisphere. *Third World Resurgence*, a journal published in Penang, Malaysia, has documented the perversity of economism in all of its expressions: from World Bank and IMF policies to the example of economists "colonizing" the policies of the Intergovernmental Panel on Climate Change (IPCC) by persuading it in 1994 to adopt a free-market approach, which in effect valued peoples' lives in industrial countries ten times higher than peoples' lives in developing countries. The economists' mission was "to capture the sustainable development agenda for the economics profession," according to John Corkindale, a British economist at the U.K. Department of Environment. The economists' argument had been simple: it is cheaper to adapt to climate changes than to stop causing them, and the right to emit greenhouse gasses should be proportional to income.[12]

Yet new indicators are emerging to correct such irresponsible, unjust theories and the old scorecards of progress such as gross national product/gross domestic product (GNP/GDP), and to add broader, quality-of-life measures reflecting social and democratic goals of human development. Sustainable development, if it can be kept from colonization by economists, can challenge the old formula of competitive economic growth. The first task in steering human societies toward healthier forms of development is that of examining old assumptions, belief systems, and paradigms that may have been appropriate in earlier, less complex times but are now dysfunctional.

GNP/GDP (which came into widespread use during World War II to mobilize the allies' civilian economies and war production) serve as narrow scorecards of money-based progress, but not of sustainable human development. Few politicians—relying as they do on their economists—have examined the premises, goals, and values underlying GNP/GDP. Military production and output of goods and services are valued highly while educated citizens, children (a nation's future), and the environment are all valued at zero. Only money transactions are tracked—while the 50 percent of productive work in all industrial countries that is *unpaid* (volunteering; do-it-yourself home building and repairs; food growing; local government service; parenting children; caring for the elderly, sick, and disabled; maintaining households; etc.) is ignored. The *Human Development Report, 1995* focused on the productivity of this forgotten half of humanity and adjusted its rankings accordingly; in developing countries, the percentage of such unpaid work is much higher. This disregard for unpaid work reflects a deep bias in economic theory: that cooperative, altruistic work is "irrational" and only humans competitively maximizing their individual self-interests are "rational." (See Fig. 8. Total Productive System of an Industrial Society [Three-Layer Cake with Icing].) Today, competition must be rebalanced with cooperation at every level—from local to global—just as these two strategies coexist in all of nature's ecosystems. The *Human Development Report, 1995* identifies four critical areas in human development: productivity, equity, empowerment, and sustainability. Cooperation

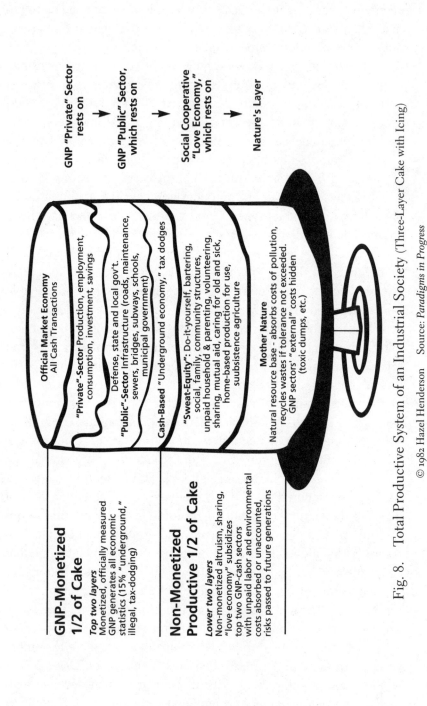

Fig. 8.   Total Productive System of an Industrial Society (Three-Layer Cake with Icing)

© 1982 Hazel Henderson   Source: *Paradigms in Progress*

GNP-Monetized 1/2 of Cake

Top two layers
Monetized, officially measured
GNP generates all economic
statistics (15% "underground,"
illegal, tax-dodging)

Non-Monetized Productive 1/2 of Cake

Lower two layers
Non-monetized altruism, sharing,
"love economy" subsidizes
top two GNP-cash sectors
with unpaid labor and environmental
costs absorbed or unaccounted,
risks passed to future generations

GNP "Private" Sector rests on →

GNP "Public" Sector, which rests on →

Social Cooperative "Love Economy," which rests on →

Nature's Layer →

Official Market Economy
All Cash Transactions

"Private"-Sector Production, employment,
consumption, investment, savings

"Public"-Sector Infrastructure (roads, maintenance,
sewers, bridges, subways, schools,
municipal government)
Defense, state and local gov't.

Cash-Based "Underground economy," tax dodges

"Sweat-Equity": Do-it-yourself, bartering,
social, family, community structures,
unpaid household & parenting, volunteering,
sharing, mutual aid, caring for old and sick,
home-based production for use,
subsistence agriculture

Mother Nature
Natural resource base - absorbs costs of pollution,
recycles wastes if tolerance not exceeded.
GNP sectors' "external" costs hidden
(toxic dumps, etc.)

and rebalancing the roles of men and women are crucial elements in each area.[13]

To achieve the necessary turnaround of industrial and industrializing economies, policymakers need to see that today's globalization processes are driven by competition: among nations, corporations, science and technological innovations, trade blocs, and financial markets, and are now leading to new forms of mercantilism. In the rush to markets and privatization, leaders must free themselves from other outdated economic generalizations, including:

1. "Free trade" is always in the best interests of everyone because it appears to lower prices for consumers; but those prices do not include full social and environmental costs. Britain's influential *The Economist* is the most dogmatic proponent of such old-time religion, based on old assumptions.

2. "Industrial policy" is always bad, even if some countries in Europe and Asia do it. Few acknowledge that the outsized military budget of the United States, with the largest arms exports in the world actively promoted by government, is a form of industrial policy. While the United States glosses over its military-industrial policy, worldviews in Washington are clouded—many dogmatic free traders still contend, as did former President George Bush's advisors, that it is irrelevant whether the U.S. economy excels in potato chips or computer chips.

3. "Investment" is always good in the private sector, whether that investment is in research to innovate a new brand of dog food or in fiber optics, whether in a new toy factory or another savings and loan association.

4. "Public-sector investment" in maintaining infrastructure (roads, dams, public buildings, airports, etc.) is classified in GNP as "spending" because, inexplicably, public facilities are not carried on the books in national accounts as capital assets. If they were, the deficit would shrink. By 1995, the only country that had reformulated its GNP/GDP to account for such capital assets was New Zealand.

Naturally, the universal focus on maximizing GNP/GDP-measured economic growth steers societies toward policies that make these macroeconomic statistics look good, including those on averaged unemployment, investment levels, interest rates, savings, deficits, and trade, while shortchanging every other aspect of progress, such as health, satisfaction, and quality of life. Social and environmental costs of dealing with the effects of such economic growth, whether unemployment, homelessness, poverty, crime, drugs, broken families, shuttered small towns, or pollution, are then *added to* rather than *subtracted from* GNP/GDP. The 1990s have, so far, seen truly unacceptable levels of unemployment in most industrial countries, forcing fundamental reappraisals. In the past few years, the dam has at last broken, and today renegade economists are joining in the now-safe general critique of economics and proliferating new indexes. Even the World Bank unveiled, in September 1995, an experimental "Wealth Index" discussed in Chapter 10. (See Fig. 9. Differing Models of Economists and Futurists.)

The macroeconomic view of life also suffers from top-down, academic abstraction and centralization. For example, measuring

Economists	Futurists/Systems
• Based on past data	• Construct scenarios
• Assume equilibrium	• Dis-equilibrium
• "Normalcy"	• No "normal"
• Reactive	• Proactive
• Linear	• Nonlinear
• Reversible	• Irreversible
• Inorganic	• Living system
• Hard sciences	• Life sciences
• "Hard" data	• "Fuzzy" data (i.e., probabilities) and models
• Deterministic	• Synergistic
• Short term	• Long term

Fig. 9. Differing Models of Economists and Futurists

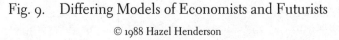
© 1988 Hazel Henderson

incomes averaged per capita conceals widening poverty gaps, and averaged unemployment rates above 10 percent, now prevalent in many countries, mask real-world problems of local regions and populations experiencing much higher joblessness. Such top-down macroeconomic statistics produce "trickle-down" assumptions: that central bank interventions in global financial markets can defend national currencies, or that easing of interest rates or tinkering with investment tax credits and capital gains tax relief will flow down to create more jobs and "jump-start" the economy.

The inadequacy of central bank intervention to defend national currency was illustrated in the U.S.-led, ad hoc $50 billion bailout of Mexico, which was hasty and highlighted the shortcomings of the North American Free Trade Agreement (NAFTA). The bailout's harsh terms were set by Wall Street, a dissenting Congress, and understandably wary voters and small investors. The bailout accelerated Mexico's business and bank failures, widened unemployment, sent prices skyrocketing, and fed political unrest, as documented by *Fortune* magazine in August 1995. These events circled back to drag down the dollar as well — even undermining its status as the world's reserve currency. Traders began referring to the three NAFTA countries, USA-Mexico-Canada, as "the peso bloc." The debate in the United States over the Mexican bailout reopened in July 1995 with House and Senate hearings challenging White House reassurances that Mexico had made a comeback. If so, said Congress members, then why should we go on spending money to prop up the peso?[14] Mexico's October 1995 repayment of $700 million was also borrowed money.

In today's global financial system, manipulation of interest rates has become a blunt instrument, domestically and internationally. High interest rates not only depress domestic businesses and employment, worsen "misery indexes," and fuel political dissent, they also either suck in too much capital (leaving the country in hock to foreigners) or, perversely, signal to canny currency and bond traders the underlying weakness of the country.

A shift in national taxation from payrolls and incomes toward overuse of natural resources and energy, together with national employment tax credits earmarked for domestic employment, would help countries create jobs at home. Consumers in many rich countries, who underpin 65 percent of the U.S. GNP, are now so debt-laden that they cannot perform the heroic feats of consumption required to buoy up the economic indicators. No wonder they rebelled at the Mexican bailout. Savings rates vary according to tax policies, but the effects of advertising must also be factored in. U.S. citizens are bombarded with $150 billion of commercials annually, urging them to consume rather than save. The U.S. household savings rate is 4 percent of disposable income, down from 8.5 percent in the 1970s and lower than many Asian and European countries.[15] *Business Week* commented correctly on another problem in an article titled "You Can't Balance Tomorrow's Budget Today." The U.S. Congress passed the 1996 federal budget, but no one can calculate from today's assumptions what will happen within the U.S. economy that will reach $12 trillion in 2005.[16]

Political spendthrifts need curbing too, but budget balancing to cut deficits must be done with great care, to avoid deflation and because governments have become "employers of last resort." Cost-benefit analyses on the costs to business of regulations ignore the social and environmental costs these companies "externalize" to taxpayers and future generations. Cutting deficits is necessary, but until we overhaul GNP accounts, we do not have an accurate measure of deficit size. Worse, the economic and social structures that GNP-growth recipes have created cannot be shifted too rapidly; budget cutting can lead to deep recessions. Billions of dollars throughout all sectors of the U.S. economy rest on calculations of the Consumer Price Index (CPI), which, if recalculated at probably correct lower figures, could be used to justify lowering interest rates and running economies at fuller employment. A recalculated CPI, lowered by 1 percent, was ordered by Congress and the Clinton administration in late 1995, largely to reduce the cost-of-living increases to retirees—a budget savings of $281 billion by 2002 according to the Congressional Budget Office.[17] However, interest rates were not reduced to reflect the new CPI. If corrected GNPs separated out long-term, capital-asset investments in infrastructure and education, deficits would be drastically lowered overnight. If we added in the full costs of environmental pollution and depletion, GNPs would be lowered and deficits would increase.

Meanwhile, laid-off employees, whose companies "improve" their economic efficiency (as measured by economists' traditional per capita productivity formulas) by automating or moving to a low-wage area, often can't buy even necessities and end up on welfare. The spread of markets worldwide since the collapse of the Soviet Union has accelerated competitive globalization. Two sets of global institutions, corporations and countries, now dominate the world. Corporations, many larger and richer in GNP terms than all but the biggest countries, roam the world in search of cheap labor and resources—touching off human economic migrations across borders (Barnet and Cavanaugh 1994). In its survey of multinationals, "Big is Back," *The Economist* reviewed the restructuring of giant companies as "globalizing their operations" and becoming "local insiders" in many countries. Multinationals' global investments are expected to increase fourfold by the year 2020, from $232 billion in 1993.[18] Countries broker their workforces—as cheap, docile, un-unionized, or well trained—to global corporations along with their natural wealth and biodiversity on the daily auction block of global capital markets—in a tragic lose-lose game. Politicians cannot devise new strategies until such dangerously short-term assumptions and measures are refuted, along with prevailing discount rates that favor present consumption over future needs.

A key task in addressing today's economically framed dilemma is to expose and redress a basic error of industrialism: pursuing narrowly defined mass-production efficiency by substituting capital, energy, and resources for human inputs of skills and labor. E. F. Schumacher (1973) and Barbara Ward (1966) wrote of the impending disaster this would cause, just as Mahatma Gandhi had warned earlier: Industrialism, guided by economists' per-capita productivity formulas, would systematically increase unemployment. For India, Gandhi urged decentralized home- and village-based "production by the masses," not British-style mass production in ever larger factories (Erickson 1969). By the 1960s, social critics and policy analysts (for example, the U.S.-based Ad Hoc Committee on the Triple Revolution) noted that increasingly mechanized and automated mass production was already increasing unemployment.

Many observers besides myself pointed out that increasingly automated mass production and unemployment need not have led to widening poverty and social disruption, if industrialized societies could have rethought their economic textbook paradigms of scarcity and the insatiability of human wants. Instead, industrial societies continued to rely on warfare, workfare, and welfare to distribute the purchasing power needed to keep up demand. Within the industrial countries of the Organization for Economic Cooperation and

Development (OECD) there were debates, often pioneered by unions, about the many ways the fruits of technological abundance could be spread more fairly and widely, as well as how the puritan "no-work-no-eat" mentality, belief in social Darwinism, and the ethics of competition, private property, and scarcity could be modified. This kind of political debate and policy innovation might have led us to accept the new material abundance, while reducing the disruptions and pain of unemployment and poverty. I was deeply involved in the debates of the 1960s and 1970s promoting worker ownership; cooperatives; smaller, labor-intensive enterprises; and forms of guaranteed minimum income. However, I insisted and still do that environmental degradation would eventually foreclose on the technological optimists' often masculine visions of utopian abundance: home robots doing the dirty work and nature providing resources indefinitely.

By the late 1970s, growing poverty and structural unemployment became too visible to ignore, and even the OECD released a report in 1978 warning that the 1980s might well be "an era of jobless economic growth."[19] In January 1993, *Business Week* worried editorially that even as the United States economy was growing again after the 1992 recession, it was "growth without jobs."[20] The editors uncomprehendingly noted that "increased output per worker had been the driving force" in the 3 percent expansion since late 1992—apparently without realizing that increased "output per worker" within the existing paradigm was simply another way of saying *increased unemployment*. It had become clear in the late 1970s that Keynesianism was unsustainable, and hyping aggregate demand to achieve full employment was becoming ever more inflationary and resource wasteful.

Meanwhile, economists rationalized away the increasing tendency toward "stagflation" (high levels of both unemployment and inflation, which the textbooks still say should be trade-offs). Worse, they also had to rationalize how unemployment seemed to remain stubbornly high or higher after each successive recession. There were no plausible theories within the economic framework that could encompass the onset of the jobless growth syndrome. Only broader, interdisciplinary policy models could have provided the explanation. Instead of opening up the debate to other disciplines, most economists closed ranks and redoubled their efforts to administer ever larger doses of the addictive prescriptions. Industrial economies became addicted first to government pump priming, then to advertising-fueled consumption, then to easy credit, then to increasing use of energy in a welter of electricity-gulping gadgets and growing material production. By the 1970s, the addiction had spread to technological innovation—as shown by Orio Giarini and Henri Louberge (1979). Increasingly, companies and nations were forced to spend more on research and development in the mad rush for often trivial product "innovation" or to compete technologically and militarily.

In the 1980s, the Keynesian economists were supplanted by the monetarists, who tried—and are still trying, along with the world's central bankers—to wrestle inflation to the mat not by correcting CPIs but, as usual, with tight money and high interest rates. They will fail and trigger a global deflation or continue to cause deepening unemployment because inflation is so often overstated in national statistics and price indexes (CPIs). Much inflation is now coming from new sources not yet described in economic textbooks: for example, the increasing complexity of interdependent industrial societies where rising social, environmental, infrastructure, and regulatory costs enter the price system indirectly and cannot be squeezed out of consumer price indexes by throttling economic activity and employment.[21] Even *Business Week* editorialized "Let's End Our Inflation Obsession" in their November 13, 1995, issue.

"Supply-siders" arrived on the scene in the United States with Ronald Reagan and simply turned Keynesianism on its head, hyping the investment/input side of production. They also hyped demand with huge military spending increases, and consumption with personal income tax cuts—covert forms of industrial policy. Deficits soared and the United States, as well as many other industrial economies, became addicted to ever larger capital investments in both public and private sectors. In December 1992, the OECD reported that the budget deficits of all industrial societies had risen to 3.8 percent of GDP, the highest in ten years.[22] By 1995, these deficits had been labeled as "structural." A footnote to the confused deficit debate in the United States was a study by Joseph Carson of Dean Witter Reynolds, Inc., a Wall Street firm, showing that government spending on goods and services at all levels hit a forty-year low in 1994. Virtually all other expenditures were interest payments on the national debt—the third largest item.[23] As in other countries, the U.S. government was at the mercy of the interest-rate policies of the secretive independent central bank, the Federal Reserve Board.[24]

During the Reagan years, the U.S. tax codes and other macro-policies were further imbalanced toward subsidizing capital inputs, which increased waste, pollution, and resource depletion. Employing people was rendered ever less attractive via regressive payroll taxes and forcing employers to shoulder burdens of workers' compensation, health insurance, and other fringe benefits. Not surprisingly, by the mid-1980s, employers, particularly in the United States, responded by speeding up automation, and in 1993 helped kill the flawed Clinton health-care plan. Often these corporate efforts added to the general inefficiency, such as the estimated $3 trillion that U.S. companies spent on inappropriate computerization that did not noticeably raise productivity (Tapscott and Caston 1992, 231). This further skewing of capital/labor ratios in the U.S. tax code simply led employers to "part-time" their workforces to avoid the costly burdens and paperwork of full-time employees. This has led to today's landscape of thirty-three million home-based and self-employed Americans and the rise of the contract workforce.

Economic models are linear and economists often do not see what systems theorists and ordinary citizens find obvious: what goes around, comes around. For example, GNP produces a short-term, cash-flow type of accounting that would lead a private company to underinvest and neglect maintenance—ending in bankruptcy. Thus the U.S. economy, on a net-worth basis, has disinvested in public infrastructure and fallen behind all its G-7 competitors. Worse, since GNP/GDP does not account for "human capital," education continues to be treated as "spending," which during the Reagan/Bush era resulted in lower U.S. functional literacy rates—below most other industrial countries and even some developing countries such as Costa Rica. The Clinton administration tried to address these problems by reclassifying such government outlays more correctly as "investments." However, the orthodox economists and their Republican and Democratic allies countered such theoretical heresies. They succeeded in reframing the entire U.S. public debate in macroeconomic terms as an exercise in bookkeeping: i.e., deficit reduction, budget balancing, and cutting all social spending, whether on health care, education, or crime prevention, to hype GNP growth—while leaving the still-bloated military spending intact.

Economists only came to dominate national policy making during World War II, when industrial countries began to accept the

notions of Britain's Lord John Maynard Keynes. Keynes was a mathematician, investor, and journalist who loved demolishing the reigning
neoclassical economists of the 1930s. He legitimized the tools of
macroeconomists to guide politicians in "fine-tuning" their fiscal and
monetary policies: taxation, money creation, government spending,
interest rates, and public and private investments to create "a rising
tide of economic growth that would lift all boats." This vivid imagery
was powerful but deeply flawed: built on mathematical formulas stand-
ing atop averaged data, teetering on unreal assumptions about the
behavior of "average" human beings. A critique of such statistical tools
in *Scientific American*, July 1995, predicted their eclipse. Economists
of the "rational expectations" school have critiqued Keynesians for
decades, offering little else to policymakers but the trivial observation
that peoples' expectations of government policies become factored
into their decisions.[25] Yet aggregate demand fueled with ever more
advertising and easy credit was still the flywheel of this economic
growth, and the pump was further primed by government spending,
increasing the money supply, and tax cuts whenever necessary.

Contemporary economic debates are still redolent with this
Keynesian imagery, even as his contribution is reassessed and his creative role in international financial institution-building is given
deserved emphasis.[26] Keynes' domestic policy prescriptions led in
part to today's addictive economies. Yet the round of supply-side market euphoria in Britain and the United States during the 1980s did
nothing to shift toward sustainability and can now also be reassessed.
The ballyhooed Reagan and Thatcher restorations tried to keep the
GNP/GDP numbers going up by running down the infrastructure,
increasing deficits, selling off public, i.e., taxpayer-owned, assets to
those who could afford the new shares, and cannibalizing the cooperative social fabric and the informal sector while overexploiting
natural resources and ignoring growing threats to the environment.
Curiously, old Keynesians often converged with supply-siders in
downplaying deficits and budget-balancing efforts. Keynesians say
that governments, like companies, must be allowed to manage their
budgets for their own or democratic goals, like employment, training,
and infrastructure investments. The key variable is the proportion of
the deficit in relation to GDP.[27] The supply-siders care more about
tax cuts—even if they unbalance budgets. Sadly, even in the 1990s,
this GNP-growth recipe went worldwide as economists spread their

nineteenth-century textbook prescriptions to the former Soviet empire and aspiring countries in the South, purveying pain to developing countries via policies of the World Bank and the IMF. In 1995 South Africa, to whom the World Bank and IMF were eager to lend, announced they were not interested in light of such failed policies.[28]

Traditional GNP-growth recipes for development have bogged down in environmental and social costs, unemployment, and widening poverty gaps. If the G-7 and other economic groups, including the WTO, are to help us escape these vicious circles, they must look beyond their economists, as 71 percent of the U.S. public agrees, and bring in advisors from other professions—systems thinkers, game theorists, cultural anthropologists, ecologists, chaos theorists, and psychologists—to help understand today's imperfect markets.[29] Economists will need retraining in all these new tools and will need to be recertified if they wish to ameliorate the social and environmental problems their former advice has so often unleashed.

Today, legions of economist jokes point to the truth—economics is not a science, in spite of the Nobel Memorial Prize money given to the Nobel Committee by the Central Bank of Sweden to bolster the prestige of economics with its own prize. Economists regularly recommend Nobel awards to each other for insights that are trivial when viewed from a broader systems theory perspective. Economists are professionals not much different from lawyers, with much less accountability. Economics is now revealed as a three-hundred-year-old grab bag of unverifiable propositions too vague to be refuted, yet parading as scientific principles. As Mahatma Gandhi wrote, "Nothing in history has been so disgraceful to human intellect as the acceptance among us of the common doctrines of economics as a science." Indian economist Nandini Joshi, author of *Development without Destruction* (1992), quoted Gandhi's statement in a letter to the Economics Department of Harvard University—where she had earned her doctorate—in which she renounced economics as "criminal."[30]

NEXT STEP: GLOBAL COOPERATION, STANDARD-SETTING, AND REGULATION

The logical conclusion to all of this mad competition and capturing of markets and resources is the $1 trillion-a-day waves of hot money sloshing around our planet today. Global forces need taming and regulating if nations are to regain some control over their political destinies. Some events that dominated the news in 1995 were the Barings Bank collapse; the bankruptcy of California's Orange County, the richest county in the United States; and the ripples felt from the simmering Mexican crisis that threatened the dollar and other currencies. At the United Nations World Summit on Social Development in Copenhagen in March 1995, several of the over one hundred heads of state in attendance, including France's then-President Mitterand, Norway's Gro Harlem Brundtland, and Denmark's Poul Nyrup Rasmussen, suggested the time had come for taxing currency transactions in order to reduce the number of transactions that are speculative (over 90 percent). *Business Week* asked "Is the Nation-State Obsolete in a Global Economy?" Quoting one financial advisor, "The ultimate resource of a government is power, and we've seen repeatedly that the willpower of governments can be overcome by persistent attacks from the marketplace."[31]

Calls for leveling the global playing field and opening up of markets can only make things worse for most of the people on the planet. What is needed is the new girder work of cooperative agreements to raise a new ethical floor under the global playing field, so that the most responsible countries and companies can win. Turning today's vicious circle economies into virtuous circles will also require additional international agreements, private-sector standard-setting, international fees for commercial use of the global commons, and fines and taxation for abuses, whether international arms trafficking, currency speculation, or cross-border pollution. It will also be necessary to harmonize national regulations and accounting standards that already exist in the capital markets of some eighty countries. The UN could well facilitate many such agreements, if its member-states would allow this.

At the 1995 G-7 Summit in Halifax, Nova Scotia, however, the G-7 countries continued the divisive practice of working outside the UN. Their focus was on new regulations for the IMF, which, like the World Bank, was originally created as a part of the UN but was quickly commandeered by the rich and powerful nations. Thus, steps toward agreements between all countries and public and private market makers to create a global version of the Securities and Exchange Commission (SEC) were initiated informally and through the IMF. The March 1995 Windsor Declaration (discussed in Chapter 12) led the way by harmonizing financial reporting and other regulations among sixteen countries, and the G-7's 1995 summit contained many similar informal proposals. Beneath the scary headlines, paradoxically, the world's competitive nations and their alarming "vicious circle" economies are now all linked on the roller-coaster of globalization and the electronic and financial commons as well. As detailed in Chapters 12 and 13, markets and commons are inextricably related: the markets' win-lose rules (i.e., competition) require managing cooperatively in new win-win games of the global commons. Yesterday's more static world of separate national economies has vanished, invalidated by the new realities of globalized technologies, trade, and information highways, which created the new financial cyberspace.

Spreading democracies and increasing information flows allow citizens in many countries to witness today's vicious-circle policies unwinding. People saw how the Mexican bailout mess was unforeseen by NAFTA enthusiasts and their economists, and how central bankers too often rely on raising interest rates to stave off raids on their currencies or curb domestic inflation—regardless of job losses and domestic pain. Citizens rightly question today's tail-chasing debates over balanced budgets and reduced deficits, carried on without fully addressing the issue of *priorities*, since someone's tax cut is always someone else's lost job or education or social benefit. No wonder voters and citizens are angry with leaders and experts and their muddled debates. No wonder even those aware of our global interconnections are confused by "economic news."

The issues have not changed very much in the past twenty years. Fundamentally, economists still take a money-centered viewpoint (too often viewing society narrowly and ecology as something out there that can be represented in their models as a "special interest group," i.e., environmentalists). Ecologists see economics as derivative, i.e., as a subsystem both of ecosystems and of human societies. My view of economics, which I have made known in print since at least 1973, still holds.[32] Economics is not a science but a grab bag of unverifiable and unrefutable propositions parading as "principles." Thus economists still prattle about various principles of Alfred Marshall, Vilfredo Pareto, A. C. Pigou, et al., as if they were analogous to such proven physical principles as Newton's Laws of Motion! Economics is a profession, more like that of lawyers; and cost-benefit analyses are not much different from a brief that a lawyer prepares for a client to justify some project. That which we reify as "economies" are merely *sets of rules* of interaction derived from the goals and values (i.e., the cultural DNA codes) of various societies as to what work is important and to be highly paid, and what work is less important (such as raising children, maintaining a household, and volunteering) to which economists assign no value.

Since the 1970s, economists (always more organized and more academically and politically powerful than other social scientists and ecologists) have proselytized environmentalists and other critics, urging them to learn economics. Many economists hastily put new labels on their old wine bottles and hung out their shingles as "natural resource economists," "social economists," "ecological economists," and "technology assessors." Most brought all their old methodological baggage (typically, welfare theory, i.e., principles of "willingness to pay" for enough clean air to breathe; "willingness to be compensated" in money if one's lungs were damaged, etc. —all measured by the principle of Pareto Optimality, which ignores the distribution of income, wealth, power, and information among people). Thus, economists, for example, view a wetland (the most productive ecosystem on the planet) in terms of how much environmentalists and average citizens would be willing to pay to keep it unspoiled—even in competition with developers with plans to profit from the wetlands when covered with condos! This is, of course, absurd, since not only are the citizens and environmentalists not trying to profit from the wetland, but they are also being expected to behave altruistically, which is considered irrational behavior in economic theory! In fact, a paper by two psychologists and an economist found much evidence that studying economics actually increased selfish and uncooperative behavior.[33]

From Earth Day 1990 onward, polls have showed that a majority of American adults call themselves environmentalists. Economists now say that they have thrown off the old theories (e.g., nature is a "free good" and pollution, in their classic Freudian slip, is an "externality") and have incorporated all the lessons of ecology, systems dynamics, and chaos theory. Therefore, people don't need to worry about leaving economists in charge of central banks, business, the stock market, national accounting, and cost-benefit analyses of local and national policies, free trade, etc. Yet most economists in charge of macroeconomic models and policy making have hardly heard of the many efforts to set prices of natural resources above zero, or to carry infrastructure on the books in national accounts, let alone to deduct social costs, pollution, and cleanup bills from corporate balance sheets and national accounts. Economists know that if all the true social and environmental costs of production were factored into full-cost prices in the marketplace, they would have to admit that they and their theories have been wrong for decades.

The Report of the Commission on Graduate Education in Economics of the American Economic Association, composed of such luminaries as Alan Blinder, Kenneth Arrow, Lawrence Summers, and others, drew data from surveys of ninety-one university economics departments, which produce 90 percent of U.S. Ph.D. economists. The report concluded that economists no longer agree on what constitutes their core discipline, that economics is often impervious to evidence (due to its deductive method and formalisms), and that 61 percent of professors agree that mathematics and statistical tools are overemphasized at the expense of substance.[34] *Business Week* pointed out in "7,000 Economists and No Answers" that flaws in economists' methods make them unable to do much to improve the real economy.[35] *Newsweek* joined in the debunking in "Dismal Science Grabs a Couch," pointing out that psychologists have a better handle on human behavior than economists.[36]

Most economists resist the new scorecards of sustainable development: the United Nations Development Programme's Human Development Index (HDI), Herman Daly's Index of Sustainable Economic Welfare (ISEW), or my own Country Futures Indicators (CFI), as well as the demands to value unpaid work in GNP from the UN Conference on Women and Development in 1995 and earlier summits. For every Herman Daly, Peggy Antrobus, Marilyn Waring, and Manfred Max Neef, there are thousands of economists who work for banks, corporations, and government agencies. Few economists work for poor people—or for the low pay environmental groups can afford. "Can Economists Save Economics?" asked Richard Parker in *The American Prospect* in the spring of 1993. His answer was probably not.[37] It has now become fashionable for academic economists, who remained silent for so long, to offer their own critiques, such as those of Richard Douthwaite in *The Growth Illusion* (1993), Roger Terry in *Economic Insanity* (1995), and others. These critiques are a welcome chorus accelerating the needed change. Another theoretical twist, Michael Rothschild's *Bionomics* (1990), personally inscribed to me with the author's "great admiration," is wildly popular with conservatives since it inappropriately analogizes market economies as "ecologies." Another coffin nail was the admission in *The Economist* in a September 30, 1995, article, "How Does Your Economy Grow?" that "Economists know surprisingly little about the causes of economic growth." This paradigm war is clearly not over yet.

CHAPTER 3

THE TECHNOLOGY TRAP

I n the 1990s, Western societies' love affair with technology
went global. Cuba became a biotech center and personal
computers became status symbols from Santiago, São Paulo,
and Shanghai, to Manila, Kuala Lumpur, Delhi, and Dakar, to
Jakarta and Johannesburg. Those inculcated in nonmaterialist
Hinduism, Islam, and Buddhism were equally enthralled. Much of it
turned out to be a masculine trip, judging from the demographics of
Internet users. As I suggested in a speech to eager U.S. technophiles
in 1976, paradigms shift slowly and transformations from pre- to post-
industrial societies are wildly uneven step functions.[1] Beyond the
Solar Age lies a future based on light waves: photonics and bio- and
nano-technologies mimicking nature's design. Will it be the wiser
Age of Light envisioned in *Paradigms in Progress* (1991, 1995) or a
replay of our Faustian past? Can we learn to see the industrial era as
a way station to a new reintegration with nature, as Duane Elgin proposed in *Awakening Earth* (1993)? (See Fig. 10. The Evolutionary
Inflection and the Stages of Development.)

Many colleagues and friends have explored these themes with me
as Fellows of the Lindisfarne Association, founded by cultural historian William Irwin Thompson, editor of *GAIA: A Way of Knowing*
(1989) and author of many other books. Jeremy Rifkin's widely influential *Entropy* (1989), *Who Shall Play God?* (1977), and *Algeny* (1984)
made him the scourge of the scientific community. Jerry Mander,
whom I met in Stockholm at the first UN Conference on the Human
Environment in 1972, seg-wayed [sic] gracefully from his Madison
Avenue ad agency to the nonprofit Public Media Center and became

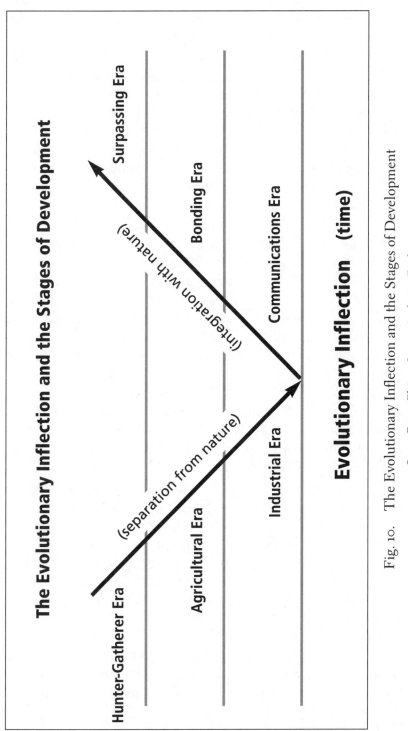

Fig. 10.   The Evolutionary Inflection and the Stages of Development

© 1993 Duane Elgin   Source: *Awakening Earth*

a philosopher in his *Four Arguments for the Elimination of Television* (1978) and *In the Absence of the Sacred* (1991). My collaboration with Fritjof Capra on *The Turning Point* (1981) continued via his Elmwood Institute, where colleagues Charlene Spretnak, Walter Truett Anderson, Joanna Macy, Ernest Callenbach, Riane Eisler, David Loye, Helena Norberg Hodge, Chellis Glendenning, Patricia Ellsberg, Carolyn Merchant, and others joined us in assessing the technology trap. My "Ph.D." course was six years on the Advisory Council of the U.S. Office of Technology Assessment and on panels of the National Science Foundation and National Academy of Engineering from 1974 until 1980.

Today the appropriate technology debate is also global. Many of us in the United States linked up (long before the Internet) with E. F. Schumacher's British colleagues, George McRobie and Satish Kumar, Petra Kelly of the German Greens, and other international leaders including A. T. Ariyaratne and his Sarvodya Movement in Sri Lanka, Indian physicists Vandana Shiva and Ashok Khosla, Maximo (Juni) Kalaw in Manila, Ziauddin Sardar and Martin Kohr Kok Peng in Malaysia, and Frank Bracho in Venezuela.

In 1995 *Business Week* celebrated the achievements of genetic engineering and the private sector "Gene Kings" who made fortunes from taxpayer-funded research. The journal lauded advances in artificial intelligence in "Computers That Think Are Almost Here." The public was told not to concern itself with social or ethical issues.[2] In 1965, Gordon Moore, one of the founders of the computer-chip maker Intel, promulgated "Moore's Law": Computer chips would double in power every two years. By 1995, Moore's Law was falling victim to an older principle that restricts the growth of such exponential curves. Even the shift to optical lithography on chips less than 0.5 millionths of a meter across would reach a limit at 0.18 according to the Semiconductor Industries Association.[3] Now, computing is shifting to the use of living DNA strands, which perform one hundred times faster than today's best serial computers, with one billion times the energy efficiency and one trillion times the storage capacity—proving again that nature is the best designer.[4]

Meanwhile, in the techno-nonsense department, a costly effort to automate highways and the cars driving on them by a group of forty U.S. universities and high-tech companies produced an automated Pontiac van, "Ralph," which steers itself, as reported in the *Business*

Week article "Look Ma, No Hands."[5] Worse, the "Glitch of the Millennium" was highlighted by *Business Week* in a November 13, 1995, editorial: "When the new century begins, most computers will interpret 01-01-00 as January 1, 1900, not January 1, 2000." As much as one-third of total global spending for information systems over the foreseeable future may be needed to rectify the glitch.[6] On the real world side, India's Development Alternatives unveiled Micro Concrete Roofing—the TARAcrete Tile—a major breakthrough in sustainable technology that cuts costs to one-third of conventional roofs and allows villagers to employ their people in locally owned enterprises.[7] As the Internet goes commercial, with the hype and price of admission increasing, the old bumper stickers return: TECHNOLOGY IS THE ANSWER, But What Is the Question? I said it best twenty years ago in the following lecture to the American Association for Industrial Arts.

OUR PERCEPTIONS WILL GOVERN OUR SURVIVAL

The days are now past when citizens automatically equate technology with progress. We are all too aware of its unanticipated consequences in daily life. These consequences range from the increasingly formidable destructive power it places at our disposal, to the ecosystem disruptions it creates and the ever-larger scale of industrial operations it produces, to the individual alienation and sense of diminished power and control that so many of us now experience.

In the past, the scale of technology was smaller and its effects were still relatively localized. Many uncoordinated technologies could still coexist without impinging on each other or affecting large regions or populations. As technological mastery increased, the increasing scale of innovations, together with the cumulative effects of many small applications, began making even more pervasive impacts on populations, social structures, and ecosystems. Today the unanticipated effects of our growing knowledge and the technologies it creates have seemingly outrun adaptive capabilities, whether psychological, social, organizational, or political. The result is the current series of unruly crises. Whether we designate them as "energy crises," "environmental crises," "urban crises," or "population crises," they all are rooted in the larger crisis of our inadequate, narrow perceptions of reality. When our perception is too narrowly focused, for example, on the city or town in which we live, we tend to lose sight of all the external factors that affect it, such as national policies, transportation, agriculture, and commerce. When one of these external factors changes, we are likely to perceive the resulting change in our city as a "crisis." For example, what was first designated as the "urban crisis" is now understood more in terms of the national policies that affect our often helpless cities: e.g., federal housing policies that, along with the Highway Trust Fund, underwrote the flight of the cities' taxpaying middle class to the suburbs; the mechanization of agriculture that drove hundreds of farmworkers to the cities; and so on.

Most humans are motivated by perceptions of reality that are quite limited in space and time. A majority are too concerned with tomorrow's food supply for their immediate family to worry about next week or their neighbors. Some, affluent enough not to worry about immediate survival, can enlarge their sights to concern themselves with their community and occasional longer-range problems. A lucky few with opportunities for travel can extend their concern to embrace national and even international affairs, and perhaps worry about the kind of world their children and grandchildren will inherit. And some extraordinary individuals, in spite of poverty and adversity, through the power of imagination, can relate to the great concerns of their time and contribute their vision to enrich our range of alternative futures.

But it is natural that most people perceive reality as their immediate environment and their personal and family concerns. And for the kind of rural, low technology world we knew in earlier times and which is still a reality for most of the world's people, such perceptions were adequate for dealing with the problems and decisions of daily life. But now that many of the world's nations are technologically advanced, global impacts and interdependencies are the rule rather than the exception; therefore, narrow perceptions become increasingly dangerous and lead to decisions based on inadequate information concerning larger and longer-range patterns of causality. Not only do we find that "crises" sneak up on us because we were not paying attention to the significant variables, but, conversely, we do not adequately appreciate how individually rational microdecisions and actions can add up, by default, to dangerous, irrational macrodecisions. This cumulative effect of the tyranny of small decisions is seen when, on a hot summer day millions of decisions to drive to the beach result in traffic jams.

How do such human perceptions become further entrapped by our very technologies? Sometimes we compound our lack of perception, as when a technology produces an unanticipated effect and we try yet another technological fix to ameliorate it, thus adding more unknown variables and increasing the impetus of social and eco-system changes. In fact, technology has now surrounded us with a human-made environment capable of insulating perceptions from direct experiences of our vulnerability and our dependence on the primary natural ecosystems. An enormous number of arguments and misunderstandings between people of goodwill seem to occur because they did not exchange some basic information about their perceptions at the outset. The dialogue can be made much easier if each of us clarifies first where we see ourselves in time and space. Where are you in the total system? Do you most often experience yourself on a planet? As a citizen of the United States? As a member of a local community? As a family member or as an individual? Similarly, what time frames do you commonly employ? In your view, is a "long time" a millennium, a century, five years, three weeks?

Learning to examine our own space-time frameworks and the mental models they generate of the system we inhabit is now of the utmost importance for our survival. "Reality" is that selective image of the external world which, as Kenneth Boulding (1956) points out, we pull in on our own personal, perceptual "TV screens." Therefore, in order to make myself more explicit, I will tell you where I think I am in space-time, and what mental models my perception has generated by which I experience "reality." I believe that I inhabit a rather undistinguished solar system in the arm of an equally unremarkable spiral galaxy, and I also inhabit a body evolved from the elements of one of the prettiest planets in this solar system. The mental models this experience of perception generates are systemic and interactive, multidimensional, balancing both equilibrium and dynamic behavior modes, and evolving over time in some purposive manner which I believe I shall never understand. There seem to be elements of subsystem expansion and contraction, ordering and disordering, entropy and syntropy, continuously occurring, along with energy-matter/information transformations.

The most puzzling aspect for me is how I am a part of this process and yet seem also to experience myself as an observer of it. But let us, for the moment, leave such mind-body, subjective-objective, observer-observed paradoxes to the adventurous physicists who are trying to deal with them as they were posed by Werner Heisenberg (1971, 96) in his famous Uncertainty Principle.[8] Science has become a religion for all too many, while human values and ethical concerns are driven into hiding because they are embarrassingly unquantifiable and "nonrigorous." Most of the academic world rewards reductionist study of less and less significant phenomena.

Many distinguished scholars have called attention to these "fallacies of misplaced concreteness," as Alfred North Whitehead called such efforts of micro-rigor, including Heisenberg in physics; Kurt Godel in mathematics; Oskar Morgenstern, Georgescu-Roegen, Kenneth Boulding, and E. F. Schumacher in economics; Lewis Mumford, Gerald Holton, Margaret Mead, Gregory Bateson, and many others in science policy; and Theodore Roszak, R. D. Laing, and William Irwin Thompson in their vigorous critiques of reductionist science. The normative nature of science is revealed in the first decision of any scientist: what phenomena to study. This choice then influences the general view of reality: where we see ourselves in space-time—a Heisenberg Uncertainty Principle at the macro, rather than the quantum, level.

Human survival now requires an awareness that transcends our very natural anthropocentrism. Each great knowledge explosion has been based on a new level of expanded awareness: from Ptolemy's geocentric view of the sun and stars revolving around Earth; to the Copernican revolution, which reduced us to a subordinate position in the universe; to Darwin's further undermining of our proud image with his theory of evolution. Much of today's new knowledge is increasingly shattering our sense of self-importance, whether studying ourselves as components of living ecosystems or as the infinitely malleable creatures of behaviorist B. F. Skinner's *Beyond Freedom and Dignity* (1971), whose most profound emotions are nothing but electrical stimulation reproducible by brain-probing instruments. Two more of our claims to uniqueness are also being debunked: dolphins and other mammals have well-developed languages, and many other species use tools, including even the lowly ant, which loads food supplies on leaf fragments and thus multiplies its transport capabilities tenfold.[9] We are just becoming aware of ecosystems as immanent intelligence; for example, it has been shown that grasses in typical grazing pastures are capable of growing themselves tougher and more unpalatable by increasing the cellulose content of their leaves in order to drive off excessive numbers of grazing animals.[10]

IMAGINATION: KEY TOOL FOR SURVIVAL

Let us not be dismayed by this new evidence of a need for greater humility, but relax, enjoy our natural curiosity, and indulge the burst of imagination and speculation it creates. Imagination, one of our most important survival tools, can help us deal with the perceptual crisis. Our species has now multiplied almost to the limits of its ecological niche on this planet. This perceptual crisis has two aspects: (1) We are experiencing an implosion, as space and resources diminish relative to our growing population. We feel the loss of frontiers, the slowing of economic expansion, urban crowding, and the evaporation of many historically defined freedoms; and (2) At the same time, we experience ourselves getting smaller and less significant as old perceptual boundaries fall away. We feel *physically* confined and frustrated, but we must deal with an expanded *mental* model of the universe. We are again facing the oldest human dilemma: a consciousness that can wander among planets, stars, and millennia, in a body with a brief span of years. As we face our own death and finiteness, the old games our cultures have provided to shield us from this reality break down. They are inappropriate for the new conditions, leaving us shorn of our psychological clothes.

Imagination can help us make some new psychological "elbow room" in diversifying lifestyles, and new images to help us expand consciousness for the evolutionary leap we must now make. Imagine that we are extraterrestrial visitors from one of the millions of planets in our galaxy that may have conditions hospitable to life. We are further evolved than the life forms on Earth. On our spacecraft, we zero in and approach this planet. It is not important where we land; it all looks the same, a sphere of blue and white with brown patches visible below. The spot where we land is apparently called by its inhabitants "Washington, D.C." We wander around (first taking the precaution of dematerializing ourselves so as not to scare the Earthlings) and peek in a large building at a gathering where they are discussing their future on this planet. They still seem to be debating whether or not their planet is a finite system. We extraterrestrials know that from the vantage point of our own highly developed technology, it is not really a closed system; but from the Earthlings' current levels of technology, it still is. The trouble seems to be that they have not yet internalized the learning experience their first costly venture into space provided. They created all that hardware, flashed back from their moon TV pictures of their actual situation, but have done little, it seems, to overhaul and reprogram their educational, political, and economic systems to conform with what they have learned.

To resume our own Earthling perspective, it is encouraging to know that this great debate is on the agenda. We are addressing at many levels our propensity to create hardware without writing the necessary software to program its orderly functioning. We have created a technologically interdependent, global economy, and now we are trying to write the program of software—monetary agreements and international rules—to operate it without catastrophic breakdowns. I have often pondered why we are so much better at creating hardware than software. At one level, it is rooted in our fear of death and nonexistence. When we build cities, dams, and factories, we provide for our material requirements, but we also affirm our existence and importance. These physical artifacts are so tangible that they reassure us of our own reality. Another root of our interest in hardware is that humans love to manipulate their surroundings, and enjoy the sense of mastery and control they derive from the expression of self found in such creation and play. Yet another explanation may be that we would rather project our inner tensions and conflicts onto the objective world than resolve them by examining our own psyches and trying to retool ourselves. Might this passion for hardware be a result of a cultural overdose of masculine consciousness? The masculine psyche does seem more attuned (either biologically or by cultural conditioning) to manipulating external things and objects, while the female psyche, by contrast, seems more attuned to interpersonal and social relationships and arrangements.

Technology, defined as knowledge systematically applied to human problem solving, means software as well as hardware. For example, the Social Security and income tax withholding systems are as much technologies as any hardware. Lewis Mumford in *The Myth of the Machine* (1966, 23) drew attention to our bias toward hardware in anthropology and archeology. He pointed out that when we dig for evidence of earlier cultures, by definition such remains are tangible—their hardware—whether arrowheads, axes, pots, or other artifacts. From the extent and elaboration of these artifacts, we infer their level of "civilization." We often forget that many cultures may have existed without leaving a trace. They could have developed highly refined technologies, but of the software variety: techniques of conflict resolution; supportive interpersonal relationships; production systems based on elaborate barter, reciprocity, and redistributive schemes; myths and taboos to regulate antisocial behavior without use of jails, clubs, or physical restraints. A culture able to elaborate such software techniques would have had little need for spears and arrowheads and might have had scant energies left over to elaborate its tools, and so we might assume too casually that because there were few tangible remains it was less "civilized."

During my 1972 visit to Japan I talked with a project director at the Japan Techno-Economics Society who was directing an effort to computer-model the value systems of the Japanese people. He pointed out that from the quantities and configurations of material artifacts and technologies created by various cultures it was possible to infer a great deal about their value systems. On one end of the scale are the Balinese, who create exquisite music, dances, rituals, stories, and clothes, but are rather uninterested in hardware. On the other end of the scale are the Americans, who are fascinated with and produce more hardware than any culture the world has ever known. We are even unable to enjoy leisure activities such as hiking without an incredible quantity of gear—let alone our uniquely energy- and materials-intensive hobbies, such as those involving snowmobiles, beach buggies, and camping vehicles. Values are the dominant variables driving not only technological but economic systems. Relationships have been established between Judeo-Christian religious beliefs and the rise of capitalism and the Industrial Revolution (Weisskopf, 1971). E. F. Schumacher, in Small Is Beautiful (1973, 50–58), describes the value system that drives Buddhist economics: labor is an output of production, rather than an input, embodied in the idea of "right livelihood"; work is a valuable mode of self-actualization while the product is of secondary importance.

Western culture may at last be awakening from that altered state of consciousness Thomas Berry calls "the technological trance" and all the unthinking assumptions underlying it.[11] The most destructive of these is our belief that innovation and technological progress consist of hardware and efficiency, and are continuous; rarely do we recognize limits or use the concept of balance. Our technological consciousness has permitted us to conquer nature (temporarily, at least), expand our ecological niche, and manage more of the variables affecting our existence. The trade-off as we proceed is the task of managing the proliferating variables, which become ever more complex until we find, as Schumacher put it, that we need "a breakthrough a day to keep crisis at bay." Some human and natural processes are not susceptible to increased efficiency. Women still understand this better than men; they know that it still takes nine months to make a baby and one hundred years to grow a mature hardwood tree. While human interactions can be increased and made faster with technology, they are rarely bettered and sometimes worsened. A companion myth is that new technologies can always be debugged if only we wait long enough.

One contemporary example of this mirage of efficiency is the effort of officials in the U.S. Postal Service to reduce inefficient human labor and replace it with elaborate, automated machines for sorting mail. After reducing the human workforce and adding to the ranks of the unemployed, and after investing millions in capital improvements, the machines are ripping, crushing, or destroying an alarming number of parcels.[12] It might have been more socially efficient to add a million unemployed workers to the Postal Service, increasing attention to customers and care in handling. Electric utilities, too, seek efficiency in larger, more automated generating plants and in nuclear power instead of less costly technologies. For this suspect efficiency, they assume risks on our behalf and trade off social efficiency, since costly police and security systems must contain and manage the deadly plutonium now and for thousands of years to come. Consumers and citizens are in full-scale revolt against these social inefficiencies.[13] The word *efficiency* is fast becoming meaningless. "Efficient for whom?" is the question in all the nuclear and technological issues. In an economy with 7 to 8 percent unemployment, clean, safe solar energy could provide an equivalent energy supply to nuclear, while creating several times as many jobs per dollar invested. Conservation itself could even become our major new energy "source."

Our economy has overshot the mark in its substitution of capital for labor. In fact, I contend that in hundreds of production and service processes, labor has now become the more efficient factor of production; and as natural resources become increasingly scarce, we must employ our human resources more fully. Operations researcher Stafford Beer points out something obvious but crucial about human social systems:

> Institutions are systems for being what they *are* and doing what they *do*. No one believes this, which is incredible—yet true. People think that institutions are systems for being what they were *set up* to be and do, or what they *say* they are and do, or what they *wish* they were and did. The first task of the systems scientists is to look at the *facts*: what is the system? What does it *do*? If the answer turns out to be something no one wants, do not go around repeating the popular but fictitious belief in a very loud voice. Do not hire a public relations campaign to project the required image. CHANGE THE SYSTEM![14]

Dr. Beer added that when people become disenchanted with their institutions, they express disenchantment with their *leaders*. "Why doesn't the leader *do* something?" This, of course, is the wrong question, because the leader is an *output* of the system. Former president J. K. Jamieson of Exxon Corporation talked of the near impossibility of shifting the course of that mammoth company. Any would-be leader who has tried to ride the tiger of such massive systems, such as the Department of Defense, understands institutional resistance to change. The appropriate question is, "Why do our institutional systems throw up leaders who seem helpless, incompetent, or corrupt?"

One of the chief reasons for our confusion over the failure of our systems to do what we designed them to do is, of course, that we do not understand them and therefore cannot design or model them accurately. Any system that cannot be modeled cannot be managed. And in today's complex industrial societies most of our large institutions fall into this category. The result is that through the filters of our myopic perception, our puny efforts at managing these systems lead to proliferating exercises in suboptimization. If you can't model the larger systems, you can take the path of least resistance and try to model the smaller, easier systems, where the numbers of variables are more manageable. Most of our societal crises today are the effects of our increasing proficiency at suboptimization—widely taught at colleges of business administration.

We must attempt to model our larger social contexts and interactions before developing ill-considered, short-range technological "fixes." For example, it is of little use merely to hire more police and buy more costly security hardware without viewing crime as part of the social cost of maldistribution of wealth and income. There is increasing evidence that violent behavior and poor eating habits are part of the social costs of the commercial structure of television in U.S. culture, just as emphysema and lung cancer are social costs of the tobacco industry. Only such a contextual view allows us to better assess which of our problems are even susceptible to a technical solution.

The often massive costs of corporate research and development (R&D) programs are routinely passed along to consumers as higher prices. Yet consumers have no control over how these funds are deployed, what new technologies are developed, and what social impacts they may cause. Narrow criteria of profitability are used for such ubiquitous R&D taxes levied on consumers. Furthermore, the engineers who design projects and the companies that get the contracts are highly organized to petition for public funds to underwrite new technological developments, but the taxpayers and consumers who foot the bills do not even get wind of these public or private proposals for months. Individuals have little information or incentive to bear the heavy financial and time costs of researching the issue and challenging such powerful forces. This syndrome is discussed by Mancur Olsen in *The Logic of Collective Action* (1965). He illustrates the difficulty of challenging any policies or proposals promoted by powerful interest groups. The potential payoffs are so large that an interest group's incentives to commit funds to win these prizes are always greater than individuals' incentives to use their own funds to try to protect themselves by organizing and applying countervailing pressure.

Technology promoters and developers and empire-building public agencies spare no expense to hire economists to prepare cost-benefit analyses to justify their plans and present them as significant advances in the public welfare. There are other more technical problems with cost-benefit analyses. They assume that adequate information is available to all parties, and they accept the existing distribution of income as a given. These two factors disenfranchise many citizens, such as those without economic or political power, or adequate information on costs, health effects, or long-range risks of a particular technology or development. In addition, cost and benefit ratios can be completely different depending on what rate of discount is used, i.e., the assumption of what interest rates will prevail over the lifetime of the project. Such arbitrary assumptions can overstate the costs and understate the benefits or vice versa and are currently the subject of hot debate among economists.

We can appreciate the relativity of all such supposedly scientific methods of analysis. The "automobilization" of the United States is an example of the cumulative effects of myopic perception, narrow analyses, and suboptimization. It has taken twenty-five years for the social and environmental consequences of the auto to reach our notice. As Ivan Illich points out in *Energy and Equity* (1974), we still measure time gained by speed as miles per hour *in the vehicle*. We forget the time spent in earning the money to pay for the vehicle, insure it, and maintain it, which in an overall view of our lives is the real measure of our time and opportunity costs vis-à-vis automobile transportation. The auto, by extending and setting in concrete our spatial living patterns and by permitting greater distances between living, working, and shopping, dictates that it will take more travel time to perform daily activities and decrees that cars shall be indispensable. By such total-system calculations, Illich estimates that our cars actually deliver us speeds of about five miles per hour, because fully one-quarter of our waking lives are spent in performing the involuntary activities associated with this automobile-transportation system. By contrast, Illich shows, in countries without highways, people walk at an almost equivalent speed, but spend only 5 percent of their time transporting themselves around.

We also often overlook the enormous tax costs of highways and police, the burdens on our court systems, the arable lands lost, crop damage, fatalities, and injuries (all quantifiable or approximatable "externalities"), not to mention the less quantifiable factors, such as the explosion of cities into wasteful, sprawling suburbs, the "disabling" of millions of citizens who cannot drive or afford cars, and the destruction of other transportation options, such as walking or bicycling. At an even broader perceptual level, we can discern that how much and what kind of transportation we have is based on how a culture values mobility and acceleration and how it assesses the trade-offs associated with these values. One sees that with a different set of values, a society could just as easily measure transportation as an indicator of the level of *dysfunction* in its system.

To control our troublesome institutional subsystems, we must recognize the extent to which their behavior is controlled by their programming assumptions and language. The programming language they use is that of economics, the discipline that monopolizes the discourse over all our national resource-allocation decisions. To understand the workings of any system one must also examine the assumptions and goals that program its activities. For example, the U.S. Constitution is the program set up by our founding fathers to provide norms for operating this social system. The judicial system performs the comparator function of measuring behavior against these norms. As we have seen, the social system's growing economic and technological subsystems are now making it increasingly impossible to operate according to the original program of the Constitution. In fact, some of our large-scale technologies, such as nuclear power, require abridgment of civil liberties and may be simply unconstitutional. As more public debates over resource-allocation decisions are forced into narrow economic metaphors, such as cost-benefit analysis, the subsystem goals of profit maximization and efficiency supplant the former goals of freedom, justice, equality, and our collective judgments as to what constitutes a good society—rather than merely a rich one.

The discipline of economics itself is now the chief stumbling block to the rational discussion that our nation must have over what is valuable and how our resources are to be allocated. Imagine, for example, how different such public debate would be if we used the discipline of biology, or perhaps general systems theory, as the language of discourse. Economics has not yet incorporated the humanistic psychology of Abraham Maslow, David McClelland, and others. It has enthroned some of our most unattractive predispositions: material acquisitiveness, competition, gluttony, pride, selfishness, shortsightedness, and greed. In his day, Adam Smith was probably right that his "invisible hand" allowed microdecisions, however selfish, to add up to a fair approximation of the public welfare. In the crowded world of today, these human tendencies are beginning to destroy us, as they become institutionalized and reverberate throughout the system, thus helping create our many "tragedies of the commons."

We see the vital need to make trade-offs in our national and individual decisions on resource allocation. Business and government leaders mask such choices by their continual pumping up of consumer and citizen expectations. Politicians win votes by promising each group the pork-barrel legislation it desires, as well as the less obvious subsidies and tax breaks that have become a continual raid of the public treasury. Corporations also inflate our expectations through the more than $20 billion[15] they spend each year on advertising, often pandering to infantile desires and fantasies and obscuring the trade-offs inherent in all of our consumption. They tell us the good news, but forget to tell us the bad news—they tell us about the sparkling dishes and clothes, but forget to mention the loss of sparkling rivers and lakes. Consumer and environmental activists bring the bad news about the inevitable trade-offs if we continue our current wasteful production/consumption patterns. If we want more—energy, cars, appliances—we must expect more emphysema, strip mines, highways, and pollution. If advertisers pointed out these trade-offs more truthfully, American consumers might embrace lower consumption lifestyles and demand that production methods be changed.

BROADENING OUR OPTIONS THROUGH CITIZEN PARTICIPATION

It is vital that citizens inform themselves and that voluntary organizations become an integral part of the process of defining technological options and helping shape the agenda of our science-policy decisions. Every well-informed layperson can ask the right questions: "Have all possible options been adequately explored?" "How will the costs and benefits be distributed among different groups and individuals?" "What are the social and environmental impacts and the future consequences?" "Will the new technology or project create irreversible changes?" "Can the goal be reached by any other means?" and, if not, "Should the goal be further examined in light of other goals and priorities?"

As we have discovered that we cannot assume objectivity with environmental impact statements, especially when they are prepared by the same agency that is promoting the project, similarly, in assessing new technologies we cannot assume the objectivity of even the most prestigious scientific panel or the seemingly most unimpeachable organization preparing technology assessments. The perceptual and organizational biases are too endemic and often below the threshold of consciousness. Therefore, public participation in every phase of such assessments is the best way to provide a rigorous watchdog function, to spur scientific assessors into broader perspectives and more thorough analyses. Diverse voluntary organizations, such as labor and consumers, and those concerned with environmental impacts, must critically examine every phase of assessment: the study design, the assumptions, the composition of the scientific team. Significant perspectives and disciplinary skills may have been omitted: occupational health to ascertain effects on workers; political science to determine whether a technology will have centralizing or decentralizing effects; ecology to investigate total energy-conversion efficiencies and whether natural systems could perform the same task without resort to massive new hardware; and welfare economists to examine any impact on the distribution of wealth and income. Voluntary groups must demand opportunities to critique the work in progress to ascertain whether major new uncertainties have emerged. If technology assessments are done well, they are bound to turn up some bad news. Vigilant public participation can assure that such findings will not be suppressed.

All human systems and ecosystems require balance: competition with cooperation, selfishness and individualism with community and social concern, material acquisitiveness with thirst for knowledge and understanding, rights with responsibilities and the striving for love, justice, and harmony. As we study nature, we infer not the absurd caricature interpretations of social Darwinism to rationalize our greed but rather the interdependence of all living things. Natural systems never maximize single variables, such as profit or efficiency. Thus, we can infer that maximizing behavior on the part of any individual or firm is shortsighted and destructive of the larger system. An extreme example is the whaling industry, which is still maximizing its catches, in spite of the knowledge that it is only a few years before most of its prey will be extinct.[16]

We must learn humility if we are to face the complexities we have created. We sense the truth that only the system can manage the system and see the airy arrogance in some of our concepts of management and administration. We examine anew the easy assumptions that sociotechnical systems are even susceptible to manipulation by legislation. We marvel once more at the ingenuity of primitive cultures, whose most obvious characteristic is the relative absence of government, because social controls have been internalized.[17] We are at a crossroads in our sociotechnical complexity. We can take the path of stepping up the computer power to model these complexities; or we can try to disentangle some of the unnecessary interlinkages and technologies themselves, and by such decentralizing of means, reduce the numbers of interacting variables that must now be managed.

It is no longer just a matter of trade-offs and budget priorities between education, transportation, health, or more private consumption; or between R&D priorities, public and private investments, capital- or labor-intensive production, or energy alternatives. Educators and professionals must deal with whether to specialize further or to expand their horizons into interdisciplinary studies, even at the expense of rigor as academically defined and rewarded. At the personal level, we all must choose whether to trade expanded consciousness for greater secular power and money. Such goals conflict, because knowledge has become the servant of power in too many cases, and our educational enterprises have too often turned out intellectual mercenaries, whose lances are for hire to justify policies of entrenched bureaucracies and interest groups, rather than to search for the truth.

At last we see that science is not neutral, nor is technology, and its pretensions to value-free objectivity are now debasing the currency of public debate and social choices. Technology now creates its own social configurations, and we must ask to what extent the continued drive toward big-bang, capital-intensive technologies simply concentrates power, wealth, and knowledge in fewer and fewer hands, while making the rest of us poorer and more powerless and actually increasing overall human ignorance. It is now clear that the free market is not working to direct technological innovation to consumer demand, as it should. If it were, we would not now have debates raging about the appropriateness of technology, which has spilled out of the market-choice arena into the realm of social and political choice. All this was predicted in 1944 by Karl Polanyi in *The Great Transformation* (1944). He demonstrated that free markets, far from being derived from some natural order or human behavioral laws, were created and designed by humans and laid the groundwork for the Industrial Revolution.

Studying market failure is necessary if we are to assess technology properly and try to simulate its consequences. Each major technological innovation redistributes power, destroys some jobs and creates others, rearranges population patterns, and creates new ranks of winners and losers. Technologies do not arise in a vacuum. There is always a force-field of institutional vested interests whose interactions may tend to promote or suppress technologies. For example, the institutional and financial commitments to nuclear power have starved solar energy for decades, as James C. Fletcher, head of the National Aeronautics and Space Administration, has pointed out.[18] Therefore, to keep technology assessments intellectually honest, their review panels must appoint representatives of potentially impacted constituencies, as I have encouraged at the U.S. Office of Technology Assessment.

The technology assessment debate can also be focused around whether technologies are producer-driven or consumer-responsive. As the shortage of capital and inflation force tougher social choices, cost-benefit and risk-benefit analyses become more difficult. A typical producer-driven technology is the computer-automated tomographer,[19] which costs about $500,000 and diagnoses rare brain diseases undetectable by other procedures. A large output of such devices seems unjustified, yet promoters sold great numbers to hospitals, which are recovering their huge costs quickly by adding this diagnostic procedure to their normal health checkup routines and charging extra fees. With limited resources, can a society permit capital to flow into this type of questionable technological proliferation, when, perhaps, health dollars spent on disease-preventive education or on other more vital but less glamorous equipment might reap greater benefits?

Most humans learn experientially. Today, in many colleges you will find that the engineering, chemistry, and physics students have steered their professors out of the lofty classroom-based conceptualizing and into the open air. There they are doing hands-on experiments with small-scale, renewable-resource, appropriate technologies: whether methane gas production from bioconversion, solar-energy collectors, wind generators, or hosts of other soft as opposed to hard technologies.[20] I have seen the sheer joy in the faces of physics professors working with their hands constructing these vital, experimental, ecologically sustainable technologies, whose great merit is their power of integration. Today, all of us must learn to study whole systems with our whole integrated selves.

The dreams of technology-based hedonism, where machines would work and people would be trained for leisure, were premature and based on inadequate ecological models. They will remain beyond our reach until we learn to control our population growth, reduce the impacts of our technology, and share our resources more equitably. It is time for the science and technology of industrialism to realize its conceptual limitations. The stakes have never been higher for human survival. We need a new scientific paradigm, one suitable for a science that stands on the brink of nuclear disaster and genetic manipulation, a science that has the potential of enhancing human evolutionary possibilities or turning us into a race of what psychologist George Leonard, director of the California-based Leonard Energy Training Institute, calls, "bionic junkies." This new scientific approach must be self-reflective. The old, innocent view—"scientist observing phenomenon"—will no longer suffice. Today we must pull back one "photo frame" and include a new composite view: "scientist observing *self* observing phenomenon." This reflective paradigm exists in psychology, where those seeking to practice psychoanalysis on their fellow creatures must themselves submit to a prior psychoanalysis. If physicist Gerald Holton is correct about the personality types who choose scientific pursuits, perhaps all scientists should also be urged to undergo such psychological evaluation.[21] Perhaps we should call for a moratorium on Nobel Prizes in controversial and dangerous areas of research—to assure incentives of questing for truth rather than ego gratification.

Possibly William Irwin Thompson (1973) is right when he notes that we need to rediscover Pythagorean tradition in science rather than continue to pursue today's Archimedean science, which seeks to control nature through prediction and experimentation. Thompson notes that the Pythagorean approach embraced a mystical view of science that was integrated with art and religion. In *The Tao of Physics* (1975), Fritjof Capra draws the same conclusions and shows how physics has progressed in this century to a more metaphysical worldview, more consistent with the direct, experiential insights of Eastern religious traditions than with the atomistic, mechanistic view characteristic of the now receding industrial age.

John Todd of the New Alchemy Institute typifies the reverence which now must inform our scientific enterprise. He sees evolution not as preprogrammed but as a continual sacred dialogue with our planet. Augmenting natural productivity and reintegrating our activities into biospheric processes is already leading to a design revolution and a rethinking of many problems of production, energy, and materials management. Architects now design "passive" houses which reduce or eliminate the need for heating units. Fertilizers can be produced by recycling animal and human wastes or by genetically engineering plants to augment their own nitrogen-fixing capabilities. Millions are transcending fragmented viewpoints by raising human awareness, and many academic fields are in ferment. We can all play our part in this human evolutionary drama.

CHAPTER 4

THE JOBLESS
PRODUCTIVITY TRAP

J obless economic growth is the result of the industrialization paradigm and its focus on narrowly accounted production efficiency and laborsaving technologies. Productivity statistics still focus on labor productivity in terms of per capita averages, thus driving economies toward greater capital intensity and mechanization — even as politicians promise full employment. Noneconomists point out that such formulas are contradictory, ignore "externalities," increase automation, and also increase unemployment — unless new jobs are created even faster than jobs are destroyed. While many government officials point to technological change as the source of job displacement, they also rely on gross domestic product (GDP) growth and "technological progress" to reemploy those displaced.

Because it focuses on narrow production-efficiency statistics in the private sector, the economists' recipe for GDP-measured economic growth disregards social and environmental costs to taxpayers and future generations. This disregard cannibalizes or reduces social and environmental productivity, leading to fewer workers with more sophisticated tools producing more goods and services — while unemployment and welfare rolls rise. (See Fig. 8. Total Productive System of an Industrial Society on page 58.) A generation of economists has been commissioned to elaborate cases where job creation in new enterprises has, over time, filled the gap. These studies are often used by corporations and investors to lobby for more generous investment tax credits, justified to spur job creation. In a burst of enthusiastic orthodoxy, *The*

Economist, in a February 1993 editorial, hailed the jobless economic growth syndrome as "the Holy Grail of economic prosperity."

The economists' formula for industrial progress, productivity, and global competitiveness initially restructures traditional society by shifting workers from rural to urban areas, from farm to factory work. As factories automate, workforces are shifted to the service sector: today's vaunted Information Society, where workers must be continually retrained for new, more sophisticated tasks that, textbooks assume, will continually increase to sop up those displaced. People migrate from sustainable rural communities to overflowing cities in search of jobs. This scenario is now playing out on a global stage, with horrendously unexpected results: service sectors are also automating worldwide, and corporations, to stay competitive, now roam the world in search of cheaper labor and unprotected resources to exploit. Even in the United States, the poverty rate for working families rose from 7.7 percent to 11.4 percent between 1977 and 1993.[1]

Companies are downsizing their middle management and creating part-time workforces in order to shed fringe benefits, while further automating their factory and office work. The workforce cuts are no longer the result of recessions, but are permanent structural changes. Unions in the United States, which represent less than 20 percent of the workforce, have responded by merging. In 1995 the United Auto Workers, the United Steel Workers, and the International Association of Machinists arranged a deal to create the largest union in the United States: 1.7 million members and a $1.2 billion strike fund.[2] Even *The Economist* now agrees that "technology has, so far, played a bigger role than trade in increasing wage inequality."[3] In *Peddling Prosperity* (1994), Paul Krugman, formerly with the U.S. Presidential Council of Economic Advisors, describes hot debates within the economics profession on all these issues, which indicates that there are no accepted policies or theoretical agreements to help government.

The North American Free Trade Agreement (NAFTA) debate, "conducted in terms of fallacies exposed 150 years ago" according to Paul Wallich,[4] was only a prelude to the global scramble for cheaper labor and its flip side: growing global human migrations as workers try to follow capital flows and job promises across national borders. Today, forces of globalization have invalidated economic textbooks and statistics, which still assume the existence of national economies

The right to work

Everybody who wants to work should be able to Every adult person. regardless of age. sex, race or religion should be able to have a satisfying job that returns a living wage It should happen that way But it doesn't

New Zealand has many laws which protect private property There is not one law which protects a person's right to work!

Certainly the dole makes sure that a jobless person does not starve, but it can do nothing, absolutely nothing, to restore that person's dignity and feeling of self worth

The desire for short term profit has meant that much economic growth has happened in industries that cannot last The automobile industry. for example. will soon grind to a halt when oil becomes too expensive to import The pulp and paper. aluminium and steel industries take 60% of New Zealand's industrial energy. yet employ less than 3% of the workforce

Is growth the answer?

To overcome downturns in the past. the system has depended on growth The mineral and energy resources that have fuelled past growth are quickly becoming scarce and more expensive Growth can no longer be used to solve what is basically an allocation problem Until we resolve the question of ownership and control of New Zealand's financial and productive resources. the human tragedy of jobless people will remain with us

the disposable worker

Unemployment is part of the system

Unemployment is a natural result of our system, where **capital employs people.** In a co-operative economy, where **people employed capital,** unemployment would be unknown

The official figures of those unemployed or on Government Relief work are near record levels. The true rate of unemployment is staggering. It would be well over 100.000 people if young people unable to register and married people whose spouse is working were involved in the statistics Most of these people are looking for work and cannot find it

Many people mistakenly believe that an economic upturn is just around the corner. They are prepared to tolerate some unemployment in the meantime. There will be **no** permanent upturn!

High unemployment will stay with us there is a basic change in our economic system.

Fig. 11.   The Disposable Worker

Source: Values Party, New Zealand, reprinted from *The Politics of the Solar Age*

with both capital and labor relatively stationary within their borders. Today, all Organization for Economic Cooperation and Development (OECD) countries face a new scenario: for example, in 1995 joblessness hovered at an average 11 percent in Europe, actually 12.5 percent in France and Belgium and 24.3 percent in Spain, while Australia had 9.9 percent unemployment. Creeping budget deficits and jobless growth are the symptoms of new structural problems, but governments can no longer apply the old remedies and unions can no longer act as a balance to corporate power.

For example, trying to strangle inflation with high interest rates sends a multiplier shock back to the consumer price index, unleashing a vicious circle that chokes off growth, jobs, and the consumer spending on which many economies rely—another vicious circle. Or as economies pick up and start restoring lost jobs, global bond traders, speculating between long- and short-term interest rates, begin worrying about inflation. The supposed Phillips Curve trade-off between inflation and unemployment and the Non-Accelerating Inflation Rate of Unemployment (NAIRU) indicator signal inflation, even though it has been largely invalidated by global and structural changes. But this hint that the Loch Ness monster of inflation has been sighted throws central bank policies and financial markets into reverse. The NAIRU indicator is now under attack for signaling nonexistent inflationary pressures, and calculations of "full employment" are now at close to 7 percent joblessness—a figure that has crept up from 2 percent over the decades during which job creation targets were not achieved. Worse, rising government debts and deficits preclude the time-honored Keynesian tools of stimulus and further pump-priming deficit spending.

NEW STRUCTURAL PROBLEMS REQUIRE NEW REMEDIES

Jobless economic growth is now recognized by the G-7 leaders as a major contradiction in their futures. At their 1993 Tokyo summit they expressed concern for their twenty-three million unemployed, stating that "a significant part" of this "is structural in nature" and agreed to a meeting to search for the causes of this "jobless economic growth"[5]—an oxymoron, since economic growth is supposed to *create* jobs, for example, the Full Employment Act of 1946, in the United States. The G-7 ministers of labor and finance convened in Detroit in March 1994 for the first Jobs Summit, but avoided the issues underlying joblessness. They could not face the new fundamentals—the unchecked forces of globalization and the exhaustion of the industrial growth recipe itself, based on "productivity" and "competitiveness" formulas of a generation of economists relying too heavily on outdated macrostatistics and models. As yet, few world leaders see a way out of today's cul-de-sac by redirecting their policies toward a new sustainable development formula that integrates economic and social development within ecological efficiency and productivity criteria.

Instead, the G-7 ministers continue backing into the future looking through the rearview mirror, by deregulating their labor markets to make them more "flexible" and by focusing on more and better training. Making labor markets more flexible has translated into calls for dismantling European-style safety nets and limiting fringe benefits, minimum wages, and social programs. The ministers favor the more "efficient" U.S. labor market with its 30 percent contingency workforce, relatively lower wages, and benefits that the London-based *The Economist* reported were the envy of Europeans. Training has been hailed as a "good thing," but few outline how training would help workers in the face of a shrinking total job base. Already, millions of Americans with college degrees are underemployed in low-wage or part-time jobs. Meanwhile, executive compensation became a political issue in Europe as well as the United States.[6]

It is true that small and family businesses in the United States still produce over half of all goods and services and create millions of new jobs, somewhat compensating for big companies' downsizing and moving offshore. And indeed, family businesses account for almost two-thirds of Western Europe's GDP and employment. But, at the same time, statistical illusions, such as counting "full-time" any job that offers twenty hours a week or more, lead to complacency. It is easy to forget that one pre-1980s forty-hour-a-week job is often now part-timed into two "new" twenty-hour-a-week jobs. While economists commenting on the 1994 Jobs Summit viewed part-time jobs as a "preference," the same view is not held by discouraged job seekers who are dropped from unemployment figures or are trying to keep their lives and families together with two or more such jobs. No wonder Southern countries are questioning the traditional Western/Bretton Woods model and indicators of "progress."

In the United States, the further skewing of capital-labor ratios in the tax code has led employers to create part-time workforces to avoid the costly burden of full-time employees. Consequently some 30 percent of the labor force in the United States today consists of contingency workers. Companies seeking productivity gains accomplish their goals by mindlessly cutting their workforces rather than reassessing their overall operations. For example, Sears, the giant U.S. retailer, in order to improve its earnings and stock market evaluation, cut sixty thousand checkout counter employees, replacing them with automated systems. Naturally, when the news hit the mass media, levels of consumer confidence fell, and to come full circle the economic outlook was pronounced to be gloomier!

Some needed reevaluation of all this corporate "anorexia" shows that investing in employees and offering them career opportunities may prove more efficient overall than the hire-and-fire model.[7] Today, even Japanese companies, most of which make lifetime employment a norm, are calling in outplacement agencies. However, in its 1994–95 slump, Japan's unemployment was still a mere 2.8 percent—demonstrating that even with high technology, a society can place a priority on minimizing job losses. The World Bank's *World Development Report 1995: Workers in an Integrated World* chose, however, to warn the world's employees that "changes in the world economy are affecting the lives and expectations of workers across the world." The Bank's advice was no surprise: "market-based strategies are the best way to raise the living standards of workers, including the poorest." The International Labor Organization (ILO), intimidated by the global spread of markets, has relied heavily on old economic paradigms and World Bank and OECD data in its mild-mannered *World Employment 1995*, while independent unions are often crushed in Asian, African, and Latin American countries.

Economists have offered politicians a promised land of economic development and industrial progress via job creation and full employment. They promised to fine-tune industrial societies so as to create those "rising tides that would lift all boats." Economists counsel politicians and their governments on how to inflate, deflate, or reflate money supplies; when to jump start, spark, spur, or stimulate; and when to step on the gas pedal or brake, as if their economies were automobiles. Their advice is to look at the car's engine—rarely to check out the design, manufacturer, or the economic engineers.

As industrial societies have become more technologically complex and structurally interlinked, the "trickling down" of the economic stimulus that the textbooks claimed would soak up those who were at the bottom, unemployed, or on welfare has been impeded. Rather than reconceptualize the textbook model, the economic goal posts were moved—full employment was initially calculated at 2 percent unemployment after World War II. As this employment target became more unattainable under existing policy assumptions, the figure was ratcheted inexorably upward toward the 7 percent unemployment officially tolerated today and counted as full employment in most OECD countries.

By July 1995, *The Economist* acknowledged, "Few economic indicators are as politically charged as unemployment rates." In "Counting the Jobless," the editors added that many politicians see persistently high rates of unemployment as a constant reminder of the failure of their economic policies. They also acknowledged that many discouraged people no longer looking for work are classified out of the labor force, while many work part-time *involuntarily*, points I and others have stressed for decades. For example, the OECD officially counted thirty-four million unemployed in 1993, but if the additional four million discouraged and the fifteen million involuntary part-timers were included, this would double the total number of unemployed in their twenty-four member-countries. In the United States this would have increased 1993 unemployment from the official 6.5 percent to 13 percent.[8] Japan's official rate hovered at 3 percent in 1995 and was broken out in *Bungi Shunju*, June 1995, showing a jobless rate among women three times higher than among men.

Whether employed at the World Bank, the International Monetary Fund, the United Nations, or at economic ministries and development agencies around the world, economists most often graduate from elite universities, such as Harvard, Yale, MIT, and the London School of Economics. Jobless growth is a failure of theory, an appalling miscarriage of macroeconomic management and a tragic waste of human resources. The answers lie under the G-7 leaders' noses. President Clinton, speaking at the 1994 Jobs Summit in Detroit, alluded to the jobless economic growth problem:

> Productivity on the farm when I was a boy meant people lost jobs on the farm, right? But productivity in Detroit meant more jobs were created in the automobile industry than were lost on the farm. Throughout the whole twentieth century, ever since the Industrial Revolution, every time we had

productivity in one area that meant that fewer people could do more work in that area, technological changes were always creating more jobs in another area. Now, that is still true today, but the problem is there has been an explosion of productivity in manufacturing—it's not stopping. And now it's in the service industry, so that banks, for example, or insurance companies, or you name it, can do more work with fewer people because of information productivities. And, at the same time, all these other countries are able to do things that they were not formerly able to do. So in our countries there is a great insecurity that productivity, for the first time, may be a job threat, not a job creator.

Politicians' defeatist mantras—"global competitiveness" and "there is no alternative"—sound more and more like the language of those who suffer from clinical depression. President Clinton, while identifying the problem, still called for economic growth and growth in the global economy via free trade and other conventional remedies. *The Economist* agreed in an editorial entitled "Workers of the World Compete,"[9] while adding that gaps between wages for high- and low-skilled jobs would continue to widen in OECD countries and require new domestic remedies from income-support programs to education.

SOME ANTIDOTES TO JOBLESS ECONOMIC GROWTH

Ever since the Industrial Revolution began some three hundred years ago, its goal has been to produce more goods with fewer people—and this goal is being achieved today on a world scale. But few now pay attention to the debates of the 1960s about how unemployed people would be able to purchase the fruits of all this productive virtuosity. Back then, ideas ranged from Milton Friedman's negative income tax and proposals for guaranteed minimum incomes, to shorter work weeks, job sharing, retraining, and new leisure industries. In Europe, labor unions called for guaranteed minimum incomes, shorter work weeks, job sharing, sabbaticals, retraining, worker ownership, and mutual funds via such means as Sweden's Meidner Plan.

After the fall of the Soviet Union, Eastern European countries have privatized state-owned companies by issuing voucher distributions of stock to employees and the general public for nominal sums.

U.S. capitalist Louis O. Kelso had called for employee stock owner-ship since the 1960s;[10] many companies are now worker owned, the latest being the employee buyout of U.S.-based United Airlines. If machines are taking people's jobs, they will need to own a piece of these machines. Britain's E. F. Schumacher and I supported most of these proposals and echoed Mahatma Gandhi's question, "Why not more decentralized production by the masses instead of ever more mass production?" Robert Theobald[11] and W. H. Ferry[12] saw the need to reframe social policy around the new technological abundance and to *welcome rising unemployment as leisure*—a bonus that could lead to wider flowering of human cultures. I launched a Citizens Committee on Guaranteed Income in the United States in 1962, call-ing for a full debate about automation and productivity formulas, wholesale rethinking of how to distribute the fruits of technology, and a full review of taxation policies.

The debate foundered on fears that people couldn't be trusted, either with free time or with guaranteed incomes designed to smooth dislocation and keep up purchasing power. Politicians went with more familiar schemes to redistribute the new wealth that technology and automation created: welfare for those who fell too far behind; warfare (increasing military budgets); and workfare (growing govern-ment bureaucracy, jobs programs, and pork-barrel politics). Today, this complex, jury-rigged redistributive industrial system is spreading around the world, but still cannot keep pace with technology-related job destruction and corporate downsizing. The *Human Development Report, 1993* shows the ominous gap in all countries between growth (as measured by GDP) and employment levels. The report warns that job growth will continue lagging ever further behind—unless coun-tries face up to the need to target job growth directly.

In the United States in 1977, a Jobs Tax Credit created 900,000 new jobs at a modest temporary cost to the Treasury. As economist Mark Goldes pointed out, it was poorly publicized since both the Carter White House and the Treasury had opposed it, and it was repealed after one year.[13] Wage subsidies and other schemes to promote employment are now being tested in Britain, Australia, and other OECD countries. Recently other policies have been reemerging, such as France and Germany implementing shorter work weeks—but often with pay reductions; Japanese companies trying job sharing; and other G-7 countries experimenting with similar projects, including retraining. Also, more attention is being given to the Earned Income Tax Credit, an approach favored by the Clinton administration in the United States.[14] The G-7 leaders, at last, must face these problems and respond to why, for instance, when between 1960 and 1987, France, Germany, and Britain saw their economies more than double, their employment rates *fell*. Worse, during the same period, less than one-third of their GDP increases were from increased labor forces while two-thirds resulted from capital investment.

I and others are calling for a wholesale rethinking of taxation.[15] Jeremy Rifkin (1995) and British economist James Robertson reached similar conclusions and also called for further debate of guaranteed citizen income in *The End of Work* and in "Benefits and Taxes,"[16] respectively. Taxes, in principle, should be designed to discourage unhealthy behavior and encourage healthy, productive activities. This principle is clearly recognized in the imposition by most governments of "sin" taxes on tobacco, alcohol, and other life-threatening substances, as well as the some eighty-five kinds of pollution taxes now levied in OECD countries.

Countries need to rebalance their tax codes to make them neutral between employment and capital investment, recognizing that excessive tax credits for capital investment in automation (now in the services sector too) are key drivers in corporate downsizing and job-less economic growth. Introducing employment tax credits, pollution taxes, and value extracted taxes (VET) to substitute for value added taxes (VAT), as well as reducing income and corporate taxes, could create conditions for both environmental sustainability and full employment. As long as employers are burdened with more taxes and employee benefits, their decisions will be skewed toward fewer full-time employees and toward unemployment. Studies by Germany's Wuppertal Institute indicate that value extracted taxes and taxation of pollution could produce so much revenue for governments that income taxes and many corporate taxes could be progressively phased out.[17] The 1995 push by U.S. Republicans for a "flat tax" was counter-productive. *Business Week* noted that those making $20–30,000 per year would pay some 25 percent more in taxes, while those making $200,000 per year would see their taxes fall by 40 percent.[18]

Since industrialization is about saving labor, the jobless growth syndrome is no mystery. The G-7 leaders' pledge to do more research will only create jobs for economists—even while their outdated economic growth formulas exacerbate the problem. Until the 1970s, overall employment levels in the industrializing countries were maintained by their growing service sectors. Indeed, most of the G-7 countries are no longer industrial but service economies—but this catchall phrase includes vastly different activities. Government-provided services grew most rapidly to coordinate all the new complexities: growing cities, public utilities, infrastructure, highways, insurance, lawyers, and regulations to deal with social costs and environmental impacts—eventually landing in what I called "The Entropy State,"[19] societies bogged down in stagflation. Private-sector services also grew: from financial and insurance jobs to the much larger increase in low-wage jobs for waiters, janitors, and other part-time occupations. In fact, we forget that if the U.S. minimum wage of $4.25 per hour had kept pace with inflation, it would now be close to $12 per hour. As jobs migrate to Mexico and China, U.S. wages are further depressed. In "A Tilt toward the Rich," *Time* magazine observed the worsening distribution of U.S. incomes and "the impact on an already polarized economy."[20]

Meanwhile, the G-7's 1993 Tokyo communiqué clung to the old economic paradigm for economic growth: productivity, competitiveness, free trade, deficit reductions, higher levels of savings, capital investment tax credits, and more efficient labor markets. These obsolete slogans map the vanishing textbook territory of domestic economies, now sinking beneath daily trillion-dollar tidal waves of hot currencies in the global casino. None of the G-7 leaders at the Detroit Jobs Summit knew what to do about these complexities. Lloyd Bentsen, U.S. Treasury Secretary at the time, noted that "the turnout, some twenty-four ministers, is a clear demonstration of the seriousness with which our nations view the jobs problem." He added, paradoxically, "These rapid advances in technology we are seeing, where computer-chip speed seems to double every week, will make us more productive."[21]

The unwillingness to examine what *kind* of productivity and the underlying per capita productivity formula indicates the paradigm problem. Total productivity formulas should include *management* productivity, *capital* productivity, *investment* productivity, *R&D* productivity, *energy* productivity, and *environmental* productivity. *Social* productivity, as Sixto Roxas (1987) points out, can be statistically highlighted by shifting the focus of GNP national accounts from enterprise production to community production. National accounts must also present assets, both human-built infrastructure as well as natural resources, so that investments in such assets can be distinct from current consumption spending so as to arrive at national "net worth" balance sheets. New Zealand is a leader in such asset accounts, which are also necessary to prevent enterprising politicians from using proceeds from privatizations to "pretty up" their annual budgets. The World Bank's paradigm shift toward accounting for national assets is discussed in Chapter 10.

THE STRUGGLE TOWARD SUSTAINABLE DEVELOPMENT

Recent G-7 summits have become little more than photo opportunities. "Breakthroughs" in trade liberalization strain credulity. Trade liberalization based on the old economics can only lead to lower wages and more joblessness on a global scale—together with worsening debt, environmental destruction, and eventually worldwide recession. Privatization can no longer be a panacea; too often it has been used by insiders to acquire assets at below market prices—or to commit any of the other seven sins of privatization outlined by the *Human Development Report*, 1993. At the 1993 G-7 Summit, U.S. estimates that tariff reductions could produce 1.4 million new U.S. jobs were based on growth assumptions by the OECD that now appear too rosy. Wildly differing estimates of jobs to be created or lost accompanied the Canadian, U.S., and Mexican debates about NAFTA. Net job losses experienced in Canada led, in October 1993, to the fall of the Mulroney government. All these issues were addressed, at least rhetorically, in March 1995 at the UN World Summit on Social Development in Copenhagen. It was, however, the citizen groups' "NGO Declaration" that outlined realistic options: taming global corporations and capital markets; recalculating GNPs by adding unpaid work and natural resources while subtracting social and environmental costs; canceling the unpayable debts of the poorest countries; reforming Bretton Woods institutions; and focusing on sustainable livelihoods and informal sectors as well as corporate job creation.[22]

Mass production economies needed advertising and credit to fuel mass consumption. U.S. "recoveries" have largely been fueled by increases in consumer debt, whose ratio to disposable income had risen to 16.5 percent by January 1994. Industrial economies have become addicted to waste of energy and raw materials. Today, they are also addicted to spurious product differentiation, technological innovation, and ever larger doses of capital investment, as they chase their own tails. In today's globalizations of technology, finance, information, work, and migration, every country will end up losing in the mad competition for production efficiency and export-led growth—auctioning off their workforces, public-sector assets, cultural heritage, and environmental resources to the highest bidder in exchange for volatile paper currencies. This is now happening as Eastern European and Russian officials adopt outdated nineteenth-century capitalism from U.S. textbooks, and as the emerging Asian players—China, Indonesia, Malaysia, and Thailand—are urged to follow suit.

Even after the Copenhagen Summit on Social Development, countries still targeted "structural joblessness issues" as caused by "excessive" wages, benefits and health costs, aging populations, and "inefficient" labor markets. Such old paradigm views also target social safety-net legislation and blame fringe benefits and minimum wages, rather than automation-favoring tax credits, for pricing labor out of markets. Yet in the United States, average total compensation (including fringe benefits) is *lower* after inflation than in 1987. The real problem, wished away in editorials in *The Economist* during 1995 and buried in a 1993 *Business Week* article, is the relative cost of labor, vis-à-vis capital—exacerbated by productivity formulas and tax incentives.[23] In a global economy investors are free to roam worldwide rather than create domestic jobs, which will require the incentive of employment tax credits. "Equities Are Disappearing," a study by Wells Fargo Bank's Gary E. Schlossberg, showed another perverse effect of taxes favoring investment—that corporate mergers and buybacks were outpacing new issues, bidding up the price of corporate shares. Schlossberg noted the reasons: "cash-rich companies were on a wave of new acquisitions to expand global market share, and . . . buybacks are . . . driven by the large gap between taxes on ordinary income and those on capital gains."[24] Thus both corporations and their shareholders *gained* from diverting cash from dividends to capital gains.

With implementation of full-cost prices for energy and raw materials, as well as a value extracted tax (VET) to discourage waste and pollution, all economies can learn to run on a leaner mix of capital, energy, and materials and a richer mix of human resources. Such a basic shift can redirect economies toward fuller employment—even if the new jobs perforce will be in pollution control, environmental cleanup, and developing more efficient, "greener" technologies, companies, and public services. Introducing VET and employment tax credits can help, particularly for small companies and the self-employed. For example, such assistance to the unemployed and self-employed in Britain has raised self-employment to 11 percent of the workforce and has created 650,000 new small businesses. In May 1994, *Fortune* magazine examined how U.S. consumers were fleeing the producer-dominated macroeconomy—bypassing retailers and holing up in their do-it-yourself, electronic home "fortresses." Such self-employed Americans now top twenty-five million, while another eight million telecommute via modem—as the Tofflers predicted in *The Third Wave* (1980).

Today's downward leveling of the global playing field sadly continues to level rain forests, shred social safety nets, and homogenize cultures in many countries. In today's global lose-lose game, as unemployment soars and wages are knocked down, declining living standards and purchasing power will prevent the heroic feats of consumption needed for traditional economic recovery. Like an alcoholic, the unsustainable global economy may "hit bottom" in an orgy of deficit- and budget-cutting before G-7 and other leaders, still focused on myopic national bookkeeping exercises, can open their eyes and shape policies to fit the new realities. Today, the global playing field must be leveled upward not downward, by negotiating treaties and agreements to raise its ethical floor.

Today's globalized economic apparatus, arguably, drives most other human institutions, policies, and activities. It has facilitated the successful spread of industrialism and its second-order effects—the marginalization of traditional societies and cultures; the restructuring of work and production; the widening of poverty gaps; the spread of pollution and unsustainable levels of consumption, waste, and resource depletion—while luring people from rural self-sufficiency into cities to look for jobs in the cash economy. As Japan's economy fell into deflation in 1995, usual pump-priming failed as its "bubble economy" of the 1980s burst. Even negative interest rates failed to boost output or employment. While both fiscal and monetary policy tools were failing, Japan's central bank might have resorted to simply printing money—a course advocated by some—including a former Bank of Japan reearcher with the brokerage firm Jardine Fleming.[25]

World leaders must shift their focus to restructuring wasteful sectors, redirecting and changing the rules of this world economic game to support sustainable development. (See Fig. 4. Restructuring Industrial Economies on page 37.) Agreements have been reached to change the scorecards by which the game of development is played. For example, in March 1995, the president of the European Parliament hosted a two-day conference on correcting GNP/GDP-measured per capita economic growth. As described in Chapter 10, a host of new scorecards, including the United Nations Human Development Index (HDI) and my own Country Futures Indicators (CFI), began appearing in the mid-1990s. These developments push leaders and citizens to change many long-held beliefs about money, wealth, productivity, efficiency, and even our notions of progress itself.

Today's global wave of speculation swamps actual trade transactions manyfold and renders bilateral trade policies and statistics, as well as the U.S.-Japan and other micro-trade showdowns, all but irrelevant. Trade became the focus of the World Trade Organization (WTO) after the conclusion of the last round of negotiations under the General Agreement on Tariffs and Trade in 1994. Yet trade now only accounts for 10 percent of world capital flows. All the issues relating to the future of the WTO and how its narrowly focused trade agreements can embrace sustainable development are updated comprehensively in *Greening the GATT*.[26] The turmoil in bond markets, which spread to stocks in April 1994, was triggered by an over-leveraged bond market. Speculators were forced to liquidate when U.S. Federal Reserve Chairman Alan Greenspan raised interest rates, reflecting most central bankers' single-minded fears of inflation. Clearly, interest rates and central bankers' focus on them to wring inflation down to zero are taking their toll, not only in jobless growth but in ratcheting up CPIs, since interest costs figure so prominently in the prices of all goods and services and raise the cost of government borrowing—yet another vicious circle. For example, Federal Reserve Board hikes in interest rates in 1995 added $125 billion to the federal deficit and $67 million to New York City's annual debt service, leading to more job losses.[27]

Meanwhile, the wage squeeze in the United States was worsening while corporate productivity and profits were up. *Business Week* pointed out that real compensation had fallen for the past five years according to the Labor Department, while other studies showed wages and benefits up—but by less. While celebrating the return of productivity to the 2 percent range, the editorial warned that all the budget-cutting was going to require even faster rates of growth and expansion.[28] Only two weeks later, the U.S. Commerce Department announced that new calculations of GDP showed less growth in productivity—a mere 1.4 percent between 1991 and 1995.[29] *The Economist* reported, "In the U.S. and Britain profits as a share of total national income are currently close to their highest level for nearly thirty years, while in most countries wages are barely keeping pace with inflation; in America, real wages continue to fall." However, the article added that companies should not be pressured by workers or governments to share their gains.[30]

The U.S. Office of Technology Assessment (OTA) had warned of structural unemployment in its 1986 report *Technological and Structural Unemployment: Re-employing Displaced Adults*, which tracked the shift of U.S. workers from the manufacturing sector— even then less than 20 percent of the economy. In 1994 the Institute for International Economics report, *The Political Economy of Policy Reforms*, reviewed the policies of thirteen countries. Despite growing evidence to the contrary, the report found that countries that had succeeded in making moves to more "liberal" deregulation of their economies, including Poland, Portugal, Turkey, Spain, and Mexico, had leaders with vision and technical economics training including Mexico's Carlos Salinas.[31] Less than a year later these countries and their leaders had lost their "star" status, another sign of the exhaustion of the GNP-growth, global economic warfare paradigm.

As fights about economic statistics broke out, surveys of the American people by the Americans Talk Issues Foundation (ATIF), showed large majorities in favor of international regulation of many sectors of today's global economy, from currency speculation to global manufacturing and arms trading.[32] The United Nations must be strengthened and reshaped to meet global situations undreamed of in 1945: for example, jobless economic growth, mass migrations, global pollution, and the need to refocus industrial growth toward sustainable development. By 1991, ATIF Survey #17 found that 77 percent of the U.S. public supported regulating global capital markets and taxing currency exchange transactions.[33] The WTO's next round could, with sufficient grassroots pressure, shift its focus to employment and sustainable development and be negotiated by multidisciplinary teams of scientists to provide needed data on missing social and ecological priorities. The WTO has already become politicized over opening financial markets at the urging of the United States. Strangely, the WTO could have devised rules to tame the global capital markets speculation. Instead of addressing this 90 percent of global flows, it chose to focus on the other 10 percent, which represented actual trade and other real transactions.[34]

In order to prepare for jobs and livelihoods in the twenty-first century, we must embrace technological shifts and global contexts. Education must be globalized and focus on life-long learning, whole systems, and the life sciences. Teachers must learn and transmit the holistic skill of learning how to learn. Universities and colleges can help legislators and funding sources to see that such broadly gauged education is far more cost effective than narrow job training in vocational skills, which become obsolete ever faster. Students can gain their balance in a changing world and learn to take risks when they see themselves more clearly within job markets and societies that are restructuring, and, indeed, within the changing planetary conditions. Beyond such needed reforms, a more fundamental understanding of money and all its functions must be a priority in public education and taught in schools. As discussed in Chapter 9, the world's people need to understand that money is not scarce, nor is credit or liquidity. They are created by banks and central bankers and myriad other public-policy directives. Neither are markets derived from God or any original state of nature, but are created by human policy.

Some of the girder work to raise a more ethical floor under the global playing field is already in place, with global agreements on worker safety and consumer and environmental protection; agreements signed on ozone depletion and biodiversity; and other provisions of *Agenda 21*, signed in Rio at the Earth Summit in 1992. All economies today are mixed, i.e., mixtures of markets and regulations, which today's economists do not understand and about which they have no theories. In reality, what we call "economies" are simply sets of rules derived from various cultural DNA codes, as we shall see in Chapter 8. These cultural DNA codes explain differing development patterns of, for example, Sweden, Taiwan, Germany, Japan, China, Russia, and Europe's social markets. This understanding of the many cultural faces of capitalism has reintroduced creativity into sterile thinking and debates left over from the Cold War. Markets, like technologies, are good servants but bad masters.

CHAPTER 5

GOVERNMENT BY MEDIOCRACY AND THE ATTENTION ECONOMY

me·di·oc·ra·cy\mē-dē-'ä-krə-sē *n* : a new form of governance based on media as the nervous system of the new body politic (still not sufficiently analyzed by political scientists, pundits, or the media themselves).

at·ten·tion econ·o·my\ə-'ten(t)-shən i-'kä-nə-mē\ *n* : a form of economy associated with mediocracies, based on the production of information, entertainment, and other goods and services that compete with politicians and educators for the attention of individuals. Attention economies are the dominant sectors in mediocracies: movies, video and audio cassettes and CDs, TV and radio, books, magazines, computers and software, advertising, tourism, education, and politics. Calculated in this way, attention sectors accounted for the lion's share of the world's GDP in 1995. It would be useful if economics, which studies scarce means applied to supposedly infinite wants, would switch its focus from money to studying the ultimate scarcity for humans: their time and attention. Spending our precious time earning inflating paper money is not worth so much of our attention.

DO WE ALL SUFFER FROM ATTENTION DEFICIT DISORDER?

Our lives are awash in info-glut: headlines, commercials, billboards, government directives, and talk-show hosts screaming for our

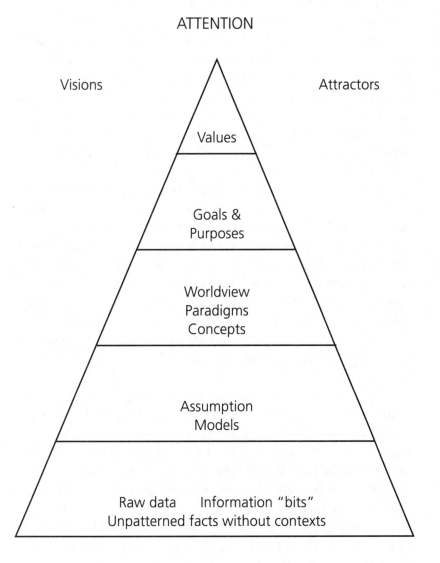

Fig. 12.   Information Quality Scale
(Meaning of information as relevant to human purposes)

© 1980 Hazel Henderson   Source: *Paradigms in Progress*

attention. Naturally, more of us each day are zapping the ads and simply tuning it all out. Is this a sign of the new malady, "attention deficit disorder," or just common sense? Are our personal priorities and values reclaiming our info-battered psyches? Or are we indeed suffering from a mental disorder now catered to by legions of psychotherapists? For better or worse, the Information Age has spawned mediocracies and the emerging attention economies. Industrial economies first grew by mass-producing goods with ever more efficient machines and by selling more products to consumers eager to spend their paychecks on all the latest gadgets. Today 67 percent of our economy rests on this consumption. But these heroic feats of mass consumption, often beyond the basic necessities, now require cajoling—with $147 billion a year of advertising—just to get our attention.

Limited "attention budgets" must be shared between job (increasingly more than one); children, spouse, and other family members; neighbors and community; politics (now global as well as local and national); career and personal development; fitness programs, sports, and club memberships; retirement and children's college planning (if we are fortunate); not to mention vacations, entertainment, TV watching, and product consumption. As most of us have found out, there are not enough hours in the day. Each of us plays a key role in the attention economy as consumers, citizens, parents, caregivers, information processors, producers, investors, savers, and community members.

Product consumption must take its turn in line. We try to save time by shopping at home from catalogues or TV, ordering even groceries by phone, and eating at fast food drive-ins. Still Americans feel harried and overloaded. Dreams of the "leisure society" promised in the 1960s as the fruits of industrial efficiency and automation haven't worked out. Americans have less free time than ever. People didn't work as many hours for their necessities in the Stone Age—when we humans were gatherers and hunters (Sahlins 1972). Clifford Stoll tells us in *Silicon Snake Oil* (1995) that he regrets the decades of his time spent cruising the Internet.

I began to study what I call mediocracies (and they certainly are mediocre) in 1969 with the publication of an article in the *Columbia Journalism Review*.[1] I became a media activist, working in New York City with Amitai Etzioni and others to pass the city law that required cable operators to set up public access channels—which then spread to many other cities. The issues have become more crucial since then: commercially profitable violence and pornography; the miseducation of children via advertising and classroom commercialism; the rise of talk-show hosts and hate-speech shows; and mad bombers who kill to demand space in the *New York Times* or blow up federal facilities to draw attention to their "causes." Today, many of the world's countries have gone from feudalism to mediocracy without ever having passed through the stages of industrialism and democracy. This new type of accidental government by media concentrates political power in ways unexplored by political scientists. Its dangerous trends toward new forms of totalitarianism, as well as its brighter possibilities are explored in Chapter 11. Attention economies have grown worldwide in lockstep with the spread of mediocracies, as satellites, the Internet, computer software giants, and media empires have expanded and conglomerated — competing for the attention of people in China and other awakening Asian societies and Latin America, which has spawned homegrown giants, such as Brazil's Rede Globo TV. The African continent has remained the last outpost of traditional life.

Opinion leader Jacques Cousteau has made a new generation aware of pollution and the pressures of overconsumption and population through his TV ocean adventures. Cousteau editorialized in "Information Highway: Mental Pollution" that people's minds were now flooded with information that increases confusion. "The mind is to be cultivated and irrigated — not flooded." He urged people to get off the information highways and back to life's side roads and byways.[2] Fritjof Capra, Jerry Mander, Joseph Weizenbaum (a computer pioneer), and many other education experts have warned against wholesale computerization of education in *The Proceedings of the Conference on Computers in Education.*[3] The Center for Media Literacy and its crusading magazine, *Media and Values*, founded by former nun Elizabeth Thoman, launched a comprehensive community education curriculum with books and videocassettes, "Beyond Blame: Challenging Violence in the Media."[4] Theodore Roszak, insightful author of *Where the Wasteland Ends* (1972) and other critiques of late-stage industrialism, sums up the debate in *The Cult of Information: A Neo-Luddite Treatise on High-Tech, Artificial Intelligence and the True Art of Thinking* (1994). As Windows 95 and Java take over the world, my own computer is still going strong: the portable one-pounder in my head, which has a multigigabyte memory, runs on carbohydrates and water, and is free.

THE ROLE OF MASS COMMUNICATION IN SOCIETY

My article, "Access to Media: A Problem in Democracy" in the *Columbia Journalism Review* in 1969, laid out issues still with us today:

The current public interest in all forms of mass communication reflects a growing understanding of its central role in our national life. We have schools of communications at many of our colleges, and an increasing body of scholarly analysis of the mass media's effects on our cultural and individual psyches, notably those of Harold Innes (1950) and Marshall McLuhan (1966). More people are at last realizing too, the awesome political power that comes with ownership or control over any medium of communication, whether television, radio, newspapers, magazines, wire services, computer networks, or any other system for moving information and ideas to significant numbers of people. Communication between all citizens and all their institutions is indeed the primary integrative force needed to turn our fragmented, uncoordinated body politic into a healthily functioning whole. The sum of all channels of communication in a society makes up its vital nervous system. The great challenge is to ensure that all the components of this nervous system are free and open conduits for the maximum possible interchange of information between the maximum number of citizens.

The channels of communication in the United States today are technologically advanced beyond those available to any other body politic. In fact, mass media are almost beginning to replace political parties in our system of government. They have informed and misinformed our citizens on national issues on an unprecedented scale, but in a largely unplanned manner. The mass media have shown the poor how the rich live, and have shown the rich what it is like to live in a rat-infested city slum. They have given us insight into pressing problems like "perspiration wetness," "tired blood," "bad breath," and "the blahs." They have made Americans interested in each other and whetted their appetite to communicate. But the only way to do this efficiently is by using the mass media, especially the air waves—that always seem to have an editor or owner, a licensee, or a sponsor between ordinary citizens and that precious microphone, not to mention the "static" of endless commercials and entertainment programming.[5]

Nonetheless, radio and television sets are the most efficient tools at hand to help us understand our race relations, why cities are decaying, what politicians are saying, and what our role in the world should be. For the underskilled, broadcasting could offer nationwide job training and basic education. For children, the air waves could provide more Sesame Street–type and "Headstart" programs, without the costs of special transportation or facilities. Mass media could become a national feedback mechanism by providing a random-access conduit for all the wisdom, creativity, and diversity of our citizens.

Our mass media are only a poor shadow of what they could be — not for lack of technology, but because of our imperfect understanding of their potential power. The mass media in the United States are still operated on the notion that they are purely businesses whose primary concern is to make profits for their stockholders, and to provide a medium for merchandising goods. We have begun to learn the considerable hidden cost to society in making advertising the chief source of revenue to sustain the operations of its mass media. Since the original decision to cede the use of the air waves to private broadcasters, we have learned that if advertisers pay the cost of putting on programs, the public must pay the price of seeing only programs advertisers feel will sell their products. Instead of the justly dreaded government censorship, we ended up with censorship by sponsors and private owners.

The advertiser's desire for the largest possible audience naturally conflicts with the needs and interests of minority audiences. It also hampers the germination of new and controversial ideas, which must break into the mass marketplace if they are to gain consideration. In a sprawling country like the United States, coverage in the mass media is the only means of gaining a day in the court of public opinion. If minority groups cannot get coverage, their only nonviolent recourse is to beg or buy advertising. But here they must compete with giant corporate-product advertisers who can afford to pay $125,000 or more a minute for prime television network time. Competition for free "public service" advertising is heating up; but here again, it has been until recently the safe causes, like "Smokey Bear" or "Give to the College of Your Choice," that are permitted to get their message through.

When civic groups "sell" their ideas and programs in competition with products and politicians, who should decide how much time and space ought to be allotted to these different purposes? Just those who own or control the media? For broadcasters and regulators, this problem is already serious. Which groups deserve free "public service" time and which must pay? If a civic group, a politician, and a product advertiser all want to buy the same limited advertising time, how will broadcasters decide whose message gets on the air and whose is blacked out? For budding civic groups, the need for publicity is a matter of life and death, and a negative decision could condemn an organization to oblivion.

Similar problems have arisen in political primaries. Politicians send advance men into an area and buy up all the available time. Other candidates arrive and find themselves blacked out. And what if a local civic group had wanted air time to raise an issue that was being inadequately covered by the candidates? Some of these matters are subject to a loose set of rules (the "Fairness Doctrine") promulgated by the Federal Communications Commission, and now continually being challenged in court, but more often these decisions are left in the lap of business.[6]

When a society is in ferment, as ours is today, pressure for equal access to public opinion through mass media increases as the old consensus splinters. New ideas and new minority opinion groups spring up everywhere. These new ideas are vital for the continual process of renewal and adaptation that prevents cultures from decaying. Such new ideas are necessarily disruptive and controversial, and therefore underfinanced and without institutional vehicles to promote them. The realization is now dawning on groups espousing these new ideas that in a mass, technologically complex society, freedom of speech is only a technicality if it cannot be hooked up to the amplification system that only mass media can provide. When the U.S. founding fathers talked of freedom of speech, they did not mean freedom to talk to oneself. They meant freedom to talk to the whole community. A mimeograph machine can't get the message across anymore.

It is entirely possible that much of the recent radicalization of American politics may be due to this media bottleneck. Minority opinion groups have discovered that whereas media ignore a traditional press release on their activities, they send reporters rushing to cover a picket line or any attention-getting "happening." Once other groups caught on to this game, the media became desensitized to mere picketing, and escalation became necessary. Now to get the media's and, therefore, the public's attention, one must hold a college dean hostage, dance naked through the streets, throw a rock, or start a riot. In psychological terms, the news media have been "rewarding" and therefore reinforcing destructive behavior, by drawing attention to it and making national figures out of those who have learned what kind of behavior keeps them in the camera's eye.

At the same time, quiet, constructive behavior on the part of all those thousands who continually work to build and heal society is punished by the negative sanction of being ignored by the media, and never reaching society's attention. Of course, there are exceptions. Many responsible publications, as well as some unusual radio and television stations, do not make a practice of exploiting sensational news. The prevalent, oversimplified journalism is based on the time-honored editorial use of "rape, riot, and ruin" as the best way to sell the news. Until we recognize its dangerous tendencies the radicalization of politics will continue. Until minority opinion groups are provided with significant rights of access to mass media, and thereby, society's group consciousness, they will continue to behave in any aberrant way necessary to get attention. Just as the labor movement had to stay in the streets until it had won the right to an orderly channel of communication (in this case, a bargaining table) for negotiation and redress of grievances, so will the new political movements disrupt until the system can provide them open and orderly channels of communication.

The battle over the public's right of access to the mass media may well be the most important constitutional issue of this decade. The issue affects every segment of society from blacks who wish to be portrayed adequately in the media to antimilitary groups vainly trying to counteract the promotional budgets of military contractors; antipollution groups wishing to counteract the millions spent on defensive advertising, public relations, and lobbying by polluting corporations; or anticigarette groups trying to neutralize the millions spent by tobacco companies to promote the smoking habit. Until very recently, there have been only sporadic skirmishes fought for this right of access by a few embattled crusaders and citizens' groups. The first real change came in 1953, with the birth of educational television. But even today, public television is still underfunded compared with commercial television, and our public television stations must still largely rely on local charity to mount their programs.

Pressures to democratize media have mounted and, as always, some critics are responsible and justified, and others are demagogic. Many civic groups have learned that they can challenge broadcasters at license-renewal hearings, held every three years by the Federal Communications Commission. Another response has been the explosive growth of "underground" media. Protest magazines and newspapers are proliferating and "underground radio" is beginning to flourish on FM bands held by churches and universities. The American Civil Liberties Union worked to broaden the interpretation of the First Amendment to include the concept of the public's "right of access" to the media. Professor Jerome A. Barron of George Washington Law School advanced this concept in an article entitled "Access to the Press—A New First Amendment Right" in the *Harvard Law Review* of June 1967. He called for "an interpretation of the First Amendment which focused on the idea that restraining the hand of government is quite useless in assuring free speech, if a restraint on access is effectively secured by *private* groups." Professor Barron thinks that the cure for suppression is government regulation through court rulings and laws to force the media to give time and space to unpopular ideas.

What can be done to democratize media and permit more citizen participation? Some broadcasters have been reexamining their policies. There have been more feedback and discussion programs on local stations, including several "ombudsman" programs to help citizens get action from unresponsive government or businesses. But efforts simply to bypass the mass media via alternative communication continue. We must remind ourselves that the present structure of our mass media was not ordained by the Almighty, but merely grew. The First Amendment should not be a cloak for our current media operators to hide behind, or to wave in our faces if we suggest anything new. We must ask, whose freedom of the press? Just the freedom of the present owners? And if so, what about citizens' freedom of the press, and our freedom to hear the maximum diversity of opinion on all issues?

If we succeed in freeing our mass media from some of their past patterns of operation, we can decide what needs to be communicated and how to use communications to build our future. First, we must have faith that new information, properly communicated, can change human perception of reality and therefore our attitudes and behavior. There must be a new, mature ethic of journalism, for both electronic and print media. Current mass journalism is still largely based on the old, fragmented Newtonian vision—where humans were the dispassionate, objective observers of their world. Even though few people still believe that humans can ever observe the world objectively because they are an interacting part of it, there is still a widespread lag on the part of our mass media in perception of this integral nature of reality.

The new, post-Newtonian journalism will be less concerned with aberrant, violent happenings and manifestations. Rather, intelligent, creative reporters and editors will face up to the knowledge that true objectivity is impossible, and therefore shoulder and acknowledge the heavy burden of responsibility thus placed upon them. They will analyze the complex structures and interrelationships which lie beneath surface events in the same way that only a handful of "little" magazines do today, and present this material simply for mass audiences. In a democracy as complex as ours, only if voters can obtain such simplified coverage of the parameters of major issues, can they hope to use their votes wisely. Mass media reporters will seek out injustices and pressures in society before they need erupt in violence or find expression in the "underground media." Just as the sensory system of primitive creatures can only signal danger or dysfunction, so our primitive mass journalism has concentrated on signaling these to our body politic. Editors will seek news of the integrative activities of people, as well as their destructive acts. Like individuals, a society needs confidence in itself, and its ability to cope with its problems. We must know of human love and courage, as well as our hates and fears.

To address adequately the need for more democratic access to public opinion, as well as to meet its huge responsibilities as our most powerful educational system, mass journalism, both electronic and print, must face up to a greatly enlarged function in a complex, mass society. If it fails, the consequences may be disastrous.

UNDERSTANDING TODAY'S INFORMATION REVOLUTION

In the 1990s and beyond, information technologies spread public knowledge and make possible new ways of revitalizing local economies starved of legal tender by central banks and other national policies. (See Chapter 9.) The same information revolution can foster the global civil society, not only through today's "narrow casting" on expensive E-mail systems or the Internet, but by expanding broadcasting capabilities and by linking television facilities and producers. Canadian-based WETV, an incipient global television consortium for sustainable development, is geared, along with other efforts, to redress global television's mental monoculture with fresh multicultural programming and news of grassroots solutions and innovations. Such grassroots TV shows can just as surely link producers in rural areas and developing countries with viewers who wish to help or to buy art and craft designs directly. There will be little need to leave the beauty of natural, unspoiled habitations and the satisfactions of traditional culture to search for a job in polluted, crime-infested urban areas. Every village could have access to opportunities, education, new technologies, and a rich variety of cultural contacts, as well as global, regional, and local news. Such grassroots, culturally diverse producers and programs are already linking the world's nonprofit television and news organizations. The currently dominant commercial television, driven by advertising to encourage unsustainable consumption and wasteful energy-intensive lifestyles, will need to be taxed rather than subsidized as in the United States.

Forms of advertising that use psychological manipulation and undercut self-esteem will need to be banned from the air waves, in spite of protestations from U.S. movie- and videomakers that this would infringe First Amendment rights of free speech. The U.S. First Amendment does not give Hollywood producers the right to encourage youths in Belize to form fighting gangs. It is also generally accepted that free speech does not include the right to advertise heroin, cocaine, or tobacco over the public air waves or cry "fire" in a crowded theater. The crowded planet, our cities, and our neighborhoods are the "theaters" now. Alternative media to cover the slow-motion good news now ignored are vital to personal development, education, and the evolution of human society and cultures. In 1997 a new Human Development Network (HDN) in the United States will carry the voices of many of the leaders and agents of transformational change already mentioned. The new healing movements and doctors, including Larry Dossey, M.D.; Bernie Siegel, M.D.; Deepak Chopra, M.D.; Carl and Stephanie Simonton; and many indigenous healers, will have air time. Many other popular inspirational authors and workshop leaders from Barbara Marx Hubbard to Jean Houston, Chris Griscom, Marianne Williamson, and Tony Robbins will communicate in the United States on HDN.[7]

In the United States, love, angels, and miracles (to recharge our imaginations) have become fashionable again in a society suffering from overcompetition and excessive individualism.[8] Many U.S. citizens have become appalled by our society's main exports to the world: weapons and the gratuitous violence in our TV, movies, music, and "entertainment." Many, like myself, who have traveled and seen the corrosive effects of such U.S. exports have been shamed into activism for media responsibility at home. This issue crosses all party lines and links powerfully with grassroots groups and activists worldwide. The ranks of planetary citizens are growing. As Margaret Mead correctly stated, "Never underestimate the power of groups of committed citizens to change the world. In fact, it is the only thing that ever has."[9]

Meanwhile, a subtle shift is occurring as the idea that many economies are no longer based on selling more goods, but are increasingly reliant on the provision of services, is dawning on policymakers, businesses, marketers, and pollsters. Obviously we need new scorecards beyond GNP—scorecards based on services and quality of life. Already the U.S. Commerce Department is overhauling GNP to reflect an economy largely based on services: from insurance, health, education, and local government to environmental cleanups and pollution control. (See Chapter 10.) In 1995, some 67 percent of our economy still rested on personal consumption; these heroic feats of consumption require ever more cajoling. Because many are reaching for higher purposes in their lives, new motivations and incentives come into play. Marketers must go beyond the fear and scarcity tactics and threats to self-esteem (you're not OK unless you buy this) typical of much of today's advertising and marketing.

Many aware Americans are protesting these manipulative approaches and are buying and spending more selectively. Does the company employ child labor? Exploit women and children in semipornographic ads? Pollute or discriminate? Sell weapons to unstable dictatorships? Does it recycle and reuse, or waste, natural resources? Socially responsible investors require that their portfolio managers, too, take these questions into account in managing their mutual funds. Many have rejected the whole "Keeping Up with the Joneses" game. A spate of new books has hit the U.S. best-seller list, including *How Much Is Enough?* by Alan T. Durning (1992), my former colleague at the Worldwatch Institute; *Your Money or Your Life* by former stockbroker Joe Dominguez and Vicki Robins (1992); and *Enough* by financial planner James D. Schwartz (1993). These authors are featured on Oprah Winfrey and other talk shows. Earth Day 1990 brought an enormous outpouring of sentiment that accepted the necessity of more frugal lifestyles. Support groups and workshops on how to reduce consumption are becoming popular.[10] Thrift shops supporting all kinds of charities are mushrooming along with cause-related marketing, "affinity group" credit cards, eco-tourism, and volunteering.

Marketers use focus groups and surveys to analyze these personal growth motivations, and why spiritual books, often self-published and promoted only by word of mouth, such as *The Celestine Prophesy* and *Mutant Message*, make the U.S. best-seller lists. As politicians and marketers begin to understand that softer selling and even personal respect are necessary to deserve the attention of today's post-industrial voters—our society and economy will change accordingly. The GNP may continue to sag, but the new quality-of-life scorecards emerging in cities from Jacksonville, Florida, to Seattle, Washington, are registering the boom of the attention economy. Personal development embraces home study and independent scholarship. Courses on video and audio cassettes and self-directed studies boom, such as Florida Community College's Open Campus on cable TV. People who have taken control of their own lives offer road maps for others, for example, Melissa Everett's *Making a Living While Making a Difference* (1995) and Ronald Gross's 1982 classic, *The Independent Scholar's Handbook*. An opinion survey by the Harwood Group for the Merck Family Fund, "Yearning for Balance," found 82 percent of Americans agreeing that "Most of us buy and consume far more than we need; it's wasteful."[11]

Attention economies may already be dominant but are statistically invisible in the maturing post-industrial societies of North America, Europe, and Japan. They augur the beginning of the end of lowest-common-denominator, instant-gratification consumerism. The attention economies began their rapid growth with entertainment, computers and software, and tourism—three of the biggest industries in the world in 1995. The growing edge of these attention markets is world music, art and pop culture, computer software and the Internet, as well as socially concerned rock stars, following the Live Aid and Food Aid concerts of the 1980s and the outpourings of eco-concern in concerts, films, and wildlife TV specials of the 1990s. Tourism is already the world's largest industry, accounting for 10 percent of global output, jobs, and investments and 13.4 percent of the GDP in the European Union.[12] Eco-tourism is the fastest growing segment—expanding annually at 25 to 30 percent.

Another segment of the attention economy is paying attention to people who need care—whether sick, aged parents or growing children. The U.S. health-care sector was 16 percent of GDP in 1994 during the great debate about paradigms and definitions of health care. The debate became too focused on the need for more money in order to support the old-paradigm material and technological base of the health-care industry. But people concerned with wellness wanted a change from impersonal, crisis-driven, expensive, high-tech intervention. They shifted the debate to prevention, and health care's nonmaterial sector became visible. Patients need human attention and one-on-one kindness and care—often in their homes and communities.

As with other sectors, this move toward the less material information and attention services means a major reclassification of national economies. Certainly if we reclassified the U.S. economy— already consisting of 80 percent services—using the attention economy model, the attention economy would predominate, including large segments of our health-care and education systems as well as information and attention services. It would also predominate in Europe, Japan, and most other OECD countries. When statistics include human rights, refugee and peace services, and volunteers (for example the eighty-nine million men and women in the United States who give five hours or more a week to community service), a new economic picture emerges. As human beings develop, attention economies will expand and mature, serving thoughtful, caring individuals, who pay attention to the health of the planet, the human family, and their own values and higher motivations.

The U.S. entertainment sector of the attention economy, regressive from a personal development viewpoint, represents $400 billion a year, or 8.5 percent of total consumption in GDP; employs 2.5 million Americans; and is a leading U.S. export. As the telecom bill that deregulated cable TV and phone companies further was signed in Washington, D.C., in 1996, many economists and experts downplayed widespread fears of monopoly. They pointed out that the technologies change rapidly and anyway, these markets are growing worldwide—so there would be plenty of competition.[13] This not very reassuring view was underscored by another story, "One More Place You Can't Escape Ads." It seems gas pumps in the United States now will have video displays of merchandise you can order with your gasoline credit card while you are filling up.[14]

In 1995, as media corporations merged, nine moguls emerged in OECD countries, whose companies now have captured the attention of the human family: Rupert Murdoch, Australia's owner of the U.S. Fox network; Europe's Sky TV; Star TV in Asia along with dozens of newspapers, magazines, and publishers; Gerald Levin, boss of U.S.-based Time-Warner, owners of *Time, Life, Fortune,* and scores of other media assets from print and cable TV to film; John Malone, head of TCI, the biggest cable operation in the United States; Sumner Redstone, boss of Viacom, a $7.4 billion conglomerate that owns Paramount, Blockbuster TV, and a chain of movie theaters; Ted Turner of Turner Broadcasting, CNN, and the Atlanta Braves baseball team; Michael Jordan, CEO of Westinghouse, who sealed a deal in 1995 to buy the CBS TV network for $5.4 billion; Michael Eisner, boss of Disney, a $19 billion enterprise after swallowing the ABC-Capital Cities TV network; Edgar Bronfman, CEO of Canada's Seagrams Distillers who bought MCA for $5.7 billion; and Michael Ovitz, the Hollywood dealmaker who brokered many of these megadeals, then accepted the presidency of Disney.[15] Lawrence K. Grossman, former president of NBC News and PBS, suggested that the public be cut in on the mega-mergers. He suggested a modest percentage of these deals could finance high-quality TV.[16]

As debates heated up over climate change, global warming, and the increase in hurricanes and floods, GNP-driven overconsumption of energy and materials by industrial mediocracies was further challenged. The Manila-based Asian Development Bank warned that a warmer planet would put much of Asia's agricultural production as well as its coastal cities at risk, while Syed Sibtey Razi, chair of India's parliamentary committee on the environment, pointed out that 25 percent of people in developed countries consume over 75 percent of many natural resources.[17]

The good news was that many of the voices for more frugal lifestyles at last found an international expression in The Factor Ten Club, composed of scientists and institutes of research from Britain, Germany, France, Holland, Canada, India, the United States, Switzerland, and Austria. Their Carnoules Declaration, made in Carnoules, France, in October 1994, calls for industrial countries to dematerialize their economies by increasing tenfold the efficiency with which materials and energy are used and to "reassess the centrality of material, energy, and land consumption in our cultures; reverse/reorient the incentive structures which presently discourage ecologically sensible behavior; and develop a new culture of learning: encourage research in sustainable technology and social change and adaptation."[18] As the calls for dematerializing industrial economies were brought before the European Parliament, the OECD, and the International Climate Convention in 1995, the shift toward attention-based economies and their further development became more visible.

PART II

SLOW-MOTION GOOD NEWS: ROAD MAPS AND RESOURCES FOR REBIRTH

Join the World of Public Entrepreneurs

There's nothing more powerful than a great idea in the hands of an entrepreneur.

Since 1978 Ibrahim has enabled over 1.7 million low-income children to

attend school—a remarkable feat in Bangladesh, where 70% of the population receives no formal education at all.

Ibrahim found that eliminating homework and enabling poor children to earn money drastically reduced drop-out rates among low-income students. He doubled class time so kids could do lessons in school, and he incorporated income-generating projects into the curriculum. The results of these simple ideas have been astounding.

If Ibrahim can get 1.7 million kids into school, what can you do? Learn how to get involved with Ashoka and our global association of over 500 public entrepreneurs like Ibrahim. Become a co-venturer. Call us, or fill out the response form below. This could be the most powerful idea you'll ever get your hands on.

> *TO: Ashoka: Innovators for the Public*
> *1700 North Moore Street, Suite 1920*
> *Arlington, VA 22209, USA*
> Phone: 703-527-8300, Fax: 703-527-8383, E-mail: Ashoka@tmn.com
>
> *I'd like to learn more about Ashoka's global network of public entrepreneurs. Please send me more information.*
>
> Name:
> _____
> Address:
> _____
> City, State, Zip:
> _____

Ashoka:
Innovators for the Public

Fig. 13. Ashoka: Innovators for the Public

© Ashoka   Source: Ashoka: Innovators for the Public

CHAPTER 6

GRASSROOTS
GLOBALISM

T oday, the most creative, energetic forces addressing the planetary problems of poverty, social inequity, pollution, resource depletion, violence, and war are grassroots citizen movements. This new form of "trickle up" globalism is very different from the approaches of national leaders at G-7 and APEC (Asia Pacific Economic Cooperation) summits, global business leaders at executive roundtables, or academics and pundits from think tanks and foundations at upscale vacation hideaways.

Grassroots globalism is about thinking and acting—globally and locally. Its problem solving is pragmatic: local solutions that keep the planet in mind. These approaches "bubble up,"[1] are often innovative, and stress positive action and role models. Some examples that address poverty, particularly among women, are micro-lending programs such as the grassroots bankers of Bangladesh's Grameen Bank, Women's World Banking, ACCION, or the Chipko movement, which saves traditional forest resources for sustainable livelihoods.

Grassroots globalism often holds nations accountable. Amnesty International awakened the world's conscience to human rights abuses, and now protects victims worldwide by publicizing imprisonment or abuse as well as nations' human rights records. Greenpeace has shown that effective media campaigns can prevent nuclear weapons tests and ocean-dumping of toxic wastes, and help save endangered species. Linking grassroots globalism to mass media is vital and can focus public concern on global and local issues that nations and corporations often prefer to ignore. U.S.-based Turner

Broadcasting and CNN, the British Broadcasting Corporation (BBC), and other mainstream media cover population issues, empowerment of women, and the environment. Yet vastly more coverage of grassroots local problem solving is needed. Nonprofit groups, including London-based TV for the Environment, Sri Lanka's Worldview, and Canada's WETV coproduce with citizen groups, and offer the needed culturally diverse antidote to the commercial media's global corporate monoculture of consumerism.

CITIZEN ORGANIZATIONS CHALLENGE THE STATUS QUO

Grassroots globalists and their organizations are often spurned by governments as amateurs, agitators, or troublemakers. Even the United Nations has warmed only slowly to citizen organizations. They are now emerging as a third, independent sector in world affairs—challenging the domination of global agendas by nation-states and transnational corporations. The global civil society, newly interlinked on the Internet and by millions of newsletters, is increasingly driving agendas of nations and corporations, which still refer to citizen groups as nongovernmental organizations (NGOs). Many grassroots globalist leaders retort that governments and corporations are NCOs (noncivil organizations). Global concerns have been on the agendas of grassroots civic groups, including churches and other organizations that have worked for food aid, peacemaking, education, culture, and youth exchange, since the turn of this century. With the founding of the United Nations in 1945, local groups affiliated as United Nations Associations (UNAs) to support the UN and its agenda.

Citizen movements and associations of all kinds—from service clubs, churches, and self-help and spiritual groups to chambers of commerce and professional associations of teachers, doctors, farmers, scientists, musicians, and artists—share a concern for human society that covers the range of human needs and crosses national borders. The rise of civil organizations is one of the most striking phenomena of the twentieth century, and is described by Elise Boulding (1988, 36) as "a major shift in the nature of the international system." Other futurists who study citizen organizations and social movements as precursors of social trends include Magda McHale, Johan Galtung, Eleanora Masini, Ziauddin Sardar, Robert Theobald, Nandini Joshi, Riane Eisler, Anthony J. N. Judge, Ashis Nandy, and David Loye. The late Barbara Ward and Robert Jungk shared my focus on the key role of citizens, as I expressed it in *Creating Alternative Futures* (1978, 1996). In addition to citizen groups, criminal and terrorist groups, urban gangs, mafia-type syndicates, drug cartels, and other violent religious and ethnic extremist groups have also proliferated. Their negative potential in the post–Cold War period is studied more by military, intelligence, and law enforcement strategists than by futurists. A notable exception is the insightful *War and Anti-War* (1993) by Alvin and Heidi Toffler. My own inquiry examines the positive potential of groups, movements, and associations, both for social innovation and for evolving human ethics and societies.

The UN recognizes these proliferating non-state actors only as nongovernmental organizations (NGOs) or international nongovernmental organizations (INGOs). Inexplicably, giant transnational corporations (TNCs) are also subsumed as NGOs or non-state actors in UN terminology. Clearly, TNCs and their national and international trade associations, such as the U.S. Council for International Business and the International Chamber of Commerce, should be excluded from the NGO category. Whenever the UN focuses its research on large corporations and their global impact—whether through its Center on Transnational Corporations founded in the 1970s; or UNCTAD (United Nations Commission on Trade and Development); or the Economic and Social Council (ECOSOC), which was supposed to be an equally powerful counterpart to the Security Council—these agencies are downgraded. The Center on Transnational Corporations was deep-sixed in the late 1980s due to pressure from the United States and other powerful member-states and their corporate and financial constituencies. Associations of small, locally owned businesses, however, which are represented by such charitable service groups as Rotary Clubs and Rotary International, do qualify as NGOs and INGOs.

In 1909 there were 176 NGOs (Boulding 1988, 35). In the 1985–86 *Yearbook of International Organizations*, published by the Union of International Organizations (UIO), 18,000 NGOs are listed, of which about 1 percent are federations of other NGOs, 8.5 percent are universal, 17 percent are intercontinental, and 74 percent are regional (i.e., European, Latin American, Asian). The *1994–95 Yearbook of International Organizations* lists a total of 36,486 international organizations in a proliferating number of categories beyond the conventional forms listed above. Anthony J. N. Judge, assistant secretary-general of the UIO, emphasizes the ambiguity of the concept of civil society, the need to review national legislation relevant to associations and collective civil action, and also notes that the European Union in 1994 outlined a plan to assist cooperatives, mutual societies, associations, and foundations.[2] CIVICUS, a global network launched in 1993, published *Citizens: Strengthening Global Civil Society* in 1994, which documents several thousand civic groups in Asia, Latin and Central America, Africa, and Europe and North America.[3]

Networks of NGOs often are freer to act and respond to humanitarian concerns than nation-states are. They can serve as precursors to new national and international government structures; for example, Amnesty International has prodded governments all over the world toward greater protection of human rights. The intellectual style of NGOs tends toward envisioning preferred futures and scenarios and organizing civic activities, as well as advocacy and "action research" (to use Kurt Lewin's term [1948]). Thus, they invoke the *possible* by mapping social potentials, rather than employing the "objective" stance of those futurists who identify trends or create scenarios driven by scientific and technological innovation. Citizen organizations and their preferred futures often are at variance with more technologically oriented forecasters because most technological innovation emerges from institutions that are culturally dominant—whether corporations or government-sponsored bodies. Citizen organizations focus on social innovations, impacts of new technologies, and "preferred futures," i.e., scenarios that are normative (implying changing values) and are often utopian. However, citizen organizations usually reframe solutions termed *utopian, idealistic,* or *naive* as more *practical* than incremental or marginal changes for human societies "in crisis."

In many cases, citizen organizations and movements can be destructive and retrogressive or led by demagogues. This type of organization often arises out of social pressures, such as the increasing migration experienced in the reunification of Germany; the painful economic transitions affecting Russia and Eastern Europe; the failures of macroeconomic management that have produced Europe's unemployment or exacerbated poverty, as in many Latin American countries; or the failure of governments as in Somalia, Cambodia, Rwanda, and the former Yugoslavia. Other movements have arisen in reaction to industrial modernization, whether they are Christian fundamentalist movements favoring isolationism or banning abortion in the United States, or other fundamentalist religious movements, particularly in the Islamic world. Many such movements also protest Western economic expansionism and its technocratic, secular domination of local cultural traditions. Indeed, there are worldwide movements of ethnic and indigenous peoples linking Brazil's Yanomami, Scandinavia's Sami or "Lapp" peoples, Native Americans in the U.S. and Canada, Basques and Catalans in Spain. Ethnic tribalism emerged in Eastern Europe and the former Soviet Union. These movements present the greatest future challenges to nation-states and to the globalization of corporations and industrialism, which many nations still espouse.

Most nations' sovereignty has been eroding from without due to forces of globalization. At the same time, nations are crumbling from within due to governments' inability to deliver on promises of progress and economic growth for their people. Increasingly, minority populations, environmentalists, and some social movements do not want their identities homogenized into the conformity of mass consumption and production required by industrialism. Western politicians and academics have reacted with alarm. Samuel Huntington, whose "Clash of Civilizations"[4] was based on an earlier study by Moroccan futurist Mahdi Elmanjdra (1992), and Paul Kennedy and Robert Kaplan, whose writings appeared in the *Atlantic Monthly* in 1994, see only anarchy and chaos in the proliferation of non-state actors and movements. Their views of this coming chaos are rarely framed within the context of the general crisis of global industrialism, whose forces continue to sweep away cultures and the borders between nations. As hot currencies slosh around the planet they continue to overwhelm the macroeconomic mechanisms: monetary and fiscal levers by which countries have managed themselves. In the ensuing devolutions of the mid-1990s everything was up for grabs—making it imperative to study social movements and citizen groups even more carefully.

The Cold War era (1945–1990) called forth much additional blossoming of NGOs focused on peace, human rights, nuclear test bans, nonproliferation, disarmament, development, globalizing of educational curricula, and student exchange programs as well as humanitarian relief—offering major new kinds of expertise to governments. By the 1960s, emerging planetary issues spawned massive citizen movements for protecting the earth's biosphere from degradation, pollution, desertification, species extinction, and resource depletion. These movements also addressed unchecked human population growth, the widening poverty gap between North and South, and the extension of human rights and fuller political and economic participation to the world's women.

The UN became a natural venue for these new national and transnational concerns. Newer organizations, such as the National Organization for Women, Friends of the Earth, Greenpeace, and Zero Population Growth in the United States, joined older NGOs, such as Planned Parenthood and the Swiss-based International Union for the Conservation of Nature, to push issues onto the agendas of national governments. Such pressure on member-states, from NGOs in both the North and South, resulted in a series of ad hoc UN conferences, notably those on Environment (1972), Population (1973), Food (1974), Women (1975), Habitat (1978), and New and Renewable Sources of Energy (1981). The more recent Earth Summit (1992) as well as conferences on Human Rights (1993) and Population and Development (1994) are discussed later. The most comprehensive source on global issues is the 1994 edition of the *Encyclopedia of World Problems and Human Potential*, a brainchild of Anthony J. N. Judge of the Union of International Organizations.

At each one of these UN conferences it became successively more recognized that the agendas had been shaped by new citizen organizations and broader social movements bringing pressure on member-states' governments. In early conferences, such as the one on the environment held in Stockholm, Sweden, in 1972, citizen organizations were grudgingly recognized with their own parallel Environmental Forum held a half-hour bus ride away from the press and the main conference in the city's center. While often ill-informed government delegates droned on at the main conference, the peoples' Environmental Forum hosted brilliant debates by many of the world's leading intellectuals from North and South, including representatives from indigenous peoples all over the world. The air was charged with excitement as NGOs hammered out their own declarations of principles and drafted treaties and protocols for protecting the Earth. This began a twenty-five-year effort to steer the course of economic development toward new values: ecological sustainability, poverty reduction, and recognition of the key role women play as the world's primary food producers, educators of children, and protectors of the environment.

Indeed, many of the policies and social innovations proposed by NGOs at the Stockholm Environmental Forum—environmental auditing of corporations, socially responsible investing, and "green" taxes to help promote research and development in renewable-resource and energy-efficiency technologies—are now government policy in scores of countries. Government and corporate elites, insulated within top-down hierarchies, often remain ignorant of such viable policy alternatives. They and their institutions are creatures of the existing order, conventional thinking, and past investments in earlier technologies. At all levels, from local to global, citizen organizations arise around the *social and environmental costs* of existing policies and industrial technologies. Status quo institutions hire most of the scientists and engineers (and futurists!), as well as subsidize universities and academic research. This leaves "early warning" feedback to a minority of dissident academics and independent researchers in underfunded, interdisciplinary programs addressing broad concerns over the direction of science, technology, the environment, and society.

Thus, citizen organizations form around social, technological, and environmental impacts overlooked by the dominant culture—for example, air and water pollution; toxic chemicals; nuclear wastes; distorted energy-intensive development policies (such as those promoted by World Bank economists); coercive family-planning programs and male-dominated foreign assistance, which reinforce social, economic, and gender inequalities. Although citizen groups often organize around problem identification, they quickly move to more positive and prescriptive agendas—often forced to innovate because existing institutions cannot respond to their proposals. For example, the U.S.-based Council on Economic Priorities pioneered social evaluations of corporate performance because Wall Street security-analysis firms did not understand this need.[5] As such social innovations become recognized as valuable, imitators spring up in academia with new proposals for "research" grants. Private-sector entrepreneurs appear with business plans to market or privatize such social innovations. More often than not, the early citizen innovators, who never thought to trademark or copyright their intellectual property and work, are bypassed or unceremoniously shuffled out of these budding markets and enterprises.

COLD WAR LABELS DAMPENED CREATIVITY

During the Cold War era, opportunities for NGOs to link up with citizens in the former USSR and Soviet bloc nations were severely limited by lack of communication channels. In addition, the co-opting of popular expression and the distorting of citizen movement agendas by government control or intervention, or by preemptive funding (such as that of the official Peace Committee in the former USSR) inhibited contacts, due to suspicions of interference. Thus, a main avenue of debate, cross-pollination of ideas, and social innovation for both capitalist and socialist models of industrialism and economic "progress" was foreclosed by this rigid Cold War ideological climate in both superpowers and their global spheres of influence. For example, in Latin America, the well-motivated liberation theology of thousands of Catholic priests and nuns and their charitable organizations became caught in the Cold War crossfire and was often unfairly labeled Marxist for espousing goals of social justice, land reform, and other poverty-alleviation efforts.

In the United States during this same period, the creativity of citizen organizations addressing the worsening social and environmental effects of traditional, free-market industrialism was often stifled by Cold War labels such as leftist, liberal, socialist, or Marxist. In other cases, citizen groups were neutralized by grant-making foundations, which exercise a deeply conservative influence because to accept a grant imposes limits on lobbying and activist approaches and reduces a group's mandate to "education." In the mid-1990s, some foundations were worried about the devolving political structures and began to fund, as an "insurance policy," civic activism: for example, the formation of the CIVICUS network was funded through grants from many major foundations. Whether foundation funding will similarly curtail activism remains to be seen.

Another Cold War perversion in the United States has been the formation of corporate and industry "front groups," which adopt names implying they are citizen based and fighting for individual freedom and property rights, when their actual function is lobbying against legislation to mandate corporate compliance with environmental or social goals. For example, under the banner of supposed citizen coalitions, the U.S. auto industry fought the corporate automobile fuel efficiency (CAFE) standards for higher mileage cars in the 1991 Clean Air Act. They use expensive lobbying, public relations, advertising, and direct mail tactics, which overwhelm genuine citizen groups' budgets. Thus, it is necessary to investigate all citizen organizations, NGOs, and INGOs to determine their sources of funding and political or corporate backers.[6]

The Cold War era, which froze the UN into impotence through the superpowers' constant use of their veto in the Security Council, also froze the vital debate about industrialism and alternative approaches to human and social development. Consequently, today we see the people of the states of the former Soviet Union and Eastern Europe struggling to recover from the failures of Stalinist-style, centrally planned socialism by adopting helter-skelter nineteenth-century capitalism. Knowledge of Western capitalistic countries was sparse and gleaned from government propaganda rather than via exchanges of information, visits, and experiences with citizen groups as well as other civilian and academic channels.

Thus, too many policymakers and citizens in these former Soviet bloc countries have unrealistic views, gleaned from outdated textbooks, about how "free" markets and "perfect" competition are supposed to work. Many academics I have met in these countries initially believed that capitalistic economies, like that of the United States, functioned almost without regulation. They were surprised to learn that there are thousands of regulations—city, state, and federal—that circumscribe all economic activities in the United States; that all the world's economies are, in fact, mixtures of markets and regulations; and that different cultural norms, ethical standards, and citizen lobbies additionally constrain free markets according to differing cultural DNA codes. (See Chapter 8.) Thus, game theorists who study rules of interaction in human societies are becoming more important and even economists are now acknowledging that rules and regulations are as fundamental as markets.

We may expect an enormous burst of creativity and social problem solving as old Cold War labels and ideological constraints become increasingly irrelevant. NGOs and their proposals are now likely to be judged on their merits rather than according to Cold War priorities. Today, citizen organizations are interpreted within the context of emerging global debates about redefining what is meant by development, and about perfecting democracy itself along the spectrum from elitism to populism. Today's concerns are about how to make both governments and global corporations more accountable to citizens, consumers, workers, investors, and the unrepresented, i.e., children, indigenous peoples, future generations, and other species, as well as the environment. In addition, if more states break up as sovereignty continues to erode, the activities and goals of emerging NGOs, INGOs, ethnic minorities, and indigenous peoples will assume a much greater significance as trendsetters for the future.[7] For example, the draft Declaration and Program of Action for the UN World Summit on Social Development held in Copenhagen in 1995 contained no fewer than fifteen references to participation, consultation, and partnerships between governments and the civil society.

Citizens are taking on new peacemaking roles, such as the California-based Foundation for Global Community's conflict-resolution efforts in Armenia and Azerbaijan in the Nagorno-Karabakh war. After missions in 1994, the group joined with others, including Physicians for Social Responsibility, Search for Common Ground, the Institute for Multi-Track Diplomacy, and Partners for Democratic Change, to explore new options with Azerbaijanis. Their assumptions are that "only people—human beings not governments—can cause people to move into a relationship of reconciliation."[8] I would say that it is not either/or but *both* people *and* governments.

Politicians in Japan's major parties are responding to grassroots pressures, both domestic and international, to ban nuclear tests and weapons. Former Prime Minister Toshiki Kaifu, leader of the opposition New Frontier Party, called for a consumer boycott of French products after the French nuclear test in 1995 at Mururoa in the Pacific. Then-Prime Minister Tomiichi Murayama of the Social Democrats announced that Japan would propose a UN resolution to end all nuclear testing.[9] All such issues and groups are covered in the *Peace Newsletter* published by International Non-Violent Peace Teams and edited by Elise Boulding.[10]

Social innovations pioneered by citizen movements are still widely resisted by the dominant culture and media as impractical; they are portrayed as frivolous or trivialized. Meanwhile, innovations in technology, production, and marketing in the private sector are slavishly reported and usually hailed as progress. This contrast is stark but understandable, since private-sector innovations arise in businesses for competitive and profit motives highly approved in all Western and industrializing cultures. Such business-sector innovation is routinely hyped in advertising and marketing and also supported by government subsidies (including contracting of weapons research and procurement for high-tech corporations) and by grants to universities, research labs, and think tanks.

Western and other industrial societies provide few resources, however, to researchers or organizations to identify the *social and environmental costs* of such private-sector technological innovations. Huge investments in inappropriate technologies, which have added imperceptibly to productivity and simply "paved old cow paths" (i.e., set old organization charts in concrete), must now be written off and replaced with more costly "second-generation" computerization. Corporate consultants gleefully assess the new expenditures required, while their corporate clients try to figure out how to create new markets to justify these investments. The social and environmental costs of inappropriate industrialization and automation, from jobless economic growth and widening poverty gaps to unsustainable resource consumption, were the focus of the NGO Forum of the UN World Summit on Social Development in Copenhagen in 1995.[11]

Research into the costs and adverse impacts of market- and industrial-policy-driven innovation still lags—often by decades. Realization of this lag led the U.S. Congress to launch the Office of Technology Assessment (OTA) in 1974 after several years of academic and political debate and grassroots lobbying efforts. As a member of the OTA Advisory Council from 1974 to 1980, I can attest to the broad opposition it encountered. The argument most often used against it was that OTA was unnecessary since markets could quite well determine the course of technological innovation for the benefit of consumers without costly government regulation or interference. This argument derives from outdated economic textbook models of perfect competition, which ignore structural aspects of mature economies.[12] OTA survived by developing links to the most highly respected academic institutions, by contracting out a portion of its research, and by appointing impeccable advisory panels representing the full spectrum of expert knowledge to steer each study. Due to its bipartisan congressional governing board and a track record of high-quality, unbiased, and innovative research, OTA overcame early opposition and spawned similar institutions in many countries. OTA came under attack from Republicans, as did multilateral aid and the UN itself, and in 1995 the Republican Congress succeeded in abolishing OTA as too liberal. The UN became a scapegoat of increasingly polarized U.S.

politics, and UN special conferences—perhaps the most successful of its programs for publicizing global issues—were excoriated as "wasteful."

The functions of OTA were anticipated and performed for over a decade by citizen groups, including many concerned professionals, which organized to research the impacts of technology on society and alternative, more benign ways of meeting human needs. Ralph Nader's Washington, D.C.-based Public Citizen and its campus spin-offs, the Public Interest Research Groups, are examples of such proto-type technology assessment research, as are the U.S.-based Scientists' Institute for Public Information, the Union of Concerned Scientists, and Physicians for Social Responsibility (now worldwide). Although such groups are woefully underfunded, they and many others have prodded governments and their in-house, scientific bureaucracies to develop their own technology assessment capabilities. These organizations also urged government agencies to utilize highly creative, alternative problem-definition methods and analyses, such as the U.S.-based Rocky Mountain Institute (which pioneered demand-side management of electric utilities and energy-efficient technologies now being adopted worldwide).[13]

Citizen organizations are a priceless social resource offering new paradigms to societies stuck in old ways or trapped, as Western industrial societies are, in wasteful consumption and production habits and technologies that are proving unsustainable. The reason independent citizen organizations provide so many innovative programs and concepts, and furnish whole new paradigms for problem definition is that they are able to tap and organize information laterally. They can network across borders as well as across corporate and government boundaries, enabling rapid syntheses of overlooked and new information into fresh approaches and paradigms.[14] They can question conventional wisdom, assess the quality of information, and point out cases where "the emperor has no clothes." The coalescing of INGOs with indigenous peoples, which began in the 1960s, has brought forth new agendas based on ancient wisdom and spiritual traditions about how to live sustainably on Earth, which industrial societies have largely forgotten.[15]

Another function NGOs and INGOs perform is to serve as nodes and magnets, attracting previously censored information as well as information from "whistle-blowers" in business and government. For

this reason, all competent citizen organizations establish good relationships with mass media and investigative journalists, who rely on
them for such bootlegged research (even if the citizen group is not
credited publicly or its general programs are labeled "too far out").
Citizen organizations such as the Kenya-based Greenbelt Movement
and India's Chipko Movement, as well as countless other environmental groups that were busy planting trees long before scientists
studying climate change began advocating the need for reforestation
and support for these programs, were ridiculed by the mass media as
"tree huggers." This uneasy, symbiotic relationship between citizen
organizations and media can lead to many policy and ethical dilemmas. Some citizen organizations "run ahead" of their research or sen-
sationalize their data to attract media attention in their search for
badly needed funds. Since Earth Day 1990, when businesses began
adopting "green" marketing policies, some citizen organizations in
the environmental movement have made alliances with companies,
even endorsing their products, in apparent quid pro quos for funding,
often thereby losing credibility.[16]

Citizen organizations, to stay true to their highest function as
social innovators, must resist constant temptations to join the dominant culture. If they do decide to join the mainstream, they should
give up their favorable tax exemptions and compete as market-driven
enterprises. Nonprofit, tax-exempt citizen organizations often create
new markets over a period of years by offering attractive new values
and lifestyles, such as the now multibillion dollar markets for green
products and technologies. As these fledgling markets become viable
through news stories and mass-media-driven public acceptance, such
NGO innovators can often gradually shift their funding base from
donations and grants to packaging their leading innovations (often
books and research reports), and move to greater reliance on earned
income. Indeed, some can become fully self-supporting.

Other groups choose to move their focus to more cutting-edge
concerns, breaking new ground, remaining innovative, and wearing
their unpopularity as a badge of honor. In my own activism with New
York's Citizens for Clean Air, which I helped organize in 1964, and
the Campaign to Make General Motors Responsible, in which I
joined with Ralph Nader in 1968, I preferred to stay on the cutting
edge. I have served on the board of the Council on Economic
Priorities since 1970 and was a founder of Environmentalists for Full

Employment in 1975. I wrote its first manifesto, which drew the support of hundreds of environmental groups, with the help of colleagues Peter Harnik of Environmental Action (now with Rails to Trails, which advocates bikeways), Byron Kennard, author of *Nothing Can Be Done: Everything Is Possible* (1982), and Richard Grossman. I helped found the Public Interest Economics Center in 1972 and recruited many volunteer economists to help citizens quantify the "dis-economies, dis-services, and dis-amenities" of many unsustainable megaprojects. I ran my own "campaign" among my activist-group allies in order to serve as the only citizen-group advocate on OTA's Advisory Council. It was after these experiences that I suspected economics was irredeemable as a policy tool for citizens groups. I saw economics lead its practitioners and citizens alike into a form of brain-damaging indoctrination. Horrified, I pulled back from activism and researched and wrote *The Politics of the Solar Age* (1981, 1988).

CITIZEN ORGANIZATIONS ARE EMERGING AS LEADERS

Nowhere have citizen organizations played a larger role than in the world's "informal economies," which are statistical anomalies spawned by the narrow paradigms of macroeconomics and its highly aggregated statistical tools: GNP and GDP; averaged rates of saving, investment, and unemployment; interest rates; trade balances; and so on. I described in *The Politics of the Solar Age* the extent of such informal economies which, even in industrial societies, represent approximately half of all production that is unpaid and, therefore, not accounted for in macroeconomic statistics. In most countries of the Southern Hemisphere, such informal sectors are much larger than the official, cash-based GNP/GDP-measured sectors—often comprising three-quarters of all production. The voluntary associations of citizens, villages, tribes, cooperatives, and families within informal sectors represent traditional, self-reliant forms of production, consumption, savings, and investment only recently recognized by Western, market-trained economists or their socialist counterparts. My analysis was vilified by economists as wrong-headed and absurd. I learned to interpret this as evidence that I was hitting home and reminded myself that in some repressive countries civic activists are jailed or murdered—as happened, for example, to Chico Mendez, the brave rubber-tapper turned activist in Brazil, and many others.

Some prototypical citizen organizations operating within informal economies are the Sarvodya Shramadana movement of Sri Lanka, which pioneered a viable form of development based on Buddhist principles in over eight thousand villages;[17] the Green Forum coalition in the Philippines, which has produced its own plan for the future of the Philippine economy;[18] and the Self-Employed Women's Association (SEWA) of India, which funds small enterprises. When such movements succeed, they are often persecuted by governments. Micro-lending programs—such as SEWA; Women's World Banking (in some fifty countries); the Grameen Bank of Bangladesh; ACCION, which lends to micro-enterprises in Latin and Central America; as well as the U.S.-based First Nations Development Institute, which lends to Native American community development groups—provide a new paradigm of sustainable development. The new development form is a "trickle-up" model—the mirror opposite of the elitist, technocratic "trickle-down" model promoted by traditional economic development theorists—better described beyond economic metaphors as the "bubble-up" model.

An unprecedented outpouring of interest in the paradigm-shifting global debates on development and democracy and in the pioneering organizations of the world's independent sectors occurred at the UN Conference on Environment and Development, the Earth Summit held in Rio de Janeiro, Brazil, in June 1992.[19] This conference boosted the growth of citizen organizations by providing a global forum for some thirteen thousand such groups and reinforced their networking activities, which were encouraged by Secretary-General Maurice Strong and his Danish-born wife, Hanne Strong, herself an organizer of the citizen organization Earth Restoration Corps. Many of the citizen organizations attending the Global Forum in Rio were already linked on computer-conferencing systems, such as Peace-Net, Togethernet, and Eco-Net.

A similar outpouring of civil society participation was evident at the UN Conference on Population and Development in Cairo, Egypt, in 1994. As at the Earth Summit and the 1995 Summits on Social Development in Copenhagen and on Women and Development in Beijing, the creative mixture of media and civil society groups focused worldwide attention on the issues and pushed the official delegates and the Action Plans beyond boundaries previously set by patriarchal leaders. Formerly "radical" notions entered the mainstream, including the ideas that the most effective contraceptive is the economic and political empowerment of women and that the best investment a society can make for development is investment in its people, particularly the education of girls.

Citizen organizations have emerged worldwide as major actors and leaders in areas such as the search for global ethics and healthy, survival-enhancing cultural DNA codes. They have staged citizen summits on vital issues wherever leaders have dragged their heels. One example is "The Other Economic Summit" (TOES), in which I have been involved, and which has dogged the G-7 nations' annual summit meetings with alternative approaches since 1984. TOES has released communiqués on subjects like the need for "trickle-up" forms of sustainable development, highlighting that the world's women produce over half of the world's food and manage 70 percent of its small businesses, but receive only 10 percent of the world's wages and own only 1 percent of the world's property.

Citizen diplomacy activities helped end the Cold War and are at last welcomed at the UN—rather than merely tolerated. In 1994, the secretary-general of the UN, Boutros-Ghali, called for nongovernmental organizations to mobilize *states*, as well as public opinion, to promote peace, adding, "The United Nations was considered to be a forum for sovereign states alone. Within the space of a few short years, this attitude had changed. Nongovernmental organizations are now considered full participants in international life . . . largely due to the quick succession of historical events. . . . Today, we are well aware that the international community must address a human community that is profoundly transnational. The movement of wealth, people, capital, and ideas is as important today as control of territory was yesterday."[20]

Electronically linked citizen groups are becoming a truly global independent sector, a third way for global problem solving, and in Boulding's phrase (1988), "a global civic culture." Dr. Howard H. Frederick of the International Association for Mass Communications Research described the burgeoning of communications-based citizen organizations, NGOs, and INGOs in *Edges*, a Toronto-based publication of the Institute for Cultural Affairs, itself a global INGO. Frederick points out the global reality that at present communication technologies are dominated by global corporations, financial markets, and global banking electronic funds transfer systems (EFTS), as well as giant information wire services, such as Reuters and the Associated Press. We still live in the world of the info-rich and the info-poor. For example, 95 percent of all computers are in the industrial countries of the North; and 75 percent of the world's people, living in the South, only manage 30 percent of the world's newspapers. The United States and the Commonwealth of Independent States (CIS), with only 15 percent of the world's population, use more than 50 percent of the world's geostationary orbits with their communications satellites, while the South uses less than 10 percent of these orbits.[21]

Two key issues signal the maturing of grassroots globalism and the growing international clout of its civil organizations. First is the new issue of legitimacy—raised by corporate executives, government officials, politicians, and competing political parties. "Whom and how many people does this group represent and are its policies steered democratically?" Civil organizations address these valid questions by opening their decision-making membership, fund-raising practices, and policy processes to public scrutiny. U.S.-based activist Ralph Nader once observed that the public, press, and scientific scrutiny given to citizen-based research reports is far more rigorous than academic peer-review. Some groups and leaders enjoy such popular support that they are suppressed as a threat to existing power structures.

A second sign of maturity is the proliferation of approaches, tactics, and goals. The biggest chasm regards funding. Groups from the well-heeled industrial countries vastly outnumber groups from the South's developing countries. This often skews global agenda-setting toward longer-term concerns coming from the North: environment, population, endangered species, biodiversity, climate change, and ozone depletion. Groups in the South worry about the environment as loss of their traditional common lands and forest resources and the livelihoods they provide; they are also concerned with injustice, poverty, hunger, lack of public health facilities, clean water, schools, and other more dire, immediate threats to their survival.

Today, grassroots globalism grows stronger as nations lose sovereignty in the turbulent seas of trillion-dollar daily global capital flows. Countries less able to manage their domestic economies to maintain employment and social safety nets must foster grassroots self-help. Even global corporations now know they cannot make executive decisions on factory closures and siting, for example, exclusively to benefit their stock- and bondholders. They now consult wider groups of stakeholders: employees, suppliers, customers, environmental groups, and now grassroots globalists as well. Politicians have also responded: for example, the British Member of Parliament Tony Blair and U.S. Congressman Richard Gephardt both offered bills to encourage companies to adopt the stakeholder model. Grassroots globalists participate at global conferences in ever-greater numbers. Gradually they have become accepted—even welcomed for their innovative projects.

Today, formerly scorned citizen groups are asked to mobilize nations themselves, promote peace, and help support United Nations activities in many new ways. Citizen organizations are not only urged to become more involved with peacekeeping, peacemaking, and sustainable development, but also with watchdogging reduction of arms sales, disarmament, and conversion to civilian economies. The new watchword to global business and government leaders in the perilous decade of the 1990s is "Lead, Follow, or Get Out of the Way." The militancy of citizen organizations is related to the evolutionary urgency they sense. Perhaps this explains why fewer citizens spend time bowling together. Many groups believe, along with INGO research groups such as Worldwatch Institute, that humans now have only a few decades to avert social and ecological disaster. In the long run and in a planetary context, all our individual self-interests are *identical*. Human responsibility and global ethics have simply become pragmatic.

CHAPTER 7

RETHINKING HUMAN DEVELOPMENT AND THE TIME OF OUR LIVES

As psychiatrists know, moving from adolescence to adulthood usually means rebellion—particularly against mom and dad. Could it be that the attacks on government, particularly in the United States, whether government is seen as the "nanny" or as the "paternal" state, are a sign that we are growing up? This idea may provide a key to our current confused politics. Yet if so, we are in for a bumpy ride. All the hot issues around government—devolution of federal regulation back to the states, unfunded mandates, welfare, taxes, budget balancing, fairness, affirmative action—stoke deep wells of passion. Men of all ages who grew up in father-deprived circumstances experienced mom as the authority figure—and now rail against government as nanny. Women of all ages who grew up in traditional "father-as-boss" families transfer their anger to patriarchal governments.

These feelings may create some of the wave of bipartisan fervor for cutting off at the knees the admittedly inept, often corrupted power of central governments. Yes, politicians and bureaucrats in Washington, D.C., and elsewhere are out of control—too far from the people and too close to the lobbyists and their special-interest PAC (political action committee) money. Yes, those bureaucracies need to be more efficient and accountable to people. Yes, the state and local levels closer to people should take more responsibility. Yes, we need more citizen and voter participation and more responsive, perhaps electronically assisted, democracy. Yes, we need to have our mass media accept responsibility as the "nervous system" of our anxious, upset body politic.

Indeed, the new, little-examined form of governance, mediocracy, now rules our lives. (See Chapter 5.) As mentioned, many countries in the world have emerged from feudalism and have gone straight into mediocracy without passing through the intervening stages of democracy or industrialism. Politicians compete with special-interest-group "spin doctors" for TV sound bytes. Candidates bypass party structures and primaries and go on *Larry King Live* to throw their hats into the ring. Endless trials, like O. J. Simpson's, preempt more important news—even in other countries. A lone newspaper in Costa Rica carried a daily box during 1995, "This Is the 365th Day We Have Not Covered O. J. Simpson." Hollywood film and video violence degrades our family lives. Kids in foreign-media-saturated Belize imitate on their own streets the gang warfare between Los Angeles' "Krips" and "Bloods" they have seen on TV programs from Hollywood. Eastern Europe's "velvet revolutions" involved capturing TV stations—rather than parliament or government buildings. Even mad bombers attract media attention to their "causes."

IS HUMANITY GROWING UP?

Welcome to the post-industrial Information Age (the Tofflers' "Third Wave"), the "Age of Mediocracy," and the emergence of the "Attention Economy." Beyond the mass production, goods-based economies of the "second wave" industrial era, by the mid-1990s politicians, corporations, advertisers, educators, and interest groups competed in mass media for the attention of increasingly jaded, skeptical, bored, or increasingly more aware and selective individuals. Are we growing up? Are voter rebellions in the United States, Europe, Japan, and other mediocracies a sign of adolescent psyches reaching for maturity? If so, we can decode the anger and unpack today's simplistic slogans. Let's take a socially therapeutic view: the United States and other emerging mediocracies are having some kind of nervous breakdown, midlife crisis, a crisis of values and cultural norms. Or are people simply growing up?

The good news is all the talk about values and responsibility. Yes, let's encourage corporate responsibility, now a big and growing investment market as described in Chapter 10. Yes, let's have responsible mass media and entertainment, responsible parenthood, more individual responsibility for wellness and personal development as well as good citizenship. And yes, let's make all levels of government responsible and fully accountable to citizens. In the 1990s citizen groups worldwide began demanding codes of conduct and drafting their own sets of principles (such as the CERES [Coalition for Environmentally Responsible Economies] Principles) of environmental responsibility, earth ethics, and earth charters—lobbying them onto startled business executives' and politicians' agendas.[1]

The bad news is that deeper issues, including the submerged, old "mom and dad" anger, remain covert. Budget balancing has become an empty bookkeeping exercise masking all the deeper issues of personal pain, values, and priorities. Men still angry with female parental authority rail against the nanny state and at tax or regulatory intrusion on their freedom of action. Their priorities are technological progress, exuberant entrepreneurship, a strong military, freedom to bear arms, and, often in the United States, free-market capitalism and more of the deregulated, untrammeled economic growth that has provided them opportunities to prosper.

Women's priorities often tend toward reforming "father"— extended to the paternal state. They seek repeal of deeply coded laws, changes in government and economic institutions that favor white men and control women's parental and other rights to choose their own lives. Women, as well as many men, favor education; Headstart; daycare; health care and Healthy Start; social security; public services and infrastructure; cultural, artistic, and recreational opportunities; consumer and environmental protection. They invest and often work in small, socially responsible companies, agencies, and media that serve all these economic sectors. Many women want to cut corporate, not personal, welfare and cut subsidies to military and other environmentally damaging, life-threatening activities.

Between these male-female emphases and priorities there is much common ground. Both sexes support personal and parental responsibility, making government and politicians more accountable, revamping the tax code toward fairness. Furthermore, both men and women want a full public debate about reinventing government and what levels are more appropriate for which public functions—from local to global. All of us seek better futures and definitions of progress, development, wealth, and satisfaction as we head into the twenty-first century. Let's get on with the politics of growing up—together—by exploring, as my colleagues Barbara Marx Hubbard, author of *The Evolutionary Journey* (1982), Jean Houston in *The Possible Human* (1982), and legions of humanistic psychologists, counselors, and therapists are now doing in the world's mediocracies.

If we are to redirect our paths to people-centered development and a newly defined global and human security, we must create a climate that fosters human creativity and social innovation. This, in turn, means fostering the global civil society and strengthening and connecting citizen organizations globally. We are talking of nothing less than reinventing ourselves, reframing our perceptions, reshaping our beliefs and behavior, composting our knowledge, restructuring our institutions, and recycling our societies. This is not an impossibly tall order. Rather, it is routine in the repertoire of human behavior. Indeed, such systemic social change is the stuff of all human history.

Humans, after all, are the most malleable of all species. This adaptability has allowed our species spectacular success in colonizing this planet. Humans invented cultural forms of evolution—bypassing the millennial time scales required for biological evolution. We can no longer remain in our current state of psychological denial of our impressive track record of changing ourselves, our societies, our cultures, and our belief systems. Today we must reaffirm our species' spectacular history of continual adaptation to changing climatic and ecosystem conditions. Indeed, we are the only global species, other than bacteria, able to create massive global ecological change visible from space.[2]

William Drayton's life work is the affirmation of exemplary human action worldwide. He runs Ashoka, a nonprofit organization that seeks out inspiring people doing extraordinary good works in their countries. Ashoka then documents these stories, profiles them in articles for the world's media, and keeps activists' spirits up by networking them together and raising funds for their causes. (See Fig. 13. Ashoka: Innovators for the Public on page 130.) Thus naysayers, cynics, pessimists, and the fainthearted can be confronted and defrocked. Yes, the agenda for change before this generation of the human family is immense—but it is clearly within our reach.

As Robert Muller, former assistant secretary-general of the UN, says, "We humans are still a young species."[3] We need to see that our new agenda can be simultaneously addressed at all levels—from the individual, to the local community, to global civil organizations. Some tasks can be best addressed by corporations in the private sector and others are best suited to city, provincial, and national governments. The largest new agenda is, of course, before the international community: the global civil society, the United Nations, and today's de facto global financial regime. Most of our long-held beliefs about money, wealth, productivity, and efficiency, and our notions of progress are rooted in immature, often infantile states of mind—easily manipulated by politicians and advertisers. (See Fig. 14. Expanding Calculus of "Self-Interest.")

Luckily, individuals learn faster than institutions and many people may already be ahead of their leaders. In the United States, surveys of the American people by the Americans Talk Issues Foundation (ATIF) show large majorities in favor of international regulation of many sectors of today's global economy, from currency speculation to global manufacturing and arms trading to new scorecards of national progress.[4] A 1994 ATIF survey of U.S. public opinion on global governance and the future of the United Nations, conducted in cooperation with the Earth Council, the Society for International Development, and the Global Education Associates, found that 73 percent of Americans thought the UN, not the United States, should take the lead when faced with future problems of aggression; 93 percent of Americans wanted the UN to be more effective in global environmental matters; and 84 percent favored UN involvement in more sustainable forms of development. Questions on UN finances found that 68 percent favored interest charges on member-states' delinquent dues; 82 percent favored the UN imposing taxes on pollution and ocean-dumping of toxic wastes; 79 percent favored carbon emission taxes; and 77 percent favored a new Development Security Council to parallel the Security Council.[5]

As the scorecards of industrial growth—GNP/GDP-based national accounts—are overhauled in line with the new *System of National Accounts, 1993* (discussed in Chapter 10), criteria for projects, lending, development strategies, and priorities will shift toward sustainable development.[6] Progress on the new scorecards, which more fully incorporate environmental costs and benefits as well as unpaid work, was watchdogged vigorously by citizen organizations. Indeed, these statistical overhauls are largely due to the vigilant efforts

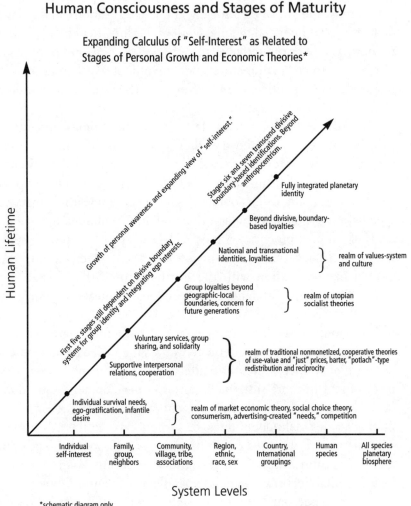

Human Consciousness and Stages of Maturity

Expanding Calculus of "Self-Interest" as Related to
Stages of Personal Growth and Economic Theories*

Human Lifetime

Growth of personal awareness and expanding view of " self-interest."

Stages six and seven transcend divisive boundary-based identifications. Beyond anthropocentrism.

First five stages still dependent on divisive boundary systems for group identity and integrating ego interests.

Fully integrated planetary identity

Beyond divisive, boundary-based loyalties

National and transnational identities, loyalties } realm of values-system and culture

Group loyalties beyond geographic-local boundaries, concern for future generations } realm of utopian socialist theories

Voluntary services, group sharing, and solidarity

Supportive interpersonal relations, cooperation } realm of traditional nonmonetized, cooperative theories of use-value and "just" prices, barter, "potlach"-type redistribution and reciprocity

Individual survival needs, ego-gratification, infantile desire } realm of market economic theory, social choice theory, consumerism, advertising-created "needs," competition

| Individual self-interest | Family, group, neighbors | Community, village, tribe, associations | Region, ethnic, race, sex | Country, International groupings | Human species | All species planetary biosphere |

System Levels

*schematic diagram only

Fig. 14. Expanding Calculus of "Self-Interest"

© 1980 Hazel Henderson   Source: *The Politics of the Solar Age*

of citizen organizations and NGOs. In another example of successful citizen effort, Amnesty International's patient, grassroots mobilizing of conscientized individuals underpinned consumer activism for human rights. Aung San Suu Kyi, the Nobel Peace Prize–winning leader of the democracy movement in Myanmar, was released from house arrest by the military junta due to a boycott by consumers and investors in companies doing business there.[7] Citizens even organized to monitor the deadly legacy of nuclear wastes in the Nuclear Guardianship Project directed by author Joanna Macy in Berkeley, California.

The Independent Commission on Population and Quality of Life and its president, Dr. Maria de Lourdes Pintasilgo, rightly emphasize population issues in their relationship to quality of life. As human populations stabilize and women have fewer children, their creativity is available for the evolutionary process. Population debates in the 1990s center around broad issues, including North-South equity and ecologically sustainable technologies, and must include the world's women in all aspects, from human rights to full participation in emerging democracies and development policies. Progress has been made since population control policy "hawks" of the 1960s tended to focus on gross population increases, particularly in developing countries of the South. The hawks' views were widely perceived as having racist and sexist overtones: the poor, women, and even the babies themselves were often portrayed as the problem. Anxieties about food, resources, scarcity, and allocation dominated. The roles of religion and patriarchal cultural traditions in pro-natalist policies in the South were downplayed—as were issues of overconsumption in the North.

North and South found new common ground at the United Nations Conference on Population and Development in Cairo, Egypt, in September 1994. Developing countries now have much support from the North in articulating their own theories: the population problem in the South is also a problem of overconsumption and wasted resources in the industrial North. To illustrate the issue, Andrew Mele's *Polluting for Pleasure* (1993) notes that in the United States "The total agglomeration of oil and hydrocarbon pollution caused by pleasure boating is 420 million gallons per year—the equivalent of as many as 40 Exxon Valdez disasters every year." Another study by F. H. Borman, D. Balmore, and G. T. Geballe, *Redesigning the American Lawn* (1993), notes that "American lawns cover some

20 million acres, claim from 30–60 percent of urban water use, while causing pesticide pollution and adding significantly to solid waste." Many in both North and South now argue that gross population figures must be corrected by adding figures reflecting per-capita resource consumption. By these calculations, the U.S. population must be figured in the tens of billions and viewed as the biggest contributor to the global population problem.

As the worldwide women's movements took off after the United Nations' Mexico City Women's Conference in 1975, research into the population issue deepened to examine more closely the demographic transitions to replacement levels of fertility that were assumed to automatically accompany industrialization and GNP growth. Women pointed out that not only did this type of development squander the earth's resources, but also the drop in fertility that occurred was more a function of the economic, social, and political liberation of women than of industrialization per se. Mature industrial societies in Western Europe began to fall toward zero population growth and even shrink in the late 1980s as women claimed their human rights and opted to have fewer children. At the same time, the cost of raising a child has skyrocketed and divorce has created legions of struggling single parents — largely women. In the United States alone, 50 percent of all children live in single-parent homes and two-thirds of all recipients of welfare are 9.5 million children.[8] By the late 1980s, policies were slowly refocusing toward women's concerns: education, pre- and postnatal health care, well-baby care, prevention of low birth-weight, breast-feeding as the most effective natural contraception method, and prevention of early childhood diseases and unnecessary infant mortality. Even *Business Week* highlighted the indispensable role women play in social and economic development, and the World Bank is coming around to this view — at least rhetorically.

Today, the main stumbling blocks to population stabilization and human development in many countries are still paternalistic policies that focus most resources on unsustainable GNP-measured industrial growth, international competition, and excessive defense budgets. As I pointed out in *The Politics of the Solar Age* (1981, 1988), patriarchal societies are organized as "protection rackets": from nation-states that provide protection from international military and economic competition down to the family, which is still too often another form of macho protection racket — where the woman is offered protection from other men sometimes at a cost of domestic domination or even violence. At last, an important paper, "What about Male Responsibilities?"[9] by the Worldwatch Institute, has addressed the lack of responsibility taken by the world's males in birth control and family planning. It underlines the extent to which women all over the world are still intimidated by men into bearing more children than they wish.

Women's groups have joined with many other grassroots organizations to advocate for environmental protection, social justice, human rights, family planning, and restructuring of hierarchical national and international institutions to include fuller participation and partnership models. Gender balance at all decision-making levels can help overthrow the protection rackets; it is also urgently needed to provide better feedback on the impact of policies and to tap the resources of the world's women. The importance of gender equity to human development has been demonstrated statistically in a three-year study, "Women, Men, and the Global Quality of Life."[10] In eighty-nine nations a correlation was found between gender equality and the quality of life of all members of the society. Similar correlations have been corroborated in the UNDP's *Human Development Report, 1995.*

PEOPLE ARE PURSUING THE CHALLENGE OF GLOBAL CITIZENSHIP

Yet women and men everywhere are behaving in an unprecedented way: audaciously taking responsibility for the whole human family and the future of life on the planet. Local communities not only organize to tame transnational corporate activity but also to establish credit unions and new forms of micro-lending, such as Women's World Banking, active in some fifty countries. Citizens who have been marginalized in industrial countries have learned from developing countries about activities such as Bangladesh's Grameen Bank, "lottery" investment clubs, and other grassroots subsistence enterprises in the world's informal sectors. Local currencies, such as Local Exchange Trading Systems (LETS), are now proliferating in many OECD countries along with computer-assisted barter clubs, radio "garage sales," and skills exchanges. Thus, global financial institutions, central bankers, and the Bretton Woods institutions must now recognize that their monopoly on money creation and credit facilities has been broken. In mediocracies, the good news is about the grass-roots — below the thresholds of national TV producers' radar.

People are taking on the challenge of becoming "global citizens," despite the scariness of protest and organizing activities and however costly and time consuming. They are discovering what Barbara Marx Hubbard calls "vocational arousal" — joining their genius to cocreate new social architecture rather than joining their genes to procreate. Availability of birth control has helped provide such opportunities and has raised new issues, as discussed in *The Pill: A Biography of the Drug That Changed the World* by Bernard Asbell (1995).

In the 1970s, Barbara Marx Hubbard, Jean Houston, and I explored the issues of emerging human potentialities for surviving and transcending the current crises of our now 5.8 billion-member human family during two weekend meetings at the Princeton Center for Alternative Futures in New Jersey, a "mom and pop" think tank I codirected with my former spouse, Carter Henderson.[11] Barbara Marx Hubbard foresaw these crises as signaling humanity's birth as an interplanetary species, an idea that she has developed in *The Revelation* (1993), and Jean Houston has continued exploring human development through The Foundation for Mind Research.[12] They and other thoughtful leaders have seeded a whole generation with their ideas, offering "new memes for the new millennium."[13]

I was always a little more reserved and offered weekend seminars at California's Esalen Institute in the 1970s on "Planetary Citizenship." I still give these seminars just to keep up my own spirits. There is nothing better than spending a weekend with aspiring planetary citizens in a state of vocational arousal to restore my faith in humanity. The phenomenal growth of self-help groups, cocounseling, twelve-step programs adapted from the success of Alcoholics Anonymous, and a wide range of new problem-solving activities — together with the huge range of self-help books and crises hotlines — is evidence that people inspire each other toward personal development. All these personal and societal development issues involve the "Decline of Jonesism," a subject I explored more deeply in the following article by that title, which first appeared in *The Futurist* in 1974:[14]

We have noted the preoccupation with hardware, technique, and the material means of our lives — all of the "How" questions that have so concerned industrial cultures. As industrialism exhausts its logic, the pendulum swings again — to a reexamination of the nonmaterial

RETHINKING HUMAN DEVELOPMENT / 159

"Why" questions. The cultural assumptions and economic arrangements associated with the game of "keeping up with the Joneses" are in for a drastic reevaluation. In a world of growing scarcity and interdependence, this sport—so popular among the middle and affluent classes in rich countries—appears to have reached its limits. Jonesism is becoming a steadily less viable motivating force for economic growth, since such mass-consumption strategies in already affluent nations require an unfair portion of the world's diminishing resources and prevent needed economic growth in the less affluent countries. The result is the growing "attention deficit" in rich countries, along with envy and greater international tensions in our global village.

There are many levels of Jonesism. Governments indulge in an international version of it with their state airlines and big-bang technologies, such as rockets. There is corporate and organizational Jonesism, typified by the proliferation of glittering glass skyscrapers, thick carpets, self-conscious art collections in the managerial aeries, sleek cavalcades of limousines and corporate jets—all sensitively tuned to the needs of status, prestige, and display. Perhaps most interesting of all is consumer Jonesism, exquisitely interrelated with and reinforced by all the other varieties. It is there that Jonesism begins and there it may end, as our individual perceptions and values change. Jonesism in all these forms is now unleashing new backlashes and counterforces. Some history may help set the stage for our inquiry into its present and probable future expressions. The conspicuous consumption of surplus has been a continuous theme of human behavior since the building of the pyramids. The excesses of kings and emperors now provide a general model for emulation by large numbers of people. Before the Industrial Revolution, a level of mass consumption beyond that necessary for subsistence was almost unthinkable. Surpluses, when they occurred, tended to be relatively small and unpredictable, dependent on cycles of harvests and military plunder. The distribution of surpluses was, therefore, hardly a central preoccupation and was often imaginative and idiosyncratic, whether dispensed in feasting and potlatches or used for conspicuous displays of the rulers' power or the groups' prestige, or for religious and artistic expression.

It was not long after industrialism began generating larger and more predictable surpluses that the first critics of the early expressions of Jonesism began to voice doubts. Marx pointed to the social hardships that industrialism created and focused on the inequities in

the distribution of the surplus that was produced. As American indus-
trialism developed into the opulence of the Gilded Age, Henry David
Thoreau, rejecting the pursuit of consumption, presented his fellow
citizens with the alternative values expressed in his famous book
Walden. Scandinavian-born economist Thorstein Veblen took up the
torch and railed against the vapid excesses of the rich in his book, *The
Theory of the Leisure Class*, published in 1899. Even economist John
Stuart Mill and the father of modern growthmanship, John Maynard
Keynes, predicted an end to the continual increase in the production
of goods and the eventual satiation of human wants. Underlying all
such critiques of materialism were the teachings of major religions,
which had always admonished against the seeking of riches and celebrated the search for spiritual values and the golden rules of cooperation, simplicity, humility, and love. The futility of Jonesism was
perhaps best expressed in the famous text, *Desiderata*, found in a
Baltimore church, dated 1692, which stated simply, "If you compare
yourself with others, you may become vain and bitter; for always there
will be greater and lesser persons than yourself."

Let us turn to the contemporary phenomenon of Jonesism and its
expression in international, national, organizational, and individual
behavior. International Jonesism is as old as the nation-state, and its
symbols, such as public monuments and buildings, new cities such as
Brasilia, well-equipped military forces, high technology, and membership in the United Nations, are all familiar. It has been widely
assumed that all nations could eventually pass through the stages of
economic growth, as described by economist Walt W. Rostow (1960),
and reach the mass-consumption phase, and even the heights of sociologist Daniel Bell's "post-industrial state" (1973). This kind of international Jonesism seems less viable in a world with a 1974 population
of roughly four billion (and set to reach some six billion in twenty-five
years) and with increasing scarcities of resources. Worldwide inflation
is making military and public-works expenditures more burdensome
while adding little increase in national security. Western-style industrial development often seems to create problems more onerous than
those it seeks to ameliorate. While the need for development in
poorer countries is indisputable, capital-intensive growth makes these
nations dependent on rich countries for both capital and technology
and renders indigenous workers inadequate, without costly training,
for all but the lowliest jobs.

With such losses in national self-sufficiency come other problems—such as migrations from rural areas to explosively growing
cities and, often, greater maldistribution of wealth and unemployment. New and expensive infrastructure must be provided: railways,
roads, communications, sewage treatment, and publicly subsidized
housing. And as indigenous consumers awaken to advertising trans-
planted from the affluent world, they often are lured into spending
their meager incomes on marginal goods, such as patent medicines,
candy, or such inappropriate substitutions as costly infant formula for
mother's milk, often with dire nutritional consequences.

Intermediate, labor-intensive technology is a viable development
alternative.[15] Capital-intensive industries can never provide enough
jobs, while simpler, less expensive technologies can create rural self-
sufficiency, raise individual productivity, stop the cancerous growth
of cities, and reduce social inequities and the dependence of poor
countries on rich ones. Such concepts of E. F. Schumacher, Ivan
Illich, Murray Bookchin, David Dickson, Francis Moore Lappé, and
others argue for development based on Mahatma Gandhi's idea of
production by the masses—not mass production. Such ideas were at
least introduced into UN conferences on science and technology in
the 1970s. The traditional goals of international Jonesism have been
modified by China's labor-intensive, rural model, which excites interest because it employs the resource that all less-developed countries
have in abundance, the labor and skills of their people.[16]

Let us turn to Jonesism as it is practiced in the affluent nations of
Western Europe, North America, and Japan, where it is encouraged
as a key motivating force in domestic economic growth. An early
example of this form of Jonesism occurred in the U.S. recession of
1958–59 when President Eisenhower approved a saturation advertising campaign that used the slogan "You Auto Buy Now!" The social
costs of Jonesism and the continual force-feeding of mass consumption through advertising and planned obsolescence were first widely
proclaimed in such books as J. K. Galbraith's *The Affluent Society*
(1958); Vance Packard's *The Wastemakers* (1960), *The Hidden Persuaders* (1957), and *The Status Seekers* (1959); and Marshall
McLuhan's *The Mechanical Bride* (1951). These critics all noticed
that our society, while well supplied with cosmetics, plastic novelties,
and tailfinned automobiles, seemed to be generating social and environmental costs, such as polluted air and water, decaying cities,

disrupted social and community patterns—as well as drug addiction, crime, excessive mobility, rootlessness, and other effects that Alvin Toffler later summed up in *Future Shock* (1970).

The idea that the world's resources might not always be equal to the task of fueling helter-skelter material consumption has come as a rude shock to Keynesian economists. The 1973 Organization of Petroleum Exporting Countries' (OPEC) fourfold increase in oil prices may be considered as writing on the wall. Other producing nations are following suit in demanding higher prices for their resources. Even if infinite substitutions can be found—as most economists hope—prudence now dictates a less-wasteful economy geared more to filling the basic needs of poorer citizens than encouraging the overconsumption of the middle and affluent classes. The continual pursuit of superaffluence in rich countries, as Robert Heilbroner speculated in *An Inquiry into the Human Prospect* (1974), may lead to increasing sabotage and international blackmail of rich countries by Third World terrorists as well as increasing the probability of wars. Barry Commoner noted in *The Closing Circle* (1971) this growing moral dilemma of rich nations, whose economies use the lion's share of the world's resources and create most of the pollution.

The coming world food shortage juxtaposed with increasingly rich meat diets of affluent consumers highlights this dilemma. Since meat production requires large quantities of feed grains, the consumers in affluent nations eat many times more grain per capita than people in the Third World. A reduction of meat consumption would release grain wastefully used to fatten livestock for direct human consumption by the world's needy (Lappé 1971). Lastly, not only must we start leveling down our own consumption of all resources, but we must also prepare ourselves for a geographical redistribution of production to other countries with indigenous resources; large, eager labor forces; and relatively unpolluted environments.

How will the decline of Jonesism affect corporations, which have played a key role as employers, producers, advertisers, and cultural standard-setters in reinforcing this human tendency? For one thing, corporations themselves will likely have to begin helping consumers get down off the Jones trip. Having raised the Frankenstein monster of demand through the over $20 billion they spend each year on advertising,[17] the corporations now increasingly find themselves unable to deliver the goods. The electric utilities have been the first hit because of their primary role in powering other production processes as well as consumer uses. Because their primary inputs of coal, oil, and natural gas are now priced more realistically (including a greater measure of their social and environmental costs), the utilities are squeezed between soaring construction and operating costs, and consumer resistance to rising rates. When it became clear to them that they could no longer increase capacity profitably, they began to reduce their advertising and promotion and started asking us not to use their product.[18] These "de-marketing" campaigns run by utilities were a forerunner of things to come. They gave a boost to the fledgling movement for counter-advertising (i.e., public service spots), and civic groups trying to obtain media time under the Fairness Doctrine to air their own views. Consumption of energy had become, like cigarette consumption, a controversial political issue rather than a simple matter of merchandising.

In the future, more and more types of consumption will become controversial and will embroil the producers in counter-advertising campaigns and political turmoils, because consumption creates as many external costs as does production.[19] In some cases, consumption of specific items will seem irresponsible, just as the wearing of furs of endangered species is viewed today. Similarly, whole classes of products that are excessively resource-intensive will be ostracized in the same way that many people reject large, overpowered cars and throwaway bottles. Corporate advertising, playing on psychological insecurities and motivations for status and visible success symbols typical of the Jones syndrome, may be called to account. Two professors of marketing at Northwestern University, Philip Kotler and Sidney J. Levy, tried to brace corporate executives for the unfamiliar world of de-marketing in a *Harvard Business Review* article entitled "De-Marketing, Yes, De-Marketing." Advertising executive Jerry Mander of San Francisco believed that if advertising is to survive as a major industry it had better get into the business of selling social issues and promoting public service organizations.[20]

When consumers have been led to expect life with limitless quantities of cheap paper products and cooks have been hooked on aluminum foil, the reaction to the withdrawal of these items is anger. The problem for companies is that we have all become inured to the daily advertising barrage and its thousands of petty deceptions. It is hard to believe companies which say that their supplies have been cut off or that prices have become too high to permit profitable manufacture of some products. The only answer for such beleaguered corporations will be to let others be the messengers who bring the bad news. This is the role that environmentalists and consumerists have been playing for years. Corporate advertising has proclaimed the good news while avoiding the bad news: it hailed the laborsaving appliances and pushed junk foods, while overlooking their effects: overweight, often unhealthy consumers. While advertisers have touted the advantages of fast cars and energy-gulping appliances, environmentalists have reminded us of the price we pay in more nuclear plants, strip mines, and emphysema. The most viable strategy for corporations will be to divert a portion of their advertising budgets as grants to appropriate voluntary organizations, whether consumer, environmental, or other community groups. These organizations can mount the needed de-marketing campaigns and serve as credible messengers to bring home the bad news. Such groups would not shirk the task of explaining the new need for hard trade-offs and choices, because they are hardened to controversy and themselves advocate changes in lifestyles, values, and economic arrangements.

Such lifestyle changes are mandated by declining energy and resource availability. Some corporations may not survive the shifting patterns and may follow the buggy-whip makers into oblivion. Others equally dependent on resource-intensive consumption may have the political power to force the taxpayers to bail them out in the manner of several aerospace, auto, and utility companies. Companies that negotiate the transition to the steady-state economy[21] will be those willing to serve public-sector needs, such as mass transit and recycling, and to minimize resource use by emphasizing durability rather than obsolescence. Corporations may also have to be content with modest profit margins because the companies will have to internalize more of the social costs of production and consumption. Energy for transportation will be more realistically valued, and overcentralized production by giant corporations will become less efficient than smaller regional and localized manufacturing serving decentralized markets.[22]

THE REVOLT AGAINST HIGH CONSUMPTION

Let us examine the individual motivations for the Jones syndrome. Sigmund Freud identified narcissism as a crucial factor in human behavior and its many expressions in display and status- or recognition-seeking as a validation of the individual's significance and very existence. We all desire to write our particular version of "Kilroy Was Here" on the course of human events and to etch some mark on the natural world around us. Norman O. Brown in *Life against Death* (1959) and Ernest Becker in *The Denial of Death* (1973) both suggest that all of our history can be interpreted as the saga of human striving to validate the importance of our existence and to overcome our fears of death and nothingness by our frantic manipulation of each other and of nature.[23]

The expressions of such drives as the material acquisition and overconsumption of modern-day Jonesism is a fleeting phenomenon associated with a relatively brief two-hundred-year span of industrialism, which may now be waning. In 1937 Karen Horney warned of the psychological toll of Jonesism on the American citizen. In her landmark study, *The Neurotic Personality of Our Time*, she noted the characteristic neurosis produced by cradle-to-grave competition to keep up with the Joneses is associated with three dilemmas: aggressiveness grown so pronounced that it cannot be reconciled with Christian brotherhood, desire for material goods so vigorously stimulated that it cannot be satisfied, and expectations of untrammeled freedom soaring so high that they cannot be squared with the multitudes of responsibilities and restrictions that confine us all.

In 1950 David Riesman examined the personality traits and sociology of an increasingly abundant and mobile society in *The Lonely Crowd: A Study of the Changing American Character*. He mentioned that as social change accelerates, values shift so rapidly that individuals, rather than relying on the "gyroscopes" of their own inner-directed principles, begin to rely on their "radar screens" and become other-directed, constantly shifting course to conform to the tastes, opinions, and values of their peers and society. As opportunities for material gain and upward mobility in consumption styles increase, other more traditional roles and niches which conferred status, dignity, and respect in other ways fall before the single, dollar-based success standards of Jonesism. In 1954 David M. Potter in his book, *People of Plenty*, provided an insightful summation of the cultural, social, economic, and individual drives that contribute to the distinctive American culture.

In the mid-1960s the rumblings against the tyranny of Jonesism became overt, built on these earlier insights and the emerging consciousness of the "beat generation" rebels such as Jack Kerouac, Allen Ginsberg, and others, whose lifestyles were sensitively examined by sociologist Robert Jay Lifton. The student revolt against what they saw as the frivolous, meaningless acquisitiveness of their parents, which exacted an exorbitant price in corporate conformity and loss of self-fulfillment and personal growth, soon led to the development of the flourishing counterculture. Overconsumption and status-seeking goals began to be viewed as obscene, and the advertisers of deodorants and grooming products, playing on deep psychological fears and insecurities, contributed to the backlash of the shaggy, gloriously unwashed "hippies." Old clothes and artifacts have become the counterculture's symbols of status, and riches in discretionary time are prized more highly than money income. Environmentalists soon joined in the movement for simplifying lifestyles as they understood the destructive role of resource-intensive production and consumption on the environment.

Swedish economist Staffan Linder's popular treatise, *The Harried Leisure Class* (1970), pointed out the anomalies of Jonesism, in that as affluence increases, time becomes more scarce. Poor people, often unemployed, have plenty of time, but the affluent come to resemble hamsters on an exercise wheel with no time to enjoy the hard-won fruits of the rat race. Linder showed that consumption takes time in the same way that production does, a point often overlooked by economists. The time required to use and maintain our cars, boats, swimming pools, campers, and gear for skiing, tennis, golfing, and hiking provides an upper limit to consumption. As time becomes scarcer for the harried overconsumer, such delights as the leisurely unfolding of affairs of the heart, tranquil reading, unhurried contemplation of where we are going and why, give way to revolving-door sexual encounters, singles bars, speed-reading, business-related vacations, and the tyranny of the clock.[24]

In *Alienation and Economics* (1971), Walter Weisskopf reached similar conclusions and pointed out that for humans, the real dimensions of scarcity are not economic but existential. Time and life are the ultimately scarce resources, because of our mortality. Such psychic needs are similar to those described by psychologist Abraham Maslow: peace of mind, love, self-actualization, community, and time for leisure and contemplation. Kenneth Boulding has highlighted our propensity to believe that the rights of private property ownership permit us to use up rather than merely to use resources, even though their utility to us is not thereby enhanced nor diminished if we reuse and recycle them. Our concerns are also moving beyond property rights into consideration of amenity rights, which are often violated by the consumption activities of snowmobilers, beach-buggy riders, hi-fi buffs, and transistor-radio lovers.

There are many signs that the need for getting down off the Jones trip is now widely understood. The energy crisis spurred the trend toward small cars, bicycles, and mass transit. Appliances are now rated for their energy economy and people are rediscovering the pleasures of home food growing and physical exercise. The popularity of survival manuals such as *The Whole Earth Catalog, Living Poor with Style,* and *Diet for a Small Planet* is not only due to their educational content on how to re-achieve basic self-sufficiency when the crunch comes, but also because they articulate the values and pleasures—not to mention the psychological relief—in store for those who kick the Jones habit.

Can we humans mature sufficiently to transcend Jonesism's basic motivations or must we be content with redirecting these human drives toward less materialistic and self-destructive goals? Perhaps it will be sufficient to alter the goals and symbols of success so that our narcissism is expressed in self-actualization and in reintegrating our self-images. Competition may be channeled into enhancement of skills, physical fitness, and well-being. Acquisitiveness may reemerge as striving for higher levels of consciousness. Status and recognition can be achieved in other ways; for example, many societies confer medals and symbolic status for social achievements. The British dispense knighthoods and peerages while the Russians and Chinese offer symbolic rewards for heroic feats of production and service to the people. In satisfying needs for display and expression, we could learn from many so-called primitive cultures in their imaginative use of body adornment, color, dance ritual, and festivals to objectify and celebrate our collective emotional and spiritual yearnings. If such outcomes were the result, then getting down off the Jones trip might open up new vistas for cultural exploration.

CHAPTER 8

CULTURAL DNA CODES AND BIODIVERSITY: THE REAL WEALTH OF NATIONS

Since the end of the Cold War, economies have moved beyond materialism, beyond the polarizations and ideologies of communism versus capitalism, and beyond left-versus-right toward the realities of globalizing markets. Now, there are many different "mixed economies" based on countries using their own markets, rules, laws, contracts, and so on, reflecting their own goals and values, traditions and cultures. Our understanding of cultural DNA codes and the human attention economy will explain and predict the economies of the twenty-first century better than old ideologies and labels. All countries seek new mixes of markets and rules to guide their development, and seek their own definitions of progress and wealth that go beyond industrialism's earlier European phase and its GNP-measured formula for growth. Many of the industrial and post-industrial countries of the Organization for Economic Cooperation and Development (OECD) now consist of attention economies focusing on "quality of life" and "human development" that are both equitable and ecologically sustainable. Many other countries, particularly in Asia, Latin and Central America, Africa, and Eastern Europe, are still industrializing and in various transition stages toward democracy and markets. All of these stages and transitions have been examined by political leaders, economists, sociologists, futurists, and political scientists in countless books and articles—many cited in this volume.

Today, we are rediscovering that values, far from being peripheral, actually drive all economic, technological, and social systems—a point I have stressed repeatedly since the 1970s. Today, we must clarify the immense political, social, economic, and technological transitions we are experiencing. How do these transitions relate to new and old multicultural goals and values, to ideas of wealth and progress, satisfaction, freedom, and development, and to the deeper spiritual and religious concerns they embody? What will be the shape of attention economies in our changed twenty-first century world, where we are all linked by globe-girdling technologies—jets, satellites, and information highways—which have given rise to the new interdependence in global financial cyberspace? As we have seen, the industrial era emphasized efficiency via material mass production, mass consumption, and technological scale—often leading to centralized cities and production, and large-scale organizations. This led to a "mental monoculture" and textbook formulas for achieving economic growth in a world of nations whose domestic economies could be separately steered by well-recognized rules of macroeconomic management.

These same countries must now deal with the effects of globalization, including lost national sovereignty over domestic affairs and increasing ecological and social exploitation by international market forces that resist regulation. How will nation-states "pool" their lost sovereignty to deal with the new globalization issues beyond the borders of any one nation: for example, trade rules, illicit drugs and arms trafficking, cross-border migration of workers looking for better jobs and companies seeking cheaper labor, cross-border pollution, resource waste, and depletion? In the late 1990s other questions include: How will societies develop to meet unmet needs and create opportunities and livelihoods for their citizens? How will societies close widening poverty gaps? Will they innovate socially by forging new partnerships and enterprises between private, public, and civil sectors? Markets spread and corporations go global, often with accountability to no one but their shareholders. We need to clarify the roles and responsibilities of business, governments at all levels, and the civil and informal sectors of society. What "codes of conduct" are socially responsible corporations accountable to and what systems of reporting to their shareholders and other stakeholders must they develop, such as social and "green" auditing?

What contributions to the future are locked in the cultural DNA codes of the world's indigenous peoples? As the Eurocentric Western model is challenged around the world, we rediscover, for example, that indigenous people were innovators—even in mathematics. Such reappraisals as those by Ziauddin Sardar (1977) of the role of Islamic science in tenth-century Europe give us new insights. Mathematician Dirk J. Struik at the Massachusetts Institute of Technology emphasizes that Greek-based Western mathematics is less advanced than we think. "Pythagoras' theorem was known in Babylon at least a millennium before the Greek gave his name to it." Struik further emphasized that Joseph Needham showed that ancient Chinese mathematics influenced Arabic and perhaps Indian mathematics and thence the mathematics of Western and other cultures. "Ethnomathematics," a term coined by Brazilian mathematician Ubiratan D'Ambrosio, illuminated the mathematical sophistication of the Incas and many indigenous peoples ignored by Eurocentrism.[1] Such fascinating studies as *Africa Counts* by Claudia Zaslavsky (1973), *The Code of the Quipu* by Marcia and Robert Ascher (1981) and *Ethnomathematics* by Marcia Ascher (1991) underline the sophistication of indigenous cultures.

CULTURE: THE DOMINANT FACTOR IN DEVELOPMENT

All these issues are well beyond the purview of economists and trade negotiators, which helps explain the rising worldwide interest in culture as a dominant factor not only in economics and development models, but also in geopolitics. Even the U.S. Council on Foreign Relations and its prestigious journal *Foreign Affairs* have come around to this view, publishing two articles in the September/October 1995 issue emphasizing the dominance of culture in development. Political and military strategists have not evolved the ability to address the geopolitics implicit in mediocracies and attention economies. Between 1989 and 1992, there were seventy-nine armed conflicts within nation-states, often around political and economic issues inflamed by ethnic and cultural differences.[2] We cannot romanticize culture and tradition; sometimes they have led to human rights abuses. It is evident from the many unique cultural faces of today's increasingly market-driven economies that they can best be understood by cultural anthropologists, social psychologists, historians, ethnomathematicians, and others in the social sciences. At least it is becoming accepted that people in these disciplines need to inform economic analyses since they can better address the underlying issues of *why* specific economies function the way they do. Economists were trained to examine *how* these specific economic systems function but not why they arose. Only with such multidisciplinary analyses of deeper cultural DNA codes can we hope to understand *why* and *how* the economies of, for example, Scandinavian countries are so different from those of other European countries, North America, Latin America, Asia, or Africa.

The extent of neglect of multicultural science is documented in "Lost Science of the Third World," a shocking indictment of Western bias in U.S.-dominated scientific journals.[3] The U.S.-based Science Citation Index (SCI), a private firm in Philadelphia, indexes articles from some thirty-three hundred scientific journals worldwide. In 1994, 30.8 percent of its citations were U.S. papers, with only 8 percent from Japan and the United Kingdom, respectively; 7.1 percent from Germany; France, 5.6 percent; Canada, 4.3 percent; Russia, 4 percent; Italy, 3.3 percent; Spain, the Netherlands, and Australia, 2 percent each; Sweden, 1.8 percent; and Switzerland, 1.6 percent. By contrast, India and China, with 1.3 percent each, were the only Southern Hemisphere or developing countries to exceed 1 percent. Every other country on the planet was represented, if at all, by less than 1 percent of the citations. Examination of the reasons for such neglect of third-world science revealed that SCI required English abstracts, purchase of a $10,000 subscription to the Index, and other onerous criteria to be met for an article to be included. A similar review of top scientific journals showed the same kind of bias.

The focus on culture has been brewing since 1988 when the United Nations declared a World Decade for Cultural Development (1988 through 1999). The UN also appointed a World Commission on Culture and Development chaired by Perez de Cuellar, former secretary-general of the UN, including many distinguished anthropologists and globally recognized intellectuals. The definition of culture used by the UN is: "Culture is the whole collection of distinctive traits, spiritual and material, intellectual and affective, which characterizes a society or social group."[4] As noted by D. Paul Schafer, director of the Canadian-based World Culture Project, viewing the development process through the lens of cultures allows a badly needed reintegration and a holistic view of these processes. Schafer emphasizes:

> There is a major battle looming in the world. It is a battle over whether cultures or economies should be the principle object and main focal point of developmental activity and national and international concern. . . . As the battle heats up and the battle lines become more firmly established, it is clear where the power lies. It lies squarely on the side of economies. Not only have economies dominated national and international thinking over much of the past century, but most governments, corporations, and national and international organizations have a vested interest in keeping things this way.5

Thus, the end of the Cold War did not mean a victory for capitalism per se — even though, quite sensibly, the use of markets began spreading along with democracy in the early 1990s. Markets are going through profound cultural changes themselves and will look very different in the twenty-first century — unrecognizable from nineteenth-century capitalism. Even Adam Smith would not recognize what we have today as capitalism. To survive in post-industrial societies, capitalism has had to put on a more "socially responsible" face. Investors, consumers, and citizens, as they reach a higher consciousness of planetary concerns and of the social and environmental impacts of private financial-market activities, demand more of corporations. Votes and full-cost prices are very useful feedback from individuals in guiding social decisions, as discussed in Chapters 11 and 12.

As I elaborated in *The Politics of the Solar Age* (1981, 1988), the end of industrialism is also coterminous with the end of patriarchy, even though this transition away from "protection-racket" systems may take many decades of struggle. Democratic forces eventually must prevail over hierarchical, instrumental, efficiency-driven corporations and governments because they cannot manage complexity and because they create such social and environmental chaos. (See Chapter 11.) Societies, as part of democratization, are revisiting the wholesale male-female polarization, which was exacerbated during the industrial period when men had to leave the home, smallholding, or village to work in factories and towns. As the production process was relocated outside the home, women and children lost power because they were not related to factory production, except as cruelly exploited, often quasi-slave laborers. Early industrialism involved regimentation and mass conformity. The intellectual tyranny of economics textbooks concerns their regularizing of industrial processes and development into formulas and algorithms concerning economic growth that were assumed to be applicable worldwide regardless of culture, tradition, values, or ecosystems. Today we see cultural diversity and biodiversity necessarily reemerging to challenge economism. It is clear today that economies and their growing attention sectors, with their different mixtures of rules and markets, are based on cultural DNA codes not economic algorithms. One size does not fit all.

Ziauddin Sardar, a highly regarded fellow futurist focusing on indigenous and Muslim cultures, talked to me recently about the inexorable march of the Western model of economism. He had decided to go to Sarawak, Malaysia, to find an "untouched" group of indigenous people. He rented a boat and poled down a river for a day and a half with his guide until finally the boat stuck to the bottom. Sardar and the guide had to get out and walk the rest of the way on the dried-up stream bed. They finally came to the village they were seeking and its bamboo longhouse. The village people were quite welcoming, and Sardar was invited to spend a couple of days with them in the communal longhouse.

After dark the first evening, everybody was sitting around and seemed to be feeling a little uncomfortable. Noticing this, Sardar asked through his guide whether they were upset by his presence and whether he should go and sleep somewhere else. The villagers replied, "Not at all," but they had become quite bored sitting around in the dark. The villagers wondered if Sardar would mind if they watched TV. So they went out and turned on the generator. After the lights came on, they found only an old BBC serial, which they had seen before, on TV. Then they pulled out the VCR and put a long scroll on the wall: a poster advertising *Terminator II*. They all sat and watched the video version of *Terminator II*. When it was over, Sardar asked what the film meant to the villagers. They said that the Terminator was like the tractors they now hear in the jungle. "They are getting closer and closer all the time and we know we are going to be overrun." The villagers had totally reframed the movie. As Sardar commented, "*Terminator II* was the Western model of development that was coming to overwhelm them."

Today, the ubiquitousness of this Western model is the driving issue for millions of citizen activists trying to limit its power and that of its corporate agents. The temptation and reach of this Western model, now dominating cultures all over the world, is provoking tremendous concern for culture and fueling the growth of grassroots globalism and the civil society. Powerful recent statements of concern include Indian physicist Vandana Shiva's *Staying Alive* (1989) and Wub-E-Ke-Niew's *We Have the Right to Exist* (1995). These books provide testimony to the disruption of the lives of countless indigenous people all over the world. This new literary genre expands on pioneering journals such as *Akwesasne Notes*, published since the 1960s by the indigenous nations of the northeastern region of what is now the United States.[6]

From the cultural perspective of indigenous people, Eurocentric industrialism, based on the Western scientific model, is experienced as alienated, rapacious theft and exploitation of people and the earth. Voices are rising in many countries and will not be silenced. Indigenous people are renouncing coercive treaties and reclaiming their ancestral lands, whether in Canada and the United States, Australia and New Zealand, Latin America, or Asia. In Europe itself, where the industrial process began, groups including Basques, Catalans, Frisians, Scots, Welsh, Slavs, and Sami peoples have been convening and networking since the 1970s. Other indigenous and rural people see the industrial Western model through gleaming advertisements and television programs and have no way of grasping its social and environmental costs and unsustainability as a path to development.

By 1995, cultural critiques of development and economism were rapidly gaining influence. In *Creating Alternative Futures* (1978, 1996), I had proposed that the United Nations set up a world data bank on cultural resources, analyzing cultural DNA codes to determine those which had proved the most survival oriented and life enhancing over the centuries. This idea and my assertions that cultures and values, far from being peripheral, were the driving forces in economic and technological systems were dismissed. Yet the cultural perspective provides sharper tools of analysis since it allows examination of assumptions and norms—including those of economists and economic textbook theories. In this light, "free trade" can be seen as a belief system rather than a scientific principle, and has been debunked by chaos theorist W. Brian Arthur (1994), myself (1991, 1995), and others.

Possibly this focus in economics on trade and "export-led" models of development arose from cultural roots in Europe, where most nations were export and trade oriented with mercantilist goals. This bias toward exploration, expansionism, and external reach led to many European wars, colonialism, and today's globalized markets. This contrasts considerably with the cultures of Asia, India, China, Japan, and others, for centuries more domestically oriented, which was a sign of backwardness to Western economists. One example of the clashes in the mid-1800s between Eastern and Western cultures was the Boxer Wars: the export-oriented, colonizing economies of Europe, such as Britain, shamefully fought for the right to sell drugs to the Chinese. In another example, the United States, which inherited this export model, arrived in Japan—Admiral Perry and his warships—demanding the Japanese open up their markets on the "principle" of free trade. Militant free-trade rhetoric about "prying markets open" with "crowbars" and other "weapons" is redolent of historical economic warfare.

Today's culturally concerned activists have joined forces with environmentalists focusing on biodiversity and with holistic women's movements around the world to provide wholesale critiques of industrialism, Eurocentric science, and the whole march to "modernization." This curiously old-fashioned word signifying the march toward industrialism is perhaps best summarized in Walt W. Rostow's perennial *Stages of Economic Growth* (1991)—a rationalization of industrial progress that has been going strong since it was first published in 1960. Another widespread response to industrialization has been the cultural movement of "post-modernism"—particularly in Europe and North America. I share much of Ziauddin Sardar's critique of post-modernism as self-indulgent, with nihilistic fantasies and hopes of rehabilitating the Enlightenment. Henry S. Kariel, a political scientist at the University of Hawaii at Manoa, Honolulu, is more sympathetic:

> The post-moderns can be understood as a *politics* for interacting with a merciless, irrevocable power, an increasingly global power that obliterates consciousness, that anesthetizes human beings, unifies contradictions, differences, and a politics that institutionalized nothing but an ongoing process of double dealing, diversity, incongruity and ambivalence. Persisting in doing *deliberately* what others do blindly, the post-moderns illuminate everyday events and obsessions. Intensifying the familiar, they exaggerate the dynamism,

thrust and range of modernity. They know that the pseudo thrills of the present are far from global, that the current technology is too soft to monitor and organize human experience comprehensively, that the prevailing quest for personal, ethnic and nationalist identity continues to enrich the weapons industry. . . . The performances of the post-moderns — my own performances included — are shamelessly fabricated realities, constructions, fictions and conceits, all designed to make the mind-blowing centers of modernity visible. They defy the optimism of the moderns. Outdistancing and outwitting the intractable realities of modernity, they acknowledge the inability to change modernity. Being sentenced to live with whatever goes on, they fully embrace it . . . more fully than robotized others who have been embedded in it. . . . The post-moderns follow Camus' *Sisyphus*, Paul Newman's "Cool Hand Luke," and the incarcerated English colonel, who at the point of death, pulls himself together to build "The Bridge on the River Kwai."[7]

As the cultural view gains ascendancy, signs of backlash from the rampant market sectors indicate that economism still reigns over policy making worldwide. An interesting case in point is the fate of a well-reasoned proposal by futurist Sam Cole of the State University of New York, Buffalo, and anthropologist Victoria Razak — an invited contribution to the deliberations of the World Commission on Culture and Development (WCCD). Professors Cole and Razak's proposal was to set up a General Agreement on Culture and Development (GACD), presumably to complement the purely commercial trade pact, the General Agreement on Tariffs and Trade (GATT), now the World Trade Organization (WTO). Their proposal directly challenged economism in advocating full-cost prices for commercial goods and services. They also called for involving indigenous, tribal, grassroots and community action groups, NGOs, private foundations, and all other major sectors in the general agreement process.

The distinguished members of the WCCD, including three Nobel laureates: Aung San Suu Kyi, Ilya Prigogine, and Derek Walcott; the former president of Switzerland, Kurt Furglar; and anthropologists Claude Levi-Strauss and Lourdes Arizpe — along with leading Latin American ministers and academics — endorsed the proposal at their Costa Rica meeting in February 1994. A press release from the United Nations Economic, Scientific, and Cultural Organization (UNESCO) announced that the proposal would be elaborated prior to its presentation to the UN General Assembly in late 1995. Other similar proposals included (1) a Marshall Plan for Culture and Development that would "reduce unproductive and especially military spending and aim to optimize public expenditures and implement new pricing policies that take noneconomic, environmental, and cultural costs into account"; and (2) an Agenda to complement the 1992 Earth Summit's *Agenda 21* and to serve as "a blueprint for the reform of cultural policies," structured around four key goals: "access to culture; control over the future in the context of revolutions in technology, including cultural and communications; preserve cultural environments, and promote creativity and freedom of expression."[8]

Since that press release, the chair of the World Commission, Perez de Cuellar, sought and failed to win the presidency of Peru, and the commission established a new secretariat. Professors Cole and Razak were informed that their GACD proposal had been "dropped completely" and that "the commission must not under any circumstances be associated with it."[9] The outline of the GACD is available, however, from *UNESCO Sources* in Paris. The GACD proposal, and presumably the others, had proven politically and economically explosive. Market players prefer their current freedom and neither government bureaucrats nor intellectuals wish to get too far out in front in such devolutions of power. During the 1980s UNESCO paid a heavy price for many of its bolder initiatives. A disapproving Reagan administration in the United States withdrew from UNESCO, and the United States only returned in the mid-1990s after much domestic lobbying by the civil society.

Other more general signs of the economism backlash include heightened worldwide efforts to create free-trade regions and multilateral pacts. The early 1990s saw the culmination of eight years of GATT's Uruguay round finally established as the World Trade Organization (WTO) in January 1995. Meanwhile, the post–Cold War reshuffling I described in *Paradigms in Progress* (1991, 1995) shifted further from the East/West rhetoric of "mutually assured destruction" to the North/South struggle over geopolitics. The rhetoric of "mutually assured development" is still unfolding. The rush for free trade, and to recolonize under the banner of freedom and democracy *equated* with the spread of markets, has continued to accelerate—as yet unchecked. Global competition has been openly advocated to curb inflation, i.e., to keep wages and prices down.

The private sector joined with business-driven governments to fuel the trade pacts. For example, expenditures by NAFTA-supporting business groups in the United States, together with some $40 million spent by the business-driven Salinas government in Mexico, to key U.S. legislators to pass NAFTA are documented in detail by the Center for Public Integrity and its fearless director, Charles Lewis, as well as by Common Cause, Public Citizen, and other civil groups based in Washington, D.C.[10] The fight over NAFTA was narrowly won by the Clinton administration. Portrayed as a bipartisan victory, it both confused and illuminated the battle lines to come and paved the way for a third political party in the United States (See Chapter 11.) Will it be top-down globalization of unregulated markets and technology making the world safe for global corporations, banks, and investors? Or will it be "grassroots globalism" with public access TV and radio bubbling up, based on local economies rooted in sustaining local ecosystems, protecting their biodiversity *and* cultural diversity, such as the model of the Philippines' Green Forum White Paper?

CROSS-CULTURAL DIALOGUES AND CRITIQUES

The new languages framing the issues qualify economics, economism, and economies—contexting their less important place within the larger cultural framework. For example, activists in Haiti reframe their goals and speak less of a culture of development and more about the development of culture. The key role of cultural DNA codes has emerged: values, ethics, and human responsibility can be refocused on the sanctity of all life and its diverse unfolding on this abundant, beautiful planet we all call "home." Elite decision makers in business, finance, and national governments still rush toward new commercial freedom in trade agreements, from MERCOSUR (Argentina, Chile, Uruguay, and Brazil) and the vision of the American Hemisphere Free Trade Zone offered in Miami, Florida, in 1994, to APEC (Asia Pacific Economic Cooperation) in the Pacific and TRAFTA (Trans-Atlantic Free Trade Agreement) to link North America and Europe. Yet all this is still governed by the competitive win-lose paradigm of market economics and its gloomy view of human nature as a "prisoner's dilemma" (i.e., because we don't trust

each other, we will continue to compete and "sell each other out"—
even though we would all do better if we cooperated). This overstated
dilemma is a core problem in game theory, discussed further in
Chapter 12. So, these regional free-trade pacts with their military
metaphors are usually defensive. Even otherwise-deluded free-trade
economists correctly point out that regional approaches simply divert
trade to their partners—rather than increasing world trade overall.

Unfortunately, most economists still miss the main issue: that the
concept of free trade is so narrow. It favors well-organized, powerful
market players and their commercial activities over virtually all other
local, national, and international concerns and goals, including
human health rights and needs, poverty alleviation, social justice,
education, local self-determination, agriculture for raising food and
fiber for local use, small businesses, local markets, the informal sectors—even the requirements for local and national infrastructure and
national sovereignty itself. Thus, a few courageous economists in the
tradition of Barbara Ward, Joan Robinson, and E. F. Schumacher—
including Herman Daly, Manfred Max Neef, Paul Ekins, and others—have begun to ridicule such narrow fixations on free trade as theology, not analysis. The economists try to slip away from their critics
by renaming their activity "geonomics"—under the new cover of
geopolitics. The widening coalitions within and across national borders against mindless "free-trade madness" are inevitably dividing old
elites and traditional politics. A despairing colleague, the well-known
Dutch environmentalist Wouter van Dieren, lamented this madness
as we were dodging huge trailer trucks on the eight-lane highway from
Brussels to Amsterdam. He noted, "These trucks are carrying local
potatoes, which go to Eastern Europe or Russia to be peeled. Then
they are retrucked to Greece or Turkey to be cut, fried, packed, and
frozen, and sent back here for sale! Flowers in our Dutch markets are
now grown in Venezuela and flown over the Atlantic daily in jets.
Soon our country will be nothing but airports and road and rail transportation corridors subsidized by Dutch taxpayers."[11]

Public understanding of the narrowness of free-trade agreements
and the absurdities they encourage goes beyond that of politicians and
elites. In 1993 and 1994, the Americans Talk Issues Foundation surveyed the U.S. public in a series of polls concerning globalization. In
questions concerning whether trade agreements should be conducted
"more efficiently by only economists and trade negotiators or made

longer and more complex by the addition of social and physical scientists concerned with broader issues and impacts," 71 percent of the public choose the longer, more complex agreements with many different experts even if they were told this might delay the creation of new jobs.[12] Even midsize companies can now only survive the cut-throat global competition by merging and sourcing their production from ever-cheaper labor. Since prices still do not include social and environmental costs, this allows for ever-wider, more ecologically destructive subsidized transportation of goods—however irrational. The concept that capital and goods and services can cross borders at will, while "labor," i.e., people, must be restricted, is now exposed as inconsistent—but the momentum is still with economism.

As I reviewed in *Paradigms in Progress*, social, cultural, and environmental backlashes emerged in Europe in the 1980s as demands for a "Social Europe" and an "Environmental Europe." The European Union, in 1995, had many environmental regulations and had partly enacted a "Social Chapter"—under fierce negotiation and opposed by the business-dominated Conservative government of Britain. Forcing their cultural critiques into economism's terminology, the grassroots oppositions in each country learned to rail against "social, environmental, and cultural dumping" (i.e., exporting cheap goods based on unfairly exploiting such resources). Grassroots groups were forced to organize internationally because the confusion now concerns the issue of levels of governance. Now that markets, finance, and mass communications have breached national boundaries, everything is up for grabs, from local, national, and regional to global. Humans, with no experience at managing themselves at current scales, are in a kind of "swarming behavior": experimenting, reshuffling, restructuring, reengineering, or simply destructuring and devolving amid rising chaos and tragic conflicts.

All this may explain the popularity among elites of Robert Kaplan's despairing essay on the decline of African living standards and ecosystems, "The Coming Anarchy," and Samuel Huntington's warnings about "The Clash of Civilizations," mentioned in Chapter 6. While all this chaos is viewed with alarm from the ramparts of the old order and the viewpoint of economism, grassroots and cultural forces see opportunities in this "breakdown zone" and niches where more sustainable societies can take root. Naturally, grassroots anger is rising at the widespread corruption of democratic governments by money and influence from entrenched special interests. In *The Politics of the Solar Age*, I referred to the two main U.S. political parties, the Republicans and Democrats, as "two football teams owned by the same owners." Now some 35 percent of the U.S. electorate that votes "independent" seems to agree. So far this does not make the emerging debate about values, family, and quality of life any easier. With commercial mediocracy in the saddle, neither political parties nor any other group that finds the right words can gain access to media, hold the floor, or even find suitable forums for the much-needed national dialogue.

In spite of all these difficulties, post-industrial societies are framing a new path to cultural development and developing human cultures. The cross-border dialogue is under way in journals such as *Cultures and Development*, published in Brussels since 1990 in three languages; the publications of the Third World Network in Penang, Malaysia; the Green Forum in the Philippines; IBASE in Brazil; and many other journals and newsletters. For many cultural grassroots groups, clarifying the issues has meant going back to basics. Brazil's IBASE (based in Rio de Janeiro and whose visionary leader, Herbert de Souza, I was fortunate enough to meet during the 1992 Earth Summit) spearheaded Brazil's "Campaign Against Hunger." Started in 1993, the campaign spread national awareness and action on all issues related to hunger and poverty. It overcame widespread cynicism, led to three thousand local committees that brought people together across all their many divisions, and today is known to the majority of Brazil's seventy million people. The campaign's message is full of possibilities for personal action, empowerment, and social transformation. Since the Earth Summit, crosscultural explorations have been increasing through networking, journals, and books, and in some cases through a new generation of sensitive diplomats, such as Venezuela's former Ambassador to India, Frank Bracho, author of *Toward a New Human Development Paradigm* (1992) and an editor of *Indo-Asiatic Encounters with Ibiro-Americans* (1992).

In Japan, cultural critiques of Western economism are growing along with people's associations and cooperatives. A 1995 conference in Tokyo brought such representatives together with those of other Asian civic and religious organizations to discuss "The Role of Culture in Japan's International Cooperation in the XXIst Century." The conference stressed that Japan had been open to foreign *cultures* from the sixth to the eighth centuries, when Chinese and Korean influences first brought in the Buddhist element of the Indian civilization. When Japan's rulers encountered the Europeans (termed "northern barbarians") in the fifteenth century, they sensed the dangers of colonialism and isolated Japan for the next 250 years. After the adoption of the Western model, the Japanese slogan became "Western technology but a Japanese spirit," which helped maintain local pride. Yet many at the conference lamented what had happened to their culture since post–World War II Americanization. A formula for future development was proposed as $D = C + U$: where D equals development; C equals commonality (i.e., common, universal values); and U equals uniqueness (i.e., cultural specificity).

Japanese participants stressed the Japanese uniqueness factor: polytheism and respect for nature, as for example in their Shinto religion. They argued, and I would agree, that having many deities should lead to a type of democracy which allows for diversity, whereas Judeo-Christian, Islamic, and other monotheistic religions may lead to a type of democracy that has more difficulty seeing ambiguity and diversity. The group discussed the dangerously unbound, Promethean side to Western enlightenment, and how this kind of development has led to increased homogenization and the uprooted "nowhere societies" of consumerism, fast foods, and video. Self-interest must be replaced, many believed, by the Golden Rule. Frequent references were made to key notions to save the world today: deep ecology, feminism, and religious pluralism, with consciousness of human duties as well as rights—according to the report of Thierry Verhelst, editor of *Cultures and Development*.[13]

Because Japan is powerful economically, its cultural role in the evolution of markets and democracy will be increasingly powerful. Since the late 1980s, Japan has been a major funder of Official Development Assistance (ODA), the World Bank, private banks, and other international financial institutions. Japanese funding of development projects in Asia, Africa, and Latin America has been accompanied by more recent funding of academic seminars, research, and study conferences on the uniquely Japanese—rather than the formerly ubiquitous European—model of capitalism. Even though the many new faces of capitalism are still more or less the faces of economism, I welcome the further elucidation of the "Japanese model." Each cultural expression of capitalism and economism offers new opportunities to enlarge the sphere of culture as prime determinant. Co-option is already rife, with "cultural consultants" offering their pat analyses to business travellers via airline magazine articles on "How To Do Business" in Thailand, China, Malaysia, Indonesia, Vietnam, or whatever country is seen as the new "target of profit opportunities" or the latest "emerging Tiger." Total private investment flows into developing countries (or as economists prefer, "emerging markets") reached $97 billion in 1994, and when Official Development Assistance (ODA) and export credits were included, totaled $169.4 billion.[14] Mexico's 1994–95 debacle caused hardly a blip on most company radar screens since the world is now their oyster and American taxpayers bailed out most of the big financial players.

Perhaps even deeper than the overall cultural critiques are the critiques of economism by the world's women. At last women began to be heard at the UN Summit on Population and Development in Cairo in 1994, and at the Summit on Social Development in Copenhagen and the Summit on Women and Development in Beijing, both in 1995. Women have been so systematically excluded from economics, economic development, and even many cultural critiques of economism that it is not surprising they reject the entire intellectual and institutional apparatus built by economics. By 1980, I had come to the same rejection, after fifteen years of effort to reform economics as a writer and activist. In *The Politics of the Solar Age*, I gave up on reform and began to study cultural DNA codes, the evolution of human ethics, altruistic behavior, cooperation and win-win solutions, and what I termed "the love economy."

Feminists, and many women who would not call themselves feminists, have picked up on my views. Some have developed their own critiques, extending mine, including Gloria Steinem in *Moving Beyond Words* (1994); Britain's Mary Mellor in *Breaking the Boundaries* (1992); and Barbara Brandt in *Whole Life Economics* (1995), which I recommend highly. Marilyn Waring, the New Zealand parliamentarian and political scientist, went deeply into the outrages perpetrated on women by economics and economists and the global systemization of economism in the United Nations System of National Accounts in her book *If Women Counted* (1988), which I joyfully reviewed. Other women thought, as I had, that they would learn economics and overcome it, but as academics from within rather than activists, like myself. Peggy Antrobus in the Caribbean, Finland's

Hilkka Pietila (1990), and other pioneers in Asia and Africa helped start the now-thriving field of feminist economics. Other women followed the Gandhian tradition of local, spiritual self-reliance, notably my colleague Nandini Joshi, author of *Development without Destruction* (1992), still a classic. London's Zed Books publishes a wide variety of books by women observers of many countries, for example, *Feminist Perspectives on Sustainable Development*, edited by Wendy Harcourt (1994).

In addition to harpooning the idiocies of economism, women have also embarked on a campaign to expose the soothing platitudes, purveyed by male leaders of the world's patriarchal societies, on the virtues of culture and tradition. At the 1995 Summit on Social Development, women challenged clauses that sought to protect cultural traditions and diversity in the draft Declaration by adding the qualifier: *"Except when such cultural traditions and practices violate human rights, especially of women and girls."* A turning point of sorts occurred in 1994 at the Summit on Population and Development in Cairo: population-control hawks in the North became convinced, however reluctantly, that population growth in societies could not be checked without the education of girls and the political and economic empowerment of women. The Roman Catholic and Muslim hierarchies, seeing this threat to their social orders, played negative roles in Cairo — throwing sand in the gears often in the name of culture and tradition. These actions, however, galvanized many Northern Hemisphere countries into a remarkable rhetorical consensus — women became the crucial factor in development, the key to sustainability, and on and on. The World Bank picked up on a 1992 statement by Larry Summers (compensating for his earlier tactlessness about the economic case for shifting pollution to the poor countries) that the best return on investment (some 18 percent) was to be found in the education of girls. Even the UN, which I was forced to describe in *Paradigms in Progress* as the most sexist organization on the planet, began to join in the rhetoric — and promoted a few women in a visible way.

Women are deeply interested in preserving traditions and culture — whenever they are benign and life-affirming. Yet women are also deeply and experientially aware of the dangers of "protection rackets," "macho" traditions, cruel "initiation" and other practices, and the corrosive effects of dominator, warrior, and patriarchal cultures such as those in early Greece documented in *Reign of the*

Phallus by Eva Keuls (1985) as well as those cultures that invaded and conquered the early Mediterranean partnership cultures described by the late Marija Gimbutas (1989), and Riane Eisler in her pathbreaking books, *The Chalice and the Blade* (1988) and *Sacred Pleasure* (1995). All this rewriting of history and *herstory* (as feminist scholars rightly emphasize) is quietly recharging our image banks and giving us new vistas and paths toward cultural evolution.

The worldwide outpouring of concern for the environment and biodiversity expressed at the UN Earth Summit in 1992 has coalesced in many ways with movements for cultural diversity, social justice, the rights of poor and indigenous peoples, women, and all those marginalized by economism. Because indigenous peoples developed cultures and coevolved with other species in specific ecosystems, an understanding of the inseparability of biodiversity and cultural diversity has been able to emerge. Destroying an ecosystem means destroying the habitats of not only indigenous people but all other unique and diverse species. Such lessons are slowly being absorbed by politicians, developers, and ecological economists. When they are fully understood, development as we have known it will no longer make human or ecological sense. Helena Norberg-Hodge (1991) is persuasive in documenting the gradual degradation of the culture and environmental conditions in Ladakh, a province in northern India, as Western models of development shattered its formerly self-sufficient economy. Edward Goldsmith, pioneering editor of Britain's *The Ecologist*, has been one of the world's more prescient futurists in alerting industrial societies to make *The Great U-Turn* (1988) to sustainability, as well as in his classic *Blueprint for Survival* published in 1972.

ANCIENT MYTHS MAY PROVIDE PATHS TO THE FUTURE

Thus, many earnest reformers in both North and South are now poring over Hopi prophesies, decoding African art, studying festivals, learning sun and rain dances, analyzing enduring stories such as that of Kokopelli in the Americas with his shoulder bag of seeds (a symbol of biodiversity), and relearning the farming methods indigenous to Asia and Africa as well as the permacultures of the nomads, gatherers, and hunters. Indigenous peoples are also reaching out to help in all this. Rebecca Adamson, a member of the Cherokee nation that inhabited the east-central area of what is now the United States, founded the First Nations Financial Project as part of the work of the First Nations Development Institute. Now based in Virginia, the group's main work is linking these first nations, some still on reservations, with responsible, caring U.S. investors who want to support local micro-enterprise, sustainable development, and eco-restoration. First Nations financial research provides a way for U.S. citizens, investors, and financial planners to learn the principles of sustainable human development from indigenous peoples. A foundation of cultural uniqueness infuses this work and is expressed in an article by Rebecca Adamson, "Indigenous Economics and First Nations":

> Although an increasing amount of research on tribal or indigenous knowledge systems is currently being conducted, literature shows that tribal knowledge is still not recognized as the product of holistic systems of perceptions, relationships, and organizational arrangements. Efforts to promote culturally appropriate development place this work within the holistic worldview and belief systems of tribal people. "Culturally appropriate" economic development, led and conducted by Native communities, does not necessarily mean the traditional, historic activities undertaken by a tribe for survival. Rather, it may mean economic development activities that are driven by a community's cultural values, based on kinship, shared responsibilities and benefits, and respect for the environment.
>
> The indigenous understanding has its spiritual basis in a recognition of the interconnectedness and interdependence of all living things. It is a holistic and balanced view of the world, in which all things are bound together, and all things connect. What happens to the Earth happens to the children of the Earth. Humans have not woven the web of life; but are one thread. Whatever we do to the web, we do to ourselves. The "environment" is perceived as a sensate, conscious, entity suffused with spiritual powers through which human understanding is only realized in perfect humility before the whole.[15] (See Fig. 15. Elements of Development.)

The first nations practiced life-affirming ways in their cultures until they were invaded and conquered by Europeans following Christopher Columbus. Kirkpatrick Sale gives a moving account of this chilling, tragic story in *The Conquest of Paradise* (1990), a book that considerably changed the nature of the Quincentennial Columbus celebrations in the United States.

Other cultural reforms of development include those inspired by Buddhist concepts of "awakening" of all members of a community, such as the Sarvodaya movement and many others documented by India's Development Alternatives, which provides well-researched concepts of alternative technologies to empower villages and local communities.[16] Indian industrialist and solar energy expert J. C. Kapur holds many conferences at his Kapur Solar Farms near Delhi. These conferences consider critical issues in human development, including spiritual development, with participants from many countries. The February 1995 conference focused on culture and development, and the report on their dialogue began with this statement:

> Development must assure the satisfaction of the minimum basic needs for food, habitat, health, education and employment, and the human quest for inner peace and self-realization. This can only be achieved if we can cultivate need-based as against desire-based lifestyles, which are not superficial or self-indulgent and are nondestructive of the environment and other cultures. These must be frugal in means and rich in ends and not beyond the reach of increasing numbers of citizens. While being equitable, development must not sacrifice initiative and excellence but be ecologically responsible, economically viable, cumulative, life enhancing, culture specific, and culturally sensitive.[17]

The potential of people's movements, such as the Kerala Sastra Sahitya Parishad in the Indian province of Kerala, to raise literacy rates and general welfare is documented in *Science in Participatory Development* by Mathew Zachariah and R. Sooryemoorthy (1994). Even optimistic futurist Buckminster Fuller in his last book, *Critical Path* (1981), made clear how far off course Western societies and their economic development models have stumbled. Fuller also reevaluated the history of human colonization of this planet as originating in Asia among seafaring humans. He believed their shipbuilding skills and knowledge of trade winds allowed the spread of their settlements in river estuaries from Bangkok, Thailand, and other Southeast Asian coastal regions to India, Africa, and beyond.

Elements of Development

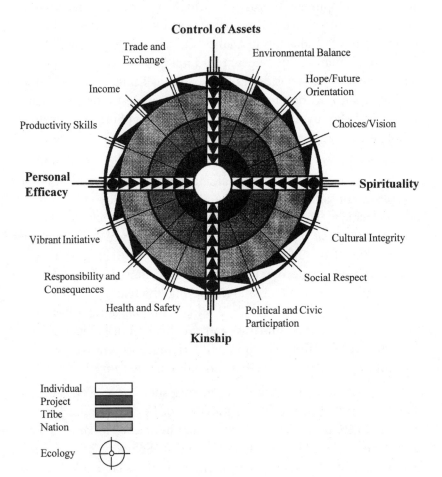

Fig. 15.   Elements of Development

Some historians and paleoanthropologists are now challenging the entire linear "human progress" paradigm, which undergirds the economic development paradigm. In *Memories and Visions of Paradise: Exploring the Universal Myth of a Lost Golden Age*, Richard Heinberg (1989) builds an interdisciplinary case for reconsidering the reigning unidirectional paradigm of human progress. Heinberg painstakingly trudges through archeology, modern and paleoanthropology, psychology, philosophy, and the world's religions and cultures, examining alternative hypotheses: for example, that ancient human societies in many ways may have been more advanced and wiser than those of today. Heinberg explores the myths in every culture of a fall from an earlier state of paradise, myths that contain encoded advice and experience. Perhaps we can learn from these stories and apply that knowledge to avert our current social crises and find healthier paths to the future. Clearly, humans are not fundamentally prone to violence and savagery or uncaring, ego-centered selfishness. We have equal tendencies toward caring, sharing, and cooperation and have existed in peaceful societies in many times and places. Heinberg assembles much evidence to show that, in many cultures, ego-centered individualism was experienced as a loss of the holistic sense of union with nature and the divine. When such ego-centered concerns become culturally reinforced, as in the Western development model, and dominate our awareness of society and nature, we can become mentally and physically sick and our societies can disintegrate.

I found Heinberg's view very insightful—that the ubiquitous myths of paradise may serve a specific function in our society, as Heinberg (1989, 241) says, "as a *design for living* embedded in the circuitry of human consciousness. All biological organisms, including human beings, contain an element of design. We know, for example, that the patterns of DNA molecules in our cells govern the basic design of our physical bodies. Perhaps we also contain within us a neurological or psychic program for the optimal design of social and spiritual relations between ourselves, the Cosmos, and Nature." Let us now turn to this deeper design element which, in the form of human DNA, faithfully replicates our miraculous physical bodies generation after generation.

As we are forced to "wake up" as a now-planetary species, with all the new stresses our technological prowess has created and all the evolutionary potential at hand, we can expand our awareness of our various cultural DNA codes as well. Indeed, competition and cooperation are key strategies of all species, along with creativity, which is the most rare and evolutionary. In human societies and in human cultural DNA codes, *replication* (i.e., tradition) is basic, as in the coding of all DNA, while *innovation* (i.e., mutation) is a much rarer phenomenon.[18] Too much innovation can destabilize a society, and as students of complex systems know, the trick is to find and study the regime operating at the edge of chaos. In *Complexity: Life at the Edge of Chaos* (1992), Roger Lewin reports how the U.S.-based Santa Fe Institute expanded its focus from global financial markets and economies to cultures. The chairman of the institute's board, Murray Gell-Mann, has adopted my concept of cultural DNA codes as a tool for researching complex, adaptive systems; chaos; complexity; and the emergent properties of such systems.

The roots of what is now pompously called the science of complexity lie in cybernetics, information and general systems theory, biology, and ecology. Complexity was explored in the 1950s at the famous Macy Conferences and well summarized at the United Nations Symposium on "The Science and Practice of Complexity" in Montpellier, France (May 1984). I was a participant, along with many of the "names" in the field from Aida, Allen, Atlan, and Boulding to Dupuy, Margalef, Prigogine, Von Foerster, and Zeleny.[19] The literature on complexity science goes back to the Russian scientist A. Bogdanov's *Treatise on Tektology*, published in Russian in three volumes in 1913, 1917, and 1920. Banned in the Soviet Union, the text was rescued by systems theorists I. Blaouberg and V. Sodowsky and republished in 1977 as *Systems Theory: Philosophical and Methodological Problems* by Progress, Moscow. It was finally translated into English and published as *Essays in Tektology* in 1984. This digression is important to context the more recent work of the Santa Fe Institute, which commenced operations in 1984. What I remember most from the Montpellier Symposium were the poems provided as instant feedback to each presentation by my late and beloved friend, Kenneth Boulding—poems that cut through the heavy jargon with his usual mischievous wit and clarity.

Research into complexity and chaos in living and nonliving systems is providing metaphors, but that research is also reaching limits, outlined in recent reports from and about the Santa Fe Institute.[20]

Rising stress may correlate with the onset of the "entropy state," where *de*-structuring and *re*-structuring are needed — not more construction on the existing structural base. I compare this de-structuring of societies approaching evolutionary cul-de-sacs to the phenomenon of paedomorphosis in species, where a maladapted adult form is discarded over time, and that species, instead, takes a new path by evolving further from its younger, more flexible, larval stage.[21] Analogies exist in the signs of devolution of unsustainable, overstructured, capital and resource intensive industrialism and its centralized control, "trickle-down" models of replication, compared with the new, still misunderstood as "chaotic," grassroots village models of "trickle-up" development, lateral information flows, networking of citizen movements and organizations — and perhaps greater wisdom.

The issue is nothing less than the direction of human social evolution on this small, ecologically compromised planet. The debate about sustainable development has become a metaphor for a complex cluster of issues; but at its core, it is a debate about values and which cultural, social, technological, and behavioral repertoires embedded in the various cultural DNA codes of the world's people actually contain the "programs" which may serve as the seeds for human survivability.

Survivability should be the overall criterion of success, i.e., those cultural DNA codes that prove to be sustainable over the longest term within their ecological contexts — by providing for material needs and by providing developmental opportunities for their people, while offering satisfying meanings, purposes, and roles, as well as coherent metaphysical and philosophical "stories." In the Epilogue in *Creating Alternative Futures*, I speculated that core values would probably be identifiable, including reverence for life and the natural world, love, honesty, and sharing — the same core beliefs encoded in all the world's great religious and spiritual traditions and on which humans can construct a win-win world. For example, one can interpret the Golden Rule, the Hindu concept of Karma, and many other expressions of human *responsibility* (as well as rights) as precise statements describing dynamic, nonlinear systems. Systems theorists will also recognize the biblical concept of "Judgment Day" as a system coming up to real time — where there are no information lags and all accounts must be settled. The global civil society and the world's indigenous peoples are today's last repositories of such common wisdom encoded in myth, spiritual traditions, folklore, art, dance, and ritual, as Jean Houston has shown in her many books.[22]

One inescapable factor is now clear: the six-thousand-year rise of cities, states, and nations has been necessitated by the enormous increase in human populations from their beginnings in Africa. Male-dominated forms of human civilization, steered exclusively with patriarchal religious belief systems, have come to prevail over almost every ecosystem on the planet, in contrast to earlier matrilineal societies based on partnership between men and women and reverence for nature. This patriarchal "spin" became exacerbated through deviation-amplification processes (as in chaos models) and eventually led to wider, even more competitive territorial expansion and the human population explosion. Obviously, women must be in control of their fertility for human populations to remain stable and within the carrying capacity of ecosystems.

Finding alternative ways to process information that has been discounted, overlooked, or suppressed is now vital for our survival. Much of this information is stored in the cultural DNA codes of groups devalued in industrial and economism paradigms—indigenous cultures and the world's women. As Walter Weisskopf (1971) pointed out, all civilizations involve different sets of *expressions* and *repressions* of the full range of human ways of being and behaving. Social revolutions always involve a "return of the repressed" onto the social scene. Gregory Bateson (1973) describes complex adaptive systems, such as human societies, as being in a constant, overall trade-off between adaptation and adaptability. If the society's store of adaptability has been depleted by too much successful adaptation to past conditions, then the society is too rigidly committed to its old structures to evolve. This "nothing fails like success" problem is stated by cultural anthropologists as the Law of the Retarding Lead, i.e., those societies less adapted to old environments will often spurt ahead as conditions change.

Today, all these dramas are being played out on a global stage. Millennial visions and apocalyptic prophesies, however we interpret them, may serve as "wake-up calls." Evolutionary paths for human societies include redesigning science: reorganizing knowledge to balance material with nonmaterial knowledge.[23] Humans must learn to live within nature's tolerances. That means designing in more feedback mechanisms from the grassroots (e.g., votes) and from the market (e.g., fuller-cost prices including both social and environmental impacts), as well as learning better methods to decode feedback from natural systems (e.g., acid rain, ozone depletion, and the buildup of carbon dioxide in the atmosphere) and creating new quality-of-life indicators to correct the deadly, rudderless drift of economism. Partnership, rather than the dominator paradigm of human organization, is a safer evolutionary path, as Riane Eisler (1988) documents. The real resources at hand for our survival require mining our storehouses of cultural DNA codes and distilling strategies to preserve and enhance diversity. Thus humans may continue coevolving within the biosphere.

PART III

BUILDING A WIN-WIN WORLD: BREAKTHROUGHS AND SOCIAL INNOVATIONS

CHAPTER 9

INFORMATION: THE WORLD'S REAL CURRENCY ISN'T SCARCE

nnovations in information technology have created a $1 trillion daily exchange in the global financial casino. In 1993, the Bank for International Settlements recorded a rise to $14.9 trillion traded between parties in derivatives of stocks, bonds, commodities, and currencies (what traders call virtual securities, swaps, puts, calls, and so on) in an attempt to manage risks in the global economy. But derivatives bring uncertainties of their own: from "bear raids" on currencies to huge losses as headlined during 1995. In July 1995, *Fortune* magazine cited these 1993 figures as the last year for which data was available, but, with derivative trading "now no doubt higher," added "the globalization of financial markets operating largely beyond the control of governments is arguably the most significant development of our times." In September 1995, *The Economist* reported that derivatives trading stood at more than $20 trillion at the close of 1994.[1]

Today's looming global financial crises have deep systemic roots in the industrialism paradigm, which inappropriately still drives the acknowledged "*post*-industrial" Information Age. New paradigms — beyond reductionism, instrumental materialism, nationalistic competition, and other fear- and scarcity-based social strategies, beyond the drive to subdue nature and perpetuate male domination — are needed. And yet central bankers and national politicians, worried by scenarios of financial collapse, are relying on failing textbook economic remedies (such as raising interest rates or trying to buy their currencies on the open markets) to support their domestic economies and currencies. By mid-1995, national players had begun to painfully maneuver toward the *social innovation* needed to match the *technological innovation* of the computer- and satellite-based global casino.[2]

TECHNOLOGICAL AND SOCIAL EVOLUTION: THE HARE AND THE TORTOISE

As we saw in Chapters 3 and 7, throughout the three-hundred-year evolution of Western industrial societies there has been a continuous lag between technological innovations and the social innovations needed to accommodate their assimilation. From the spinning jenny and the steam engine to the automobile and computer, new technologies have always outpaced and eventually called forth responding social innovations: double-entry bookkeeping and accounting protocols; national currencies and central banks; standardization of rail gauges, highway signs, and electrical fixtures. The computer industry, which underpins the global casino, is still in its competitive, market-expansion phase. It is facing a paradox of technological evolution often experienced at this stage of the innovation cycle: incompatibility and mismatches between software, operating systems, and other components. This diversity of design—originally a competitive advantage to individual firms—begins to hinder further market expansion into more system-wide applications.

Market competition or, in game theory terms, win-lose strategies, begin to *limit* market penetration. For example, in the 1800s, railroad track gauges were incompatible as were the multiplicity of bank-issued currencies, and in the 1970s there were a dozen or so different, separately developed machine-readable product code systems. This incompatibility often leads to chaotic conditions. As I detailed in *Paradigms in Progress* (1991, 1995), a systems approach would view the win-lose market framework as entering a transition phase where cooperation (i.e., win-win strategies, such as Sematech and the Universal Product Code) could expand opportunities for all by standardizing a regulatory regime. Paradoxically, textbook market theory often *inhibits* the social innovation response, which could widen market penetration, as "interference in free markets."

These competing paradigms of competition and cooperation now rage over the Internet. Will Microsoft and Intel continue providing their private, costly de facto standard: Windows and Intel—or Wintel—almost a monopoly? Or will new software like Java, a breakthrough in simplicity for users pioneered by Sun Microsystems, win by rapidly licensing Java at below cost to Netscape and all the new developers of software for navigating the Internet and its World Wide Web? Will Java then become a new Internet standard—set by private, monopolistic market power? How should governments relate to, much less regulate, the Internet?[3] John Heielmann summed up the issues as an epic battle between the paradigms of U.S. Vice President Al Gore and House Speaker Newt Gingrich, both self-styled futurists and Information Age proponents. Will it be Newt's libertarian, market-set standards or Gore's public-access rules and regulatory standards?[4]

Social lag-time actually allowed the rapid germination of the Industrial Revolution in eighteenth-century Britain. Millions of small, diverse decisions, seeded by the fertile minds of individual inventors, changed the social scenery. No one thought that their individual activities were also helping to change the world irreversibly. Further, social mores provided a nurturing context: the Enlightenment championed philosophies of individualism and material improvement via scientific and technological progress. As chaos theory shows, those initial conditions allowed for easy diffusion of early technological innovations. Clearly, computer industry CEOs understand the benefits of rapidly capturing markets and standard-setting, as recently documented by W. Brian Arthur in *Increasing Returns: Path Dependence in the Economy* (1994).

In addition, several Western cultural DNA code "strands" provided a climate that accelerated further the technological "colonization" of British, European, American, and eventually many other societies. These strands included a culture that rewarded scientific curiosity, the desire to dominate nature, and instrumental Cartesian/Newtonian reductionism, within a framework of patriarchy (which, as Boulding [1976] pointed out, forced generations of women inventors to take out their patents in their husbands' names and banned women from scientific societies and pursuits). The Luddite movement in Britain, famous for breaking the early machines because they took away jobs, was anything but mindless. Early industrialists were quite honest in their desires to "discipline" workers via fear of technological unemployment (Dickson 1974).

Thus it is not surprising that social efforts are still lagging behind and unable to control the rate and direction of technological innovation. Western societies are still unsuccessful in channeling these now powerfully institutionalized technological drives toward systemic, social, and ecological goals—despite social inventions such as the U.S. Office of Technology Assessment. Nowhere is this widening lag in social innovation more visible than in the growing gap between the explosion of computerized information highways, the Internet, multimedia, and the as-yet unregulated global financial trading. In 1995, Electronic Share Information, Ltd. (ESI) was launched in London; it bypasses stock exchanges and brokers and offers any personal computer (PC) owner access to trading small holdings at one-tenth the cost of the London Stock Exchange.[5] A similar firm, E-Trading, opened on Wall Street and offers trades directly to PC users at $19.95 per transaction. So far politicians, including U.S. Vice President Al Gore and Republican Speaker of the House Newt Gingrich, Britain's Tony Blair, and others have hailed these new technologies almost as social panaceas, overlooking monopolistic dangers of private companies capturing standardization processes—rather than standards being set by public, legal agreements. Presidential science advisor John H. Gibbons cautioned that regulation oversight was behind the curve, and tax evasion and money laundering would create new problems.[6] The "gee whiz" approach is also useful for diverting voters' attention from more intractable problems, such as the widening gaps between rich and poor—ironically evident in cyberspace as well.

Politicians, finance ministers, bankers, and international bodies, such as the Bank for International Settlements (BIS) and the International Monetary Fund (IMF), were forced by the 1995 headlines to beef up the needed regulatory regimes. This new regulatory framework is now essential; it must be global and as "real-time" as the markets themselves. Other issues concern privacy, electronic surveillance, encryption standards, copyright, and civil liberties.[7] Market players, including Bankers Trust former chairman Charles Sanford, envisioned the consequences of global information networks that can now bypass banks—allowing entrepreneurs seeking capital to simply upload their business plans onto the Internet.[8] Similarly, I predicted that financial TV channels will offer shows like "The Venture Capital

Show" and "The Initial Public Offering Show," complete with 800-numbers to complement existing electronic trading systems, such as Instinet, AutEx, and Reuters. By 1995 the Internet boasted its first electronic "E-cash" and "virtual bank," while business plans and small-cap companies were touted in the home pages of informal market makers, tip-sheet editors, and speculators—all beyond the reach of the Securities and Exchange Commission (SEC) and other regulators.[9] As the proletariat flocked to buy PCs and get on the traffic-jammed Internet, the big players switched to vBNS, the Very high-speed Backbone Network Service with 155 megabytes per second, run by MCI for the U.S. National Science Foundation. The vBNS, at ten thousand times the speed of the Internet, is for big science players who are "bored with the net."[10]

CRISES OF THE GLOBAL CASINO AS PARADIGM PROBLEMS

Today's abstracted world trade/global competitiveness model has alienated financial markets from the real economy of Main Street (where actual people in real factories produce real shoes or build real houses and grow real food). Thus, the global casino is now spinning off into cyberspace, divorced from any understanding of the whole picture: human societies cooperating and competing while interacting within webs of other species and ecosystems in a fragile, ever-changing biosphere. Emerging use of dynamic change models and systemic, ecological, and chaos paradigms can allow social innovation to catch up with rampant technological innovation, whether in computerized global financial markets or in cyberspace, to address the globalization of markets and industries and the management of common resources.[11] Such new paradigms, including those from game theory and psychology, extend beyond individualistic, scarcity/fear-based economic models of maximizing self-interest as "rational" behavior. The new paradigms reintegrate intellect, empathy, intuition, stewardship, and vision in caring for future generations, which allows a rebalancing of motives toward win-win cooperation. The new paradigms are now *conditions* for the shift of our financial systems, and increasingly cyberspace, too, from GNP-based, "trickle-down" economic growth to diversified, decentralized, "bubble-up," sustainable development, which reincentivizes mutual aid and cooperative informal sectors.

These paradigm shifts begin with rethinking scarcity, abundance, needs, and satisfaction, and lead inevitably to wholesale redefinitions of money, wealth, productivity, efficiency, and progress. However mind-blowing, a prerequisite of this new worldview is the understanding that *money isn't scarce* and that its apparent scarcity is itself a major social regulatory mechanism. Money systems were a major social innovation. When functioning well, money provides a beneficial circulatory system for wider human exchange beyond face-to-face barter. This brilliant social invention—designing markets as predominant resource-allocating systems—was adopted in seventeenth-century Britain by Parliament in a fiercely contested package of social legislation, over which a civil war was fought (Polanyi 1944). While Adam Smith noted correctly in his *An Inquiry into the Nature and Causes of the Wealth of Nations* (1776) that humans had, from the earliest times, exhibited "a propensity to barter," marketplace exchanges were localized. An often forgotten fact is that Adam Smith also recognized the need for rules and legislation, i.e., he held that markets could only function properly if (1) all players met in the marketplaces with equal power and information, and (2) no harm was caused to innocent bystanders. Humans make rules for their interactions as readily as they make markets.

In the eighteenth century, money transactions had only begun to replace earlier systems of human interaction and exchange: reciprocity, kinship, potlatches, mutual aid, and Aristotle's "just prices," as well as redistribution by kings, lords, the church, or simple fiat (feudalism, conquest, and slavery).[12] Kenneth Boulding (1968) noted that there are three basic kinds of human interactions: (1) *threat*, based on fear; (2) *exchange*, based on barter and reciprocity; and (3) *love*, based on gifts, altruism, and more comprehensive, long-term value systems. Humanistic psychologists have also noted that economic models based on scarcity fears can erode natural feelings of well-being and abundance, and even regress whole populations into excessive anxiety, stress, and unrealistic motivation for power, "success," wealth display, and other addictive behaviors.

Many of the operating principles derived from industrial paradigms remain unexamined: technological innovation is encouraged and subsidized; social innovation is suspect as "planning" and occurs only after crisis, such as the Great Depression. Society is assumed to be divided up into a private sector (market competition) and a public sector (government and nonprofits) with a Berlin Wall inhibiting interaction (buttressed by antitrust laws). Government is enjoined from "competing" with private-sector business. Meanwhile business lobbies governments to capture regulatory processes and tax codes: the familiar foxes guarding the chicken coop. Much creativity and inventiveness is dammed up behind the rigid definitions and restrictive institutions that operationalize the industrial paradigm. In preindustrial and traditional societies, most land and natural resources were held communally and known as "the commons"—i.e., the village green—as the common grazing land of England was known. From a systems viewpoint, markets are open systems with abundant resources that can be used individually and competitively, while commons are closed systems where resources are used indivisibly, such as national parks, air, oceans, satellite orbits, and the earth's electromagnetic spectrum. (See Fig. 20. Differing Models of Markets and Commons on page 271.)

Debates regarding the information superhighway typify the now bankrupt public-versus-private and market-versus-regulation polarization and are becoming confused and schizophrenic. For example, Wall Street analysts devoted to free markets characterize the telecommunications sector as balkanized and fragmented and needing national standardization in order to develop further. In addition, freedom in cyberspace attracts conservatives, such as U.S. House Speaker Gingrich, author George Gilder (a father of supply-side economics), and former Reagan science advisor George A. Keyworth, Jr., along with more futurist-oriented authors Michael Rothschild, Lewis Perleman, and Alvin and Heidi Toffler.[13] The Progress and Freedom Foundation, a U.S. neoconservative think tank aligned with Gingrich, promotes principles for the Information Age at conferences dominated by white, middle-class males—the predominant promoters and users of cyberspace. Most still see the issues in either/or terms: *either* rules and regulations, *or* freedom and markets. Not surprisingly, *The Economist*, while admitting that networks need common standards and acknowledging the dangers of private corporations like Microsoft capturing those standards, still opined that "For the time being at least, it may be more sensible to trust the market."[14]

Cyber-libertarians, who oppose regulation of the global information superhighways, use transitional hybrid paradigms. They justify deregulation by reimposing laissez-faire ideas and equating free enterprise technological evolution with the natural evolution of ecosystems. Meanwhile, they invoke chaos theory and system dynamics to prove that regulatory intervention is too unpredictable and that private regulation of the new networks, and even the capture of standard-setting, is simply the wisdom of the market. Yet regulation of cyberspace is inevitable. By 1995, the Internet was politicized by commercialism, junk mail, fraud, and theft involving dozens of lawsuits.[15] Even wealthy Telluride, Colorado, a pioneer of the information revolution reluctantly set regulations for its free public computer system, the InfoZone, after racist, pornographic, and libelous messages began proliferating.[16]

The chaotic global financial casino too, as well as the other new technological domains in cyberspace, will likely become even more unpredictable without some regulatory intervention. *The Economist*, in a July 1, 1995, survey, "The Internet: The Accidental Superhighway," projected various scenarios for the future of such open networks. Hybrid paradigms have grafted a dynamic update onto the "invisible hand" of neoclassical economics. Ironically, arbitrary forms of private regulation and censorship are becoming a real problem. As commercialism invades the Internet, regulators are rushing to devise "rules of the road" that limit freedom on information highways and in cyberspace—just as they have already done on commercial radio and TV. Will cyberspace be regulated as a new kind of common carrier (i.e., a commons) in order to prevent arbitrary, private rule making by servers such as America Online and Compuserve, or to prevent the capturing of standards by big players like telecommunication companies (telecoms) or Microsoft?

The tug-of-war in the United States is between regulation by the Federal Communications Commission (FCC) and successive waves of mergers and acquisitions leading to de facto national standardization via a private-sector oligopoly with little public accountability. In 1995 such mergers and captures of standardization by telecoms and media giants in the United States and Europe had consolidated their geopolitical power in the mediocracy. There is a long history of antitrust laws to prevent such centralized powerful monopolies from controlling and administering prices of essential utility services—in the United States and other OECD countries. Capturing the standard-setting process with a new industry or technology confers enormous, often monopoly, market power. However, an equally long history of government-owned or franchised *regulated* monopolies has shown similar abuses of power, special-interest influence, and price gouging. Today, the *potentially* decentralizing effects of information technology are jeopardized by the huge rewards these technologies confer on early entrants and standard-setting colonizers. Yet as discussed, in all human societies at all levels, rules of interaction are fundamental. It is only a matter of who, what, when, why, where, and how we choose to regulate ourselves. The "invisible hand" is a projection—obfuscating our own responsibilities and choices. Only more power to and feedback from users, voters, and organized civil society consumers can exert a democratizing influence.

The spreading democratic revolutions, also spawned by information technologies, are restructuring hierarchical, bureaucratic, monopolistic institutions—whether private megacorporations or malfunctioning government agencies. Yet unless we apply new paradigms, systemic models, and win-win standards and regulatory agreements, we cannot transcend the public-sector versus private-sector dichotomy. The rush to commercially colonize multimedia by telecoms, cable TV, and computer and entertainment companies, which resulted in the rash of mergers of the mid-1990s, is creating oligopolistic market situations. As mentioned in Chapter 5, giant communications conglomerates now control the world's attention. By late 1995, Disney-Capital Cities-ABC; Time-Warner; NBC-General Electric; Rupert Murdoch; and CBS-Westinghouse had emerged as the global giants. In all the hype around such mergers, the biggest of which was Disney-Capital Cities-ABC, there is hardly a mention of the need to upgrade content and public access, the possibilities of electronic town meetings, or how these technologies could perfect democracy and foster cultural evolution.

With information technologies we could design new methods of multilevel decision making within organizations based on systems principles, plugging in feedback and feedforward from users in a more democratic Information Age. Furthermore, the world's peoples could be linked at every level as producers and consumers by *information exchanges,* the world's new currencies. Information, unlike material goods, isn't scarce, which explains why economic theory based on scarcity cannot encompass information well. If you give me information, you still have it, and we are both richer for having shared it—a win-win proposition. In the Information Age, win-win games will gradually eclipse win-lose games.

More expansive, systemic frameworks are essential to reconceptualize today's great globalizations and the restructuring processes they engender. Three changing concepts help to put the rise of information societies and the eclipse of industrialism and its now dysfunctional economic paradigm into context:

1. The shift from conventional, materialist, equilibrium-based economics to chaos and systems modeling and game theory— i.e., the view that evolving, adaptive human information societies and their cultural DNA codes and decision processes exist within equally dynamic ecological systems governed by both positive and negative feedback loops. (See Fig. 2. Two Cybernetic Systems on page 14.) The worldwide rush of politicians to adopt markets and democracy is instinctively correct: complex societies are best governed by feedback from individual actors to decision centers at every level. As mentioned in Chapter 8 the two key forms of such feedback are *prices* and *votes*. But prices must be corrected to reflect social and environmental costs, while democracies must reflect choices of voters rather than rich, powerful, special-interest groups. Other forms of feedback are now necessary, including new indicators and statistics to measure outcomes and signal early warning, as well as mass media to amplify and spotlight such new issues and concerns. All economies today are "mixed," i.e., mixtures of markets and regulations.

2. The shift from equating human progress with quantitative GNP growth to embracing more complex goals related to quality of life and sustainable development. (See Chapter 10.) This requires reclassification of the economy beyond public versus private sector and beyond free market versus regulation, to encompass the rise of information-rich service and attention sectors. Examining the total productivity of social systems expands the mapping of productive sectors to include the civil society, the unpaid love economy, and the productivity of nature, all of which are currently hidden subsidies to the GNP-money-denominated public and private sectors. (See Fig. 8. Total Productive System of an Industrial Society on page 58.) Each society sets up the boundaries between sectors and rules of interaction according to its specific cultural DNA codes.

3. The shift from an economic model that views the private market and the public sector as totally separate to a systems model reflecting a view of markets as *open* systems and commons as *closed* systems. (See Fig. 1. Three Zones of Transition on page 10.) This shift clarifies policy options and new strategies for entrepreneurs. Most enterprises geared to meet today's needs and those of future sustainable development will require restructuring and cooperative linking in networks and consortia of *both* public and private actors as well as partnerships with civil society institutions.

BREAKUP OF THE GLOBAL MONEY CARTEL

Today we see the rise of nonmoney, information economies (local, regional, and global networks for barter, countertrade, reciprocity, and mutual aid) wherever macroeconomic management is failing in societies. From G-7 countries, including Canada, Britain, and Italy, to Russia and Eastern European countries, people are creating their own local information societies on the Internet and other networks, where users are increasing 25 percent per month. In the Washington, D.C., area, small businesses in bartering networks have increased from twelve hundred in 1990 to thirty-five hundred since 1995.[17] Businesses are issuing discount coupons and other scrip, just as cities all over the United States did during the Great Depression of the 1930s.

As democracy sweeps the planet, people everywhere see on satellite TV how politics, economics, money, and cultural traditions interact to control human affairs from the global to the local level. The global civil society, now linked electronically, is challenging both governments and corporations. Many in government and people at the local level realize the implications of the global Information Age: *money and information are now equivalent—if you have one, you can get the other.* In fact, information is often *more* valuable than money. Today, money often *follows* information (and sometimes misinformation). Markets are revealed as less than efficient because they ignore social and environmental costs and assume that people are rational only if they maximize their self-interest, rather than being driven by multiple, complex motivations. Indeed, psychology and game theory now often explain markets better than economics.

In 1994, I described how the global money monopoly was breaking up as it became more unstable with bouncing currencies, derivatives, and increasing volatility.[18] Governments can now go around the money monopoly and conduct sophisticated barter and countertrade deals directly (as do corporations) using computer-based trading systems similar to those that Chicago's commodity traders use. Since the mid-1980s I had been asking Southern Hemisphere officials why they did not act on this knowledge. Indeed, up to one-quarter of all world trade is already done this way according to some industry estimates. Thus, the "need to earn foreign exchange," which has hung over governments like a sword of Damocles, can now be lifted. Complicated four-, five-, and six-way trading deals between multiple partners can be executed with almost the ease of money. Computers record the audit trails of who promised to "pay" for which commodity in exchange for what other commodity on what dates—which is what money is and does anyway. I concluded that Western paradigms had dominated the minds of finance ministers in the South—unless they simply dreamed of *joining* the international financial "old boys network."

Money, essentially, is a unit of account entered on various ledgers to track and keep score of human production, services, and transactions as they interact with each other and nature's resources. As central bankers know, money is not scarce, and it can serve as a stable store of value if its supply is controlled to correspond with and track expanding production and exchange transactions. When governments and central banks supply too much money and spend or invest too much (beyond tax receipts) in short-term or unsustainable projects and public services, money loses its purchasing power: i.e., inflation. Budget deficits and minimal rates of inflation have been accepted by governments since John Maynard Keynes (1934) showed that some investment might be necessary to "prime the pump" for national economies, which could sink into an equilibrium at well below full employment. Economic theory is, however, notoriously deficient in providing any workable, repeatable formulas for how to invest *wisely* in creating future societal assets (whether the goal is healthy, educated citizens, productive infrastructure, or maintenance of natural resources and environmental quality). This is because economic theory still deems so many social and environmental costs "externalities"; these costs are not internalized on corporate or government balance sheets to arrive at full-cost prices.

As discussed in Chapters 2 and 4, national macroeconomic management tools (i.e., fiscal and monetary policies) become ever more erratic as national borders are swamped by waves of hot electronic money. People everywhere are realizing that money and credit are used also as *political tools* to create incentives and substitute for regulation. Aware grassroots globalists also know that money can no longer effectively be used as the major tool to denominate broader indicators of quality of life and progress or provide accurate data to manage national economies or the world trade system. Thus, grassroots nongovernmental organizations (NGOs) all over the world are now challenging the political underpinnings of the global financial system. This system has not been overhauled since its founding under the United Nations in 1945 at the famous Bretton Woods conference.

The Bretton Woods institutions—the World Bank, the International Monetary Fund (IMF), the General Agreement on Tariffs and Trade (GATT), as well as the Bank for International Settlements (BIS)—were hammered out to reflect conditions in the post–World War II era. Many compromises were made, such as excluding some countries from the GATT rather than creating a democratic, inclusive International Trade Organization (ITO) as was originally envisioned. Today these institutions still form the political machinery that undergirds the global economy. They are widely accused, not only by NGOs but also by many governments, of being undemocratic and skewed in favor of the already rich and powerful. Such views first consolidated in the Group of Seventy-Seven meeting in Lome, Togo, in 1972, where the global financial community heard the first shot ring out demanding a New International Economic Order (NIEO). OPEC then quadrupled the price of oil in 1973—the second salvo challenging the assumptions of the global money game.

Calls for democratizing the World Bank, the IMF, and the GATT (now the World Trade Organization or WTO), as well as opening up the still private BIS have grown out of the failure of the United Nations Third Development Decade (the 1980s). Instead of progress, this decade saw development in Africa, Asia, and Latin American bog down in mountains of unrepayable debt (often incurred by cronyism among international elites), widening gaps between rich and poor, and ecological devastation. The World Bank and the IMF's "structural adjustment loans" were conditional upon painful belt-tightening within the indebted countries so they could maintain interest payments on their debts. Given the undemocratic structure of many governments, such austerity programs squeezed the poor and powerless while protecting affluent, influential groups from hardship (Rich 1994).

South African banks provide an example of the use of new banking technologies to make things worse in poor neighborhoods. Standard Bank's new E-Bank and Nedcor Bank's Peoples Bank offer limited, automated services to the poor. Using state-of-the-art technology to replace labor costs with machines, they offer their customers plastic smart-cards that are recognizable by thumbprint in their cash machines. The government underwrites some of these banks' risks even though they only offer minimal services and a few small home loans.[19] In the United States, First Chicago Bank's attempt to further automate by imposing a $3 fee on all face-to-face customer transactions misfired. This new service charge resulted in many withdrawals.[20]

The demands for overhauling the UN's Bretton Woods financial institutions culminated in 1994 with the global, grassroots campaign "Fifty Years Is Enough" to actually shut down the World Bank. This campaign did produce some reforms by 1995. Protests will become more strident as more people see that money is not in short supply and that credits and liquidity often follow politics. Relief in the form of credit, debt cancellation, or a new issue of Special Drawing Rights (SDRs), sometimes known as "paper gold," could be made available more widely and equitably through the IMF and the World Bank, instead of just to governments or to shore up powerful national alliances or pander to central bankers, bond traders, and other special interests.[21] Democratic reformers seek wider access to credit for private groups, local enterprises, villages, and many other NGOs and communities for local "bubble-up" development. Campaigns to democratize the secretive governance of the World Bank, the IMF, and the WTO will persist until their political assumptions are teased out of their economic models and their relationships with governments, banks, securities traders, stock exchanges, and bond holders are made clearer.

LOCAL INFORMATION SOCIETIES CAN BECOME NEW SOCIAL SAFETY NETS

As the crises and failures of macroeconomic management become more evident worldwide, people at the grassroots are rediscovering the oldest, most reliable safety net: the nonmoney, pure information economy. All human societies are information societies and have always operated on sharing information — from gestures to language, from smoke signals to today's telephones, faxes, and the Internet. Information is thus more basic than money to human transactions and trade (Henderson 1981). As described, over half the world's production, consumption, exchange, investments, and savings is conducted outside the money economy — even in industrial countries. For example, eighty-nine million American men and women volunteer an average of five hours each week, saving taxpayers millions in social programs.[22] (See Fig. 8. Total Productive System of an Industrial Society on page 58.) Meanwhile, OECD countries face stubbornly high average unemployment rates.

In many developing countries, the official money-denominated economies tracked by national accounts and GNP are less than one-third of all the economic activity of these often traditional subsistence economies and societies. No wonder many World Bank and other development projects failed when they overlooked these nonmoney sectors. Worldwide, people are responding to economic "shock treatments" and worsening national debt pragmatically — by reinventing barter, alternative currencies, community exchange, consumer-contracted agriculture, and mutual aid, often assisted by computers, radio, and phone banks. Most economic textbooks excoriate such informal local economies as backward or inefficient and ignore the rich history of such information-based alternatives to central banks and national currencies.

Independent, urban money systems have always flourished whenever central governments mismanaged national affairs. Such alternative currencies are catalogued in *Depression Scrip of the United States* by Ralph Mitchell and Neil Shafer (1984), which documents the hundreds of American cities and cities in Canada and Mexico that recovered from 1930s unemployment by issuing their own money. Earlier examples were based on the theories of economist Silvio Gesell and included the City of Worgl in Austria and the Channel Islands of Jersey and Guernsey off the southern coast of Britain. All three became enclaves of prosperity and survived botched national policies of the period. Today, Jersey and Guernsey still survive as examples of how independent, local credit and money systems can maintain full employment, public services, and low inflation.

In the United States in the 1890s, a local barter system flourished in Cincinnati, Ohio, called the Time Store—a forerunner of many of today's local exchange systems. Other local currencies in the United States included the "constant" issued in Exeter, New Hampshire, in 1972 and 1973 by economist Ralph Borsodi and World Business Academy fellow Terrence Mollner, following the monetary theories of Irving Fisher. The equivalent of $160,000 was in circulation. The constant was to have been backed by a basket of commodities, but Borsodi's death ended the Exeter experiment.[23] Another U.S. commodity-backed currency was "energy dollars" issued by the Technocracy movement that flourished in the 1950s. In addition, a large network has grown in the United States in the past decade seeking to reform debt-backed, bank-created U.S. dollars, to smooth the boom-bust cycles they create, by reforming the Federal Reserve Act of 1913, which handed over to the twelve private member-banks of the Federal Reserve System the power to issue currency and to return the exercise of that power to Congress.

Today, ordinary people are not sitting idle hoping centralized economic managers can help them. Local communities see the confusion at the top and are not waiting. In Russia, as the ruble declined, barter and flea markets became pragmatic substitutes. Oil flows from Kiev, Ukraine, to Hungary in exchange for trucks, and Russian engineers design power plants in exchange for Chinese coal. The big lesson of the Information Age is being learned: information can substitute for artificially scarce money. Information networks operate barter systems in the United States worth $7.6 billion per year. The number of U.S. companies engaged in barter services has increased from one hundred in 1974 to six hundred in 1993. These barter companies, according to AT WORK newsletter, range from the Barter Corporation, a trade exchange network in the Chicago area, to Ron Charter of Costa Mesa, California, which exchanges recycled appliances and sports equipment for Green Card credits good toward payment for goods and services at more than two hundred participating businesses in Orange County. Some of these exchanges are for education and health care of employees. Goods bartered range from trucks, office furniture, and carpeting to clothing, travel, hotel rooms, and dental and optical services.[24] At the local level, barter clubs now keep track of credit, investment, and exchange transactions. These information networks function like commodity exchanges, just as payment unions and trade agreements do for governments. These nonmoney and scrip-based economies are leading indicators signaling the decline of macroeconomic management.

Such decentralized, local ingenuity still alarms bankers and central monetary authorities. In the past, local currencies and ad hoc, alternative economies have been stamped out by governments as illegal or as tax dodges. Yet whenever local producers and consumers are faced with hyperinflation of national currencies or jobless economic growth policies, they resort to pragmatic ways of clearing local markets, creating employment, and fostering community well-being. These new local information societies are not only attempts to create safety nets and homegrown economies, but are a resurgence of kinship systems. Thus they are understood better from anthropological and cultural perspectives than from an economic viewpoint as financial/currency systems (an excessively reductionist view).

Local information societies are rooted in the love economy; they derive from systems of reciprocity, mutual aid, and self-reliance in traditional societies and are based on attempts to reknit community bonds.[25] Now that information has become the world's primary currency both on international computer trading screens and in local PC networks and exchange clubs, people are at last beginning to understand money itself. For example, grassroots groups in many countries have endorsed a Global Resource Bank (GRB) whose charter is based on that of the IMF, except that the new GRB will make credit available to individuals, towns, and enterprises—not just national governments.[26]

Organizers of local and informal economies have realized that if central bankers, the "croupiers" of national economies, can't provide the needed "chips" (i.e., money supply, credit, and liquidity) for local people to complete their trades and transactions, then alternative local chips and information systems can fill the gap. When commercial barter is profitable, local groups are even willing to pay taxes to municipalities in local currencies, and to national authorities in cash, even though exchanging community services in mutual aid is generally exempt. While it is potentially useful to amplify these grassroots exchanges and extend their benefits to more communities, immediate problems arise in interfacing with the more powerful, competitive market and financial institutions. Governments will want to tax local exchange, while banks and companies may see these new grassroots networks merely as potentially profitable new markets—thus missing their love economy traditions of trust and mutual aid.

Today economists and bankers, after fighting such local initiatives, may need to rely on them to stabilize sputtering national economies. But attempts to co-opt or competitively exploit these homegrown, safety-net systems will rapidly shrink them or drive them underground. As with all currencies, trust is the factor that gives value. We must believe in our money or it becomes worthless. Interfaces with market sectors can develop only as far as trust is established: market competitors must respect the community's cooperative codes of conduct and honor community concerns and values. For example, decision making and rules must be democratic and participatory; management and transactions must be open and transparent; scrip currencies must be free of manipulation, brokering, and other inflationary influences; and grievance procedures, as well as all relevant codes of conduct and rules, must be clear and posted.

Following are some examples of this new global trend:

- One of the oldest, most sophisticated, member-owned cooperative exchange systems is Switzerland's WIR-Messen, now fifty years old. Its thousands of members receive the full-color, glossy monthly *WIR Magazin*, replete with hundreds of ads for a vast range of goods and services from insurance, banking, credit, and transport to manufactured goods: computers, furniture, and luxury items from furs to antiques. These are all offered for sale in the cooperative's scrip: WIRs. In 1993, trades conducted in WIRs were equivalent to 19.7 million Swiss francs. Articles in the *WIR Magazin* celebrate such statistics as well as the group's achievements in creating thousands of jobs and many new businesses, and fostering community self-help programs in Bern, Zurich, St. Gallen, Lucerne, Lenzburg, and other Swiss cities. WIR-Messen maintains a very low profile, even though its network now includes as members a large number of Swiss companies willing to accept WIRs at least partially interchangeably with Swiss francs.

  A problem of inflation of the WIR currency did occur as some of the member enterprises accumulated the scrip and began trading WIRs at a 40 percent discount for Swiss francs, according to economist Hank Monrobey.[27] WIR-Messen's management responded with aggressive action against members' unauthorized trading—causing dissension in the cooperative. Nevertheless, this middle-class WIR network has continually interfaced with the dominant market economy while managing to maintain its cooperative value system.

- The Seikatsu Club of Yokohama, Japan, is a consumer cooperative founded by Japanese women over twenty years ago to contract with local farmers to produce organically grown fruits and vegetables. Seikatsu has now grown into a multimillion-dollar network of farmers, canners, food preparers, and distributors linked directly by truck deliveries to hundreds of thousands of consumers. Its principles include a holistic view of life and world harmony based on cooperation, not competition. The club is committed to small farmers and producers; a safer, healthier environment (through use of their nonpolluting soap products); and empowerment of workers and women. Costs of organically grown and prepared foods are kept minimal via collective buying contracts and by offering a single brand of each of the club's four hundred food products.

  Seikatsu is one of about seven hundred similar co-ops in Japan and one of Japan's larger investors in nonprofit production companies. Seikatsu has spread into many local, autonomous groups composed of from six to thirteen families called *han*. By 1987, thirty-one Seikatsu members had become elected public officials in Yokohama, Tokyo, and Chiba. Seikatsu has also been able to blend with Japan's dominant, competitive economy without losing either its social concern or its vision of building a cooperative, peaceful world. Indeed, Seikatsu's members travel the world articulating their vision at many meetings and forums.

- In Britain, over two hundred Local Exchange Trading Systems (LETS) are either operating or in the launch process in such regional towns as Bristol, Cardiff, Manchester, Sheffield, and Swindon, according to LETS LINK.[28] The Totnes, Devon, LETS now provides instruction on ecological economics, taught by this author and others at Schumacher College. LETS, founded in Vancouver, Canada, by social entrepreneur Michael Linton, links communities via phone banks and personal computer bulletin boards where people post notices of the services and goods they need and have to offer in trade. The computers keep account of the transactions and each system names its own unit of account, such as "links" instead of pounds. Some two hundred LETS systems are operating in Australia, where the First National Conference on LETS was held in 1992. In New Zealand, the largest LETS is in Auckland and now has over two thousand members and a forty-five-person staff, all paid in its own currency: Green Dollars.

• In the United States, where at least fifty million consumers participate in cooperative enterprises,[29] a new scrip system— Service Credits or Time Dollars, invented by law professor Edgar Cahn of the University of Miami—has been introduced in retirement communities in Florida and in New York City.[30] Time Dollars allow people who wish to help their neighbors and volunteer for community service to register their hours worked in a central computer account system. Then they may call on the system when they need help and arrange for another Time Dollar volunteer to assist them.

The potential of such service-credit systems is enormous for cities wishing to put unemployed people to work on local rehabilitation and community service programs. For example, city governments could issue City Credit Cards to unemployed people who sign up. As they earn work credits on city projects, people could use their City Credit Cards to ride local public transit or for admission to parks, libraries, recreation facilities, and any other city-supported training and education programs. This would allow cities to capture fuller value from their tax- and bond-issue-supported local infrastructure and services— many of which have periods of underutilization as well as "peak load" problems. A vacant bus seat is a loss that can be partially recovered—even if it is filled by a rider using discounted Time Dollars or a City Credit Card. Local Chambers of Commerce, restaurant associations, and others could cooperate in City Credit Card programs by offering cut-rate tickets to local cinemas and attractions or discounts on meals at participating restaurants during slow business periods. The same is true for private-sector hotel rooms and, of course, airline seats—now being filled by private scrip systems, i.e., frequent flyer programs. All such scrip, whether discount coupons or other awards, rebates, and so on, are subject to abuses, such as unauthorized resale.

The City of Curitiba, Brazil, and its innovative mayor, Jaime Lerner, became world famous for instituting many such local programs linking the city's unemployed and poor to unmet city needs, such as street cleanups and garbage recycling, and at the same time allowing citizens fuller use of city buses and services in return. In 1986 at a public symposium, "Money, Myth, and Manna," sponsored by the Dallas Institute of Culture and Humanities, I urged the city of Dallas, Texas, to create a "Dallas Money Card" program. At that time, the city's economy was depressed by low oil prices and high unemployment—but the concept was too unfamiliar.

Fig. 16.   Ithaca Money

For information on how to start a local version, write to
Ithaca Money, P.O. Box 6578, Ithaca, New York 14851.

• *Ithaca Money* is a community newspaper/directory in Ithaca, New York, the hometown of Cornell University. The directory lists all businesses and services that accept payment in Ithaca Hours, ranging from architects, accountants, car repair, computer services, catering, and chiropractors to grocery stores, heating and air conditioning services, sheet metal work, restaurants, and trucking. The Alternatives Federal Credit Union, in operation since 1980, has over a thousand members and makes loans in Ithaca Hours (worth $10 each). This cooperative exchange system has received nationwide attention on television and from the libertarian radio news syndication, "The Paul Harvey Show." Key theorist and organizer, Paul Glover, reports that three hundred kits designed to help other communities have been sent out. Grateful letters of thanks have come in from places as diverse as Ulan Bator, Mongolia; Ankara, Turkey; Bujumbura, Burundi; Ferguson, Missouri; and the Kootenay Barter Bank in Nelson, B.C., Canada.[31] By 1995, Ithaca had inspired Lehigh Valley Barter Hours in Bethlehem, Pennsylvania, while Boulder Hours in Colorado, Santa Fe Hours in New Mexico, and Kansas City Barter Bucks still flourish along with others networked by local Green Parties and other activists, including Tom Greco, author of *New Money for Healthy Communities* (1994).

- In Ahmedabad, India, Nandini Joshi, a Harvard Ph.D. economist who wrote *The Challenge of Poverty* in 1978, now helps a nearby village to barter their local goods, services, and employment via the Hank Bank, which stores the hanks of local cotton grown and spun in the village. Dr. Joshi has designed a much-simplified version of Gandhi's famous spinning wheel, which any poor or unemployed villager can make with wooden sticks and simple fasteners. Thus, even children, shut-ins, the old, or the infirm can meet their needs by spinning—a task that many enjoy. They exchange their hanks of thread for rice, flour, and many other local foods and commodities. Such simple solutions to local self-reliance are invisible to World Bank economists.[32]

- Commonweal, Inc., of Minneapolis, Minnesota, is a privately held, for-profit corporation founded in 1993, now in its experimental phase. Commonweal's founder, Joel Hodroff, has developed an innovative dual currency that combines service credits with a scrip called CEDS (Community Economic Development Scrip, pronounced "seeds"). The scrip will be backed by the to-be-contracted discounted goods and services provided by a variety of local businesses. This system combines the best features of several alternative currencies into a Currency Exchange Network (CEN). The CEN pilot project has gained important local endorsers, including bankers, trade associations, and the influential Minnesota Center for Corporate Responsibility. Like other local exchange systems, the CEN links the city's consumers, workers, and volunteers in church and service clubs and the United Way with employment and consumer opportunities via a special plastic debit and credit card that accesses all members of the network.

The CEN can organize diverse sectors of Minneapolis' economy into a "win-win" commons, where all parties benefit. Businesses gain new customers while utilizing overhead fixed costs more fully for greater profitability. Citizens find productive work and increase their buying power. Sponsoring organizations (schools, churches and synagogues, labor unions, etc.) earn referral fees every time one of their members makes a purchase with the card. The CEN modifies such standard business tools as frequent flyer miles and cause-related marketing (e.g., buying Girl Scout cookies), and encourages consumers, as in a buying club, to make purchases within the network to benefit the community. The CEN requires neither tax nor charitable subsidies because it leverages excess productive capacity, whether in businesses or hospitals, colleges or restaurants, to produce needed goods and services at affordable prices while creating additional jobs. Commonweal, Inc., is patenting its computer software that keeps track of the service credits people earn and handles all of the plastic card transactions.

Like all other local exchange systems, the success of Commonweal, Inc., will hinge on the preservation of its kinship, love-economy base and the cooperation of all the diverse members, which will require clearly spelled-out codes of conduct, rules, and principles, which have been found essential in operating such systems elsewhere.[33] The new information currencies are shattering all our former assumptions about central banks, money, credit, liquidity, and trade, as well as rearview-mirror efforts to reimpose scarcity and reinvent traditional money on the Internet. Fast-moving information has end-run fiscal and monetary tools, and calls into question how deficits should be calculated as well as other macroeconomic management models, statistical apparatus, and conventional measures of progress. The debate about democratizing the global financial system and the Information Age has begun in earnest—joined by all the grassroots pragmatists who bring their experience in solving its shortcomings on the ground.

CHAPTER 10

REDEFINING WEALTH
AND PROGRESS:
THE NEW INDICATORS

Companies and the marketplace are assuming new roles and responsibilities in all mature industrial countries. In Europe, the United States, and some other countries, they call it stakeholder capitalism or the social market; in Japan it is "Japanese capitalism"; while Scandinavian countries have their own distinctive brands of mixed-market economies. Markets are developing both social conscience and environmental awareness. As privatizations continue in the European Union, Eastern Europe, Russia, Latin America, Asia, and increasingly in Africa, we see many cultural ways, means, and faces of a new kind of hybrid capitalism. How can linear balance sheets and economists' categories keep track of communities of stakeholders and seamless circular processes? By the 1950s, social scientists and statisticians together with natural scientists began documenting social costs and the systemic, circular nature of complex economies. Certainly, domination of the news by the single, money-based scorecard of GNP/GDP exacerbates the problem.

Many entrepreneurs and small-business owners ask, "Is there nothing beyond endless competition in today's global economic rat race?" "Must the spoils continue to go to the fastest players with the cheapest labor force, those who care least about human rights, community, and environmental values?" "How could a socially responsible company operate, let alone remain profitable in such a competitive global playing field?" To these questions from concerned young capitalists and many leaders in the public and private sectors and the civil society add

"Whose responsibility is it to keep score and set the rules of the road in the new global financial markets and cyberspace of the Internet?" "Who is responsible for volatile markets and currencies?" "Domestically, should the national, state, or local levels of government be responsible to set standards for health, human rights, poverty, law enforcement, immigration, working conditions, and consumer and environmental protection?" Citizens ask, "Under what circumstances should investors be bailed out by taxpayers? We have endured the Savings and Loan mess, the financial meltdown in Orange County, California, and the Mexican peso debacle; we have watched the dollar nose-dive and the collapse of Britain's Barings Bank."[1]

Government officials, business executives, academics, and hundreds of thousands of civic organizations are beginning to agree that we humans have been confusing *means* (i.e., GNP growth) with *ends*—human development and the survival and further progress of our species under drastically changed planetary conditions. The current recipe for economic growth has been increasingly questioned, along with scorekeeping methods that compare national GNP (or the narrower domestic version, GDP). Statistics, however objective and accurate, are never value free but draw attention to what various societies deem important goals and values. We measure what we treasure and vice versa. Statistics change our worldview and what we pay attention to. Global events are driving changes in scorecards, statistics, and quality-of-life indexes, which will redefine wealth and progress and change the future direction of human societies on earth.

For example, in 1993 the speedup of global currency speculation forced the IMF to shift from per-capita-income-denominated GDP to purchasing power parities (PPPs) in order to compare actual living standards (i.e., how much a loaf of bread costs a Russian compared with the cost of a similar loaf in the United States). This change catapulted China into third place, after the United States and Japan, in the world economy. In addition, waves of privatizations in many countries in the past decade have made adding capital assets into GNP more urgent, as well as to account for public infrastructure and investments—currently expensed as "spending." So far, only New Zealand and Switzerland have launched new net-worth GDP accounts. Capital asset account budgeting, such as that of state governments in the United States, allows more accurate deficit calculations and is now being debated in the U.S. Congress, but is not yet included in national GNP figures.

Costs of GNP growth are now obvious—from felled forests, pollution, exhausted soils, depleted natural resources, and holes in the ozone layer, to disrupted cultures and communities. At the 1992 United Nations Earth Summit in Rio de Janeiro, 178 countries signed the *Agenda 21* agreement to halt and begin to reverse this disruption of natural and social processes by correcting their GDPs. Furthermore, GNP/GDP figures do not allow for easy cross-country comparisons on important policy issues, such as ratio of military to civilian spending within a budget or spending on education, health, and so on, since the figures are an aggregation. These policy concerns created a market for the successful Human Development Index (HDI), of the United Nations Development Programme (UNDP), discussed on page 233 of this chapter. The 1995 UN World Economic and Social Survey records an average 7.2 percent decrease in military spending in all regions between 1988 and 1993. The biggest drop was in the former Warsaw Pact countries, averaging over 22 percent per year, while in the United States the drop was 4.4 percent. The Latin American countries are the lowest military spenders at less than 2 percent of GDP.[2]

Press stories underline today's political and cultural confusion as we redesign our statistics, reengineer our corporations, reinvent our government, recycle our concepts and material resources, and reshape our public debate to fit new realities. Rapid global change has caught us with our paradigms down. Bipartisan national opinion polls in 1993 and 1994 by the nonprofit Americans Talk Issues Foundation found that over 79 percent of Americans said "yes" to the statement, "In the same way we've developed and used the Gross National Product to measure the growth of the economy should we develop and use a scorecard of new indicators for holding politicians responsible for progress toward *other* national goals, like improving education and health care, preserving the environment, and making the military meet today's needs."[3]

Following are some of the news headlines and stories that illustrate the need for a broader set of benchmarks to clarify our public discourse.

A $150 Billion Question: Is the CPI Accurate?
—John M. Berry, *Washington Post* (February 12, 1995)

The CPI (Consumer Price Index) is often used by the Federal Reserve Board to signal coming inflation. Many economists agree that the CPI overstates inflation from .5 to 1.5 percent. However, some argue that if the CPI were to be adjusted downward, the Federal Reserve Board would also have to recalibrate its NAIRU (Non-Accelerating Inflation Rate of Unemployment). This would allow the economy to move closer to full employment before the Federal Reserve would need to damp things down by hiking interest rates.

On the other hand, as this *Washington Post* story points out, instead of recalibrating the NAIRU, Federal Reserve chairman Alan Greenspan called for using the downward revision of the CPI as a means to hold down Social Security benefits and other cost of living increases and thereby to reduce the deficit. "House Speaker Gingrich warned that if the Labor Department bureaucrats (who calculate the CPI) could not 'get it right' they should be 'zeroed out' in thirty days." Another headline in *Business Week* countered "The CPI: Why Politicians Should Butt Out," pointing out accurately that the CPI overstates some inflation, but understates other sources, as I and others have pointed out, since it does not account for environmental goods.[4] This paradigm debate became part of the 1995 budget battle.

Two Families' Stories:
In the Middle of the Middle
— David Wessel and Bob Davis, *Wall Street Journal*
(March 29, 1995)

In this story, the lives of Jim and Ann-Marie Blentlinger and Dennis and Martha Ann Kerley, all of whom live in Chattanooga, Tennessee, are compared. Who is living better—the Blentlingers, who earned about $43,000 last year, or the Kerleys, who earned about $12,500 a year two decades ago?

"By most material measures life in the middle today is better than back in 1974. Contrary to popular belief, incomes for husband-and-wife families have risen. The inflation-adjusted income of the typical two-parent family has increased 10 percent since 1974. Still, there is this economic reality too: things required to produce a modern middle-class life—two working spouses and more debt—create anxiety. Americans living on median incomes see—rightly—a widening gap between themselves and the best-off Americans." The story goes on to describe this gap, mostly in terms of the quality of their lives.

Myth: Americans Are Working More.
Fact: More Women Are Working.
—Gene Epstein, *Barron's* (April 3, 1995)

"Are Americans overworked with less leisure than they had twenty years ago? Yes and no." A study by economists at the Federal Reserve Bank of Cleveland cites the gender gap: "When a married woman moves into the workplace, her total number of hours worked (including housework) increases substantially. But whether or not a man's wife works, his work week remains about the same. . . . In 1988 when a woman chose to enter the labor force her total hours worked jumped from 32.2 to 57.3 hours per week. But her husband's total hours worked increased from only 50.2 to 52.2 per week. Who said life was fair?"

The Issue Isn't the Deficit: It's Wealth and Well-Being
—James K. Glassman, *Washington Post* (February 13, 1994)

This story points out that GNP focuses on cash flows in the economy and does not as yet have a separate capital asset account to show national wealth on our balance sheet: roads, ports, public buildings, parks, and other infrastructure owned by all taxpayers.

"Congratulations. You're rich! Yes, according to the just-released Budget of the United States Government, you, Mr. or Ms. Average American, have a net worth of $195,300. This $50 trillion estimate of our total net worth (the pie from which our individual $195,300 slices are cut) puts the subject of deficits in perspective.

"The deficit—the annual difference between what the federal government spends and what it collects in taxes—represents less than 1/2 of 1 percent of the nation's assets. Even the national debt, which is the total of all the deficits of all years of this country's existence, is a mere 8 percent of our wealth.

"To evaluate this level of debt, consider that for a corporation, a debt-to-equity ratio of 40 percent is considered pretty good. The point of the exercise, which was conducted by the Office of Management Budget, was not to play down the perils of deficits but to construct a framework—a scorecard—for determining whether government operations have contributed to the nation's current and future well-being."

Price of Pleasure: New Legal Theorists Attach a Dollar Value to the Joys of Living
—Paul M. Barrett, *Wall Street Journal* (December 12, 1988)

"The best things in life may be free. But the way Stanley V. Smith figures it, they can be worth a bundle, nonetheless. The simple joys of living—baseball, hot dogs, apple pie and such—have real and substantial monetary value, the 42-year old Chicago economist and former investment advisor believes.

"And because he is willing to swear to that in a courtroom, he is stirring up more than a little conflict inside the legal establishment these days. . . . Mr. Smith is the high-priest of 'hedonic damages' urging juries in death-related law suits to award huge sums to the estates of victims deprived of the pleasure of life.

"Usually, payment in death cases is based on what the victim might have earned in the future. But life is more than a paycheck, argues Mr. Smith: 'We are worth more than we earn.' "

The World Bank Announces a New "System of National Accounts"
—World Bank Press Release (February 1994)

This new system of national accounts (as the GNP is known officially) had been developed by the World Bank in cooperation with major international statistical agencies. The Bank stated: "A new focus on the role of people in the economy is embodied in social accounting. . . . Environmental concerns are recognized, such as the use of depleting natural resources and the costs of environmental degradation which adversely affect human health."

The Wealth of Nations: A "Greener" Approach Turns List Upside Down
—Peter Passell, *New York Times* (September 19, 1995)

The World Bank's September 1995 release of its new Wealth Accounting System dealt another death blow to the now increasingly discredited GNP. The World Bank's new index includes four kinds of assets as the real wealth of nations: (1) Natural Capital: natural environmental resources; (2) Produced Assets: factories, infrastructure, financial assets; (3) Human Resources: educated, healthy, productive people; (4) Social Capital: families, communities, institutions. These new rankings identify at least 60 percent of the wealth of nations as human and social resources, with some 20 percent attributed to the assets of nature, and the balance of 20 percent or less attributed to "produced assets" on which economists and national policies have hitherto focused almost exclusive attention.

The World Bank's wealth rankings (using 50 percent of market prices for natural resources) bumped Australia and Canada to the top ranking of per capita wealth. This kind of market evaluation is certainly more realistic than GNP's zero. Using replacement costs will prove optimal for long-term evaluation. The first "green" GDP in the United States, released in 1994, accounted for natural wealth in perverse ways, which triggered the current debate about whether placing market values on natural assets would *accelerate* rather than slow their depletion. This was a hot button at the World Bank's October 1995 conference on measuring sustainable development—defined as development that meets the needs of the current generation while maintaining similar opportunities for future generations to meet their own needs.

The news that major statistical agencies have published new guidelines for figuring GNP is welcomed. The U.S. Commerce Department announced yet another overhaul of GDP in July 1995, which showed a slowdown in growth and productivity, amid howls from the business community that the department was still under-counting the new information sectors.[5] Clearly, hard work and much public debate will be needed in every country in the world before GNP accounts are recalculated to reflect the great global changes that now need incorporating into updated scorecards of national progress. Meanwhile, the International Accounting Standards Committee is working hard to harmonize national accounting rules by the end of the century, so that investors can better compare companies' performance.[6]

NEW INDICATORS ENCOURAGE SUSTAINABILITY

The emergence in the mid-1990s of new indicators redefining wealth and progress alerted us to new problems and is slowly changing the direction of human societies toward sustainability. Preeminent is the Human Development Index (HDI) of the United Nations Development Programme (UNDP), which ranks 173 countries by a measure that combines life expectancy, educational attainment, and basic purchasing power. The UNDP's public dissemination of its annual HDI editions since 1990 has created unprecedented levels of press attention. Wide interest in the HDI has included much controversy: for example, its Human Freedom Index was criticized by many developing countries as being biased toward Western values. *Human Development Report, 1992* brought indicators of the global poverty gap to public view; *Human Development Report, 1993* identified jobless economic growth; *Human Development Report, 1994* highlighted human security and sustainable development criteria; and *Human Development Report, 1995* dealt with global gender inequalities. The re-ranking of countries according to such noneconomic quality-of-life factors received major media coverage. There are now domestic Human Development Reports in thirty nations, announced by James Gustave Speth, UNDP's administrator, in August 1995.

Some developing countries see human rights and other social and environmental indicators as leading to another set of conditionalities that the World Bank, the IMF, and Northern bankers could add to their loans—increasing the pain of structural adjustments of their economies. Yet in eighty-seven countries, as noted in Chapter 8, human rights, particularly for women, are now correlated with improvements in everyone's quality of life. Such indicators can also pinpoint problems, such as the 8.5 percent rise in the prison population in the United States in 1994—up to 1,053,738, the highest in the world.[7] The new indicators can help expose the current hypocrisy of the Bretton Woods institutions, pointed out by K. Tomasevski in *Rethinking Bretton Woods* (Griesgraber 1994); the institutions have become vulnerable to logical and moral demands for greater democracy, financial accountability, and the restructuring that they have prescribed for others. As they incorporate the new social and environmental indicators, the Bretton Woods institutions themselves can be held more accountable.

Another issue raised by the new indicators is how to value people, at last seen as the real wealth of nations, in national accounts called "human capital." Clearly, the shift from material to service and attention economies makes this change urgent. Here again, economics was an obstacle, valuing people by the money they earn: those who earn more money are more valuable people than those who earn less. Many economists have now linked value with education—a better approach.[8]

The milestone *System of National Accounts, 1993,* published in February 1994, reflects the official rethinking of its sponsoring organizations, the World Bank, the IMF, the OECD, the European Commission, and the United Nations Statistical Division. The new System of National Accounts (SNA) offers many useful protocols for integrating social and environmental statistics into expanded national accounting frameworks. It still has many shortcomings, however, including its treatment of labor force participation, the informal sectors, household services, women's work, and the vital and equal role women have played and will continue to play in human development, as pointed out by Lourdes Urdaneta-Ferran (Griesgraber 1994).

Indeed, a paradigm shift has occurred at the World Bank (not yet translated into action): women are now seen as key actors in development, and investment in their education is seen as bringing high payoffs. The North-South Roundtable, in its report *The United Nations and the Bretton Woods Institutions* (September 1993), recommended a new UN Agency for the Advancement of Women. Similarly, population demographers and policymakers now acknowledge that empowering women is the best contraceptive. Women in the United States now own 8 million businesses, emplying 18.5 million, or one in four American workers[9] and start new businesses at twice the rate of men. While big businesses employment in the United States declined by over 7 percent between 1987 and 1992, employment in small, locally based firms grew by 5 percent, and such female businesses now account for 10 percent of all new U.S. jobs according to Dun and Bradstreet.[10]

The *System of National Accounts, 1993* still emphasizes market-derived data with highly imperfect pricing, translated into money coefficients that undervalue environmental resources and obscure the full dimensions of "defensive" expenditures. For example, the pollution control/environmental industry, a major new employer, is estimated worldwide as increasing from $200 billion in 1990 to $300 billion by the year 2000 just to ameliorate the "bads" that come along with the goods. Some of these costs will be subtracted from GNP/GDP so as to arrive at new net indexes. The OECD reports that the United States spent 2 percent of GDP on environmental protection with no evidence that it has affected national economic growth and competitiveness.[11]

The UN's Statistical Division's new *Handbook of National Accounting*, 1993 addresses some of these issues with a new statistical alphabet soup that offers EDP (Environmentally Adjusted Net Domestic Product); ENI (Environmentally Adjusted National Income); SNI (Sustainable National Income); and FISD (Framework of Indicators for Sustainable Development). The UN's Statistical Division, the World Bank, and many national bureaus of economic analysis agree that many social and environmental statistics cannot and should not be aggregated into expanded GNP-type single indexes, such as EDP. Instead, they recommend new data be offered as "satellite accounts," unfortunately implying less importance. Peter Bartelmus addresses the new issues for the UN Statistical Division:

> EDP could be used to define sustainable economic growth in operational terms as: increases in EDP (which allows for the consumption of produced and the depletion and degradation of natural resources), assuming that the allowances made can be invested into capital maintenance and taking into account that past trends of depletion and degradation can be offset or mitigated by technological progress, discovery of natural resources, and changes in consumption patterns.[12]

Such tortured definitions still beg a host of questions about such single indexes: how will the public be told about such assumptions underlying EDP, or how economists and bureaucrats weighted all of these factors? How will balance sheet boundaries be drawn between aggregate production and tax-supported social programs dealing with family stress and illness that increase with rising unemployment due to corporate layoffs to bolster productivity and profits? All of the public and private costs economists call "defensive expenditures" are still averaged into GDP as more economic growth (because they do create jobs and profits), even while compounding rates of environmental and social disruption. Here, the paradigm problems concern the linear, input-output models of economics and their compartmentalizing of highly interactive circular economic processes in arbitrary boxes and boundaries. Similarly, GNP/GDP double-entry bookkeeping concepts and other macroeconomic categories can no longer clarify what is a "cost" and what is a "benefit." Only interactive systemic models, which can reflect dynamic changes, can help in managing such new complexities. (See Fig. 5. Vicious Circle Economies on page 39.)

A fuller review of the background on overhauling the GNP/GDP-based Systems of National Accounts and the role social scientists and environmentalists have played is in Chapter 6 of *Paradigms in Progress* (1991, 1995). By the 1950s, social and natural scientists emerged in a movement to apply broader indicators in the United States, Canada, and Europe as they documented social costs. By the 1960s, the social scientists were critiquing GNP's simplistic averaging of incomes, which often meant a few hundred more millionaires with most people left out or worse off. In the 1960s, Emile van Lennep, former secretary-general of the Organization for Economic Cooperation and Development (OECD), attempted to introduce social indicators into that organization's preeminently economic analyses. Van Lennep encountered objections that such social indicators were "normative"—even though, of course, economic indicators are also normative.[13]

Early examples of alternative indicators are the Index of Social Progress (ISP) devised by Richard J. Estes, begun in 1974 and summarized in his *Trends in World Social Development: The Social Progress of Nations, 1970–1987* (1988), and the Physical Quality of Life Index (PQLI) developed by David Morris for the Overseas Development Council of Washington, D.C. Neither received much attention at the time. As a member of U.S. President Jimmy Carter's election campaign Economic Task Force in 1975, I recommended expanding the President's Council of Economic Advisors to an inter-disciplinary Council of Social Science Advisors, and expanding the Federal Reserve Board of Governors to include representatives of consumers, employees, and environmentalists. At that time, Vice President Walter Mondale was a champion of social indicators and of an expanded Council of Social Science Advisors. In 1973, my research in Japan examined efforts at deducting environmental costs from GNP. At least one economist, Hirofumi Uzawa, had written a paper on the need for adding a capital-consumption account to GNP to measure depletion of national resources.[14] Other early efforts by economists, such as the Measure of Economic Welfare (MEW) of James Tobin and Richard Nordhaus, and several UN papers and other studies are summarized in Chapter 6 of *Paradigms in Progress* and Chapter 13 of *The Politics of the Solar Age* (1981, 1988).

Other indicators have received less attention than the high profile HDI. The World Bank has still to translate the *System of National Accounts, 1993*, its 1995 Wealth Index, and other social and environmental indicators into its operations and projects. The OECD, due partly to van Lennep's early leadership, is still producing additional useful work on environmental indicators. A working paper by John C. O'Connor provides a recent overview of current work at the World Bank, the OECD, and other agencies.[15] The IMF's *World Economic Outlook, 1993* received much attention when it converted to PPPs in order to correct for currency fluctuations. The PPP's comparable "basket" of goods approach is also controversial. The Western-biased "Big Mac Currencies" promoted by *The Economist* measure purchasing power in Beijing, Zurich, London, or Tokyo by the price of a Big Mac hamburger. In 1995 it showed the Chinese yuan as the most undervalued and the Swiss franc as the most overvalued currencies.[16] Currency devaluations have continued to make real comparisons of living standards difficult as countries have resorted to this kind of lose-lose competition. Money itself, as well as its use as a measure, has been politicized.[17] Many private groups produce global indicators and data, notably Reuters and other on-line services, the London-based *The Economist* and other business publications, as well as the World Resources Institute's *World Resources* (five volumes published since 1986) and the Worldwatch Institute's *Vital Signs* and *State of the World Reports*.

Implementation to overhaul national accounts will be coordinated through the UN, the World Bank, the IMF, the OECD, and the European Union—joint promulgators of the *System of National Accounts, 1993*. Maintaining a level playing field for statistics, indicators, and accounting standards is vital for global financial, business, and government decision making. In April 1994, a year after the Clinton administration ordered the U.S. Commerce Department's Bureau of Economic Analysis (BEA) to begin the work of overhauling U.S. national accounts, the first "Green GDP" was unveiled, but only as "Integrated Economic and Environmental Satellite Accounts" (IEESA). It is replete with many problems: for example, it shortchanges future generations by using traditional discount rates, which value future consumption as successively less important. Also, in treating newly discovered oil and minerals as additions to capital assets, it allows high current-consumption levels to appear *more sustainable* than if these resources had stayed off the books.[18] In fairness, BEA director Dr. Carol S. Carson had cautioned earlier against over-expectation:

> Gross Domestic Product (GDP)—widely used around the world—is a measure of market-oriented economic production. In turn, the level of production largely determines how much a community can consume. While the level of consumption of goods and services, both individually and collectively, is one of the most important factors influencing a community's welfare, there are many others—the existence of peace or war, technology, the environment, and income distribution, to name a few. Because these other factors do not enter into the measurement of GDP, additional measures are also needed to evaluate welfare or make policies regarding welfare. It would take a philosopher king to "add" all the measures relevant to welfare into a single indicator useful for all times and communities; until then, a variety of measures will be needed along with GDP.[19]

THE POLITICS OF INDICATORS

Sustainable development became the rallying cry of some twenty-six-thousand nongovernmental organization (NGO) representatives and activists at the Rio Earth Summit in 1992 and at its Global Forum. This popularized the demand for new indicators and provided the opportunities for coalition building among four major global constituencies:

1. environmentalists who promote for "green" indicators;
2. women who push in almost every country to have household management, parenting, home enterprises, and subsistence agriculture accounted for in GNP/GDP;[20]
3. citizens and NGOs that are concerned with social justice, urban problems, human rights, and corporate and government accountability; and
4. developing country policymakers who are learning how to exploit the new bargaining power they have over the North regarding environmental and social issues worldwide. This

power is based on logic and ethics: "Why should developing countries have to arrest their own development, when it is Northern Hemisphere industrial countries that have caused the lion's share of pollution and depletion?" Statistics abound on the vast asymmetry between North and South in relative emission of pollutants, energy consumption, and so on, which indicate that industrial countries owe an equivalently large share for the cleanup costs and must reduce their own wasteful consumption.

In 1989, then-President Carlos Andrés Pérez of Venezuela challenged the economism of the IMF's structural adjustment requirements by gathering statistics on the adverse effects on children, social programs, and the environment.[21] At the Earth Summit, many Southern Hemisphere NGOs came up with estimates of the Northern Hemisphere's "pollution debt" to the world at between $15 and $20 trillion. This was put on the negotiating table at the Global Forum along with discussion of the South's debt to Northern banks and governments, and the issues of cleanup costs and the transference of green technologies.

The continued global linking of citizen organizations has accelerated the formation of new constituencies for global change and support for the United Nations as the only global actor with any mandate for addressing global issues. Citizens and NGOs have grasped the paradigms and new criteria to operationalize alternative paths to more sustainable development. They know it is not enough only to point to the effects and symptoms of the existing unsustainable global economic and geopolitical system (e.g., desertification, pollution, poverty, injustice). They now also highlight the causes and the structural barriers to achieving ecologically sustainable, equitable human development; increasingly, they offer creative solutions and social innovations.

Citizen groups and coalitions such as the "Fifty Years Is Enough" campaign point to an inequitable global economic order reinforced by the outdated workings of the World Bank, the IMF, and the WTO—as well as unequal terms of trade, dominance over the UN by big powers, and the global arms race, which still accounts for some $750 billion annually. *Human Development Report, 1994* documents a decline in the arms trade of an average 3 percent per year since 1987. As mentioned earlier, the resulting "peace dividend" was lost in budget deficits in most countries, largely because it was statistically invisible. Today, the United States, Russia, and the major G-7 armaments producers—the United Kingdom, France, and Germany—are still selling weapons to every tin-pot dictator and warlord around the world. This underlines the usefulness of the HDI's indicators of military to civilian budget ratios (see Fig. 3: Military Spending and the Peace Dividend on page 29.) and the groundbreaking work of Ruth Leger Sivard and her reports *World Military and Social Expenditures* (1991). The World Game Institute in Philadelphia, Pennsylvania, collates and juxtaposes many indicators that relate global arms expenditures to global needs.

New levels of subtlety are now in focus. Such issues as the *values* undergirding economic systems are unavoidable. Indicators of "progress" and measures of "wealth" such as GNP/GDP naturally have become targets of popular attack by constituencies for change and grassroots activists. Because such indicators were promulgated behind official facades in government agencies, their formulas for weighting often incommensurable statistics were devised in arcane economic and computer models and were maddeningly inaccessible to activists. For example, in the United States, a brewing conflict concerns the percentage of children versus the percentage of elderly living in poverty—with children under six now 25 percent of the poor and adults over sixty-five down to some 11 percent. Such are the dangers of highly averaged statistics.[22] Even when challenged by public-interest advocates in the scientific community, economists employed in these status-quo bureaucracies obfuscate—claiming that economics is a science and that only those with Ph.D.s in economics can understand the construction of such indexes. Traditional academic etiquette stops many experts in other disciplines from invading the economists' "turf," and even motivated social and ecological scientists often lack the time, courage, or resources to perform needed critical analyses.

The HDI program at UNDP encountered considerable hostility from economists, even some at the UN's own statistical offices, architects of the GNP/GDP-based United Nations System of National Accounts (UNSNA). A "not invented here" reaction as well as defensiveness emerged as HDI's indicators revealed long-term patterns that the per-capita-averaged UNSNA glossed over, such as widening poverty gaps and jobless economic growth. HDI was further

politicized in 1995 as it became an ever-sharper tool holding governments accountable for actual results in achieving more sustainable
human development. Some UN member-governments actually
debated shutting down the *Human Development Report* and the
HDI—a sure sign of its usefulness. By then, such censorship was too
late, since the Report and the Index had found a global audience and
were published by Oxford University Press. The Reports and Index are
now valuable intellectual property—demonstrating again the social
usefulness of markets.

Professional economists who focus on concerns of lenders and
capital markets still predominate at the World Bank, in spite of yeo-
man work by Herman Daly (now at the University of Maryland),
Robert Goodland, Ernst Lutz, Mohammed el Ashry, and others in the
Environmental Department of the Bank. In 1994, the Bank's
Department of Sustainable Development convened what was billed,
rather autistically, as the First International Conference on
Measuring Sustainable Development, offering few new approaches.
The department's head, Ismail Serageldin, who understands the
issues well, advocates indicators based equally on economic, social,
and environmental data. The Bank's *World Development Report*
(1994) did break new ground by focusing on the huge sustainable
development payoffs from investments in health and education. But
on the whole, for reasons inherent in the Bank's structure
(Griesgraber 1994), it is still heavily oriented toward neoclassical economic views similar to those of Harvard-trained economist Lawrence
Summers, its former chief economist. Summers' now infamous internal memo about *encouraging* dirty industries to relocate in poor countries[23] illustrates the conceptual problems of neoclassical economics
in coming to grips with broader concepts such as sustainable development. Traditional GNP/GDP economists' unwarranted desires to
cling to old data and formulas "for historic comparability" are now
being overcome. Others, including myself, point out that this can be
overcome by introducing the new national accounts and various satellite accounts *in parallel* with GNP/GDP for as long as necessary.

Inertia and fierce resistance in powerful quarters to reformulating
GNP/GDP will continue holding up the shift to sustainability.
GNP/GDP indexes have become a chief bulwark sustaining existing
power centers in both business and government and among academic apologists. GNP/GDP measurements underlie the entire

Western/industrial way of life. Existing SNAs have powerful vested-interest champions in academia, since shifts to new indicators would require wholesale rewriting of economic textbooks and revamping of courses in universities everywhere as well as in prestigious business and management programs. There are literally tens of thousands of tenured Ph.D. economists on powerful faculty committees and editorial boards of journals who will still attack any deviants as "lacking rigor" or "unprofessional." Such academic sniping and turf-battling was witnessed publicly during the confirmation of Laura D'Andrea Tyson, chair of U.S. President Clinton's Council of Economic Advisors, who is a fairly conventional structural economist and hardly a sustainable development innovator.

Progress in developing and using indicators of sustainable development demands that the new indicators be generated through an *interdisciplinary* process. Economists, who usually resist interference in their domination of macro-policy, have conceded and hired a few social scientists and environmentalists. They still insist on retaining control of the policy models and frameworks, however—and they have vastly superior access to funds—helping them to maintain this control. Gauging the progress of complex societies and the many dimensions of quality of life using a single disciplinary approach is, on the face of it, absurd. Sustainable development indicators require not only economists but statisticians from many disciplines: for example, from the World Health Organization (WHO) for health care; from UNESCO for education and literacy; from UN Population and Family Planning for gender-specific issues; from the International Consumers Union for consumer/environmental impact statistics; from the International Labor Organization (ILO) for workplace issues; and from the United Nations Environment Program (UNEP) for environmental statistics. Nancy Rodriguez, M.D., president of Venezuela's Institute for Advanced Study in Caracas, favors such broad indicators, including additional measures of child development, in *Redefining Wealth and Progress*.[24] Other multidisciplinary approaches include such successful indicators as Jacksonville, Florida's Quality Indicators of Progress, operating since 1983.

UNBUNDLING THE AGGREGATED INDEXES

The unbundled scorecards of all major aspects of quality of life (including economic data) give a holistic overview—allowing voters to do the weighting by focusing on whichever indicators concern them. Jacksonville uses this approach, often with as many as eighty to one hundred indicators, which are recalibrated annually with input from citizens. The Sustainable Seattle Indicators, the Report Card for Vermont, and others construct their data with input from voters who are also involved in regular reviews of civic progress toward the goals targeted. The London-based New Economics Foundation has launched a similar project in British cities with local United Nations Associations.

At all levels of human societies there is a new push to redesign healthier cities. Spearheaded by Dr. Ilona Kickbusch, the World Health Organization has encouraged and documented "Healthy Cities" indicators worldwide, which now can be accessed on the Internet.[25] The International Association of Architects held a world-wide competition in 1993 to develop criteria and models for designing sustainable communities, and a new movement with similar goals is growing rapidly in North America. Even London's *The Economist* publishes a host of social and environmental indicators—albeit, trivializing them as a guide for tourists and relocators on "Where to Live."[26] New indicators of quality of life are becoming increasingly important to the business and investment community as predictive tools for longer-term asset evaluation.

The National Center for Economic Alternatives in Washington, D.C., takes an interdisciplinary view. Its 1995 "Index of Environmental Quality" covered physical effects of pollution and depletion of resources on the environment in seven industrial countries: the United States, Britain, France, Japan, Italy, Canada, and Germany. The proliferation of new indicators, both economic and aggregated like GNP as well as those that are multidisciplinary, should be welcomed as expanding the emerging debate.

Most business and economic journals regularly cover the new issues around "green" accounting, taxation, and life-cycle analyses of products—all signposts on the road to internalizing costs formerly externalized. The goal is to correct prices, and the new green accounting on thousands of corporate balance sheets, as well as reports and books on environmental and social auditing, reflects new constraints, environmental and resource realities, legislation, and insurance liabilities. The municipal bond rating firms, Moody's and Standard and Poor's, now use such quality-of-life indicators in rating municipal bonds, and the Calvert Group, Inc., managers of over $1 billion in socially responsible mutual funds, has joint-ventured with me on a version of my Country Futures Indicators (CFI): the Calvert-Henderson Quality-of-Life Indicators for the USA. (See Fig. 17. Country Futures Indicators.) In the European Union (EU), environmental auditing is a widely used management tool and companies seek "accreditation" under the EU's eco-management and audit regulations.[27] *Fortune* magazine recently published a green scorecard, citing the ten best and worst companies, with data compiled from the respected nonprofit public interest research group, The Council on Economic Priorities of New York.[28] A spate of new volumes on green accounting has appeared: for example, *Green Reporting* edited by Dave Owen (1992); *Coming Clean: Corporate Environmental Reporting*; and "Green Accounting," a special volume of the *Accounting, Auditing and Accountability Journal* edited by Rob Gray and Richard Laughlin.[29]

The new indicators measure real-world results: for example, parts per million of particulates in urban air, literacy rates, infant mortality rates, ratios of soldiers to teachers, poverty-gap data, energy efficiency. One Dutch-based global company, BSO Origin, has produced since 1990 an annual report with full "state-of-the-art" accounting of its environmental performance. Its CEO, Eckart Wintzen, crusades in Europe to change the cumbersome value added tax (VAT) to the more ecologically and actuarially correct green levy he terms a value *extracted* tax (VET), mentioned in Chapter 4.

The main weakness of HDI is its use of economic methods and mainly traditional weighting to aggregate diverse elements in order to come up with a ready-made eye- and media-catching analog of GNP/GDP. Herman Daly and John Cobb (1989) acknowledge this problem with their Index of Sustainable Economic Welfare (ISEW), the basis for the Genuine Progress Indicator (GPI) released for the United States in 1995 by the "green" group Redefining Progress of San Francisco, on whose advisory board I served. A U.K. version of ISEW has been published by The New Economics Foundation of London. The ISEW is being promoted in Europe in *Taking Nature into Account* (1995), a volume edited by Dutch environmentalist Wouter van Dieren and to which I contributed. The trade-off is difficult. A single-number index will gain more media coverage — but at the cost of obscurity since no one can unpack all of the arcane assumptions

COUNTRY FUTURES INDICATORS – CFI™

Beyond money-denominated, per-capita-averaged growth of GNP

Reformulated GNP to Correct Errors and Provide More Information:

- PURCHASING POWER PARITY (PPP) corrects for currency fluctuations
- INCOME DISTRIBUTION: is the poverty gap widening or narrowing?
- COMMUNITY-BASED ACCOUNTING: to complement current enterprise-basis
- INFORMAL, HOUSEHOLD-SECTOR PRODUCTION measures all hours worked (paid and unpaid)
- DEDUCT SOCIAL & ENVIRONMENTAL COSTS: a "net" accounting avoids double counting
- ACCOUNT FOR DEPLETION OF NONRENEWABLE RESOURCES: analogous to a capital consumption deflator
- ENERGY INPUT/GDP RATIO measures energy efficiency, recycling
- MILITARY/CIVILIAN BUDGET RATIO measures effectiveness of governments
- CAPITAL ASSET ACCOUNT FOR BUILT INFRASTRUCTURE AND PUBLIC RESOURCES (Many economists agree this is needed. Some include environment as a resource.)

Complementary Indicators of Progress toward Society's Goals:

- POPULATION: birth rates, crowding, age distribution
- EDUCATION: literacy levels, school dropout and repetition rates
- HEALTH: infant mortality, low birth weight, weight/height/age
- NUTRITION: e.g., calories per day, protein/carbohydrates ratio
- BASIC SERVICES: e.g., access to clean water
- SHELTER: e.g., housing availability, quality, homelessness
- PUBLIC SAFETY: crime
- CHILD DEVELOPMENT: e.g., World Health Organization, UNESCO
- POLITICAL PARTICIPATION AND DEMOCRATIC PROCESS: e.g., Amnesty International data, money-influence in elections, electoral participation rates
- STATUS OF MINORITY AND ETHNIC POPULATIONS AND WOMEN: e.g., human rights data
- AIR AND WATER QUALITY AND ENVIRONMENTAL POLLUTIONS LEVELS: air pollution in urban areas
- ENVIRONMENTAL RESOURCE DEPLETION: hectares of land, forests lost annually
- BIODIVERSITY AND SPECIES LOSS: e.g., Canada's environmental indicators
- CULTURE, RECREATIONAL RESOURCES: e.g., Jacksonville, Florida

Fig. 17.   Country Futures Indicators™

© 1989 Hazel Henderson   Source: *Paradigms in Progress*

behind a one-number index. In principle, the World Bank's Ismail Serageldin, Ignacy Sachs, I, and many economists concerned with sustainable development, even including Herman Daly, agree that societies should not use such overall indexes. Worse, they tend to reinstate economism. The rise of global investing has brought new demands for better government statistics. *The Economist* pointed out that "huge investment flows were based on the flimsiest of economic statistics." Governments often released figures to put the best spin on their performance or timed them for their own advantage.[30]

DEMOCRATIZING THE INDICATORS AND THE POLITICS OF MEANING

Democratizing the indicators of human progress and sustainable development fosters a new politics of meaning based on a broader, longer-term bottom line that can better measure results and thus hold politicians accountable. In the United States, Michael Lerner, editor of *TIKKUN* magazine, also advocates a politics of meaning, but seems to have less interest in all the ways new scorecards could *operationalize* such a politics. Mass media must help by breaking themselves of their fear of advertisers and their addiction to single indexes amenable to sound bites. To address the problem of overaggregation and mystification, my Country Futures Indicators are unbundled so as to be transparent, multidisciplinary, and accessible to the public. Editors and reporters need to be made aware of today's debate over sustainable paths to development. In my press briefing on "Redefining Wealth and Progress" for my fellow journalists at the National Press Club, Washington, D.C., in May 1993, I was encouraged by the size of the group of media attendees and their thoughtful questions and comments.[31]

Creative producers are needed to design serial news and documentary formats for radio and television. For example, a "Country Scorecards" program could cover on a regular basis cross-country and domestic comparisons of the full range of quality-of-life indicators. The time is ripe, since indicators are now becoming a fad, often with catchy graphics such as those of the daily newspaper *USA Today*, the witty juxtapositions of diverse indicators in *Harpers* (a New York–based monthly), and increasing focus on such data in other popular magazines, such as *Atlantic Monthly*.

Country Futures Indicators (CFI) include all major categories and subcategories I deem necessary to form a generic, country-comparable model. Any city, province, or country can delve into the CFI and develop its own indicators according to its needs, values, and goals. Truly sustainable development will require at least (1) inclusion of *all* CFI categories; (2) an interdisciplinary group of statisticians; and (3) unbundling the indicators so that all the separate data is released to the public media—rather than mystified aggregations such as GPI. The approach of the first version of CFI—the Calvert-Henderson Quality-of-Life Indicators for the USA—launched in 1996, is as a public education service of the Calvert Group, Inc. Devising indicators of sustainable development does not involve "rocket science." It requires excellent research to survey and collate the wealth of diverse indicators and data already available, often languishing in the public domain at the United Nations and other public agencies.

National statistical needs of developing countries are also multi-disciplinary; all countries have their own cultural DNA codes around which specific indicators can be designed. The South Commission took this approach in its report, *Challenge to the South* (1990), as did Nandini Joshi in *Development without Destruction* (1992), which describes the rural, informal sector-development model in India. Regional variability can be instructively highlighted, such as the superior performance on social development by the state of Kerala, India, belied by its $300 range GDP.[32]

Thus, sustainable development indicators will diverge methodologically in many ways from traditional economics-based national accounting that uses money coefficients and weighted formulas. The fears of many Southern policymakers, mentioned earlier, are understandable: that HDI and green indicators are normative, like all such measurements, in the sense that they focus on what societies hold important. GNP is revealed by all the new debates and indicators as normative, nontransparent, and unaccountable to electorates, thus preempting the very processes of democracy.

Economists are not sitting idly by as their markets are being invaded by other statisticians and corporate reformers such as the World Business Council for Sustainable Development, which published *Changing Course* in 1992. The council's 1996 report, *Financing Change*, on making capital markets truly efficient by overhauling capital asset pricing models (CAPMs), will accelerate the shift of financial markets to full-cost pricing of such assets. In the professional sense, economists are being entrepreneurial. Some are putting new labels on old wine bottles. Others are reformatting their resumes and business cards to catch the lucrative new green and social markets— as ecological economists, natural resource economists, social economists, or what have you. These are often speciously quantitative, pseudo-rigorous approaches to specific environmental indicators.

Some macroeconomists are still trying to expand GDP into welfare indexes by pricing environmental amenities and costs, including David Pearce and Partha Dasgupta in Britain and Robert Solow in the United States. The International Institute for Ecological Economics and its journal *Ecological Economics* use similar as well as broader interdisciplinary approaches.[33] Frances Cairncross uses this approach also in *Costing the Earth* and *Green, Inc.: A Guide to Business and the Environment* 1995.[34] Cairncross, however, falls into economism traps: for example, she agrees with traditional economists' valuation of human lives, promotes pollution-license markets, and agrees that it is better to "adapt" to global warming than prevent it— whatever the real costs in poor countries. Herman Daly and John and Clifford Cobb, designers of ISEW, are at least helping to illustrate their differences with GDP in their media-friendly approach.

The main intellectual problem with the "ecological economics" approach is the general assumption that if a natural resource—a rain forest or whatever—has a value somewhere between zero and infinity, then an ecological economist can be awarded a contract to calculate what the price should be using "willingness to pay" or "willingness to be compensated" formulas to calculate "contingent prices." Thus, to arrive at such a "shadow" price for valuing a marshland (one of the most productive ecosystems on the planet), economists poll voters and residents. Often citizens have no motives other than appreciation for marshes and their nonmonetary or aesthetic values or a desire to preserve them and the rare species they might contain. Such contingent prices, *of course*, would be lower than those offered by a hotel developer with profit motives or by a biotechnology firm that had identified species in the area which could be used for pharmaceutical products. (See Chapter 2, page 71.)

The problem is that all the fancy math hides the ecological economist's neoclassical assumptions, e.g., the "principle" of Pareto

Optimality (which ignores disparities in wealth, income, power, and information between people and countries, as well as issues of who wins and who loses, job loss, the unpaid informal economy, and so on). This is not to say that environmental resources should continue to be treated as "free goods" or priced at zero as they still are in GNP/GDP, but only to caution against this narrow evaluation method, since economists believe deeply in money coefficients and prices, however imperfectly derived from imperfect or even fictitious markets. Such pricing, especially for essentials such as water, discounts poor people's needs and concerns since they cannot afford to pay or participate. Here, the price system should be subordinated to more democratic decision making, i.e., *voting*.

Similar concerns challenge economists advocating pricing and market trading of licenses to pollute, instigated in 1991 in the United States by the Chicago Board of Trade (CBOT). Companies can trade such pollution licenses without consulting citizens living in the areas surrounding their plants who need to breathe. Indignant voters cite the U.S. Constitution, which assures the human right to breathe, i.e., *survival*, as well as the pursuit of happiness. Tragically, even otherwise savvy, environmentally concerned groups, including the Natural Resources Defense Council and Working Assets of San Francisco, actually used charitable funds to "purchase" some of these licenses to pollute the public air—in order to "retire" them. Such aberrant do-goodism only reinforced the illegitimate concept that the public should pay to breathe and bribe corporations not to pollute.

The saddest case was the hoodwinked sixth graders at a public school in Glens Falls, New York. Their misguided teacher, Rod Johnson, persuaded them to raise $3,171 to buy twenty-one pollution credits on the CBOT and retire them. These pollution credits are offered by the EPA to private utilities to give them more time to reduce their emissions of sulfur dioxide. The children's money, $151 for each credit, bought the equivalent of 151 tons of sulfur dioxide from the utilities, which they otherwise might have sold to other companies. Most CBOT traders and corporations don't mind such misguided philanthropy. It simply drives up the prices of the remaining credits. The Glens Falls students plan to purchase more credits in 1996.[35]

I had warned in *Paradigms in Progress* how such aberrations as the trading of pollution licenses (or "credits" as polluters prefer to call them) grow like noxious weeds from economics textbooks. These arcane theories have befuddled a new generation who can no longer see that companies don't own the air we breathe—any more than media companies own the public airwaves. A final irony is that these pollution license schemes are not working as forecast—trading has made acid rain problems worse than if a simple law had been passed.[36] Furthermore, utility companies are leery of them for financial and public relations reasons. The only useful role for such trading may be to compensate the developing countries by allowing them to "sell" their unused "global pollution rights," up to Northern levels, to the rich countries. A Bank for Environmental Settlements to arrange such compensation has been proposed by Chilean economist Graciela Chichilnisky at Columbia University in New York, but it might work better as a Barter Treaty.[37]

Economists have little training in truly understanding social systems or the productive functions of ecosystems. Economic approaches should, at least, jettison neoclassical welfare and market formulas and try to price such truly priceless resources as biodiversity or rain forests at the cost of replacement. This, of course, is an unresolvable dilemma and pits economists against environmentalists and those concerned with human and aesthetic values. Most social and natural scientists, as well as voters, believe that economics must now take its place within interdisciplinary teams of statisticians from health, education, energy, environmental, and other social policy fields.

The new national accounting methods being redesigned to correct GNP/GDP will function like healthy cultural DNA strands newly spliced in to govern healthier, more normal development patterns for human societies. Just as *quantitative* growth is dominant as children grow to adulthood, once physical maturity is reached, *qualitative* growth prevails: education, social skills, broad awareness, even greater ethical understanding and wisdom. The statistical shift from GNP/GDP to sustainable indicators mirrors this growth and maturation process in societies. Human beings must now develop new goals and traits at an accelerated pace if we are to restructure our societies for sustainability.

Narrow views of the value of environmental and natural resources can also shortchange other needed correction of GNP/GDP on the social front (e.g., unpaid work, poverty gaps, etc.). This will further alienate the Southern Hemisphere, where there is not yet much long-term thinking on environmental preservation because, as they see it, poverty is the greatest pollution problem. Such reactions and possible opposition from the South would be justified and could jeopardize the whole movement to adopt new indicators. Thus, the useful work of Robert Repetto of the World Resources Institute in valuing forest resources in Indonesia and Costa Rica; of Robert Costanza in valuing wetlands (based on Howard T. Odum's net energy analyses at the University of Florida); and of Ernst Lutz, Salah El Serafy, John Pezzey, Joachim von Amsberg, and others at the World Bank must be viewed as a partial aspect of sustainable development indicators.

An example of the problem of excessive focus on environmental indicators is the case of Costa Rica, where valuing and subtracting of extracted rain-forest resources was not done within the context of GDP's still missing asset account. Thus while commercial exploitation of the forests was correctly valued as a deduction from GDP, the enormous value of the forests *should also have been estimated at replacement costs and added on the asset side*. More attention should have been drawn to the missing asset account. Well-meaning environmental economists helped to portray the Costa Rican economy negatively. The partial social innovation in its national accounts was less than rewarding—giving the false impression in GNP rankings that Costa Rica's economy was no longer "progressing." Similar studies of extraction of forest resources could just as easily have shown the same kind of lowering of GDP in the United States.[38] In 1995, the GPI showed a somewhat arbitrary lowering in the United States, to mixed reviews.

Ecological economists need to forge methodological links with more holistic, social approaches like those of the HDI team, the Society for the Advancement of Social Economics, the research department of the Calvert Group's Calvert Social Investment Funds, and Canada's Green Indicators. Meanwhile, the ecological economics community does advocate green taxes—certainly preferable to the tradable emission rights they also promote. Green taxes have the advantage of correcting prices to reflect more fully the costs of production, formerly externalized from company balance sheets, thus redirecting corporate enterprises. As mentioned earlier, Ernst Ulrich von Weizsäcker's *Ecological Tax Reform* (1992) is a reference source on green taxes, and his Wuppertal Institute is doing groundbreaking work on indicators and ecological taxation. Global green taxes (on carbon and other air, water, and land pollution) could also be collected by the UN to fund grassroots sustainable development. It seems clear that the World Bank should relinquish management of the Global Environmental Facility—even though the 1995 UN bashing had the effect of strengthening the World Bank's stranglehold on environmental lending. Even comanaged with UNEP and UNDP, World Bank lending is still steeped in old economic paradigms and may continue destroying local communities and forcing additional millions to relocate in the path of its dam-building projects—producing even bigger environmental disasters. Such projects, including the cancellation of a big dam in India in 1995 due to grassroots efforts, are monitored in Asia by *Development Alternatives*, published by the nonprofit Development Alternatives institute, New Delhi, India.[39]

Indicators of sustainability will not be set in concrete, but will evolve and continue to have dimensions that are country specific. The textbook formulas for economic growth fail precisely because there are no "correct" rates of savings, investments, or exports. As mentioned, some economists are broadening their analyses from equilibrium-based macroeconomic models to systems and chaos theory in order to better capture accelerating rates of change and restructuring. Courses on sustainable development indicators should include reviews of all major efforts in this fast-moving field, statistical source material, evaluation of data reliability, critiques of different approaches, and overall development paradigms. It remains for economists to relinquish their colonization of national policy via macroeconomic statistics. More broadly focused economists can continue collaborating with the worldwide interdisciplinary effort to promote indicators that can help put all countries on paths to sustainable development.

For fifty Cold War years the superpowers and their blocs of states competed militarily. In the uneasy 1990s, religious, cultural, and ethnic groups conflict, along with competing trade blocs, within the same old games of global competition and economic warfare. Another dilemma that humans have not encountered in all their history on this planet: how to manage ourselves in societies and cities of such unprecedented numbers on a small, polluted planet. The WTO could, by adopting the broader criteria and indicators reviewed here, help level the global playing field *upward* with multilateral agreements, so that the best managed and most responsible countries and companies can prosper.

As we humans prepare for the twenty-first century, we can grow markets that serve our highest aspirations and our deepest beliefs. A twenty-first-century capitalism worthy of the noblest ideals of the whole human family can evolve on our small, beloved blue planet— Earth. Broader quality-of-life scorecards can expand holistic, in-depth analyses of trends and serve as larger, many-dimensional sets of indicators. The Calvert Group, Inc., of Washington, D.C., on whose advisory council I have served since 1982, manages mutual funds that offer socially concerned investors solid financial returns and the chance to express their social values: a "double bottom line." The Calvert-Henderson Quality-of-Life Indicators serve its investors and all Americans in their life roles: as citizens, employees, investors, consumers, and family members. These new indicators supplement more familiar indicators including Dow Jones, Standard and Poor's, and the Domini Clean Yield Index.[40] Many other mutual funds in the United States, Canada, and Europe also offer clean, green, and other ethical portfolios to aware investors and planetary citizens.[41]

The new scorecards allow us to move beyond old ideologies—to measure results directly and scientifically. These scorecards can help hold our business and government leaders accountable for implementing progress on all the major goals of individual stakeholders, voters, consumers, and investors. The new scorecards can help broaden national debates and trade negotiations to include sustainable development criteria; they can help define a twenty-first-century capitalism worthy of our highest goals and most enduring values; they can help level the global playing field upward to make markets more orderly for investors by including social and environmental costs. The preventive, early-warning, feedback function of quality-of-life indicators makes the global ball park safer for everyone—today and for future generations. People everywhere can join in raising the global economy's "ethical floor," encourage corporate codes of conduct, and expand democratic debate in a deeper politics of meaning.

CHAPTER 11

PERFECTING DEMOCRACY'S TOOLS

Within this century human beings must make a quantum leap to enable us to manage our now accelerating global affairs. The human family will soon comprise six billion members—a condition beyond the experience of leaders, academics, and indeed anyone alive today. Humans now gobble up an unprecedented 40 percent of the primary production of all other species. Ninety-eight percent of the planet's other species are green plants that humans and all other mammals and insects use for food and depend on for survival. Millions of refugees now flee collapsing societies and depleted ecosystems.

In *Paradigms in Progress* (1991, 1995), I viewed the history of the twentieth century as a series of ghastly experiments in managing larger and larger numbers of people in cities, states, and mega-states, while dealing with the cruel legacy of nineteenth-century colonial organizations. Most of these tragic experiments cost millions of lives—from Hitler's Third Reich, to Mussolini's and Franco's fascism in Italy and Spain, to Lenin's and Stalin's USSR, to Mao Zedong's China. The Cold War aftermath of World War II subtly changed the nature of these experiments in organizing human affairs, with a shift toward the idea of industrial "progress" that included technocratic visions of material plenty espoused by economic theories from left to right. Karl Marx and Adam Smith were in fundamental agreement about such goals; they differed only on the means to achieve them.

The transitions and restructurings at the seven levels discussed in Chapter 1 have involved shifting patterns of governance, power, and decision making. The vectors have been the six great globalizations, and the transmission belt of these changes has often been money flows. In the 1980s, nations began breaking into smaller states, with their former power migrating *upward* into global treaties and corporations as well as regional alliances and trade blocs, and *downward* to rebellious provinces, grassroots communities, and growing cities. In the United States, Canada, and Britain devolution was the rage—often the goal was to shuffle the funding of social and budgetary responsibilities, or to redesign, shift, or repeal regulations or enforcement. In Britain, by 1995, half the population lived in households receiving a means-tested welfare check—twice as many as in 1979.[1] The last gasps of domestic macroeconomic management sank into budget and bookkeeping battles and empty debates as to whether governments should inflate, reflate, deflate, deregulate, reregulate, privatize, or nationalize their overaggregated, statistically fictitious economies. None of the transitional experiments were stable or working very well. No one knew what an optimum size might be for a nation: where a trade-off between economies of scale in delivering public services and security to citizens could be balanced with population diversity—although two ambitious economists tried in "The Number and Size of Nations."[2]

China, the emerging superpower, was an interesting case. During the 1980s Deng Xiao Ping had triggered new dynamism and markets, allowing Guangdong Province and Shanghai's commercial power to challenge the political power of Beijing's "mandate of heaven." Shanghainese Jiang Zemin and Zhu Rongji became president and vice premier, respectively. The slogan of the often-Moscow-trained Beijing bureaucrats was, "Socialism will save China." The joke in Shanghai, which accounted for 25 percent of China's GDP, was "China will save Socialism." By the 1990s, as China emerged with the world's third largest GNP/PPP (purchasing power parity) ranking, its leaders, jockeying for Deng Xiao Ping's succession, were further challenged by the Confucian dictum: "If you can rule your whole country, who dares insult you." Beijing's demands for respect in the world were well founded, not only in its booming economy but in its increasing influence in Asia.

Meanwhile, Japan's miracle was eclipsed despite second-place GNP ranking. Its bubble economy of the 1980s precipitated bank crises, recession, and the end of the sedate political control of the ruling Liberal Democrat Party with its many campaign finance and other scandals. The United States, ranked number one, with plenty of internal troubles of its own, took on both Japan and China in trade disputes and inept political maneuvers based on old paradigms and bilateral statistics.

MONEY AND POLITICS IN THE GLOBAL FAST LANE

Everywhere money and politics were tightly entwined as economic restructuring broke up old parties and coalition governments. Small, breakaway nations proliferated, including Slovenia, the Baltic States, Moldova, the Czech Republic, Slovakia, Armenia, and the tragic state of Bosnia. Another "failed state," Sudan joined in the fate of Somalia, Rwanda, and Yugoslavia, sinking into savagery.[3] Breakaway movements also multiplied, from Canada's Parti Québecois, to the enclaves on Russia's Caucasian and southern borders, to Norway's rejection of membership in the European Union. France's statist market "mixture" failed its young, 25 percent of whom were unemployed.[4] Retiring French President François Mitterand, when asked what was the most important quality for a politician, replied, "I would like to say it was sincerity. It is in fact, indifference."[5] Italy's revolving-door governments led, in 1993, to a full-blown mediocracy with the election of media mogul Silvio Berlusconi, whose rule was *based* on TV ownership and media manipulation. Mexico provided the world a short course in all the tangled issues of money and power in the global fast lane. Prospering cities challenged national governments, while those in decline demanded bailouts. Rural provinces and communities, labor unions, and the poor often rebelled in their backwaters, depleted by national policies favoring urban elites and large corporations. From Chiapas, Mexico, to Central America, Peru, the Philippines, and the antifederal militias in the United States, people were rising up and demanding participation in new forms of governance.

Despite all these difficulties, there are also seeds of hope in our technologies—*hardware*, i.e., electronic communications, aviation, and space faring—have shrunk our world to a global village. We must now develop *software*, i.e., the rules of interaction, knowledge, values, ethics, and morals that can allow us to organize for survival and further development. Democracy has emerged as a necessary process to manage the complexities of reorganizing human societies for this next quantum leap. Warren Bennis and Philip Slater pointed out in the 1960s that complex human organizations, whether corporations or countries, *require* democratization of their decision making, i.e., democracy is inevitable.[6]

To steer today's complex societies, democracy now requires systemic, cybernetic models, self-regulated by thousands of feedback loops at all levels. As systems theorists know, the more complex a system, the more feedback loops are required. Living systems, such as cities, corporations, nations, and the United Nations, are the most complex of all. Thus it has been a triumph of common sense that so many politicians, regardless of ideology and tradition, have begun moving toward democratization and markets, amplified by freeing mass media to help guide inevitable restructurings.

A new danger is in simply *equating* democracy with other forms of decentralization, privatization, and markets. There is also widening confusion between the two key individual signals from people to their decision makers in government and business—*votes* and *prices*—as feedbacks to guide and correct decisions. These two vital forms of feedback are failing to deliver enough timely information on the effects of policies and multiple restructurings to adequately guide and correct decisions. Votes every two or four years are too slow and cannot refine voters' feedback on multiple issues, while prices cannot guide markets without incorporating the fuller social and environmental costs of products and services.

In the United States, democracy has atrophied. Over two hundred years of experience with both votes and prices has not advanced the model of democratic, privately driven, self-organizing processes. In *Creating Alternative Futures* (1978, 1996), I noted that the two hundredth birthday of the United States in 1976 was a good time for us to examine the state of our lives, our beliefs, and our values, so as to illuminate which were deep—even eternal—and which were transient or merely fashionable. What might be "excess baggage" and what would we continue to cherish and carry with us into our third century? Could we clarify the cultural confusion over rights and responsibilities, preserving individual freedom in relationship to family values, our desire for community, and a broader national identity?

At the time of the U.S. bicentennial, expectations were high that all these problems could be addressed through the institutions inherited since the country's founding. In 1976 most U.S. citizens saw their country continuing to grow richer—with each generation aspiring to and achieving better living standards than those of their forebears. The American Dream, however, sparked similar dreams via movies, TV, and radio all over the world. In the mid-1990s, the United States also encountered the hurricane of change unleashed by the great globalization forces. There were increasing disagreements over priorities in budgeting and even over constitutional rights to "life, liberty, and the pursuit of happiness" under the rapidly changing conditions. Yet as I described in 1970 in "Computers: Hardware of Democracy," technologies to help perfect U.S. democracy—high-speed data processing, electronic communications, call-in radio, TV, electronic town meetings, polling—had all been available, even then, for over two decades.[7] Well-grounded fears of misuse of such instantaneous forms of democracy had stifled the debate on how to design these potential tools of democratic participation so as to avoid abuse and new forms of totalitarianism.

How can we humans shape *hardware* technologies that have shrunk our world by consciously designing the needed *software* and social innovations now vital for our survival and cultural evolution? This developmental lag in social software and architecture can be seen in the twentieth century's triumphant political model: democracy. Nation after nation has come to acknowledge democracy as a necessary component for managing complex, modern social and political structures. South Africa, now an emerging powerhouse of leadership on that continent, has made a historic transition to democracy. Mechanistic models of eighteenth-century representative democracy, however, can no longer solve our ever-more-complex web of social, cultural, political, and economic problems.

First, we must accept that electronic hardware (largely developed for commercial markets and research *about* people and their habits) will continue to be used and abused. We cannot repeal these technologies. We can redesign and adapt them from elitist to populist purposes (1) to help people understand more about their societies and the new threats and opportunities in today's global village; and (2) to collect and steer feedback and informed consent or opposition back to all decision-making levels: community groups; school boards; local, state, and national governments; and international bodies.

The challenge, as usual, is in designing the software to manage these potential feedback technologies. We must restructure their

manipulative, top-down, "big brother" aspects, which currently reinforce hierarchical institutions in both public and private sectors, as
well as today's mindless mediocracy politics. The design principles we
need to follow to gear the technologies to encourage the evolution of
democracy include *prevention* (foresight); *cooperation* (finding consensus and balancing markets' emphases on competition); *acceptance
of diversity* (a basic principle of living systems); and *clarification of
underlying assumptions* (beliefs, goals, values) as the first step in the
search for unifying global concerns and ethics. Emerging global
ethics include respect for life, fairness and equity, aspirations for
future generations, openness and freedom of information, and a love
of one's homeland as part of the Earth (rather than mere allegiance
to nations, leaders, or flags).

Genuine democracy must close the gap between elitism and
populism and embrace a commitment to the proposition that people
can govern themselves. Deeply held views about human nature color
politics: whether humans are viewed as basically untrustworthy and
morally flawed or whether they are deemed intrinsically good. This
kind of deeply rooted either/or polarization plays out as *either* conservative, authoritarian, benevolent, or dictatorial elitism, *or* visionary
idealism, populism, democracy, or anarchy. The wretched "Law of
the Excluded Middle" (i.e., A cannot equal Not-A) that Western
societies inherited from the Greeks still underlies our language and
polarized, gridlocked politics.

My view is that human nature has equally positive and negative
aspects. Thus the good-natured, life-affirming tendencies *and* the
bad-tempered, selfish, greedy ones are reinforced (for better or worse)
by feedbacks from family and community relationships, economic
rules, and social and cultural life, as well as the politics of nations. As
Western societies have become more technologically complex and
interdependent, the simple either/or, conservative/liberal polarity
and its familiar two-party politics, such as in the United States, cannot channel the multiplicity of issues and multidimensional debates
that are necessary. I theorized in *Creating Alternative Futures* and *The
Politics of the Solar Age* (1981, 1988) why the protest movements of the
1960s could not find expression in U.S. politics via the traditional
transmission belts of the two parties. I diagrammed U.S. political
movements of that time, not on a polarized single axis from "left to
right," but as a spectrum. The movements of the sixties and seventies

encompassed multidimensional issues, crosscut by concerns about centralization and devolution, globalism and localism. On this political spectrum, grassroots anarchists were comfortably akin to conservative libertarians. This spectrum, in reality a hologram, persists today. (See Fig. 18. Changing Political Configurations.)

Either/or, two-party politics are beloved by industrial era political theorists. Their simple mechanical models are reminiscent of Isaac Newton's clockwork universe. But as the complexities and interdependencies of post-industrial societies in the twentieth century have grown, inevitably, two-party politics has not been able to reflect the range of new issues. As mediocracies developed in the 1980s and 1990s, political parties were simply bypassed by mass media and shrank in numbers and significance. Both parties are about money. In the United States, for example, Republican and Democratic politicians in these "pork and bacon" parties became the "political entrepreneurs" we are familiar with today: wheeling, dealing, fund raising with interest groups and lobbyists for their own accounts and to advance their individual careers.

This view of politicians reflects the conservative viewpoint taught in law and economics departments at the University of Chicago and elsewhere, but also captures and reinforces today's cynicism. One result of this type of thinking has been the polarization of politics and issues in ever more simplistic ways, which politicians see as their only recourse. They have resorted to sloganeering, sound bytes, and flowery rhetoric—casting complex issues in terms of fundamental principles and values. This has only served to polarize media editors and talk-show hosts in the "Crossfire"-type formats that copycat the popular "left/right" program on CNN. Mainstream media were shocked by the new angry populism and its some six hundred radio outlets in 1995.[8]

All this further polarizes voters, who become even more angry and cynical—leading to the widespread alienation discussed in Chapter 5. This, in turn, opens up possibilities for a third party to organize the 35 percent of the disgusted U.S. electorate that call themselves "Independents." These are the voters who deposed George Bush in 1992 by casting almost 20 percent of the swing votes for Ross Perot, and in 1994 turned their wrath on Bill Clinton. By contrast, in coalition governments with multiparty systems such as are common in Europe (particularly the Nordic countries and the Netherlands), issues are always in dynamic play and can be triangulated, shaped,

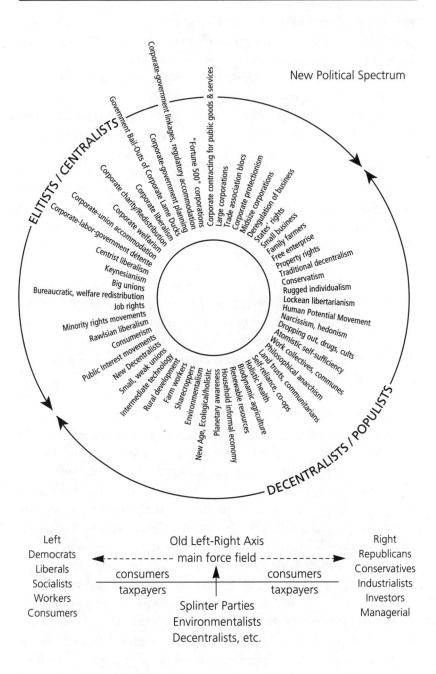

Fig. 18. Changing Political Configurations

© 1978 Hazel Henderson   Source: *The Politics of the Solar Age*

and reshaped to achieve multiparty coalition governments and much wider consensus. Citizen movements and pressure groups have much less difficulty in achieving parliamentary representation for their views, as occurred with the rise of the Greens in Germany leading to Europe's now flourishing green parties.[9] Lack of proportional representation in Britain and the obsolete electoral college in the United States crippled budding green parties, which are still condemned by the U.S. political structure and its money-dominated politics to remain a movement.

As all countries restructure under globalization pressures, two-party politics will increasingly give way to coalitions and new parties as the old centers cannot hold. All three political parties in Britain, combined, have fewer members than the Royal Society for the Protection of Birds. Britain's Citizen's Charter, created to woo voters and hear complaints, was judged in a 1995 MORI poll, which found that less than 25 percent of petitioners even received apologies for deficient public services.[10] Governments began calling in management gurus as they experimented with reorganization—but soon learned that politics and government are very different in nature and goals from business.

DEMOCRACY'S FUTURE: CITIZENS WANT TO SET PRIORITIES

The abortive 1992 U.S. presidential candidacy of Ross Perot was a dress rehearsal for raising all the right questions about democracy's future. Yet in the millions of words written on the Perot phenomenon, few examined historical experience with electronic town meetings (ETMs) and public opinion polling, or efforts already underway to prevent abuses and perfect such new feedback channels provided by technology. Much has already been learned from ETM experiments in New Zealand in 1980 to clarify that country's goals and values as well as a similar electronic referenda conducted in Hawaii by political scientist Theodore Becker. Many such experiments in anticipatory democracy have been documented by Alvin Toffler in *The Third Wave* (1980), David Loye in *The Healing of a Nation* (1971), Thomas E. Cronin in *Direct Democracy* (1989), Clement Bezold in *Anticipatory Democracy* (1978), Christa Daryl Slayton in *Televote* (1992), and my own *Creating Alternative Futures* (1978).

Professors Becker and Slayton, based at Auburn University in Alabama, reported in 1995 in "Teledemocracy Action News Network" that little progress had been made in 1995 in this area in the United States. Nothing had advanced citizen empowerment even though some attention had been given to creating "pressure valves" to relieve citizen frustration. An example was the U.S. version of University of Texas Professor James Fishkin's 1994 and 1995 series of TV programs on Britain's Channel 4, a process he called "Deliberative Polling." Fishkin teamed up with the U.S. Public Broadcasting System, which convened a similar representative sample of six hundred U.S. citizens who were exposed to presentations of two or three issues by experts — with polls taken before and afterward. These formats are a pale imitation of what is technologically possible, and the results are highly sensitive to the way the issues are framed. The Kettering and Public Agenda Foundations suffer similar problems from rigid "containment" of the issues. Indeed, they trivialized the process by fragmenting the debate into such rigid Cartesian boxes as health care, environment, and so on, rather than choosing a holistic crosscut, such as the Federal budget, which would allow participants to *set priorities* across the entire range of issues.

The opportunity to set priorities is what a majority of U.S. citizens want, as the consensus locator survey method of the Americans Talk Issues Foundation (ATIF) determined. When ATIF asked if citizens would like to have sent to them, along with their income tax forms, a questionnaire on how they would like government to spend their tax dollars (i.e., a de facto nonbinding referendum on overall priorities), 79 percent approved.[11] The Clinton administration considered experimenting with a small sample of tax returns — then opted out because "the administration might lose control of the budget process."[12] This, of course, was the idea.

Professor Becker reported an advance in Canada, where the Reform Party captured 16 percent of the 295 seats in the Parliament after the 1993 rout of Mulroney's conservatives. The Reform Party, in 1994 via an ETM, had sampled districts in Calgary on the issue of physician-assisted suicide, which the party opposed. They promised to abide by an electronic referendum where voters with PIN numbers called in massively in favor. The party changed its position and supported physician-assisted suicide. In Nova Scotia and British

Columbia, some parties elect their leaders by phone. Similar projects have been conducted in Finland, while Oregonians vote by mail.

Another useful form of anticipatory democracy is the "futures search" conference, pioneered by Eric Trist and Fred Emery and described by practitioners Marvin R. Weisbord and Sandra Janoff in *Future Search* (1995). Search conferences were originally used by organizations, but their application to cities, counties, and states was fostered by the Washington-based Institute for Alternative Futures, and many local efforts have been documented by its founder Clement Bezold. Another approach is that of the Idaho Centennial Conference and Survey *Visualizing the Future: Idaho's Second Century*, which surveyed voters' quality-of-life preferences on a broad range of issues in 1990.[13]

Building on his research in designing communication systems, mathematician/entrepreneur Alan F. Kay has also broken new ground in public-opinion surveying on policy issues. Kay's Americans Talk Issues Foundation (ATIF), founded in 1987, discovered that scientifically random telephone polls sampling a national statistical cross section of one thousand Americans can often identify a genuine "wisdom of the people" on many complex issues. Often the public chooses farsighted, globally aware policy alternatives not offered by either political party or any mainstream political figures, experts, or pundits. ATIF's method is in fact a social innovation, far less expensive than ETMs, and can be used to prevent abuses in town-meeting and call-in programs. The opinion surveys are nonpartisan, designed to broaden the range of policy alternatives offered, and provide essential, unbiased information on each policy issue, prepared by many experts on all sides. Questions often range well beyond the current debate.

A 1991 survey broke ground on issues of globalization. One of its fifty questions was, "Would you support a proposal for the UN to monitor and tax international arms sales with the money going to famine relief and humanitarian aid?" Even after hearing arguments against as well as for the proposal (another ATIF method), an average of almost 70 percent remained unshakably in favor of this proposal in a series of seven polls from 1991 through 1995, where this question was included. I have cited results from ATIF surveys on a broad range of national and domestic issues throughout this book since I serve on its board and consider ATIF the best available source of public-opinion data in the United States.

Many rules emerge from experiments in gathering such data, including the vital need to randomize all feedback, whether in opinion polls, via studio audiences, or on electronic town-hall-type programs. Similarly, such randomized feedback can balance incoming phone calls to call-in radio and television shows (which are always biased) by comparing the calls registering crude yes or no votes with a scientific, random sampling of all Americans. Indeed, this randomizing feedback rule is one of the reasons we should trust the general public *more* than leaders, politicians, and elites. The U.S. Congress is gridlocked by special interests, political action committees (PACs), and other campaign donors, and by limited information from biased lobbyists. ATIF random-sampling feedback from all Americans can "damp out" such distortions and often identify common-ground solutions.

We also need more democratic access to TV, radio, and print media, now dangerously concentrated in commercial, and increasingly global, corporate ownership. The hope that cable would open up TV channels died in a plethora of old movies and sitcom reruns. Public Access TV, hard won by activists in the 1960s, has been frittered away by cities and communities unaware of its political potential. The Perot movement, United We Stand America (UWSA), is about taming Washington's arrogance; "restoring the United States to its rightful owners: the people"; access to media; and fuller participation in politics.[14] Perot demonstrated the possibilities in the new communications technologies for end-running the political parties and short-circuiting the old electoral processes. Yet Perot, too, became manipulative. His March 1993 "electronic town meeting" turned out to be a half-hour infomercial (i.e., a paid political or commercial program). It starred Perot asking seventeen simple yes/no questions and urging people to call in or write to him at UWSA. As mentioned in Chapter 5, rebels in many countries learned that coups were best accomplished by capturing radio and television stations rather than legislative or government buildings. In another example, frustrated voters in the United States have bought stock and swarmed to annual meetings to engage in proxy fights over companies doing business in apartheid South Africa and Myanmar, pollution, animal rights, and unfair labor practices. When democracies fail to channel voters' feedback, new channels and forums are politicized, as I pointed out in 1971 in "Toward Managing Social Conflict."[15]

Citizen movements have grown by learning to feed news media and capture TV time even as they found out how unresponsive traditional politics was to their new issues. "Politics-by-other-means" has become the watchword of the sixties generation as U.S. citizens have politicized shopping, investing, banking, corporations, education, talk shows, music, movies, sports, and lifestyles with politically correct campaigns or boycotts. By the 1970s people had learned to recruit rock stars for fund-raisers and create their own media-reportable events such as Earth Day, Live Aid, Food Aid, and Farm Aid concerts. One of the most imaginative was the 1976 People's Bicentennial, which produced books and public service spots on U.S. history that shamed the crass commercialism of the official American Bicentennial Committee. (See Fig. 19. America's 200th Birthday?)

Today's frustrated efforts to redesign and expand democracy must now be channeled by every means possible at all levels, so that viable third parties and broader coalitions can emerge to break the stranglehold of special interests on the majority parties. In 1995, the University of California at Berkeley's Center for Community Economic Research introduced a new computer simulation game on its Internet Web page: Balance the Federal Budget. The game allows users to play a congress member's role and prioritize, cut, add, or otherwise balance the U.S. budget. Twelve hundred users logged on, including one from the White House.[16] A radical reform proposed by Ernest Callenbach and Michael Phillips in A *Citizen Legislature* (1985) would overcome special interests by random selection of congressional members in the same way that juries are selected. In all the restructuring between levels of governance, the overarching principle for the new democracies is that articulated in the European Union (EU): <u>subsidiarity</u>, i.e., policy making as close to the people as feasible. Feedback from the grassroots is, at last, reclaiming issues and problem solving from distant, indifferent, or uninformed elites, as feisty, intelligent Danes demonstrated in refusing to ratify the EU's Treaty of Maastricht.

Another democratic principle: transparency underlies efforts to redesign the too-highly averaged statistics of macroeconomics, which has allowed political issues and vital clarification of values to be obscured by cost- and risk-benefit analyses, i.e., portrayed as technical or economic matters on which the public was deemed "unqualified" to comment. Broader, quality-of-life indicators for health care,

Is this what America's 200th birthday is all about?

I hope we shall crush in its birth the aristocracy of our moneyed corporations, which dare already to challenge our government to a trial of strength and bid defiance to the laws of our country.

Thomas Jefferson

1814

Fig. 18. America's 200th Birthday?

Source: The People's Bicentennial Commission, reprinted from *The Politics of the Solar Age*

literacy, air and water quality, cultural amenities, democratic participation, and human rights are becoming essential tools of democracy, as well as better predictors of truly human development.

The nature of computer and communications systems makes them ideally suited to collecting, analyzing, and delivering the "feedback" of voters' viewpoints to the political system. As the voter becomes more dissatisfied with outmoded hand tools for political expression — the ballot, the pen, and the periodic election of representatives — we are seeing evidence of the short-circuiting of these traditional methods by the use of highly simplistic, partisan polls to take the voters pulse on current issues. Yet as *The Economist* has editorialized, "the opinion poll is, in a sense, a prototype for interactive politics."[17] An ATIF poll on "Improving Democracy in America," April 3, 1993, found U.S. citizens favored by 70 percent the following statement: "Require Congress to fund an independent office, set up to conduct scientific, nonpartisan, large-sample surveys of public opinion on all important national issues AND to promptly release the results to the media so that Congress and the public will know what most Americans want for legislation." This survey was part of the reason Congressman Ron Klink introduced a bill that would set up such a Congressional Office of Public Opinion Research and Assessment (COPORA).

The instant electronic referendum is already technically possible and the hardware, the television set as the citizen's information-receiving device and the telephone as the political-input unit, is already in place in almost every home. ATIF Survey #24, "Steps for Democracy: The Many Versus the Few," March 25, 1994, found 70 percent of U.S. citizens favored national referenda *binding* on Congress — while only 59 percent favored nonbinding referenda. As *The Economist* rightly notes, referenda may be a better way to deal with lobbying and special interests — since the people rather than politicians must be lobbied.[18] Yet the referenda process is often corrupted by money, special interests, and media campaigns such as those of the tobacco lobby and the interests that defeated the 1990 California environmental referendum: Big Green.[19]

Before we are overwhelmed by fears of the tyranny of the majority, let us clarify two U.S. beliefs: (1) citizens should participate in social decision making in a democratic society; and (2) voters must communicate their views to one another, to the organizations in which they are involved, and to elected government officials. The rationale lies deep in U.S. history in the ever-more-liberally inter-preted premise of its great social experiment: wisdom, creativity, and common sense are qualities distributed quite randomly throughout our population. Biology has not found us mistaken in this belief. This central premise, that an informed citizenry is capable of self-government, is not to say that the citizen will have all, or even some, of the answers to often complex, technical issues. But nonspecialized viewpoints can discipline technocrats by raising broad, humanistic questions, thereby helping experts structure problems, justify their projects, and think through long-range consequences more carefully.

Opening up existing and new channels of communication in commercial and noncommercial mass media is the key to assuring that citizens are sufficiently enlightened to vote wisely. Already U.S. citizens and those of other OECD countries are the most broadly educated populations in world history—and mass communications can raise this level even further. More continuous public affairs pro-gramming, such as on Britain's BBC and C-Span in the United States, is essential. Free, equitably apportioned time for political candidates and public and private officials is also vital and available in many OECD countries. By contrast in the United States, this free and equal time provision as well as the Fairness Doctrine were repealed, as men-tioned, by pressure from commercial broadcast lobbies. While speak-ing on a platform with him, I asked New Jersey Senator Bill Bradley about reinstating these former provisions of the Federal Communications Commission. Bradley ducked this issue and said that he favors a constitutional amendment to limit campaign donations.

Higher education could be available to all via the airwaves, as in Britain's Open University. Education no longer needs buildings, only the voluntary communion of the minds of our greatest teachers and of all who thirst for knowledge and understanding.[20] Indeed, in the past two decades highly educated citizen groups, with their academic advisors in tow, forced onto national agendas: (1) energy efficiency standards, conservation, and renewable energy sources (solar, wind power, etc.); (2) recognition of biodiversity as a fundamental natural resource; (3) self-determination for the world's indigenous peoples; (4) human rights; (5) equitable, resource-efficient, sustainable forms of development mindful of future generations; (6) restructuring of the

World Bank and the IMF; and (7) overhauling of the gross national product (GNP) to deduct social and environmental costs.

Collecting and analyzing individual viewpoints is already common practice in the commercial world; it's done by market sampling of consumer preferences and by use of data banks containing credit information or medical histories. We see it too in the statistical studies so prevalent in the behavioral sciences, and of course in the increasing use that politicians make of opinion polls. Yet the private use of information-gathering on credit or medical records has itself become a threat—with individuals' rights to challenge or correct erroneous data now protected by law. In the United States, commercial Neilsen ratings of audience size have been disastrous for quality television. Such methods tend to screen out of consideration new or random ideas, which are a vital component of an innovative society—just as money corrupts politics.

DEMOCRACY AND TECHNOLOGY: UTOPIA OR DYSTOPIA?

To illustrate all these issues I ended my 1970 article, "Computers: Hardware of Democracy," with this scenario:

> It is an early February evening in the year 2023, and John and Jane Doe are relaxing before the TV wall in their home communications center. The newly elected president of the United States is having her first "fireside chat" with her fellow citizens. She maps out the main issues the voters have presented to her administration, together with the widest range of options suggested by citizens from all walks of life. These options have been winnowed and tabulated by computers as to priorities. Priority number six has been flagged for resolution now to meet long-range planning goals. Priorities one through five, while of global importance, need further information input and analysis. "Priority number six" the president continues, "concerns future development plans for U.S. Region Three, which was formerly known as Appalachia; and five major options have been developed from both random voter feedback and scientific and specialist feedback, with votes from the affected region having additional

weighting over the rest. The options will now be summarized and simulated on your home screen."

The first option is displayed in a series of colorful simulated maps and diagrams. It would designate the whole region as a national park, and the chief recreational playground for the two great adjacent megalopolitan regions: to the east, BOSWASH (formerly known as the northeastern seaboard from Boston to Washington), and to the west CHIPITS (formerly the great industrial region of the Ohio River between Chicago and Pittsburgh). The plan entails six new towns of 250,000 people each, to serve as spas and cultural meccas. Their chief industries would be leisure and tourism, health and beauty maintenance, and the performing arts. Now charts appear showing that the economy of the region would grow at 10 percent per year for the first five years, and would require capital expenditures of half of one percent of current gross national product. Then, expected influxes of construction engineering and planning personnel are shown for the first five years of building; and, thereafter, the needs for increasing numbers of recreational managers and workers, doctors, health therapists, beauticians, physical education personnel and, of course, performing artists of all kinds.

"And now to Option Two," the president says. The second option would designate the area primarily as a natural resource bank, with a secondary use as wilderness recreation. The plan calls for filling the old mines with plastics, iron, copper, rubber, and other materials salvaged from the nation's waste disposal plants; these items would be stored until needed for recycling into production. A network of small towns would be necessary; their economies would be based largely on caretaker and inventory control functions, while also providing for campers and hikers using wilderness areas. As each of the additional combinations of alternatives was presented, a new computer simulation would appear on the Doe's screen. The president reappears and makes her formal declaration that the referendum on these development plans for U.S. Region Three would be made at 7 P.M. one week hence. She adds, "Each voter can, of course, receive their own detailed printout of the plans from the U.S. Government

Printout Office by dialing 555-4707 on their computer phone terminal."

At 7 P.M. one week later, John and Jane Doe—having discussed the plans with neighbors, and at their community town-hall meeting—have made up their minds. The telecast begins and the president says, "Good evening, my fellow citizens. I hope you have all done your homework, and that those of you who are registered voters will now give America the benefit of your informed, collective wisdom in tonight's very important national referendum on the long-range development of U.S. Region Three. To refresh your memories, we will again simulate on our home screen the five alternative plans prepared with guidelines from your previous feedback. Please have your voting cards ready for the optical scanner to verify. At the end of the review of the five plans, please place your voting cards in the scanner and then punch in your choice of options, one through five, on your computer phone digit buttons."

After voting John and Jane relax while the returns are being tabulated. It has been a grueling week of study for both of them, even though the standard work week has been reduced to two days—a result of machines and other capital instruments largely taking over production of wealth. Apart from the U.S. Region Three plan, they have had to study an important local education proposition involving three options on the "mix" of educational services their growing town will need in the next decade; they also have had to fulfill their voluntary community commitments. The red indicator light comes on, and the Does return to their home communications center. They learn that Option One for U.S. Region Three has passed.

Next month, their tasks will include determining a ten-year transportation design mix for their own U.S. Region One, monitoring a new study course given by the University of the Air, and beginning work to establish priorities on national resource allocation for the second phase of the twenty-five-year plan—for the years 2025 through 2050.[21]

"Utopia or nightmarish Dystopia?" I asked in my article. Was this the way democracy and technology might be headed? As automation produced more unemployment and shorter workweeks, would citizenship itself become more demanding so that for many it would be a full-time job and for others an overwhelming burden? Or will complex societies simply extend what de Tocqueville in 1835 called their "manufacturing aristocracies" worldwide? Are existing decision makers afraid that if citizens have too much undistorted information, and the means of channeling too many informed decisions into all levels of the political process, this will change the system itself? The more legitimate fear, shared by the founders of the United States, is just as real: that a truly direct democracy could not sufficiently filter the emotions of the voters and might lead to a tyranny of the majority. In computer terms, would too much participation make the social system too sensitive to feedback and produce rapid overcorrections, which could lead to destructive oscillation, loss of equilibrium, and chaos? In short, are humans too irrational to build a rational society?

In Chapter 8 we looked at human societies and their cultural DNA codes and saw that *replication* (i.e., tradition) is basic (as it is in the coding of all DNA), while *innovation* (i.e., mutation) is a much rarer phenomenon. Too much innovation can destabilize a society and too little leads to decay. Failed development models have proved to be overcentralizing, resource-wasting, often poverty-exacerbating, ecologically unsustainable, and finally have led to today's global debate about what we mean by "development." Archeologist Joseph Tainter (1988) identified precursors to the onset of collapse of earlier human civilizations. He noted a flurry of collective activity, often involving construction, just prior to the collapse of both the Roman Empire and the Mayan civilization, as if the societies were trying to counter rising stress. Today we see countries using massive public works projects to hype growth and we see growing megacities in construction booms that *The Economist* noted approvingly attest to their *vitality*.[22] These trends, whether debated as positive or negative, were the focus of the UN Habitat II Conference in Istanbul in 1996. I compare this de-structuring of societies approaching evolutionary "cul-de-sacs" to the phenomenon of "paedomorphosis" in species. (See Chapter 8, pages 190 and 191.)

History shows how earlier human attempts to organize growing populations repeatedly derailed. Hierarchies collapsed and leaders toppled because of lack of feedback from the governed, i.e., the feedback lacked the requisite complexity and leaders received too little valid, reality-tested information. This corresponds to my Entropy State: the growing organization reaches a stage where more effort is spent in coordination than in useful, productive output, and the society bogs down in transaction costs. The operational metaphors are "only the *system* can manage the system" and its corollary, "only the system can model the system." *The Economist* described this phenomenon in the growth of government bureaucracy and the numbers of lawyers in similar terms.[23]

De-structuring and devolution are about a key issue: how to flatten or replace old hierarchical structures by substituting lateral, networked, real-time information flows to allow all parts of a complex system to coordinate and align their knowledge of changing environments and move their activities toward flexible, adaptive responses. Political scientist Benjamin R. Barber points the way in *An Aristocracy of Everyone* (1992). Joseph Tainter adds, "Complex, differentiated industrial societies are an anomaly. For over 99 percent of our history as a species, we lived as low density foragers or farmers in egalitarian bands or villages of no more than a few dozen persons. . . . More complex societies are more costly to maintain than simple ones, and require greater levels of support per capita. . . . Moreover, to maintain complexity depends on continuous assessment of energy and other resources. It takes energy both to become complex and to remain so."[24]

I came to a similar conclusion: that the three-hundred-year industrial era has been a unique one—based on consuming a large percentage of the fossil fuels that were laid down in the Earth's crust over sixty million years ago. Thus, I saw the march toward increasing social complexity as a sign that industrialism had reached the evolutionary cul-de-sac I termed the Entropy State. This would mandate a shift toward renewable resources that I envisioned in *The Politics of the Solar Age*, and hopefully a new, wiser Age of Light. This would require relearning the arts and sciences of sustainability and *non*-material forms of development.

Meanwhile, even the European Union (EU), with its past successful cooperation and unification of twelve western countries and its 1994 inclusion of Austria, Sweden, and Finland, is in turmoil. The 1992 Maastricht Treaty and the move toward a single European currency were little more than an attempt to make Europe safe for global banks and corporations. Like the Norwegians, who opted not to join the EU at all, the Danes saw few safeguards within the EU for

Denmark's distinctive culture, social programs, and environment. Elites, which continue to see their independent sectors as rabble-rousers, know-nothings, or NIMBYs (not-in-my-back-yarders), will miss the point. If citizens' feedback is not taken seriously by politicians and media and channeled positively, their only recourse will be to simply continue resisting to get attention. Today, there is much new soul-searching by "Eurocrats" in Brussels about how to democratize: how to implement the principle of subsidiarity and share power with the elected European Parliament. Danish diplomat J. Ørstrøm Møller in *The Future European Model* (1995) sees simultaneous processes of economic internationalization and cultural decentralization.

National politicians and trade negotiators still believe that the global economy, world trade, and financial anarchy can be tamed by deregulation and by leveling the global playing field via the powerful but narrow commercial pacts of the World Trade Organization (WTO), while they lay off bets by forming new regional trade blocs. Yet these experiments in suboptimization simply *widen* social and environmental costs and *strengthen* protest movements and isolationist politicians. The North American Free Trade Agreement (NAFTA) ran into resistance from labor, environmentalists, and social movements including the uprising in Chiapas, Mexico, and so far has cost almost one million lost U.S. jobs, according to the *New York Times*.[25] Meanwhile, five giant corporations dominate citizens' attention in the global mediocracy. A headline concerning Rupert Murdoch's empire simply read, "Man Buys World."[26] Only when the UN is reshaped, together with other needed global institutions, can a more limited but effective form of sovereignty be exercised by nations—in new partnerships with both the private and civil sectors.

CHAPTER 12

NEW MARKETS
AND NEW COMMONS:
THE COOPERATIVE
ADVANTAGE

Today's Information Age networks function best on win-win principles, but they are still dominated by the global economic warfare paradigm. Bribery and cutthroat competition have become a large part "of a nasty, multibillion dollar war being waged over global markets."[1] Speculators have raided weak currencies almost at will: whether Mexico's 1994 peso meltdown or the 1992 trashing of Britain's pound and the European Monetary Union. Nervous investors, following each other in herds and trying to avoid currency risks, churn the world's stock exchanges. In the past, to deal with military thugs and threats, countries formed alliances such as the UN and made allies as in the Gulf War. Nations faced with raids on their currencies and bond markets by "economic thugs" who stampede investors will need to form new alliances against "economic aggression." In the United States, Republicans and Democrats in Congress joined populists and revolted against the $50 billion bailout of the Mexican peso, cobbled together by "old boys" at treasury departments, central banks, and the IMF. The populists cited the free market. Why should taxpayers take the hit rather than private banks, bond dealers, brokers, speculators, and other holders of Mexican debt just taking their losses as they did their earlier profits? Governments must share the blame for Mexico's woes.

THE CHALLENGE TO COOPERATE

Footloose money crossing national borders every day is one of the most destabilizing offshoots of the world's new electronic information-highway system. No government alone can withstand the hordes of currency and bond traders at their computer screens, executing the orders of large-scale speculators. As yet, there are no global "rules of the road"—let alone fees on these gambling transactions. As game theory and dynamic chaos models supersede economics, people can begin to see that rules of interaction are as fundamental as markets in human societies. Information Age networks function optimally with standardization of technologies and rules, while allowing democratic, equitable access to these new kinds of "common carriers."

Highways need traffic cops and stoplights. Gaming casinos must take a small percentage to operate the house. Today's global financial casino needs rules, and fees on transactions to pay for these necessary regulations. We need not repeat globally the bad old days of Wall Street in 1929, where the lack of rules, along with stampeding speculators and panicky investors, brought on the market crash and the Great Depression. In the 1930s, Wall Street's speculators were tamed and abuses were criminalized. A system of regulations was finally codified in 1933 as the Securities and Exchange Commission (SEC) to oversee the game. Confidence slowly returned—but not before the crisis brought misery and unemployment to millions of ordinary people on Main Street who had become dependent on Wall Street and banks in faraway capital cities.

After the Cold War, more competition, not cooperation, was hailed along with individualism and spreading markets as the preferred, inevitable path to a better future. Either/or thinking prevented the ancient Eastern concepts of balance and yin-yang complementarity from reframing the global situation—equally in need of cooperation as competition, similar to all of nature. As noted in Chapter 8, humans are equally capable of both behaviors, as well as creativity in new situations. In Chapter 9, we began to explore social aspects of competitive markets and cooperative commons and how, in truth, all markets *require* cooperative rules to function. (See Fig. 20. Differing Models of Markets and Commons.) Without cooperative rules, competitive markets will eventually self-destruct in cutthroat competition, oligopolies, or monopolies, or simply fill up all available niches and transform themselves into commons. For example, when

Economists	**Futurists/Systems**
Markets Private Sector . . . • Individual decisions • Competition • Invisible hand • Anti-Trust	**Open Systems** • Divisible resources • Win-lose rules • (Adam Smith's rules)
Commons Public Sector . . . • Property of all • Monopoly under regulation • Consortia • Networks • Standards	**Closed Systems** • Indivisible resources • Win-win rules • Cooperation • Agreements

Note: One must remember that all such schematizations are, at best, approximations and often culturally arbitrary.

Fig. 20.   Differing Models of Markets and Commons

© 1988 Hazel Henderson   Source: *Paradigms in Progress*

entrepreneurs and investors establish themselves in virgin territory (an unexploited wilderness or a traditional, nonmoney-using culture), they can compete as long as the "market space" allows. Then, similar to ecosystems, as more competing firms (or species) arrive, all the available niches in the market (or ecosystem) get filled. At this point, species and firms must shift to symbiotic, cooperative strategies and learn to coevolve, as in evolutionary biology.

As systems theorists know, if a problem looks insoluble from *within* the system—however deeply diagnosed—one must look at the larger enfolding system to search for causes that may be driving the problem. Nations have not fully learned this lesson—even after two devastating World Wars—they are still trying unsuccessfully to address global competition between them. In 1945, a social innovation, the UN, was founded, and warlike nation-states once again addressed their common problems of expansionism, mercantilism, beggar-thy-neighbor trade policies, and "hot" wars. Nations, however, had neither diagnosed themselves nor questioned their values and their institutionalizing of competitive protection rackets at all levels. National leaders, like many corporate chiefs, did not see their hierarchical competitive structures and their dominance/submission games as part of the problem. The competition paradigm was unquestioned. Many had pointed in this direction, from management gurus Warren Bennis, Charles Handy, and the late Eric Trist, to James Robertson in *Power, Money and Sex* (1976), William Irwin Thompson in *The Time Falling Bodies Take to Light* (1981), and Fritjof Capra in *The Turning Point* (1981), as well as myself in *The Politics of the Solar Age* (1981, 1988) and Riane Eisler in *The Chalice and the Blade* (1988).

Immediately after the Second World War, civil society groups kept alive hopes for world peace based on international cooperation, but they were officially shunned as naive idealists and, during the Cold War, as security risks. Most diplomats and international experts accepted the warring nation-state model of human societies as a given. They rarely took alternative analyses seriously, such as those of game theorist Robert Axelrod in *The Evolution of Cooperation* (1984), Fred Thayer in *An End to Hierarchy: An End to Competition* (1973, 1981), Alfie Kohn in his imaginative *No Contest* (1986), or Roger Fisher and William Ury in *Getting to Yes* (1991). A notable exception was Mikhail Gorbachev, who used game theory's tit-for-tat models as a negotiating tool to end the Cold War. In the late 1980s, in a series of moves that baffled the Reagan administration's military and political strategists, the last president of the USSR repeatedly challenged the United States to cooperate.

Currency speculation and the inability of the global securities and financial industry to address the mounting risks to all players has been another lesson in the limits to competition and the vital complementary role of cooperation. Economics is so immersed in the competition paradigm it consistently overlooks cooperation, the commons, and allocation theories—except when commons can be owned as property. Most of the governance and allocation issues perplexing human societies involve competition inappropriately extended into the global commons. And now yet another competitive market has integrated: the twenty-four-hour global casino has transformed from a marketplace of win-lose competition to a new form of electronic commons, where each "rational actor's" self-interested behavior can endanger the entire system—unless rapid, cooperative, win-win collective action is taken.

The vulnerability of tightly interlinked global financial market systems operating without overall rules has been repeatedly illustrated by examples such as Germany's Herstatt Bank failure and later the U.S. savings and loan crisis. Both these episodes were addressed by cooperative agreements and government intervention. Steven Solomon describes such behind-the-scenes global financial cooperation in *The Confidence Game: How Unelected Central Bankers Are Governing the Changed World Economy* (1995). The 1990s losses by banks and corporations in derivatives and hedging strategies raise concerns that risk reduction for individual players increases risks in the whole financial system; 1995 was a watershed year that forced governments to consider new global rules. Even otherwise free-market economists, including Fred Bergsten, Jeffrey Sachs, and Lawrence Summers, urged the formation of a "GATT for investment and finance."[2] Clearly, the UN can and must have a key role in fostering such innovations, together with the WTO.

Worried central bankers trying to stave off further crises are inhibited by the competitive paradigm from thinking outside of textbook economic remedies—such as raising interest rates or buying efforts, both zero-sum games—to support their domestic economies and currencies. Japan, facing deflation, tried another tack in August 1995 when it helped lower the overvalued yen by relaxing its regulations on Japanese investing in other countries. In the global commons, competitive zero-sum games reverberate into vicious circles where everyone loses. Not every country can run a positive trade balance or grow via export strategies without new win-win rules to end poverty: i.e., create new customers and manage the commons cooperatively. National players, handicapped by eroding sovereignty, maneuver painfully toward the *social innovation* needed to match the advance of the global casino's computer and satellite-based *technological innovation*. The UN in its preeminent role as global norm-setter, broker, networker, and convenor is well suited to fostering such social innovations in the new electronic commons.

Bankers, brokers, and bond and currency traders themselves — along with growing numbers of finance ministers, parliamentarians, and regulators — see the need for new rules to create more orderly capital and currency markets. Rules and standards extend, not limit, market regimes and inspire confidence and trust — the bedrock on which banking and money itself rests. The "circuit breakers" introduced on Wall Street after the 1987 crash damped the destabilizing effects of computerized program trading. Finance ministers acknowledge the loss of domestic controls to global competition as well as diminished tax revenues, which came with the financial deregulation of the 1980s. But their market paradigm hampers vital cooperation to address their collective dilemma. Bond markets more concerned with inflation than unemployment limit any one nation's "pump-priming" projects and jobs while reducing options for social safety nets to zero. Some central banks even tried to join the zero-sum derivatives trading game — on occasion with heavy losses. One entrepreneurial U.S. government agency, "Fannie Mae" or the Federal National Mortgage Association, capitalized on the weakness of the dollar in 1995 by successfully launching an offering of global bonds worth $720 million — in Deutschmarks. *Business Week's* Bill Javetski opined a new currency "marriage" between Germany's Deutschmark and the U.S. dollar, which is no longer seen as a reliable global reserve currency. Since the U.S. Republicans were looking to subcontract out government functions, he added "Why not let the Bundesbank run the Federal Reserve?"[3]

Only global agreements and standards for accounting, capital investment, currency exchange stabilization, and the restructuring of the IMF, World Bank, and World Trade Organization (WTO) can address today's paradoxes so well described by Jeffrey Sachs in *The*

Economist. However, his prescriptions for closing "the big holes [that] remain in the legal fabric [which] may yet threaten global economic systems," fall far short of addressing the dilemma of national governments squeezed between currency speculators and bond traders on the one hand and the perils of angry domestic voters and protests of IMF structural adjustments on the other. Sachs assumes "in 1994 the world is closer than ever before to the global *cooperative* [emphasis added] free market arrangements championed fifty years ago by the visionaries who met at Bretton Woods."[4] However, cooperative agreements do not emerge automatically from free markets and must be designed by human rather than invisible hands.

The continuous lag between technological innovations and social innovations, now evident in the computer industry as it is automating service sectors worldwide, underpins today's Internet and global financial cyberspace. Such cyberspaces are still viewed as markets by all the players, and their current win-lose competition, unchecked by rules or cooperative agreements, has begun to disorder social structures. Social innovations and new agreements, which often come from a systems approach, are seen as "interference in free markets." Yet in France, under a socialist government, MINITEL terminals were distributed freely, achieving much more rapid market acceptance of computers than in the United States. In France, after the 1995 strikes, there is also a widening debate about shortening the workweek to reduce rising unemployment.[5] Systems approaches suggest new strategies as win-lose markets grow into transition phases where cooperation (i.e., win-win strategies) can improve the game for everyone by establishing standards and rules at the global level. Mainstream corporations embraced global standard-setting in an advertising insert in *Business Week*, October 16, 1995, "American Competitiveness: Gaining an Edge through Strategic Standardization." Competing by cooperating and standard-setting will hallmark twenty-first century economies.

The lag between the explosion of computerized global financial trading and the regulatory efforts of finance ministers, bankers, and international bodies is widening. Capital-market regulations in individual countries must be harmonized into a single "global SEC," resembling the functioning of the SEC that regulates Wall Street in the United States. Many ad hoc efforts have been going on behind closed doors in studies underway at the IMF, at the BIS (Bank for

International Settlements), at meetings of the G-7, and in academia. National legislators can only respond to global speculation, hedging, and derivatives with ineffective domestic legislation. Meanwhile, the Europeans were still redesigning "convergence criteria" for their European Monetary Union (EMU), which had been derailed by speculators, strikes, and public skepticism. For example, the EMU's central bank board of directors might be fired if it didn't control inflation.[6] Market responses are equally suboptimal, such as increasing the contracting out of hedging and risk-management activities to banks (including Bankers Trust and Tokai Bank Europe) or private consulting firms such as Emcor Risk Management Consulting, U.S., the largest player.[7]

This outsourcing is driven by the complexity and costs of the computer programs and "rocket science" experts in such hedging strategies—now beyond the capabilities of most company treasurers. Such outsourcing creates even greater risk to the system as a whole since the few providers of such services may lead to a de facto "cartelization" of them. George Soros, one of the largest derivatives players, states in *Soros on Soros* (1995) that "all derivatives traded by banks should be registered with the BIS through various national regulatory agencies," and that "knock-out options should be banned." Soros has changed from believing markets are always right to assuming they are always wrong; he also states that economic theory assuming markets act on "perfect information" is false. I assume Soros has switched to systems and chaos theory, particularly now that he has become more of a global philanthropist. Meanwhile, Nobel Prize economist Gary S. Becker urged more old-time religion: "competition among currencies [to] help discipline irresponsible governments."[8]

Many traditional banking and financial leaders are still unable to transcend their competitive models to visualize needed social innovations, beyond maximizing self-interest as "rational" behavior. Regulation was fiercely opposed in the United States by the 1995 Republican "Contract with America," which stated that free-enterprise technological evolution was fundamental to American values and that regulatory intervention was too onerous on businesses. *Business Week* found the opposite to be the case—often regulations force companies to find cheaper and better manufacturing processes.[9] Regulations can also push companies to find new uses for effluents, recycle former wastes, and occasionally save money as with 3M's

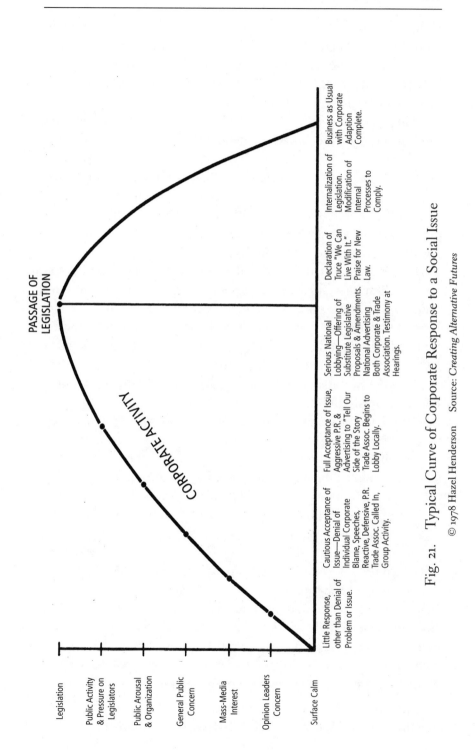

Fig. 21.   Typical Curve of Corporate Response to a Social Issue

© 1978 Hazel Henderson   Source: *Creating Alternative Futures*

Pollution Prevention Pays and other programs, confirmed by management guru Michael Porter.[10] The demand that cost- and risk-benefit analyses should arbitrate over regulations at an additional cost to taxpayers of $25 million was also debunked in *Business Week*, which pointed out well-known flaws in these methods.[11]

The Republicans had learned little from the savings and loan (S&L) bailout of the 1980s where the limits of competition had led to what bankers call "moral hazard," i.e., regulations acting to serve and protect competitors' risky searches for higher rates of return. In the case of the S&Ls, the repeal of "Regulation Q," which had limited the interest they could pay for deposits, set off a fierce competition for new depositors at ever higher interest rates. While still holding old low-interest mortgages from the past, the S&Ls made ever riskier real estate investments trying to make their "expensive" new deposits profitable. All this risk-taking in real estate speculation, however, was still buttressed by government-guaranteed deposits and insured by the Federal Savings and Loan Insurance Corporation (FSLIC). Several hundred billions of taxpayer dollars were thrown into the bailout—adding to the budget deficit.

In 1995, just as the need for a global SEC was being seriously debated, the Republicans took aim at none other than the U.S. Securities and Exchange Commission—as part of their budget cutting and downsizing of the federal bureaucracy. Even *Business Week* decried such reckless deregulation of the agency that had tamed Wall Street and made financial markets safe for U.S. investors—hinting at "revenge" motivations since SEC Chairman Arthur Levitt had raised over $3 million for Bill Clinton's presidential campaign.[12]

As debates over the need for regulating global capital markets could no longer be contained, central bankers and other gatekeepers of the old order resorted to "reliable experts" and lobbied the financial press to buttress their zero-sum views. *The Economist* ran articles defending speculators and free trade. No effort was more transparent than an invited article by Martin Feldstein, hailed as "distinguished Harvard economist" and president of America's National Bureau of Economic Research, in a section of *The Economist* on Global Capital Flows.[13] As I pointed out in a letter to the editor:

> Martin Feldstein's arguments and evidence do not support his thesis that "Too Little, Not Too Much" capital crossed

national borders (June 24, p. 72). Feldstein's semantics obscure the fact that he is making virtually the same critiques as many others who point to the same effects of today's $1 trillion daily capital flows: most are not "patient capital" (i.e., they are short-term and speculative).

Inconceivably, Feldstein missed the underlying reasons for this dearth of "patient capital"—the dearth at the global level of reporting, disclosure, rules, information, and the kind of policing by which the SEC regulates U.S. markets—which would reduce the risks of foreign investments. It is such national regulations that foster domestic capital flows within countries, as Feldstein must know.

Most of the specific reasons Feldstein cites in the case of Mexico, including the role of the U.S. Federal Reserve Board, are correct. They are also cited by others, including myself, who argue for a "global SEC" (i.e., international harmonizing of national securities regulations, in which task the International Organization of Securities Commissions [IOSCO] is leading), as well as other measures including overhauling the IMF and levying small (.003 percent) currency transaction fees. Only with such international agreements can we expect portfolio managers, other fiduciaries, and "patient investors" to venture into the global fast lane.

Feldstein simply avoids all these issues, now widely discussed, including by the G-7 at its 1994 and 1995 summits. One cannot mandate enforced savings by employees in government-franchised pension funds either, unless their portfolio managers can protect those investments from undue global financial risks.

Clearly the paradigm shift toward cooperation was not coming from the old money centers. However, the tacit discussion of both cooperation and the fact that all financial markets and money itself are undergirded by nothing more than *trust* was surfacing. Even the WTO was urged by *The Economist* to get involved in helping devise "investment principles" rather than just prise open markets. Some regional trade blocks do contain such codes and principles, including the eighteen-member Asia Pacific Economic Cooperation forum. *The Economist* pointed out that "regional deals will not suffice. A global accord will eventually be needed," and rich countries would have to curb their use of investment incentives (such as tax holidays, etc.).[14] In December 1995, I participated in a Geneva meeting hosted by Mikhail Gorbachev to discuss with business and government leaders and top officials of the WTO how to take such global codes, principles, and standards into account so as to focus on sustainable development.

After California's Orange County was forced to declare bankruptcy in 1995, this seismic shock reverberated to municipal bond markets. Lawyers for Orange County took refuge in the Chapter 9 Municipal Code of the U.S. Bankruptcy Law, which allows a municipality to declare bankruptcy and keep all its essential services intact, unlike the Bankruptcy Laws' Chapter 11 for private corporations. Holders of federal tax-free municipal bonds have always considered them the safest investment, since cities and counties do not go into liquidation. But Orange County's lawyer, Bruce Bennett, declared that the fine print in some of the bonds made them Certificates of Participation, i.e., not really bonds at all, but a form of lease. This makes it easier for any town or county in California to walk away from such obligations, including Orange County and its $1.9 million debt.[15]

Before the 1980s debt crisis, banks had also believed that nations' debts were as good as gold. In the 1990s, nations tried to protect their domestic safety nets in global financial markets, just as counties tried to protect their citizens from a *national* bond market. Yet if trust in any of these markets was undermined, the investors these cities and nations depended on would flee—causing financial meltdown. For example, in the U.S. budget battle of 1995, *Business Week* warned in "What If Uncle Sam Defaults?" that "the consequences should give pause to Gingrich's gang. A default would mean dumped bonds, a weaker dollar, and higher interest—just for starters."[16]

All this shows that trust and cooperation are already the key, but unacknowledged, underpinnings of all such domestic and international markets. The Orange County mess led *Fortune* magazine to investigate the $1.2 trillion U.S. market in tax-exempt municipal bonds subsidized by $20 billion a year of federal tax revenues. Widespread corruption, shady deals with local politicians to fund their pet urban construction projects, overcharging, and other irregularities were discovered.[17] What further proof is needed that markets must be regulated to protect the trust and cooperation intrinsic to their functioning? Once again, it is never a matter of *either* rules and regulations *or* freedom and markets. In human societies making rules of interaction is as natural and fundamental as the propensity to barter noticed by Adam Smith.

RECONCEPTUALIZING THE GLOBAL CASINO

The world trade/global economic warfare paradigm and financial markets have divorced themselves from the real economy of Main Street. The global casino has begun spinning out of control. One looming scenario is that of global recession as central bankers have tried to force countries to cut back their real Main Street economies whenever external raids by currency traders devalued their currencies. New spectacles have allowed some paradigm shifts. Downward mobility in the United States, Europe, and Japan have forced many to rethink scarcity, abundance, needs, satisfaction, and the value of their time. Many have begun paying attention to their own inner values and redefining money, wealth, work, productivity, efficiency, and progress. The key to the global puzzle is understanding that money is about trust; it isn't scarce and can no longer serve in its present form as a major, albeit covert, social regulatory mechanism.

Money, when functioning well, provides national circulatory systems for wider human exchange and purchasing power beyond face-to-face barter. But in globalized, competitive financial markets, national domestic economies will experience turbulence, recession, further restructuring, and even breakup. If central bankers continue to read out of their "zero inflation" hymnbooks, this might trigger a global slump. Driving countries into recessions with old remedies such as raising interest rates could ratchet rates up competitively. Or such "monetary mercantilism" could cause simultaneous recessions as each country tries to respond by "putting its house in order" with deep budget cuts and deficit reduction.

The Economist noticed this possible slump scenario in a June 1995 editorial, "Where a Slump Might Start." If the U.S. economy's 1995 growth kept slowing at the same time that Japan was experiencing negative growth and a painful savings and loan crisis of its own banking system, these two largest economies alone might trigger a global contraction. The institutional transmission belt of global money flows makes such scenarios possible. A large Tokyo bank, the Cosmo Credit Corporation, experienced a run in August 1995 when depositors drew out $900 million, forcing the Japanese government to put together a bailout while eyeing the $2.36 trillion savings of its citizens in Japan's Postal Savings Bank. Furious voters called for the resignation of Prime Minister Tomiichi Murayama. His Social Democratic Party persuaded him to hang on,[18] but he has since departed.

Nations have not recognized the crucial role of cooperation internationally or domestically and are still divided into private sectors (market competition) and public sectors (government and nonprofits)—even when they are obviously inextricable, as the Orange County, Mexican, and Japanese bank-bailouts showed. Competition's logical conclusion—global economic warfare—was proving its unsustainability. In Chapter 9 we saw how most preindustrial and traditional societies held land and natural resources communally—the village green (as the common grazing land of feudal England was known). In "The Tragedy of the Commons," Garrett Hardin pointed out the problem that occurred when individuals could maximize their self-interest (win-lose) by putting more of their sheep to feed on the commons—leading to overgrazing and destruction of the commons for all (i.e., lose-lose).[19]

Hardin, however, failed to dispel the confusion among economists between the commons as "property" and the commons as "closed systems" that are accessed collectively.[20] (See Fig. 20. Differing Models of Markets and Commons.) Either communities can agree on rules to fairly access the commons (win-win) or the commons can be enclosed as private or group property and plots to be traded in a market. In either case, issues of equity and freedom always have to be adjudicated, while the poor and powerless tend to be denied fair access. The world's oceans, the air we breathe, the planet's biodiversity are also commons—not property. They can only be managed with agreed upon rules to prevent exploitation. This is also true for the emerging electronic commons. The concept of private property (from the Latin *privare*) began as meaning all those goods, lands, and resources that individuals wished to *withhold* from the community and *deprive* from common usage.

Today, commons are still widely evident in traditional agricultural societies and many developing countries. Indeed, the march of industrialism has involved the enclosure of commons, begun by force in seventeenth-century Britain when peasants were driven off common lands by the Enclosure Acts, as described by Karl Polanyi in *The Great Transformation* (1944). Today, market forces seek to enclose such declining commons as ocean fish stocks (by arbitrarily allocating property rights to fisheries) and biodiversity (by continually encroaching on natural habitats and by patenting life forms and species)—shortchanging future generations via current market discount rates.

Such preempting of commons and simply declaring them common property or markets by fiat denies due process to indigenous people who have fostered natural resources and biodiversity for generations. Markets are the focus of economics textbooks, since economics arose as an epistemological justification for early capitalism and industrialization. Commons are still barely examined, even in much more recent "green" economics texts, except as common *property*.[21] The global electronic commons of finance, computer, and other communications networks are based on trust, standards, and informal cooperation as much as on competition.

In Chapter 9 we saw that from a systems viewpoint markets are merely open systems with abundant resources that can be used individually and competitively, while commons are closed systems where resources are used indivisibly, such as national parks, air, oceans, satellite orbits, and the earth's electromagnetic spectrum. (See Fig. 20. Differing Models of Markets and Commons.) Yet economics textbooks see these commons as only rationally managed if *owned* by somebody as "common property." Thus, economists rely on private ownership and property rights schemes, and lobby for market-based regulations, taxes and subsidies, or tradable "licenses to pollute." But the issues of markets-versus-commons and their enabling regulations still concern equity, accountability, and democratic access to public assets and essential services.

This state of affairs typifies the myriad players in the global casino: banking, brokerage, and insurance services, which now are merging; ad hoc groups such as the Paris Club; as well as the International Organization of Securities Commissions (IOSCO), the BIS and its 1988 Basle Accords, the Committee on Inter-Bank Netting Schemes, and others.[22] These public- and private-sector actors in the global casino can be convened. For example in 1995, Mary L. Schapiro, chair of the U.S. Commodity Futures Trading Commission (CFTC), helped convene officials of the securities regulatory commissions of sixteen nations in Britain, under the auspices of IOSCO. Their ensuing Windsor Declaration pledged to do the following:

1. Increase surveillance of big risks taken by market players.
2. Better disclose how well customer money is protected by foreign rules and regulations when it ventures abroad.
3. Establish strict accounting by brokerages and exchanges to distinguish client money from brokerages' funds.
4. Improve information available about bankruptcy laws in each market so investors will know how difficult it may be for them to get their money if their broker fails.
5. Establish a crisis team to provide other regulators with quick information at any time of the day or night.[23]

Similarly, systemic theoretical frameworks, as discussed in Chapters 9 and 10, can help reconceptualize the global casino, as well as the restructuring processes it has engendered:

1. The shift from measuring human progress as quantitative GNP growth to quality of life and sustainable development using the new scorecards discussed in Chapter 10.
2. The shift to reclassify the economy beyond the binary public and private sectors to include services; attention sectors; the unpaid, informal economy; and the productivity of nature.
3. A systems view of markets as open systems and commons as closed systems, to clarify policy options and new strategies. Systems theory shows how markets saturate (i.e., all niches are filled), and they turn into commons. A sign of the need to reorganize a market from win-lose competition to broader win-win rules for all players is the pervasive appearance of cutthroat competitiveness, i.e., lose-lose, such as today's competitive global economic warfare, conflicts over the earth's cluttered electromagnetic spectrum, or spreading global arms sales, which make no one more secure.[24]

Most institutions geared to meeting today's needs and those of future sustainable development will require restructuring and cooperative linking in networks and consortia of both public and private actors and civil organizations. Cold War ideological categories still divide Western industrial societies into public and private sectors. Public-sector organizations are expected to be socially concerned, cooperative, and less than efficient, while private-sector organizations are encouraged to be greedy, competitive, self-interested, and even rapacious. Happily, this wall is also coming down, as the voluntary civil society is being widely recognized as a third sector. Many hybrid, public-private organizations now address needs too large for any one company: for example, COMSAT and INTELSAT in telecommunications and SEMATECH, a consortium of computer-chip makers, share research and development costs, thus allowing them to compete globally. Even U.S. antitrust laws, which have enforced the ideology of competition, are now recognizing that competition and cooperation are equally valuable strategies — even as the people of the former USSR have recognized the limits of enforced cooperation and the bureaucratic welfare state.

There will be as many new types of enterprise charters as human imagination can devise: joint-stock companies, consortia, employee stock ownership plans, worker-owned enterprises (such as Trans World and United Airlines), holding companies, profit/nonprofit institutions and franchise chains, private/government corporations (such as the World Bank), community development banks, cooperatives (such as Ace Hardware), team-based decentralized enterprises (such as Swedish-Swiss Asea), networks of cooperating small businesses (such as those in Italy and Denmark), task forces of all kinds, and virtual corporations: i.e., networks of self-employed entrepreneurs and consulting groups. As appropriate to the Information Age, the new productive institutions will be knowledge intensive, communications intensive, and increasingly widely distributed both locally and globally. The key to all these new productive institutions will be their internal cultural DNA codes: their rules, values, and goals, as well as codes of conduct, which may be initially voluntary and self-proclaimed but are precursors to wider accountability.

These new enterprises and networks and their rules can help organize many of today's currently failing or saturated "win-lose" markets into "win-win" commons, such as that created in Kalundborg, Denmark. These new enterprises will be "thinking bigger" as they reconceptualize today's large-scale systemic human needs and sort out how those needs can be served through markets or reorganizing commons: peacekeeping, reforestation, desert greening, community health and care giving, public water supplies, clean air, etc. (See Fig. 22. The Evolving "Global Playing Field" on page 294.) Economics textbooks need to reflect systems theory and teach how to recognize when markets saturate (i.e., all niches are filled) and turn into commons.

In Chapter 9 we discussed the rise of nonmoney, information economies (local, regional, and global networks for barter, counter-trade, reciprocity, and mutual aid) wherever macroeconomic management is failing in societies.[25] The implications of the global Information Age of attention economies and mediocracies are that money and information are now equivalent. Information is often *more* valuable while money markets are no longer so "efficient." Indeed, psychology and game theory now often explain markets better than economics, as the 1994 Nobel awards in economics attest. The global money monopolies will continue to break up in the turbulence they create and as grassroots communities and small businesses retreat to their own local information societies and currencies. Socially innovative corporations, governments, and citizens go around money monopolies ever more easily using computer-based trading systems and the Internet.

Demands for democratizing and restructuring the World Bank, the IMF, and the WTO as well as opening up the still private BIS, culminated in the clashes in Madrid in 1994 between developing and industrial countries over fairness and special drawing rights (SDRs), paper gold that the IMF can issue. Protests will become more strident as more people see that money, its issuance and the regulation of its supply, and the availability of credits and liquidity, are not due to an invisible hand or market forces. Money is created and regulated by national governments and their central banks—which often heed other bankers, bondholders, and players in the capital markets more closely than they heed employees, villages, or women in the world's informal economies. In mediocracies, people now see on financial TV shows how market players wait with bated breath to hear of the interest rate decisions of the U.S. Federal Reserve Board or Germany's Bundesbank. Democratic reformers seek transparency and access to these "technical" decisions so that local enterprises, villages, NGOs, and communities can operate on the same real-time basis as the market makers.

As the crises swamping macroeconomic management become more evident, it is clear that money systems need rethinking and redesigning. The daily aggregated global money tsunami rolls around the world with inadequate sluices, dams, and holding ponds and is too immense, volatile, and liquid. It washes away vital catchments, familiar eddies, stream beds, and eventually the delicate membranes surrounding each human community "cell." Free traders do not understand such concepts from cell biology: that all cells must have membranes. This is not the same as advocating protectionism. All cells have *permeable* membranes, but if these are swept away, the cells' internal processes are unable to function. Living human communities are akin to cells in requiring such permeable membranes — based on local cultural DNA and ecosystems.

We saw in Chapter 9 how independent, urban money systems have always flourished whenever central governments mismanaged national affairs. Local money is needed, too, until global casino money fire hoses are capped. Such alternative currencies fostered local employment in the 1930s as mentioned in *Depression Scrip of the United States* (Mitchell and Shafer 1984). As we saw, many of these new forms of "money" are simply information networks and function like commodity exchanges, just as payments unions and trade agreements do for governments. These nonmoney and scrip-based economies are leading indicators of transition to a much more diverse socially and ecologically compatible future.

Different kinds of money at different levels are necessary to preserve a measure of autonomy and diversity in communities, cities, and nations. When I first visited China in 1986 I remember congratulating officials on their use of "village money," i.e., the renminbi currency, which was not easily convertible to the yuan or to the Foreign Exchange Certificates issued to visitors. The nonconvertibility of the yuan in international markets for many years thereafter allowed China to grow domestically without the daily destabilizations that are the curse of weak convertible currencies.

Now that the dollar is suspect, a truly global currency is needed, as Keynes advocated in 1945 at Bretton Woods: one which does not depend on any one or two national currencies. This vital global currency — probably backed by a basket of commodities — has been debated for many decades and was also proposed by Ralph Borsodi along with his local currency, the constant, as described in Chapter 9. The idea of a global currency backed by a basket of commodities resurfaced in the 1980s as a proposal by then-U.S. Treasury Secretary James Baker. Other refinements on global currency proposals, discussed in *Rethinking Bretton Woods* (Griesgraber 1994), include using SDRs and other variations on buttressing a commodity-backed global currency by managing buffer stocks of the world's key commodities and gold. In 1990, I collaborated on and hand-delivered in Moscow such a proposal for a national commodity currency to parallel the ruble. At a seminar at the then-Soviet Academy of Sciences Department on World Economy, it was studied by the group and sent to President Mikhail Gorbachev's advisors—but rejected in the rush to make the ruble convertible. At that time, the exchange rate was six rubles to the dollar. In 1995, the rate fluctuated around 4,500 rubles to the dollar.

The transitional Eastern European economies have done much social innovating in devising specialized forms of money for government use. These include the vouchers issued in the Czech Republic, Poland, Hungary, and later, Russia, to all adults for nominal sums for the "purchase" of privatizing assets of state-owned enterprises. These privatizations, when conducted fairly and openly, were far more equitable than many of Europe's privatizations or those in Mexico and Latin America. In Britain, for example, water and telephone companies, railroads, and other assets built and owned by all taxpayers were sold on stock exchanges to those who could afford them. This allowed well-off players to acquire them—while the proceeds were sunk into annual budgets or went to reduce deficits and pay off interest and old bondholders.

Other vouchers, for student loans, rent, daycare, and so on, along with food stamps and low-cost credit for micro-enterprises, are a form of government money. Social security checks, Earned Income Tax Credits (EITCs), corporate subsidies, and tax expenditures are also special kinds of money with limited uses and convertibility. The other major kind of money needed is local, as described in Chapter 9. All these different kinds of money are essential to optimize the functioning of human communities, their trading and productive enterprises in all sectors at all levels from global to local. These new kinds of currencies, some pure information exchanges, are emerging in mediocracies and attention economies. They can create safety nets and homegrown economies, and allow a resurgence of kinship systems and cultural perspectives beyond today's economies and financial/currency systems.

NEW MARKETS TO SERVE BOTH GLOBAL AND LOCAL COMMONS

The United Nations itself is best positioned to serve this new global Information Age. Information technologies, communications corporations, and well-motivated private-sector innovators are waiting to play. Mutual- and pension-fund managers are faced with huge flows from small investors and employees. These funds are overhanging domestic stock markets—driving up prices—while good opportunities to invest in entrepreneurs in South Africa, Asia, East Europe, and Latin America are too risky. For example, Marshall Carter, a former Peace Corps volunteer and CEO of the Boston-based State Street Bank, which serves as fiduciary manager for some $3 trillion of employee pensions in 70 countries, has been pondering the role of over $6 trillion in such pension plans, and how to responsibly manage them for the overall benefit of their beneficiaries—the world's workers. Thus Carter and the CEO of Boston-based Fidelity Investments, Ed Johnson, with some $200 billion in assets, joined with *WorldPaper*, also of Boston, and offered to host with UNDP a meeting in connection with the 1995 UN Summit on Social Development in Copenhagen. They wanted to explore what private, financial players could do to help fund social and sustainable development. The reverberations of that meeting are discussed in Chapter 13.

The UN, seeing itself as a "club" of nation-states, has often ignored or been suspicious of private-sector corporations. Only after corporate profits have been sanitized as pure financial flows via the World Bank and the IMF have UN agencies dealt with private banks and debt markets, country's sovereign bonds—often haggling over restructuring the uncollectable debt-overhang from the 1980s. The Cold War congealed such attitudes: private capitalism was excoriated in many countries with socialist-leaning governments, while governments—however venal and incompetent—were always part of the UN club.

If the UN could break out of this ideological box, it could reframe its activities as partnerships with globally concerned, private-sector players, with technological and social innovators, and with the creative forces within civil society. I had crassly suggested that UN administrators might imagine the entire organization in global corporate terms: i.e., the United Nations as the world's best known and respected de facto "global brand name." Such a concept was, of course, scandalous and I did not commit it to paper until 1995. The UN had already been approached countless times by profit-maximizing corporations wanting to "ride" on its logos and the fine work of its agencies in child development, health, human rights, and peacekeeping—just to boost their own corporate images and marketing.

Yet the watershed events of 1995 pushed UN leaders to rethink their old public/private-sector dichotomies, too. At the Copenhagen

Summit, the roles of the private sector and the civil society were acknowledged. The idea of a multiplicity of pragmatic partnerships between all three sectors took root. This helped break a fifty-year logjam. Thousands of innovative proposals could, at last, be structured into real business plans and new partnership organizations. Those seemingly insoluble problems of the commons could be reorganized and some of them could be addressed by new charters of authority from the United Nations. The UN could very carefully "license" its precious "global brand name" under public scrutiny and oversight.

This is similar to the early corporate charters that kings and nations "subcontracted" to private-sector innovators to trade, produce, and serve needs, as for example in Canada's many Crown corporations. Yes, it is risky and it will take years to design such semiprivatized activities with all the necessary rules, regulations, and oversight. But by contrast, what already exists is worse—a world of unregulated financial casinos and global corporations chartered to exploit the global commons and even capture further standard-setting and regulation from governments with no concern other than profiting their stockholders. The "fast-tracking" of private interest groups cooperating in trade pacts is described by Raymond Vernon and Debora Spar in *Beyond Globalism* (1989)—without a single reference to the United Nations.

Worse, the UN has been called upon daily by its member-countries to assume ever-larger burdens, from Cambodia to Cypress to El Salvador. UN Secretary-General Boutros Boutros-Ghali has noted in *Agenda for Peace* (1992) and *An Agenda for Development* (1995) that a strengthened UN, which can meet the new burdens, requires more secure and predictable financing. But the countries making the most demands (notably the United States, which owes the UN some $1.3 billion) are collectively in arrears by over $3 billion. The UN Charter mandates these dues and penalties for delinquents. Logically, the UN should impose penalties on arrears and be able to collect fees for its services: for example, on commercial uses of the global commons—the oceans, the atmosphere, and the electromagnetic spectrum, whose shipping lanes, air traffic routes, and radio frequencies the UN oversees. The UN should also be able to collect fines for abuses of these commons, such as arms trading, pollution, and currency speculation, or even create partnerships to privatize some of its services and share in the revenues produced. The UN has been providing hundreds of valuable, unique services for member-countries and private sectors. These services could yield new sources of sufficient revenue to fund all the UN programs, from peacekeeping to health, education, and humanitarian aid.[26] Yet if the United States paid up, the UN's "funding crisis" would disappear.

Issues of restructuring the UN for greater accountability are cru-cial to its new role. The UN could then downsize and focus on its roles as global networker, norm and standard setter, convenor and broker; it could continue its vital services to the international com-munity and receive proper compensation. Or the UN could assist in organizing agreements and partnerships and, where possible, contract out some of its services on behalf of the global commons. Only such agreements, painstakingly forged and ratified by governments and parliaments, can foster the organization of new markets to *serve and not control* these commons—the biospheric heritage of all people and species. Traditional diplomats and international experts at first dis-missed such ideas as impossible. Yet we also witnessed in 1995 the for-mation of the WTO—a massive multinational agreement ratified by no less than 120 countries, which have pooled some of their former sovereignty in much less accountable ways.

Global capital markets can be tamed *and* made more efficient by shifting taxes onto resource depletion, inefficiency, waste, and pollu-tion while reducing income and payroll taxes (calibrated to meet each country's tax code differentials between labor and capital). Such a tax formula could correct prices (by internalizing social and environ-mental costs) and run economies with a leaner mixture of resources, energy, and capital and a richer mixture of employment. Globally, taxation of currency speculation, collected automatically by all gov-ernments as proposed in 1978 by James Tobin, is winning new sup-port.[27] This tax should be less than the .5 percent originally proposed since the volume of speculation is now so huge. Some currency traders are comfortable with a tax of .003 percent or less—even though their trades often involve spreads of only a few basis points. Even U.S. Treasury Under-Secretary Lawrence Summers supported the tax in 1989, when he was an academic.[28] Economist Rudi Dornbusch supports a cross-border tax on all financial transactions instead of just on currency trades, which could be collected also by national governments.[29]

There are few good arguments against the UN being able to issue its own bonds. The $700 billion socially responsible investment market in the United States demonstrates that many globally concerned investors and bond traders would make a viable market in such UN bonds—underpinned by mandatory dues. The UN has become a mature global institution that provides its 187 member-countries with indispensable services. There is no reason that companies and individuals who benefit from these services should not share costs: from airlines and their passengers to investors, corporations, banks, accounting firms, bond dealers, hotel chains, and the tourist industries and entertainment sectors. Should not all of them pay small royalties for the privileges of using the global commons and doing business in a peaceful, orderly world assured by a properly funded United Nations?

Unfortunately, a high-level advisory group on UN financing convened by the Ford Foundation in 1993, representing many players in the now-dying global financial order (including former central bankers Paul Volcker of the United States and Karl Otto Pohl of Germany's Bundesbank), rejected new UN funding mechanisms. Nevertheless, the debate about democratizing the global financial system in the Information Age has been joined. Social innovations to enhance UN functions and provide secure financing is the subject of Chapter 13. Many new markets and new commons will provide opportunities in the emerging global playing field. The UN has already modified its concepts of sovereignty to embrace global changes and to address the new humanitarian concerns in world public opinion, which no longer sanctions national dictators who oppress their own people.[30]

All of these concepts were researched by members and expert advisors of the Global Commission to Fund the United Nations. The commission released its first report at a press briefing at the UN Summit on Social Development in Copenhagen in March 1995, *The UN at Fifty: Policy and Financing Alternatives*, coedited by Harlan Cleveland, myself, and Inge Kaul, all of whom serve on the Global Commission. In addition, new agreements can raise the floor under today's global playing field by building on the girders already in place, such as the *Agenda 21* and other UN treaties and agreements. We humans *can* build a win-win world; indeed we *must* if we are to survive.

CHAPTER 13

AGREEING ON RULES
AND SOCIAL INNOVATIONS
FOR OUR COMMON
FUTURE

Let us now examine more closely 1995, a watershed year in global affairs. Millennial anxieties and hopes were focused on the fiftieth anniversary of the UN. Clearly, the UN needed reinvigorating, restructuring, and reforming. Almost since its founding in 1945, the Cold War had slowly warped its politics and structures in the ideological crossfire of the superpowers, and the veto had often crippled the decisions of its Security Council. The General Assembly had become a forum for the rest of the world—an important function and safety valve for the world's unsolved problems and human agendas. Too often this led the more powerful nations to bypass the General Assembly and the Economic and Social Council (ECOSOC), which was designed to be an equal counterpart to the Security Council. ECOSOC and other agencies of the UN, like the Commission on Trade and Development (UNCTAD), had become forums for what were then called "Third World" issues and withered; some agencies— the International Labor Organization (ILO) and the Economic, Scientific, and Cultural Organization (UNESCO)—were politicized.

Meanwhile, the UN's powerful member-states had commandeered the World Bank and the International Monetary Fund (IMF) and, together with financial and corporate interests, dominated the endless GATT (General Agreement on Tariffs and Trade) rounds of trade liberalization that led to the World Trade Organization (WTO).

New markets

- Attention, information, media sectors
- Telecom services
- Desert greening
- Pollution control
- Renewable energy
- Recycling, ecoresource management
- "Caring" sector (day care, counseling, rehab, nursing)
- Infrastructure (extending transport, telecommunications, etc.)
- Ecorestoration, bioremediation
- Conflict resolution
- Personal growth, education
- Human social development

New commons

- Biodiversity
- Space, Earth systems science
- Electromagnetic spectrum
- Oceans, water resources
- Atmosphere, ozone layer
- Security, peacekeeping
- Forests, ecosystems
- Health
- Global economy, financial casino
- Cyberspace, networks
- Antarctica

Fig. 22.   The Evolving "Global Playing Field"

© 1981 Hazel Henderson   Source: *Paradigms in Progress*

These industrialized states also formed their own "clubs" outside the UN—the Organization for Economic Cooperation and Development (OECD), the G-7, the G-10, and others—while their central banks coordinated through the Bank for International Settlements (BIS). The North-South dialogue fizzled. Launched in the late 1970s by the Group of 77 developing nations, it had gradually broken down after the Group proposed a more equitable New International Economic Order (NIEO).

The Cold War struggle had politicized the whole world—increasingly terrorized by the superpowers' nuclear and conventional arms stockpiles. In 1995 Alice Slater, director of Economists Allied for Arms Reduction (ECAAR), estimated the cost of the nuclear age to U.S. taxpayers at $4 trillion since 1945. Since 1984 the United States has spent $36 billion on Star Wars, and the 1995 budget was estimated to include between $25 and $40 billion more.[1] NASA's $3.4 billion plan for a 1997 launch of the Cassini space probe powered by 72.3 pounds of plutonium (while European launches already used benign solar cells) extended the nuclear madness. From 1947 until 1990, the United States spent over $11 trillion on the military.

Yet the UN's special agencies had pressed on quietly—fostering scores of agreements and treaties: from nuclear nonproliferation through the International Atomic Energy Agency (IAEA), to airline routes through the International Air Traffic Association (IATA), and postal rates through the Global Postal Union. As Harlan Cleveland (1993) described, the members of the UN—working around Cold War confrontations—had been gradually "pooling their sovereignty" in such cooperative agreements for their collective mutual benefit. It is on these and other foundations that "We the Peoples"—not just the *nations* seeking freedom from "the scourge of war," as stated in the UN Charter—must continue this task of building a win-win world.

Many nations still competitively manipulate the UN for their own national purposes: withholding their annual dues (in 1995 the total arrears were $3.4 billion), walking out of UN agencies of which they disapprove, or using the UN as a "fig leaf" or a "scapegoat." Yet the UN has continued doing much of the work the world wanted done through its humanitarian and development agencies and various peacekeeping missions. The U.S. government's role—for better or worse—has always been pivotal: whether in the cold-shouldering of the UN during the Reagan years, with its back dues still $1.2 billion in arrears by 1995, or in the sudden almost commandeering of the UN in 1991 to support President Bush in the Gulf War. The high point of U.S. "approval" of the UN was marked by its controversial role in the Gulf War, although the war was deeply opposed by many other states.

In the intervening run-up to the UN's fiftieth anniversary in 1995, thousands of civil society organizations (CSOs), study groups in academia, and assorted commissions prepared reports and recommendations to reshape the UN for its next fifty years. Some reviewed the UN charter and pointed out that it contained no language on major contemporary concerns such as the environment, global corporations, refugees, terrorism, money laundering, and global currency flows. The widespread supposition behind these mostly useful and constructive recommendations was that the UN was here to stay—in fact, indispensable. It was unthinkable that its fifty years of often unappreciated work on "We the Peoples" agenda concerns—human rights, education, health, children, poverty reduction, safety standards for employees and consumers, peacemaking, and environmental protection—would not continue and expand. While there had always been UN detractors in many countries, they were considered backward, isolationist elements. Yet in the United States, such elements had often thrown Congress into reverse on internationalism and had triggered the U.S. pullout from the doomed League of Nations after World War I.

Tragically, in the general celebration worldwide of the UN's fiftieth anniversary, the United States again became the spoiler. The Clinton administration, weakened by the 1994 Republican capture of the U.S. Congress, became ambivalent in its UN commitment. Meanwhile, the reactionary Senator Jesse Helms took on congressional oversight of the UN and global concerns as chairman of the Senate Committee on Foreign Relations, which joined with the House of Representatives in proposing deep cuts in UN peacekeeping contributions and "foreign" aid. The old two-party consensus had splintered, and often-muddled "third party" opposition to NAFTA and GATT permeated both Republican thinking (via Pat Buchanan) and that of Democrats (via Ralph Nader-led consumers, labor leaders, and environmentalists) as discussed in Chapters 4 and 11.

The alienation and job insecurity described in Chapter 4, as well as the confusion over domestic terrorism and violence, led to extreme, anti-UN fringe elements such as the network of Washington-hating, armed "militias" capturing the attention and support of some five million Americans, far in excess of their actual numbers. Amplified by mediocracy politics, these groups—many sounding paranoid—demanded cuts in U.S. funding of the UN. Some even called for the United States to pull out of the UN as they fantasized that UN blue helmets were lurking in the U.S. backwoods, "maneuvering" their "foreign troops" to "take over America." In spite of such baseless ravings and other untruths, Washington politicians often pandered unconscionably to fringe opinions. A bill calling for a U.S. pullout from the UN, filed in late 1995 by a Florida Republican freshman, gained over a dozen cosponsors. Even presidential candidates, from Robert Dole, who should have known better, to isolationist Pat Buchanan, adopted such rhetoric. Dole stirred up a phoney flap about the UN and in 1996 introduced his own bill to pull the United States out.

The debacle in Bosnia proved to be a flash point for much arguing and reassessment. UN Secretary-General Boutros-Ghali, in an interview published in the *San Francisco Examiner* on 30 June 1995, laid out the whole truth. Responding to questions about the horrors in Rwanda and Bosnia for which the UN was blamed, Boutros-Ghali responded, "The Security Council and the UN are the member-states. . . . The UN has no army, no money, no infrastructure. The UN is a kind of symbol, a forum. If they [the member-states] are not able to work together, the UN can do nothing . . . and in the case of Bosnia, they are not able to work together." The next question: "Doesn't Article 42 of the UN Charter allow you to raise an army from member-states?" Boutros-Ghali replied, "Yes, but the member-states have never accepted giving an army to the UN. . . . The member-states still don't know what they want to do with the UN. . . . If member-states will not decide, it will just become a debating society."

This unbelievable scenario was looming: U.S. politicians talked recklessly about the UN's irrelevance while its brave blue helmets were dying in Bosnia's cross fire. The 1995 Dayton Accords bypassed the UN in a U.S.-led NATO (North American Treaty Organization) operation—even though U.S. public opinion rejected the role of "world policeman." Bosnia became the best argument for UN "rapid-reaction forces." Member-states, not the UN, were revealed as impotent.[2]

When an Americans Talk Issues Foundation (ATIF) survey questioned the U.S. public about the U.S. role in the UN and what might happen to U.S. leadership in the world if the United States actually left the UN, 58 percent said the United States would lose its world leadership—either because there would be no world leadership (38 percent) or because U.S. leadership would be taken over by other countries (20 percent). A frightening 39 percent said it would make no difference, but this must be seen in the context of the survey, which showed that some 71 percent of Americans mistrust their own government to do the right thing. By contrast, Americans have more faith that the UN is doing the right thing (at least 52 percent). By a two to one ratio, Americans also think that "U.S. troops should only take part in military operations under U.S. command," a plank in the Republicans' Contract With America.[3] As the United States was sending its own troops to Bosnia under NATO command, many wondered how many returning body bags seen on U.S. TV screens it would take to push U.S. leaders into reaffirming the UN's role in global peacekeeping. In many cases, UN soldiers already in Bosnia simply exchanged their blue helmets for NATO ones.

Perhaps we humans need to go right to the brink and look over the precipice before we pull back and devise more appropriate strategies. The Bosnian tragedy accelerated U.S. and NATO administrators' attempts to find partnership and common cause with nongovernmental organizations (NGOs), which they had previously patronized. The September 1995 forty-eighth annual NGO conference addressed "Global Issues, Global Actors, Global Responsibilities." UN Secretary-General Boutros-Ghali stated, "NGOs are a basic element in the representation of the modern world." The conference invited not only NGOs/CSOs and media but also the business and financial community, trade associations, and local authorities. Meanwhile, U.S. and NATO operations in Bosnia were budgeted at $6 billion, and it was belatedly acknowledged that another $6 billion would be needed to cover the costs of civil society conflict resolution, organization of elections, care for refugees, and resettlement operations, in which the UN would be indispensible.

NEW APPROACHES TO FUNDING THE UN: MAKING THE WORLD SAFE FOR SOCIAL INNOVATION

Clearly the dues system of funding the UN must be augmented by these methods:

1. Assessing interest payments on arrears and suspending voting rights for member-states in arrears.

2. Exploring with the private sector the issuing and marketing of UN bonds.

3. Levying a .003 percent fee on all international currency trans-actions to shift markets toward longer-term investments; to reduce speculation; to allocate proceeds in a transparent, accountable manner to UN programs for human development; and to pay for computer programs to collect the fees.

4. Stepping up research on fees for use of the global commons, as well as global "sin taxes" on pollution, ocean-dumping of toxic wastes, excessive depletion of natural resources, and energy-waste, in order to correct prices with fully internalized social and environmental costs and lower the relative cost of labor and payroll taxes.

5. Downsizing and restructuring the World Bank and IMF while bringing them back into the UN fold: make their governance equitable and transparent and retarget their missions toward social development and environmental sustainability, starting with cancellation of debts of the most indebted countries.

6. Reducing, by fines or other means, international arms and drug trafficking, and authorizing the proposed new public-private UN Security Insurance Agency (UNSIA), which would offer countries wishing to remain secure while lowering their defense budgets, contractual insurance policies for peacekeeping forces—the premiums for which would be used to permanently fund a professional UN conflict-resolution and peacekeeping system.[4]

Meanwhile, I had become a founding commissioner of the Global Commission to Fund the UN (GCFUN) in August of 1994, along with concerned experts, officials, and NGO leaders from over thirty countries. The GCFUN was a unique expression of the grow-ing global civil society, since no heads of state or UN bodies had com-missioned or funded it and it operated as a "virtual organization." GCFUN's two-person secretariat simply networked its already active, powerful, and committed commissioners around strategic global con-ferences, G-7 meetings, and other media-reportable events to draw attention to its agenda.

This agenda was evolutionary and rested on a three-pronged approach to financing the UN and building a win-win world. First, the commission's name signaled that funding the UN was no longer only a concern of its member-nations but also of the civil society, i.e., "We the Peoples." If the member-states would not shoulder their UN Charter responsibilities to pay their UN dues, then others in the progressive private sector and in the civil society would devise additional ways to fund the UN. Secondly, the UN itself would need to be restructured in order to be reinvigorated and fully financed to address all the tasks the world demanded, and the many new problems of the global commons which no nation alone could address. Thirdly, the commission intended to show, via the global media, that there was no shortage of money in the world to meet the real needs of "We the Peoples." The commission would demonstrate that it was a matter of old paradigms, misplaced priorities, malfunctioning governments and bureaucracies, and lack of cooperative international agreements. Most commissioners favored proposals that small fees and royalties should be collected on the so-far untamed workings of global financial markets and rampant private and corporate exploitation of the world's common, biospheric heritage of millions of years of evolution.

The commission's charter—drafted and ratified by its own members—was designed to make the world safer for social innovation. The commission would seek out or generate outside-the-envelope proposals in the emerging paradigm of global cooperative advantage: agreements to halt the slide toward global economic warfare. The charter included, for example, encouraging and researching all possible ways of funding the UN and of furthering sustainable human development by the international levying of fees and licenses for all the private, commercial uses of the global commons. The charter defined these commons as the world's oceans, atmosphere, satellite orbits in space, electromagnetic communications spectrum, Antarctica, and the newest global commons—the world's information highways, financial cyberspace, and the now seamless interdependent world economy. By levying fair commercial fees for profitable use of these resources and fair taxation on their abuse—such as pollution, arms sales, and currency speculation—legitimate revenues could fund the UN many times over *and* address all the needs of the human family as outlined, for example, in "What the World Wants and How to Pay for It."[5]

As mentioned in Chapter 12, the commission's first report, *The United Nations at Fifty: Policy and Financing Alternatives* (Cleveland et al. 1995) was released to the two thousand journalists who covered the UN World Summit on Social Development in Copenhagen in 1995. The report, now in its second U.S. edition, helped force all these proposals and others onto the world agenda—via the world's media and also because they were hand carried by NGO leaders to their national politicians and officials. Heads of state at the Copenhagen Summit added some of the new agenda items to their speeches, including ubiquitous calls for redirecting GNP growth into a "new development paradigm." Many of the leaders and delegates called for international taxation, particularly of currency speculation, which filled the headlines during the conference.

UN Secretary-General Boutros-Ghali had issued his *Agenda for Peace* (1992) and *An Agenda for Development* (1995), chartering a new course for the UN emphasizing its development and humanitarian role in *preventing* conflict—above the more limited role in after-the-fact peacekeeping. Development, redefined as people-centered and ecologically sustainable, would be the strategy to prevent conflicts. The UN itself, in spite of its current problems, is still the world's major networker, broker, and convenor of new global negotiations. The G-7 is too elite and only represents 12 percent of the world's population. The Bretton Woods institutions are undergoing their own restructuring—responding to criticism and trying to rebuild confidence in their development strategies. The OECD is also unsuitable as a convenor since it only represents the world's industrial countries. The Nonaligned Group of 77 and the Group of Fifteen represent the developing countries. All these organizations illustrate the fault lines of the declining post–Cold War world, together with ad hoc groups such as the Paris Club and other debt-renegotiating groups.

Leaders at the UN were galvanizing. One example is Ambassador Juan Somavia of Chile, who steered the Copenhagen Summit into addressing the issues of the global commons and the need for a new paradigm of development. UN Administrator James Gustave Speth restructured the United Nations Development Programme (UNDP) along the lines of partnerships in its programs, with multiple actors and grassroots NGOs. The UNDP's *Human Development Report* kept the agenda of "We the Peoples" before world public opinion. In 1994, UNDP published a number of innovative proposals, including

Dr. Oscar Arias Sánchez's Global Demilitarization Fund; James Tobin's Currency Exchange Tax; the idea for a new Development Security Council; and the 20/20 Compact (between donors and recipient countries), which proposed that 20 percent of all aid funds be directed toward poverty reduction and social needs.

These visions of the possible, along with others such as a World Criminal Court to bring to public judgment dictators who oppress their own people as well as other perpetrators of crimes against humanity, caught the attention of the world. By the end of 1995, this new court had issued indictments of war criminals in Bosnia, and a World Environmental Court was proposed by many NGOs. The world's image banks — even those still controlled by giant corporations and mediocracies — began to be recharged with new paradigms, possibilities, and viable paths to the twenty-first century. For example, the world learned that in 1991 governments spent $1,877 on their militaries for every $1 spent on peacekeeping; by 1993, governments had reduced this sum to $250 spent on the military per peacekeeping dollar.[6]

Simultaneously, in the UN's fiftieth anniversary year, all the reports of semiofficial bodies and mainstream NGOs were released or received renewed attention, including the Commission on Global Governance, *Our Global Neighborhood* (1995); the Independent Commission on Population and Quality of Life, *Toward a New Multilateralism: Funding Global Priorities*; and academic reports from the Worldwatch Institute; the North-South Roundtable; the Yale University report, *The United Nations in Its Second Half-Century*; and those of many NGOs, including the World Federalists, the United Nations Associations, and others. Earlier publications on UN reform by Erskine Childers and Brian Urquhart (1990, 1991), both commissioners of GCFUN, added to the mix of socially innovative proposals. Some reports were bureaucratic,[7] designed to offend no one and keep further foundation grants coming — while others such as the GCFUN report contained signed articles that were clearly outside the envelope. Additional groundbreakers were Worldwatch Institute's *Budgeting for Disarmament: The Costs of War and Peace* (Renner 1994), and *Partnership for the Planet: An Environmental Agenda for the UN* (French 1995).

The Commission on Global Governance called for a World Summit on Global Governance to complement the World Federalists' proposal for a Citizens Summit. In 1993, 1994, and 1995, the civil-society-managed World Convocations on Global Governance had set the stage and helped network many organizations. Proposals for an elected "Peoples Chamber" of the UN (similar to the European Parliament) were widely discussed in many countries and approved by 44 percent of U.S. citizens in an ATIF survey.[8] Meanwhile, concerned legislators caucused with members from eighty parliaments worldwide, via their own Parliamentarians for Global Action.[9]

Not surprisingly, it was the grassroots globalists who pushed the old structures with the most innovative reports and actions. Some fifty NGOs petitioned the 1995 G-7 Summit in Halifax, Nova Scotia, with their reform proposals, *Making the International Institutions Work for People and the Planet*. Seven global NGOs arranged for a public hearing on 27 June 1994 at the European Parliament in Brussels on "The Political Responsibilities of the European Union for the International Financial Order in View of Sustainable Development and Social Cohesion."[10] The International Coalition for Development Action (ICDA) published its 1995 *Update on Trade-Related Issues, Focusing Grassroots Globalists on the Need to Lobby Reforms at the New WTO*.[11] Grassroots globalists successfully lobbied the European Parliament, which rejected a law that would have allowed companies to patent life forms. UN advisor Mahbub ul Haq, pioneering innovator of the *Human Development Report*, published his own no-holds-barred *Reflections on Human Development* (1995). Two innovative ecological economists calculated the Generational Environmental Debt (GED) that Sweden's current generation owed to its descendants at $32 billion as of 1990.[12] Other innovative reports included *Sustainable Netherlands* by the Netherlands Friends of the Earth in Amsterdam, and a host of new *Green Plans* (Johnson 1995).

THE BUSINESS COMMUNITY BEGINS TO BUILD BRIDGES

One of the more interesting innovations at the 1995 World Summit on Social Development in Copenhagen was the deliberate involvement of the financial and business community. Maurice Strong had pioneered this kind of involvement at the Rio Earth Summit in 1992 by inviting his friend Stephan Schmidheiny and the World Business Council for Sustainable Development to produce their own report, *Changing Course* (1992). At the Copenhagen Summit, a Business Council for the Social Summit (BUSCO) was organized by Oliver

Giscard d'Estaing, cofounder of INSEAD, the "Harvard Business School" of Europe, based in France. The BUSCO brought many high-level corporate leaders to Copenhagen and they released their own report, *The Evolution of the Market Economy*. The German Foundation for International Development's Policy Forum also produced a report, *Innovative Resource Management for Social Development*. Many of these reports were included in the GCFUN's *The United Nations at Fifty* (Cleveland et al. 1995).

The GCFUN Report also reviewed many of the new "codes of conduct" promulgated by business groups, such as the Caux Roundtable, the CERES Principles, the Calvert Social Investment Fund's Principles, and the Minnesota Principles of Corporate Responsibility. These codes of conduct and standards can be dismissed by cynics, but they do tend to gradually solidify via legal precedent and form the basis for international protocols. The World Business Academy's Brian Bacon helped forge a historic cooperation between business and the ILO, launching business-labor partnerships for social development in Bombay, Tokyo, Nairobi, Bangkok, Dubai, Vietnam, and Mauritius.[13] Indeed, Robert L. Howie, Jr., vice president of International Systems Services Corporation, stated in *Business Week*, October 16, 1995, "There are only two kinds of corporations: those that have embraced the global standards process and those that will."

The group of financial players convened in Fredensborg's historic Stor Kro Hotel, near Copenhagen, by WorldPaper, State Street Bank, Fidelity Investments, and the UNDP explored how best to steer pension funds and other managed assets, particularly those in socially responsible, clean, green, and ethical funds, into real grassroots local development. Their two-day international inquiry, "Money Matters," emphasized in its invitation that "the social pressures facing human societies on the eve of the twenty-first century are abundant. In the information technology age with more wealth visible—and transferable—than ever, issues of unemployment, poverty, and human security still threaten the fabric of society."[14] Governments alone cannot address these issues, as their autonomy is ceded further to the financial cyberspace of global capital markets. Business, particularly the financial sector, is seen by many not only as a source of capital and jobs but also as a source of technological and social innovation, which can create opportunities for sustainable human and social development.

The Copenhagen Summit provided an ideal opportunity for a frank exchange of views between sectors and began the process of finding ways to insure more orderly international markets and investor confidence. A more predictable international climate in global capital markets is now a prerequisite for financing new enterprises, greener technologies, needed infrastructure, and a new era of sustainable human development. Investors and portfolio managers in North America, Europe, and other OECD countries have invested broadly in today's global, emerging markets. They have found many new opportunities for meeting human needs and social development while making good returns on their investments—despite escalating currency risks.

All investors, large and small, in mutual funds as well as those vested in pension plans, are anticipating college educations for their children and secure retirements for themselves from these investments—as they pour their funds into such managed portfolios. These funds now overhang domestic stock markets in most OECD countries. After the Mexican peso crisis, this overhang increased since many burned investors withdrew from global markets. Portfolio managers, however, trying to increase their competitive yields by diversification, increasingly turn to global investments—relying on ad hoc rescue packages such as that for Mexico. Until firmer plans emerge for a global SEC, such portfolio managers can only *increase* their use of hedging instruments—one more vicious circle.

Today all players seek common ground and win-win solutions to this looming "prisoner's dilemma": a virtuous circle, where agreements between all major public and private institutions can be harmonized and global currency and market risks can be reduced for all players. This, in turn, could help reduce reliance on hedging instruments, derivatives, and currency trading—further lowering risks.

Such win-win strategies could make global markets safer for all investors. For example, the Clinton administration in the United States unveiled a voluntary code of business ethics and workers' rights for U.S. companies, which Secretary of State Warren Christopher promised "will bring about a worldwide standard for the conduct of American business."[15] When I published "Should Business Solve Society's Problems?" in the *Harvard Business Review* in 1968, there were few MBA courses on business ethics. By 1995 such courses were standard and often compulsory.[16] Just as important, these same kinds of win-win strategies could reduce the daily hot money flows. Many public officials and financial and business leaders are advocating cooperative approaches, which will also help to restore a measure of domestic autonomy to national macroeconomic managers, government leaders, and central banks.

Loss of control has made it more difficult for leaders to govern; to meet voters' expectations; and to make long-term investments in domestic infrastructure, in the health and education of their people, and in the retraining of workers, as well as in reasonable social safety nets and sound environmental resource management. If a measure of control were restored, public- and private-sector leaders could capitalize on potentially positive trends (while minimizing the negative trends) in global capital markets and national economies. At the Money Matters meeting in Copenhagen, many players agreed that there is no dearth of funds seeking sound investment opportunities, particularly if governments cease subsidizing unsustainable practices and businesses. Then both public and private sectors could build stronger bridges and new partnerships for sound, long-term investments in socially responsible development.

The following were among the issues discussed at the Money Matters meeting in Copenhagen:[17]

1. Policy measures that could attract long-term, private-capital investment to an increasing number of developing countries, while insuring that the investments take "root" and promote broad-based participatory development.

2. The role of pension funds in mobilizing domestic savings, and how these funds could be used for social development, including credit for small-scale entrepreneurs.

3. How businesses and governments, as well as the civil society, can play their roles more effectively. Social development is a joint responsibility without which there will be no stability, peace, and growth, and hence no "good investment climate."

4. How to go beyond the financial services' enlightened, self-interested policy approaches and discuss additional policies, including currency exchange fees, which might help improve the orderliness of global capital markets and reduce volatility.

5. Ways and means of encouraging private enterprises to be environmentally sound and socially responsible, such as by

promulgating ethical principles and codes of conduct. A review of "best practices" in the business sector shows how socially responsible, ethical mutual funds, unit trusts, and limited partnerships can be financially successful. Many corporations have moved beyond compliance with existing regulations and are no longer merely driven by rising insurance costs and liability, but see their future profitability in longer-term economic calculations.

6. The changing values of investors, and marketing to the fast-growing segment of ethically, socially, environmentally, and globally concerned investors. This segment of the securities market represents over $650 billion in the United States alone. The demographics of such U.S. investors (concerned with "quality of life," college-educated, affluent, internationalist, and 60 percent or higher female) have allowed portfolio managers to create today's many successful "screened" portfolios, as well as innovative "high-social-impact" funds that invest in community development loan programs (combining their lower-than-average risk with slightly below-market return).

7. Creative legislative responses geared to encourage social investing and corporate responsibility. For example, Congressman Richard Gephardt, U.S. minority leader, has introduced legislation to recognize socially responsible companies that voluntarily use "best practices" and publicly promulgate social and ethical codes of conduct. Such companies would face less frequent financial reporting schedules: from a quarterly to an annual basis to encourage their longer-term views of profitability. The 1996 UN Summit, Habitat II, held in Istanbul, Turkey, hosted a World Business Forum that brought together a large gathering of corporations, socially responsible business groups, and trade associations concerned with global standards, best practices, codes of conduct, green auditing, and eco-labeling of products. The forum launched a Steering Committee on Global Standards.

This first Money Matters inquiry spawned others: in Boston, Kuala Lumpur, and Cairo. In June 1995 a group of private-sector leaders met with ECOSOC in Geneva for a historic exchange of views—leading to a reinvigoration of this important council. In January 1996, the World Business Academy–International Labor Organization leaders in Partnership for Social Development met in Hyderabad, India, hosted by the Nagarjuna Group of companies. Other efforts include the Progressio Foundation, a three-way, public-private-civil partnership to bring venture capital and foundation funds into the new hybrid enterprises of the civil society. Its founders, P. H. L. Kloppenborg and M. A. G. Palazzi, have been involved in the establishment of the Social Venture Network Europe in Amsterdam and the New Academy of Business, recently founded in cooperation with Schumacher College in Devon, U.K., which will offer executives, according to its prospectus, "a new kind of business education required for the greater role that business plays in society." The five-hundred-member Social Venture Network, established in 1987 in the United States by entrepreneurs and companies, released *Seventy-Five Best Practices for Socially Responsible Companies* (Reder 1995) and promulgates auditing of its standards.

Of course, the new social concern coming from small, progressive, young companies does not make a revolution. Most of the business world is still on the dog-eat-dog paradigm. And the mainstream business press is always waiting to pounce on any story that shows progressive enterprises may not be "walking their talk"—*as they should.* In addition, more exposés and investigations of media companies and their ethics are needed, as well as codes of responsibility for owners, editors, publishers, and journalists. The key issue in corporate responsibility remains the unaccountability of media giants in the global mediocracy and attention economies.

The more public airing of these issues, the better for everyone. Exposés in *Business Ethics,* a journal that covers the socially responsible business scene, have skyrocketed it to fame, increased its circulation, and won it a journalism award. For example, it ran a story investigating Britain's Body Shop, which was rejected by another publication, while informing its own investors of the increase to be expected in its own market position as a result. Some companies such as AES, which constructs cleaner, more energy-efficient cogeneration electricity facilities, have made headlines by planting trees to offset the carbon dioxide emissions they cause. AES planted a million trees in Guatemala in such an offset—while on the downside the company dabbles in ethically dubious trading of pollution licenses with other utilities.[18] Enterprises today offer transition strategies at best—all are rooted in unsustainable industrial sectors and beholden to profit-maximizing financiers and stockholders, not stakeholders.

Science ventures, too, have become more cooperative, as documented by the U.S. Office of Technology Assessment (OTA) in *International Partnerships in Large Science Projects* released in July 1995. The report points out that the use of treaties to formalize such partnerships is too cumbersome a vehicle for structuring scientific projects and will not necessarily guarantee funding stability. An important insight into the new partnership structures is that governments can rarely initiate such agreements—since their intergovernmental and treaty processes are too slow for such innovation. The private and civil sectors can move faster and innovate freely—precisely what their limited liability charters encourage.

Just as national governments have always franchised or chartered such activities under social contracts and legal authorizations where feasible, so international bodies, from the UN to the EU to the OECD and others, can franchise or charter new limited-purpose activities as well as franchise their well-known "global brand names." Governmental bodies and nations can then continue their roles in selecting and authorizing the best of the models. They can assess results, shape protocols and agreements to institutionalize standards, oversee compliance, and ratify the resulting treaties. We sometimes forget that this is the way COMSAT, INTELSAT, SEMATECH, the World Bank, and other hybrid, public-private corporations began.

EARLY INNOVATORS CONTINUE TO CHALLENGE OLD PARADIGMS

Once a paradigm begins to shift, often triggered by recognition of a looming crisis, the process resembles the critical mass phenomenon in physics or the sand-pile model in chaos theory. There is a sudden, often chaotic, slippage. (See Fig. 21. Typical Curve of Corporate Response to a Social Issue on page 277.) In human organizations this process is marked by a flurry of activity as growing numbers follow the path of the early innovators and challenge the old paradigm (both from within and without). Then, aware "early followers" rapidly reposition themselves for the new game—reworking research and grant proposals, recasting their resumes to highlight any relevant experience, however minuscule, refocusing their business plans, rewriting their courses, and reinterpreting their journal articles. Finally, the dam bursts, and the majority become imitators, adopters, or adapters. Often, in companies and large bureaucracies, management gurus and consultants midwife these change processes. They are hired to both train and familiarize people with the changes or to outplace those employees marked as part of the downsizing, or as outplacement firms prefer to say: right-sizing of the organization.

One recent sign of paradigm slippage was the Third Annual World Bank Conference, held in October 1995 and organized around environmentally sustainable development. The ninth president of the World Bank, James D. Wolfensohn, a former U.S. investment banker and arts patron, had taken over in June 1995 with a radical new agenda. Wolfensohn intended to shift the Bank's focus from giant dams and other big projects, hated by the large populations they displace, for which the Bank had been loaning money to governments for fifty years. The new focus would be on enabling private investments, with the Bank acting as a consultant and advisor.

The Third Annual Conference reflected this change—illustrating the speed with which paradigm shifts can occur in hierarchical organizations if they start at the top. Invited speakers included some old critics and even some passionate activists who had organized opposition to past Bank projects. Four volumes of environmental studies coauthored by Mohan Munasinge, chief of the Bank's Environmental Economics Division, were widely circulated, including one on "Economywide Policies and the Environment," a formerly taboo subject,[19] as well as the new Wealth Index mentioned in Chapter 10. An adjunct conference was jointly sponsored by the Bank and the Center for the Respect for Life and the Environment, an organization based in Washington, D.C., on "Ethics and Spiritual Values and the Promotion of Environmentally Sustainable Development."

During the 1970s and 1980s, there had been a small cabal of innovators within the Bank who invited me on several occasions to address their informal "prayer breakfasts" on the almost-taboo topic: "Values in Development." The cabal included Morris Miller, an executive director of the Bank, Ismail Serageldin, Mario and Sophia Kamanetsky, Pushpa Schwartz, and others. By 1993, Ismail Serageldin had emerged as the Bank's new vice president for Sustainable Development, while Morris Miller and Mario and Sophia Kamanetsky had left to write books on new models of development.[20]

The Bank became schizophrenic under the onslaughts of 1993 and 1994. On the one hand, it hired Herb Schmertz, a hard-ball public relations man formerly with Mobil Oil, to counteract the Fifty Years Is Enough campaign that had been instituted by environmental and sustainable development activist groups, and then echoed by U.S. conservatives and free-marketers at the Cato Institute who just wanted to shut the Bank down. On the other hand, the Bank began to hire some of its critics, including Joan Martin Brown, formerly of the United Nations Environment Program (UNEP) and John Clark of OXFAM (a private NGO aid agency) in the United Kingdom and author of *Democratizing Development* (1990). Evelyn Herfkens, the courageous, outspoken Dutch parliamentarian, had been appointed with her government's backing as one of the Bank's executive directors—and proved a key inside player for reform.

Thus, the early innovators either had left or were now able to advance within the new Wolfensohn presidency, while the outside academics and contractors hastily repositioned themselves. The staff imitators changed official pronouncements and public representations of the Bank's policies with bewildering speed—often denying that these policies were even new. The sign of organizational adaptation was when employees were instructed to announce that the Bank had always been right and had understood the new paradigm all along. A later, final stage is when organizational history is rewritten to show that the early outside critics and bearers of the new paradigm had been "too extreme" or deficient in some way. At the World Bank, in the Sustainable Development Department at least, adaptation was under way, even though many insiders told of a civil war of paradigms between orthodox economists and those espousing sustainable development.

In societies, the process is messier and involves everyone, i.e., it becomes political as well as economic and cultural. For example, in democracies and mediocracies, a torrent of new books formerly rejected are published and find audiences. Early innovators within political parties, trade associations, government agencies, academia, corporations, and civil society carry the new messages. They organize seminars and conferences and propose new courses, training, and restructuring. New entrepreneurs proliferate and their new enterprises are capitalized. Sclerotic old corporations downsize, restructure, merge, or are liquidated. Eventually, the ferment is reflected in traditional politics: first at the more permeable local, city, and state levels and then in national parliaments and governments, which become short-circuited internationally by grassroots, globalist NGOs and mass media. The confusion of political party realignments, conflicting polls, and differing interpretations of election results is seen, only in hindsight, as a political watershed—left for the historians to chronicle and debate.

Thus humans and their societies have always evolved. What makes us think this process will stop now? It is easy to laugh or be cynical at all these well-recognized human foibles. But we are an immature species and faced with organizational change processes at an unprecedented scale. We are all involved in these processes and cope as best we can—justifying our actions by defenses and rationalizations that best portray our own life changes. We have to remember the diversity principle—there are enough different roles for all the different souls—so that everyone can find their niche in the ecology of change.

Meanwhile, the high-risk, early social innovators plow on—together with their equally high-risk, but much more highly rewarded, private-sector technical innovators. The contrast is often startling. High-risk social innovators, such as former New York representative Bella Abzug, founder of the Women's Environment and Development Organization (WEDO); former New Zealand parliamentarian Marilyn Waring; and Indian physicist Vandana Shiva, all struggle on with few funds in their courageous, nonprofit organizing. Meanwhile, on August 9, 1995, two technological innovators who invented software for more efficient browsing on the Internet launched Netscape Communications in an initial public offering on Wall Street. The sixteen-month-old company, which had yet to earn its first dollar, was floated at $28 a share and soared to $74 ¾ by the end of the day.

Netscape Communications is a perfect example of a new enterprise in a mature mediocracy's attention economy sector. Its closing price gave Netscape a market value of $2.3 billion—more than Bethlehem Steel, Wendy's, and Maytag. According to Roger McNamee of Integral Capital Partners, Netscape Communications was pronounced by eager traders "the Microsoft of the Internet. . . . And everyone wants to own the next Microsoft," he added ebulliently.[21] The two innovators received instant high rewards: James

Clark's 9.7 million shares were valued at $566 million, and his partner Marc Andreesen's 1 million shares and options were worth $58 million.

Indeed, far from these kinds of instant rewards, social innovators are often punished—by death in countless cases: from Mahatma Gandhi and Martin Luther King to Chico Mendez. Sometimes they are forced to recant their groundbreaking work, as in Galileo's case where he was only acknowledged long after his lifetime. Other social innovators are arrested, jailed, and threatened, such as Myanmar's democratic leader, Aung San Suu Kyi, and Rigoberto Menchu of Guatemala. They, like some other social innovators, have the protection conferred by the Nobel Peace Prize. Others are only recognized posthumously after much ridicule and denouncing by their peers, as in the case of Buckminster Fuller.

These phenomena are related to the strong forces in human organizations for homeostasis: the wondrous, vital process that keeps our bodies from losing their structural integrity and vital functions. In our bodies "innovation" can appear as an invader to the immune system or as a mutation (possibly retrogressive) in a species. In societies, too, innovation is highly combustible and replication is the stabilizer in cultural DNA codes—just as in the DNA in our bodies. Elise Boulding has noted that sometimes less than 5 percent or even 3 percent of a population can shift an entire society in a new direction—*if* these people are active organizationally and become catalysts and enzymes of social change.

This phenomenon is mirrored in many dynamic systems studied by psychologists and chaos theorists, from the herd behavior seen in stock markets to the role of lone inventors of technologies that create new industries and change whole societies. In Chapter 11 of *The Politics of the Solar Age* (1981, 1988), I describe how dynamic systems are highly sensitive to initial conditions, as well as positive and negative feedback and their respective deviation-dampening and deviation-amplifying effects. I cite the example of the insurance industry's growing vulnerability to uninsurable risk-underwriting: by the mid-1980s the insurance industry was caught in many uninsurable debacles, with some companies near bankruptcy for writing "ticking time bomb" policies on classes of risk subject to dynamic change processes.

As the rate of global change has accelerated, social innovators who had been patiently "tilling the fields" in grassroots activism have become more visible. There are many examples. The late Jerry Mische and coauthor Patricia Mische, working with Global Education Associates, had for decades networked positive images and exemplary local solutions. Mildred Robbins Leet and Glenn Leet's "Trickle Up Program" has spawned thousands of small businesses in Africa, Asia, and Latin America. Mohammed Yunus' Grameen Bank in Bangladesh; Women's World Banking, founded by Michaela Walsh, Esther Ocloo, Ela Bhatt, and other pioneering women now represented by its president Nancy Barry; Southshore Bank, with its groundbreaking lending in poor neighborhoods—all are de rigueur organizations at World Bank meetings on the "new development paradigm." As Japan's political consensus splintered, Buddhist leader Daisaku Ikeda's long-time work for peace and human security became more visible through his position as international president of Soka Gakkai.[22] E. F. Schumacher's inspiration has lived on after his death in 1978, on the way to one more meeting. Appropriate Technology International of Washington, D.C., the U.S.-based clone of Schumacher's Intermediate Technology Development Group in Britain, went from punishment under the Reagan administration to being hailed as a technology-and-small-enterprise model of the new development paradigm.

Mikhail Gorbachev, who had done so much for the world in bringing perestroika and glasnost to the Russians and freedom to Eastern Europe, has become a global statesman. Gorbachev, through his Gorbachev Foundation, organized dozens of world leaders to examine new ways of thinking and fostering social innovations for humanity's twenty-first century. In September 1995, Gorbachev launched the first Annual State of the World Forum in San Francisco, California, bringing together heads of state, business leaders, authors, and those in the arts to address the great transition to the new century. I was privileged to be invited to convene the roundtables on "Twenty-First-Century Economies." Former U.S. President Jimmy Carter founded the Carter Center in Atlanta, which has become a mecca for social innovation. Ashok Khosla, who had given up a career as a Princeton-trained Ph.D. in physics to form the nonprofit Development Alternatives institute in his native India and convene the NGO forum at the Earth Summit, has now become an invited expert at World Bank meetings. The tireless work of Sixto Roxas and Maximo Juni Kalaw in the Philippines, as well as Kumar Rupesinge of International Alert in London, and many other such "servant" leaders has been recognized, along with others whom CIVICUS has documented.

After recognition of Senegal's late President Leopold Sengor and Czech President Vaclav Havel, heads-of-state have felt freer to quote poets and visionaries. In April 1996, President Havel hosted a Conference on Socially Responsible Business in Prague. Japan's former Prime Minister Murayama, on the anniversary of the end of World War II in August 1995, apologized before the world's media, the Emperor and Empress, and a football stadium of dignitaries in Tokyo for Japan's aggression. After Costa Rica's President Oscar Arias Sánchez was recognized with a Nobel Prize in 1987, he has tirelessly pursued preventive ways of peacemaking. Maria de Lourdes Pintasilgo, former prime minister of Portugal, and Canada's Pierre Elliott Trudeau forged similar exemplary paths as global citizens working for peace, justice, and sustainable development. Other heads of state began realizing that setting examples, in peacemaking and in their own lives, could win wide public admiration. Even U.S. Senators Jesse Helms' and Robert Dole's knee-jerk opposition to the UN was denounced and modified in more constructive terms—toward enabling the organization for its future role in the world.

After foot-dragging at the Copenhagen Summit on Social Development, the U.S. Clinton administration State Department issued a fact sheet, "Accomplishments of the World Summit on Social Development," emphasizing First Lady Hillary Clinton's and Vice President Al Gore's participation. The State Department reiterated its formerly lukewarm support citing five of the action items:

1. The commitment to reduce overall poverty in the shortest possible time and to eradicate absolute poverty by a target date to be specified in each country.

2. The commitment to achieve equality and equity between women and men.

3. The need to establish a framework that could improve the quality of life for workers . . . to safeguard the basic rights and safety of workers . . . to enforce the prohibition on forced and child labor . . . to support freedom of association, the right to organize and bargain collectively, and the principle of non-discrimination.

4. The need to equalize opportunities so that people with disabilities can contribute to and benefit from full participation in society.

5. The importance of key commitments made at recent UN conferences on the environment (Rio de Janeiro, 1992), on human rights (Vienna, 1993), and on population (Cairo, 1994), strongly endorsing the central role of sustainable development.[23]

The last UN conference of the century, on South-South cooperation, was set for 1997 and will provide welcome enrichment of development paradigms beyond global competition.[24]

Of course all of these signs of shifting positions can be dismissed as the ravings of a naive optimist or a blue-sky idealist. I respond these days by saying that I have studied human pathology for a quarter of a century—and still do. Later, I decided to map human societies for their potential, for signs of wellness, exemplary actions, local solutions, and where and how people were living out pompous creeds and walking their talk. In mediocracies and attention economies, where violence and degradation still are sold as "entertainment," some of us must seek the good news.

EXPLORING OPTIONS FOR TAMING THE GLOBAL CASINO

A full exploration of all the different ways to tame the global casino has been undertaken by the commissioners on GCFUN's Committee on Global Financial Markets, the research program at Yale University under Professor Bruce Russett, the University of Pennsylvania's Lauter Institute under Professor John Eikenberry, and the Centre for the Study of Global Governance at the London School of Economics under Professor Megned Desai. At the same time, groundbreaking work at the International Organization of Securities Commissions (IOSCO) and the Commodity Futures Trading Commission (CFTC) has continued. One of the most creative researchers on the subject of international financial regulation is Professor Ruben Mendez (1992), official historian of the UNDP and a Professor at Yale University.

Professor Mendez has proposed a social innovation that may work in conjunction with a currency exchange fee or as an alternative to it, and is now actively under review.[25] Mendez proposes a not-for-profit foreign exchange facility (or FXE) to perform foreign currency exchange transactions.[26] The FXE would be set up as a public utility, possibly franchised by a group of governments and the UN to offer a little healthy competition to the small group of private money-center banks that now exert a virtual monopoly on foreign exchange trading (known as "forex"). Experts in computer-based markets and trading systems believe this proposal is technologically feasible and even politically viable—if private markets continue unregulated and untaxed. The public utility FXE could simply offer lower prices per transaction and, since central banks and sovereign states still retain a measure of control over the currencies they issue, they could, if they cooperated, carve out a chunk of this global exchange. While costly to set up, the FXE would pay for itself rapidly and might be administered as a partnership with participation by the UN, the IMF, and the BIS, and might well generate revenues for UN programs.

Imagine walking through an airport looking for a booth to exchange your money and finding a new booth where a percentage of the exchange fees would go not to a private bank, but to the United Nations Children's Fund (UNICEF). A lot of travelers would appreciate the choice. Or how about buying UN bonds instead of expensive toys for your grandchild? Many grandparents would enjoy this option. A working group of bond dealers might jump at the opportunity if authorized informally by a high-level group of treasury officials in important member-states. They might, in private consultation with top UN officials, approve a study of such a new bond market. After all, if the member-states don't like paying their dues or do not wish to tax their voters but still value the UN's role in the world, they should welcome such funding alternatives.

World trade, as described in *Paradigms in Progress* (1991, 1995), is still shifting from hardware to software: cultural exports, music, art, design, expertise, and social innovations such as democracy. In some cases, such as truly complementary trade in a level global playing field of markets regulated for the highest ethical standards and using full cost prices, competition can work well. In other cases, cooperation is the advantageous strategy—for example, whenever resources must be used indivisibly, such as air, oceans, the Internet, and global financial trading systems. Another step in the right direction was the 1994 agreement between industrial and developing countries to restructure and share control of the World Bank's Global Environment Facility via its council of thirty-two nations. In a global commons, social innovators who want to push societies beyond the envelope of national protection rackets and global economic warfare have to be more audacious, and think bigger as well as smarter. Already, NGOs are campaigning to bring the WTO, with its nineteenth-century trade regulations, into the realities of twentieth-century global financial markets where speculative flows swamp trade in goods.

The currency exchange tax proposed by James Tobin in 1978 was derived from the writings of John Maynard Keynes.[27] Originally suggested at .5 percent or 1 percent on international currency trading (which is now the world's largest market at over $1 trillion per day), it would theoretically produce about $2 trillion annual tax revenue. This amount is probably much larger than the actual revenue that would be produced since the tax would deeply curtail reported trading, and exceeds manyfold the profits of that group of currency traders who derive income from facilitating (and hedging) legitimate international transactions, principally the money-center and large regional banks. All the rest of currency trading (estimated at 93 percent of the total) is a zero-sum game for speculators. Looked at from other points of view, the .5 percent to 1 percent tax also seems unrealistically large since it is far greater than typical spreads between bids and offers. For a standard trade (a typical trade for money-center banks is U.S. $5 million), a 1 percent tax amounts to a sizable $50,000, which would reduce currency trading drastically and dry up liquidity. Traditional arguments against such taxes cite the problem of avoidance, i.e., moving operations offshore or through quietly created loopholes.

Such a tax would certainly do what Tobin said it would, namely, "throw sand in the gears" of the speculative markets to slow them down. His goal was sensible: to make capital markets orderly and predictable enough to foster international trade and longer-term investment, which unbridled speculation might make so chaotic as to shrink currency liquidity drastically and ultimately bring chaos to national economies. Nation-states, in spite of their fears of driving forex markets offshore, still suffer from problems created by international capital markets since the widespread discontinuance of fixed exchange rates and other means of currency stabilization that have been tried and failed over the years.

The time is ripe for a much smaller fee than Tobin proposed (in the range of .001 percent to .003 percent). This would not harm trade in real goods and services or longer-term investments—but would mount up rapidly on the short-term daily transactions of speculators. The fee would be easy to collect according to computer experts, and some companies are interested in the task of adding a chip to trading screens. The smaller fee would still yield upwards of $50 million per day. This would pay for its administration, while a percentage would be retained by the collecting governments, with the balance replenishing currency stabilization and development funds. The Commission on Global Governance, many GCFUN commissioners, and others support this very small fee. A report in October 1995 from a group of influential economists convened by UNDP supported a Tobin fee of between .05 percent and .25 percent, collected by national governments.[28]

A firestorm of protest against a currency exchange tax arose from traders, central banks, and finance ministers after the March 1995 Summit on Social Development in Copenhagen. Even though the subject of global instabilities in capital markets was on the agenda of the June 1995 G-7 Summit in Halifax, Nova Scotia, Canadian Finance Minister Paul Martin, Trade Minister Roy McLaren, and Bank of Canada Governor Gordon Thiessen all rejected the tax proposal of Canadian Human Resources Minister Lloyd Axworthy, who had raised the issue with many others at the Copenhagen Summit. A flurry of editorials in the business press called for rejecting such a tax—using all the conventional arguments: it would dry up liquidity, be impossible to collect, invite offshore forex operations. The *Toronto Globe and Mail* rounded up many naysayers including Peter Sutherland, outgoing director general of the WTO, Ralph Bryant of the U.S.-based Brookings Institution, and David Longworth of the Bank of Canada. UN High Commissioner for Human Rights Jose Ayala Lasso had joined Lloyd Axworthy, however, in endorsing the tax, and events and popular protests kept the tax alive.[29] In April 1995, with the dollar still nose-diving, G-7 finance ministers met in Washington for five hours—but could not agree on any common action to stabilize the currency markets. Thus the whole issue landed at the Canada Summit in June.

As civil organizations rallied in Halifax to welcome the G-7 leaders with their demands for action to stabilize and tame the global casino—including imposing the currency tax—the G-7 countries issued an unusually frank communiqué and Background Document:

Review of International Institutions. It examined "the need for changes to the architecture of the international financial institutions"—i.e., the IMF, the World Bank Group, and the regional development banks. The Document noted all the new conditions in the integrated global capital markets and the new risks and challenges, among others, to "correct imbalances that engender financial and exchange market instability; adapting institutional mechanisms to a world of large and highly mobile private capital; and promoting more effective, sustainable development and poverty reduction." It rejected currency exchange taxes and capital controls, but allowed that "There may also be a need to look at other mechanisms that might usefully be considered in situations of financial crisis," calling for "an improved early warning system . . . to avoid financial shocks . . . an ongoing system of surveillance of national economic policies and development" by the IMF, which "should be more open and transparent." An "Emergency Financing Mechanism" was proposed within the IMF with a doubling of the reserve sums for currency stabilization (cleaned out by the Mexican bailout). The Document called for "strengthening financial market supervision and regulation" and a new "one-time special allocation of SDRs . . . to reduce inequities in the system"; it also asked the multilateral development banks for "a stronger focus on primary education and health care or the environment . . . such investments are not only economically sound but typically demonstrate high social rates of return as well."[30]

This Background Document is required reading for global grassroots activists as it adopts many of their demands. Amusingly, behind the scenes at the IMF, the research department had been ordered to bring out the heavy guns against the Tobin tax. A confidential memo on "International Capital Markets: Note on 'Sand-in-the-Wheels' Taxes on Foreign Exchange" approved by Morris Goldstein, 13 July 1995, was faxed to me by a grassroots activist group. In the memo, all the usual objections were trotted out again—based on the .5 percent original tax, which Tobin had revised downward to below .01 percent to account for today's much larger volume. The argument that traders would "fly the coop" to offshore jurisdictions is easily countered: if over 120 countries can agree on the WTO, surely they can add another clause on currency exchange fees. These would be universal and make any residual offshore efforts unlikely; if some small ones appeared, they could be outlawed as is money laundering. The memo asserts that little relationship has been shown between the level of transaction taxes (quite common in financial and other markets) and asset price volatility (not the main point—which was sheer *volume* of transactions—which *would* go down as admitted). Then the memo argues the opposite: i.e., the smaller tax now proposed would have little effect on volume or in deterring a speculative attack on a country's currency, and anyway, a tax would violate the IMF's Articles of Agreement (an obvious red herring—these can be changed).

Thus, the IMF had not yet heard of the "circuit-breaker fee" suggested by GCFUN Commissioner T. Ross Jackson, a mathematician and CEO of the GAIA Currency Funds, which manages hedge funds and currency portfolios. The circuit-breaker fee would be analogous to a similar one on Wall Street and could be used in conjunction with halts in trading (common on all stock exchanges) if a currency came under speculative attack. Jackson's proposal is a genuine social innovation because it offers national governments and central banks a new domestic macro-management tool to insulate their currencies and economies from attack—without having to raise interest rates and subject their citizens and businesses to a recession. Jackson's Working Paper and many others cited here are available from the Committee on Global Capital Markets of GCFUN.[31] They complement the group of proposals, published in *Rethinking Bretton Woods* edited by Jo Marie Griesgraber (1994), all innovative, equitable, and doable—highly recommended reading.[32] In late 1995, the Group of Twenty-Four (finance ministers from important developing countries) commissioned UNCTAD to study taxing global financial flows, and influential economist Rudi Dornbusch's verdict was a cautious endorsement.[33]

Another social innovation was proposed by Kimbert Raffer from the Kreisky Forum in Vienna in 1994: "What's Good for the United States Must Be Good for the World: Advocating an International Chapter 9 Insolvency." Raffer quoted no less than *The Financial Times* of London for context: "It is now well known that countries politically incapable of meeting their liabilities need some sort of bankruptcy procedure that ensures all creditors share the losses."[34] Recalling the Orange County bankruptcy, discussed in Chapter 12, we can see that many nations face analogous situations.

Indeed, G-7 meetings since the 1988 Summit in Toronto had been calling for more write-offs of debts of the poorest countries in

Sub-Saharan Africa. Most commercial banks had written off these kinds of loans years ago—with their stockholders taking the hit. The exception was the World Bank, which stubbornly refused—citing its charter—as if such things cannot be changed. Thus, the World Bank had entered into a punishing round of ill-conceived lending to such indebted countries—just to pay the interest on these uncollectable loans. No private banker could get away with such lunacy. The application of Chapter 9 of the U.S. Bankruptcy Law would be logical and doable, and would force the World Bank to adhere to the same good business practices it is fond of urging on everyone else. I expect to see such Chapter 9 proceedings initiated as test cases—since they can protect all vital services to the people of a country—just they protected the people of Orange County.

A new proposal by Howard M. Wachtel, author of *The Money Mandarins* (1990), calls for the coordination of interest-rate policies among the G-3: the United States, the European Union, and Japan. This cooperation would enable countries to pursue their own interest-rate objectives, but not at the expense of potential destabilization from other nations' competing interest-rate policies induced by the foreign exchange rate transmission belt.

Another quite practical innovation is the Blue Planet Lottery. Some airlines, including Swiss Air and British Airways, are considering the proposal that passengers be offered lottery tickets to benefit the global environment. Promoters, the Blue Planet Group of Canada, got the concept from TV producer Robert Duffield of the BBC. Canada's innovative International Development Research Centre is funding its assessment by an expert team from McGill University in Toronto.[35]

SOCIAL INNOVATIONS TO ENCOURAGE DEMILITARIZATION, PEACE, AND SUSTAINABLE DEVELOPMENT

The UN could authorize yet another social innovation: set up the proposed new public-private agency modeled on INTELSAT. The proposed United Nations Security Insurance Agency (UNSIA) could provide a substantial source of revenue for peacekeeping and peacemaking while providing member-states more security for less money, and it is supported by 62 percent of the U.S. public.[36] Initial calculations suggest that UNSIA could eventually cut countries' defense budgets by as much as 50 percent; provide enormous new markets for insurance companies; and allow former defense budgets to be redirected toward investments in health and education—now recognized, at last, by economists to be keys to development. The disarray of UN initiatives in Bosnia and elsewhere are arguments in favor of, not against, UNSIA.

UNSIA would negotiate agreements guaranteeing UN peacekeeping support to countries paying an annual premium for this protection. UNSIA would work closely with the country seeking protection, the UN, and the Security Council, all of whom must approve an agreement to make it binding. There would be separate agreements between UNSIA, the UN, the Security Council, and countries supplying the peacekeeping forces, whose costs would be actuarially covered out of the premium pool. A country seeking protection first would pay UNSIA to investigate its insurability, to assess its military risks, to determine the premiums required, and to define such insurable threats to its security, as invasion by neighbors, that would trigger specified levels of peacekeeping or other UN interventions. UNSIA may require that the country reduce its aggressiveness or curtail its military expenditures before it would be insurable, or it may suggest that if an adversarial neighbor also obtains UN protection, premiums for both countries would be greatly reduced. UNSIA would continually monitor compliance, contracting with civil society groups for their professional conflict-resolution services, and make recommendations on renewal.

UNSIA coverage would be particularly suitable for the forty or so smallest nations that would clearly be more secure if they had guaranteed UN protection, and might thus safely eliminate their military forces altogether. It may also be attractive to countries in regional hot spots who, after years of spending far more than they can afford in order to achieve, at best, an uneasy peace, are almost desperate for some way to break out of the dead end. The UNSIA proposal has been welcomed by Dr. Oscar Arias Sánchez as another useful approach to demilitarization and peacekeeping. Other endorsers include Nobel chemist John Polanyi of Canada and Nobel Peace Prize winner Betty Williams of Ireland; as well as Kumar Rupesinge, secretary-general of International Alert; Harlan Cleveland, author of *Birth of a New World Order* (1993); Jonathan Dean, author of *Ending Europe's Wars* (1994); UN advisor Mahbub ul Haq; and others. UNSIA has been assessed as "feasible" by the U.S.-based Center for Defense Information, which cites its applicability to NATO as an alternative to requiring prospective new Eastern European members to spend millions on upgrading their militaries to meet NATO standards.

Another social innovation toward global equity, which I proposed in *Paradigms in Progress*, is a North-South Population Credit Bank that would reward successful population and development policies. Using IPAT (see page 15), or similar Indian Equivalent measures, "sustainable development credits" would be due and could be further extended to countries for their lesser impact on global resources. I also proposed a Global Energy Bank to underwrite the shift to sustainable, renewable solar energy and conservation—since at that time the World Bank was funding ever more unsustainable energy projects. Construction of the massive ENRON fossil fuel energy plant near Bombay, India, was halted in 1995 though local and global grassroots action protesting overcharging and noncompetitive bidding. U.S. Ambassador to the UN Madeleine Albright floated an innovative proposal of her own: to complement existing groups of nations—the G-7, the G-10, the G-77, and others—there should be a Group of Democracies with the best rankings in the HDI. Hopefully, many in both North and South can find such new common-ground policies in the 1990s as we humans learn that managing our global commons will require many such "win-win" negotiations.

In 1995, the UN Commission on Sustainable Development accelerated schedules for implementing *Agenda 21* with agreements to Combat Desertification, strengthen the Climate Treaty, adopt a Fisheries Convention, and set up an Intergovernmental Panel on Forests; the commission also involved itself in the financing of sustainable development.[37] *Agenda 21* is a uniquely important global document signed at the 1992 Earth Summit in which 172 governments committed to implementation of a cooperative, multifaceted program to shift human societies toward partnership for healthier, more sustainable forms of development. To operationalize such shifting of gears, *Agenda 21* realistically calls for unprecedented levels of cooperation between countries, institutions, groups, and individuals.

Agenda 21 lays out the cooperative agenda for sustainable development. Developing countries, where large numbers of people still live in poverty, are accorded the necessary priority. Specific commitments are made to:

- reduce and write off unpayable debt;
- implement the official UN target for countries to make .7 percent of their GDP available for Official Development Assistance (ODA);
- address inequities in the structure of the global economy;
- increase cooperation in implementing environmentally sound technologies and making them available, particularly to developing countries;
- improve domestic policies; and
- make sure that World Bank and IMF-imposed structural adjustment programs do not cause further social and environmental costs and are applied fairly to all countries, both developing and developed.

All these commitments are fair and realistic bare minima in the global shift to sustainable development. *Agenda 21*'s more detailed agreements are equally vital:

- to overhaul economic indicators and systems of national accounts to more accurately value environmental damage and costs as well as resources;
- to institute user fees and other forms of green taxes on pollution, resource depletion, and waste.

Agenda 21 focuses on consumption patterns and draws the inescapable conclusion that industrial countries have patterns of consumption underlying their GDP growth that are unsustainable and unjust. A 1995 opinion survey of Americans found 82 percent agreeing that "Most of us buy and consume far more than we need; it's wasteful."[38] A UN tax-collecting authority could be set up for peacekeeping and sustainable development and to implement *Agenda 21*. This tax-collecting agency was called for in the 1980 proposal of the Brandt Commission to tax at a rate of 1 percent all arms trading (representing in 1995 some $800 million). As mentioned, 70 percent of U.S. citizens already support such a tax.

Additionally, the Information Age has opened up hosts of new opportunities. The UN global TV service could televise proceedings of the World Court and tribunals on genocide and criminal conduct. The World Court's new arm, which investigates criminal acts by leaders, could be on global television — just as the breakthrough program

"Human Rights and Wrongs" today airs cases of political repression, wrongful imprisonment, and torture of individuals—often uncovered by the tireless work of Amnesty International. Another social innovation, the proposed U.S. Congressional Office of Public Opinion Research and Assessment (COPORA), could help perfect the machinery of all democracies by consistently polling voters on major policy issues and instantly releasing the results to the media, as outlined in Chapter 11.

A social innovation proposed some twenty-five years ago by K. Helveg Peterson, the visionary former minister of education in Denmark, is even more important today. He proposed setting up a UN-authorized "rapid deployment" information force. A distinguished panel of highly recognized media editors and expert commentators would continually scan the planet's existing and potential political trouble spots. They would report to the relevant UN and government agencies on emerging potential crises or the rise of "crazy leaders," such as occurred so tragically in Yugoslavia. The panel would also release the information as newspaper columns and TV and radio reports to the growing "world court" of public opinion. For example, in the case of Yugoslavia, the world would have known soon after the fall of the USSR that old rivalries might be exploited by unscrupulous politicians such as Slobodan Milosovic, who preached his ugly "ethnic cleansing" on hundreds of radio stations. Similarly, rumors spread by radio fomented some of the atrocities in Rwanda. Irresponsible use of media can be counterbalanced by high-quality fact-finding broadcast rapidly worldwide.

The report issued by the Independent Commission on Population and Quality of Life, "Towards a New Multilateralism: Funding Global Priorities," contains forty-four important recommendations and assesses the current chances of most of the social innovations reviewed here and many more. Each is carefully examined and its considerable merits highlighted. While the commission's president, Maria de Lourdes Pintasilgo, former prime minister of Portugal, is a scientist and innovator, the authors, Dragoljub Najman and Hans d'Orville, are international experts and diplomats, and judge the likelihood of acceptance from a "rearview mirror" perspective.[39] Thus, social innovations can be slowed by historically bound ideas of the possible. With the best will in the world, fatalism can also lead to self-fulfillment. We humans have very powerful minds. The dreams and visions of yesterday have concretized—for better or worse in the structures we exist within today. We shape our buildings and institutions and then they shape us. This is why visioning and social innovations are so vital. They must be fostered so they can compete with dysfunctional beliefs and images and the malformed structures they create.

The biggest paradigm breakthrough for national leaders and international diplomats and experts would be reframing the international taxation issue. Beset by angry voters, most politicians and administrators have been in full retreat on domestic taxes and pushed further into tax and budget cutting. Thus, they have been averse-conditioned and deaf to any discussion of international taxation. Even collecting small and justifiable *fees* for commercial use of commons' resources and taxing their abuse, waste, and pollution has been a hard sell. Leaders have found it hard to see the good news: that by extending the WTO and other international agreements to include such fees and fines and by collecting such cross-border levies or designating the IMF, a UN agency, or other collection authority, they would have access to a new revenue stream. Just as nation-states have been devolving activities and "block grants" to their own provinces, cities, and states, the international agency collecting the new commercial fees and fines would disburse them by agreed formulas, as block grants to nation-states, international development, peacekeeping, and other agreed purposes. National governments would then disburse these block grants to localities. With the tax burdens of defense reduced by UNSIA and these other levies, and other external activities funded in this way, nations' domestic taxes could be lowered and still cover domestic investments in their own citizens and civil infrastructure.

Will the nation-states see the foolishness of their self-imposed "prisoner's dilemma"? Will they review the cases where cooperation confers greater advantages than competition? Will their advisors show them the difference? Possibly, we may be moving from today's unipolar world to a new bipolar world, with the United States outside of the UN. The pettifogging in Washington, D.C., by Senators Bob Dole and Jesse Helms concerning the UN and its alternative financing is not just a new politics of the absurd; the possibility of the United States pulling out of the UN was taken seriously around the world.

In January 1996, the fifteen-nation European Union had already proposed a new UN dues system by which the U.S. share would decline from 31 percent to 28.75 percent—a reduction of some $56 million annually.[40] Such a formula would increase the dues of other prosperous countries to bridge the gap, including Japan, Germany, and some of the rapidly growing Asian countries. The EU's proposal included a quid pro quo: delinquent members (including the United States) would be required to pay their dues on time. If they didn't, they would be assessed late payment charges and face a ban on all UN purchases from their corporations and on UN hiring of their citizens. The UN spent 19.5 percent of its budget with U.S.-based companies in 1994, for a total of $737 million. The delinquent countries would also face suspension of their voting rights.

New scenarios have begun proliferating. In recent discussions in the United Kingdom, Switzerland, India, and with many knowledgeable policymakers, North and South, a new view has been emerging that it might be a blessing if the United States withdrew from the UN. For example:

- If the United States were not present to veto it, the UN Security Council could be expanded to include countries such as India, Brazil, Germany, Japan, South Africa, and others as permanent members. UN dues could be reallocated to cover the U.S. arrears, reflecting the larger contributions and influence of the new members of the Security Council. The veto itself could at last be phased out.

- The UN headquarters could be moved to Geneva or to a friendly Asian city, reflecting the new and powerful role of Asia in the world's economy. The UN facilities in New York City could be sold or rented.

- With such improved finances, the UN might not need new sources of funding. At the same time, the UN would be free to enter into the long-standing debate on the many well-researched proposals for future financing of development and other preventive peacekeeping operations without further interference from the United States.

- The debate on managing the planet's common heritage resources—the oceans, the atmosphere, Antarctica, the electromagnetic spectrum, the information highways, and financial cyberspace—could continue in an open academic climate of free speech.

Is this what Senators Dole and Helms had in mind with their bill in the U.S. Congress to pull the United States out of the UN? As the old proverb goes, "Be mindful of what you ask for—you may get it." As long as the thinking of leaders remains trapped in their "prisoner's dilemma" of mistrust, they avoid the needed confidence-building and cooperation. As they inch toward new "win-win" paradigms, a view of all the possibilities in the cooperative advantage grows clearer. A win + win + world is not easy or certain—but it is possible.

NOTES

CHAPTER 1: GLOBAL ECONOMIC WARFARE VERSUS
SUSTAINABLE HUMAN DEVELOPMENT

1. World Commission on Environment and Development, *Our Common Future* (New York and London: Oxford University Press, 1987).

2. See, for example, Robert Kaplan, "Coming Anarchy," *Atlantic Monthly,* February 1994.

3. See, for example, Bart van Steenbergen, "Global Modeling in the 1990s," *Futures* 26, no. 1 (Jan./Feb. 1994): 44–56.

4. Gerald O. Barney with Jane Blewett and Kristen R. Barney, *Global 2000 Revisited: What Shall We Do?* (Arlington, Va.: Millennium Institute, 1993). Write to: Millennium Institute, 1117 North 19th Street, Suite 900, Arlington, VA 22209.

5. For additional information, contact the United Nations University, Tokyo 150, Japan; Fax: 89-03-3499-2828, or Washington, D.C., 202-686-5179.

Level 1

6. United Nations Population Division, *World Population Prospects: The 1992 Revision* (New York: United Nations, 1993), 153.

7. See, for example, Jon Erickson, *The Human Volcano: Population Growth as Geologic Force* (New York: Fax on File, 1995).

8. United Nations Population Division, *Long-Range World Population Projections: Two Centuries of Population Growth, 1950–2150* (New York: United Nations, 1992), 14.

9. *Business Week,* 12 June 1995, 28.

10. International Conference on Population and Development 94, "Investing Directly in People," *Newsletter of the International Conference on Population and Development,* no. 7 (New York: United Nations Population Fund, June 1993), 6.

11. EarthAction is a network of one thousand citizen groups in 126 countries. Address: Antonia Lopez de Bello, 024, Providentia, Santiago, Chile: Fax: 56-2-737-2897.

12. Sharon S. Russell and Michael S. Teitelbaum, *International Migration and International Trade* (Washington, D.C.: The World Bank, 1992), 15–17, 26–27.

13. *Business Week*, 3 July 1995, 30.

14. *The Economist*, 15 July 1995, 30, 18.

15. United Nations Population Division, *Urban and Rural Areas, 1950-2025* (New York: United Nations, 1993).

16. Carl Haub, Demographer, Population Reference Bureau, Washington, D.C., 1993. As quoted in World Resources Institute, "Population and the Environment" *World Resources, 1994–95: A Guide to the Global Environment* (New York and Oxford: Oxford University Press, 1994).

17. United Nations Population Division, *World Urbanization Prospects, 1950-2010* (New York: United Nations, 1993).

18. *Human Development Report, 1995* (New York: United Nations Development Programme, 1995).

19. Boris G. Rozanov, Viktor Targulian, and D. S. Orlov, "Soils," in *The Earth as Transformed by Human Action*, ed. B. L. Turner, William C. Clark, Robert W. Kates, et al. (Cambridge: Cambridge University Press, 1990), 213.

20. World Resources Institute, *World Resources 1992–93* (New York and Oxford: Oxford University Press, 1993), 111–118.

21. *The Economist*, 25 November 1995, 41.

22. *The Green Scissors Report*, Friends of the Earth and the National Taxpayers Union, Washington, D.C., 1995.

23. Harry E. Schwarz, Jacque Emel, William J. Dickens, et al., "Water Quality and Flows," in *The Earth as Transformed by Human Action*, ed. B. L. Turner, William C. Clark, Robert W. Kates, et al. (Cambridge: Cambridge University Press, 1990), 254.

24. *The Economist*, 10 June 1995.

25. World Resources Institute, "Population and the Environment," *World Resources, 1994–95: A Guide to the Global Environment* (New York and Oxford: Oxford University Press, 1994).

26. Stephen S. Morse, ed., *Emerging Viruses* (New York: New York University Press, 1993).

Level 2

27. Andrew Vayda, "Maori Conquest in Relation to New Zealand Environment," *Journal of the Polynesian Society* 65, no. 3 (1956), 20411; and Colin Turnbull, "Plight of the Ik and Kaiadilt Is Seen as Chilling Possible End for Man," *Smithsonian Magazine*, November 1972.

28. See, for example, David Loye, *The Healing of Our World: A Science of Moral Transformation* (Carmel, Calif.: Center for Partnership Studies, forthcoming); Wendell Bell, "Using Religion to Judge Preferable Futures: An Assessment," *Futures Research Quarterly* (fall 1994); Anna Lemkow, *The Wholeness Principle*; and Riane Eisler, *Sacred Pleasure*.

29. Americans Talk Issues Foundation, Survey #23: "Structures for Global Governance" (10 May 1993); and Survey #25 (July 1994). For copies of all sur-

veys write to: Americans Talk Issues Foundation, 10 Carrera St., St. Augustine, Florida 32084.

30. *Directory of National Commissions on Sustainable Development*, compiled by the Earth Council, the Natural Resources Defense Council, and the World Resources Institute: Washington, D.C. (1st edition, May 1994); Fax: 202-638-0036.

31. See, for example, *Newsweek*, 10 April 1995, 46; and Gregg Easterbrook, *A Moment on the Earth*.

32. Fundacion de la Paz, San Jose, Costa Rica.

33. *The Economist*, 22 July 1995, 44.

34. See the *Human Development Index* (New York: United Nations Development Programme, 1990–1995).

35. *Human Development Report, 1994* (New York: United Nations Development Programme, 1994), 59.

36. See, for example, Boutros Boutros-Ghali, UN Secretary-General, "Agenda for Development" (speech to the United Nations, New York, March 1994; available as a booklet from the United Nations, New York, N.Y. 10017).

37. See, for example, Harlan Cleveland et al., *The United Nations at Fifty*; and the Commission on Global Governance, *Our Global Neighborhood*.

Level 3

38. Thomas F. Malone, *International Networks for Addressing Issues of Global Change* (Research Triangle Park, North Carolina: Sigma Xi, The Scientific Research Society, 1994).

39. Hazel Henderson, "Citizen Movements for Greater Global Equity," *International Social Science Journal* 28, no. 4 (1976), 713–788, Paris.

40. See, for example, Ronald Inglehart, *The Silent Revolution*.

41. James Gustave Speth, "From Rio to Istanbul: UNDP and Opportunities for Partnership with Civil Society" (speech to the United Nations Development Programme, New York, 23 June 1995).

42. *The Economist*, 22 July 1995, 42.

43. Write to: Appropriate Technology International, 1828 L Street, N.W., Washington, D.C. 20036.

44. *The Economist*, 22 July 1995, 42.

45. See, for example, Paul Craig Roberts, Cato Institute, "Development Banks: An Idea Whose Time Has Gone," *Business Week*, 11 July 1994.

46. See, for example, *Business Week*, 29 August 1994.

Level 4

47. *Business Week*, 7 August 1995, 84, 46–56.

48. Mikhail Sergeyevich Gorbachev, general-secretary of the Communist Party of the Soviet Union (speech to the plenary session of the 43rd UN General Assembly, New York, 8 December 1988).

49. Americans Talk Issues Foundation, Survey #28, August 1995.

Level 5

50. Frances Cairncross, *Costing the Earth* (Boston: Harvard Business School Press, 1992). *Coming Clean* (London: Deloitte, Touche, Tomatsu International, 1993).

51. These new statements of principles are summarized in Harlan Cleveland et al., *The United Nations at Fifty.*

52. *The Economist*, 20 August 1994, 53.

53. Emanuel Epstein, "Roots," *Scientific American* 228, no. 5 (May 1973): 48–56, as cited in Hazel Henderson, *Creating Alternative Futures.*

54. Hazel Henderson, "The Entropy State," *Planning Review* (May 1974).

55. "Sun Up at Last for Solar," *Business Week*, 24 July 1995, 84–85.

56. Ibid.

57. See Hazel Henderson, chap. 7 of *Paradigms in Progress.*

Level 6

58. See Hazel Henderson, "Eco-Tourism," *Futures Research Quarterly* (fall 1994): 19–33.

59. Contact the Sustainability Resource Institute, Takoma Park, Maryland 20913; phone: 301–588-7227.

60. Quality Indicators for Progress, prepared for the Jacksonville Chamber of Commerce by the Jacksonville Community Council, Inc., JEA Tower, 11th Floor, 21 West Church Street, Jacksonville, Florida 32202.

Level 7

61. See, for example, Abraham H. Maslow, *Toward a Psychology of Being.*

62. Briefing before the National Press Club, 12 May 1993; broadcast 13 May 1993. Tape no. 35326 can be ordered from C-Span, Viewer Services, 400 N. Capitol Street, N.W., Washington, D.C. 20001; phone: 202–626-7963.

CHAPTER 2: JUGGERNAUT GLOBALISM AND THE BANKRUPTCY OF ECONOMICS

1. "Twenty-first Century Capitalism," Special Report in *Business Week*, December 1994.

2. *Human Development Report, 1994* (New York: United Nations Development Programme, 1994), 47.

3. "Total Debt of Heavily Indebted Poor Countries," IMF-World Bank internal memo of 6 February 1995.

4. *The Economist*, 1 April 1995, 59–60.

5. "Twenty-first Century Capitalism," Special Report in *Business Week.*

6. *Business Week*, 1 May 1995, 57–58.

7. McKinsey Global Institute, "The Global Capital Market: Supply, Demand, Pricing and Allocation," November 1994. See also "The World Economy" (survey), *The Economist*, 7 October 1995.

8. *The Economist*, 13 May 1995, 71.

9. See, for example, Harlan Cleveland et al., *The United Nations at Fifty*, second edition available from the Global Commission to Fund the United Nations, 1511 K Street, N.W., Washington, D.C. 20005 for $12.95.

10. Americans Talk Issues Foundation, Survey #28 (August 1995). For copies of all surveys write to: Americans Talk Issues Foundation, 10 Carrera St., St. Augustine, Florida 32084.

11. See, for example, "Electronic Money," *The Economist*, 26 November 1994, 21.

12. *Third World Resurgence*, no. 49 (September 1994), 2.

13. *Human Development Report, 1995* (New York: United Nations Development Programme, 1995), 23.

14. *Washington Post*, 21 July 1995.

15. *The Economist*, 21 January 1995, 68.

16. *Business Week*, 10 July 1995, 35.

17. "Deflating the CPI," *Business Week*, 30 October 1995, 53.

18. *The Economist*, 24 June 1995.

19. See Hazel Henderson, "Workers and Environmentalists: The Common Cause," chap. 9 in *The Politics of the Solar Age*.

20. "Why This Upturn Still Has This Empty Feeling," *Business Week*, 25 January 1993, 25.

21. Hazel Henderson, "The Entropy State," *Planning Review* (May 1974).

22. "Hark the OECD Angels Sing," *The Economist*, December 1992.

23. *Business Week*, 13 May 1995, 26.

24. "In a Fix at the FED," *Business Week*, 26 June 1995.

25. See Hazel Henderson, "Dissecting the 'Declining Productivity' Flap," chap. 10 in *The Politics of the Solar Age*.

26. See John Maynard Keynes, *The General Theory of Employment, Interest and Money*; and Robert Skidelsky, *John Maynard Keynes*.

27. See, for example, economist Harvey D. Wilmeth, *Milwaukee Journal*, 19 February 1995.

28. "Biting the Hand That Squeezed Them," *The Economist*, 21 October 1995, 48.

29. Americans Talk Issues Foundation, Survey #21: "Global Uncertainties" (18 May 1993).

30. Nandini Joshi, personal conversation and correspondence with the author, September 1995.

31. *Business Week*, 17 July 1995, 80.

32. See, for example, Hazel Henderson, "Economists versus Ecologists," *Harvard Business Review* (July–August 1973); *Creating Alternative Futures*; and "A Look Back: Economics As Politics in Disguise," part 2 of *The Politics of the Solar Age*.

33. Robert Frank, Thomas Gilovich, and Dennis Regan, "Does Studying Economics Inhibit Cooperation?" *Journal of Economic Perspectives* (spring 1993).

34. See "Report of the Commission on Graduate Education in Economics" and W. Lee Hansen, "The Education and Training of Economics Doctorates" (statistical annex), both in *Journal of Economic Literature* (fall 1991).

35. *Business Week*, 14 January 1991, 36.

36. *Newsweek*, 10 April 1995, 41.

37. Richard Parker, "Can Economists Save Economics?" *The American Prospect* (spring 1993), 148.

CHAPTER 3: THE TECHNOLOGY TRAP

1. The material in this chapter, with an updated introduction, is the Damon Lecture, given by Hazel Henderson at the annual convention of the American Association for Industrial Arts, Des Moines, Iowa, April 1976, with original footnotes.

2. *Business Week*, 8 May 1995, 72; 17 July 1995, 68.

3. *The Economist*, 15 July 1995.

4. Thomas A. Bass, "DNA Computer: Gene Genie," *Wired*, August 1995, 114.

5. *Business Week*, 14 August 1995, 80.

6. "Glitch of the Millennium," *Business Week*, 13 November 1995, 54.

7. Development Alternatives institute, B-32, Tara Crescent, Qutub Institutional Area, New Delhi, India 110016.

8. Heisenberg's Uncertainty Principle states that the accuracy of measurement is limited in principle, i.e., as one tries to measure smaller and smaller particles or phenomena, the act of observation itself affects the object or process under observation. Heisenberg (1901–1976) founded quantum mechanics, for which he received a Nobel Prize in 1932, and was director of the famous Max Planck Institute for Physics from 1946 until 1970.

9. "Two Zoologists Find Ants Using Tools," *New York Times*, 4 April 1976.

10. Eugene Odum, "The Strategy of Ecosystem Development," *Science*, 18 April 1969.

11. Rev. Thomas Berry, "Future Forms of Religious Experience," Information Paper #50, Futures Planning Council, Episcopal Diocese of California, 1976.

12. "Postal Officials Say They Miscalculated on Postal Damage," *New York Times*, 26 March 1976.

13. "Three Engineers Quit G. E. Reactor Division and Volunteer in Anti-Nuclear Movement," *New York Times*, 3 February 1976.

14. Stafford Beer (keynote speech before the Canadian Operations Research Society, Ottawa, Canada, 1974).

15. Now over $150 billion per year.

16. For a comprehensive overview see Peter Weber, "Net Loss: Fish, Jobs and the Marine Environment," Worldwatch Paper #120, Washington, D.C., July 1994. For even more current data, Lester R. Brown, Nicholas Lenssen, and Hal Kane, *Vital Signs 1995*, 32–33.

17. Edward Goldsmith, "The Family Basis of Social Structure," *The Ecologist*, January 1976.

18. James C. Fletcher, administrator of the National Aeronautics and Space Administration (speech to the National Academy of Engineering, Washington, D.C., 10 November 1975).

19. Now called the CAT scanner.

20. For additional comparisons see Hazel Henderson, "Characteristics of 'Hard' v. 'Soft' Technologies," fig. 12 in *Creating Alternative Futures*, 366.

21. Gerald Holton, "Scientific Optimism and Societal Concern: Notes on the Psychology of Scientists," *Hastings Report*, New York, December 1975.

CHAPTER 4: THE JOBLESS PRODUCTIVITY TRAP

1. *The Economist*, 8 July 1995, 23.

2. *Business Week*, 7 August 1995, 34.

3. *The Economist*, 2 April 1994, 69.

4. Paul Wallich, *Scientific American* (January 1994).

5. G-7 Communiqué, Tokyo, Japan, 1993.

6. "Fat Cats and Their Cream," *The Economist*, 22 July 1995, 19.

7. "Career Opportunities," *The Economist*, 8 July 1995, 59.

8. *The Economist*, 22 July 1995, 74.

9. "Workers of the World Compete," *The Economist*, 2 April 1994.

10. Kelso Institute for the Study of Economic Systems, San Francisco, California. Louis O. Kelso and Patricia Hetter's book, *Two-Factor Theory*, launched employee stock ownership plans (ESOPs). Patricia Hetter Kelso, Louis Kelso's coauthor and life partner, now continues the work, spreading ESOPs in Russia, Eastern Europe, and China. Their last book together was *Democracy and Economic Power*.

11. Robert Theobald, *Committed Spending*.

12. W. H. Ferry, "Caught on the Horn of Plenty," *The Bulletin* of the Center for the Study of Democratic Institutions, 1962.

13. Mark Goldes, personal interview with the author, March 1994.

14. *The Economist*, 20 August 1994, 55.

15. See Hazel Henderson, "Greening the Economy," chap. 7 in *Paradigms in Progress*.

16. James Robertson, "Benefits and Taxes," March 1994, The New Economics Foundation, London.

17. See, for example, Ernst U. von Weizsäcker (president of the Wuppertal Institute) and Jochen Jesinghaus, *Ecological Tax Reform*.

18. *Business Week*, 4 December 1995, 51.

19. Hazel Henderson, "The Entropy State," *Planning Review* (May 1974).

20. "A Tilt toward the Rich," *Time*, 30 October 1995, 62.

21. Communiqué from the Jobs Summit, Detroit, 1994.

22. Copenhagen Alternative Declaration, 8 March 1995. Available from NGO Forum '95, Njalsgade #13C, DK-2300 Copenhagen, S, Denmark; Fax: 45-32-96-8919.

23. *Business Week*, 12 July 1993.

24. *Business Week*, 12 June 1995.

25. *The Economist*, 15 July 1995, 55.

26. Daniel C. Esty, *Greening the GATT* (Washington, D.C.: Institute for International Economics, 1994).

27. "The Feds Unfunded Mandate" *Economic Reform*, Toronto, August 1995, 70.

28. *Business Week*, 17 July 1995, Editorial, 104; Cover Story: "The Wage Squeeze," 54–62.

29. "Suddenly the Economy Doesn't Measure Up," *Business Week*, 31 July 1995, 74–75.

30. *The Economist*, 24 June 1995, 68.

31. John Williamson, ed., *The Political Economy of Policy Reforms*, (Washington, D.C.: Institute for International Economics, 1994).

32. See, for example, Americans Talk Issues Foundation, Survey #17: "Perceptions of Globalization" (1991).

33. Americans Talk Issues Foundation, Survey #28 (August 1995).

34. *The Economist*, 15 July 1995, 58.

CHAPTER 5: GOVERNMENT BY MEDIOCRACY AND THE ATTENTION ECONOMY

1. Pages 116 through 121 of this chapter are excerpted from Hazel Henderson, "Access to Media: A Problem in Democracy," *Columbia Journalism Review* 8, no. 1 (spring 1969).

2. Jacques Cousteau, "Information Highway: Mental Pollution," *Calypso Log* (August 1995): 3; The Cousteau Society, New York, N.Y. 10017.

3. *The Proceedings of the Conference on Computers in Education* is available from the Center for Ecoliteracy, Berkeley, California, 1995.

4. "Beyond Blame: Challenging Violence in the Media" is available from the Center for Media Literacy, 1962 South Shenandoah Street, Los Angeles, CA 90034; phone: 1-800-226-9494.

5. See, for example, Neil Postman, *Amusing Ourselves to Death*; Jerry Mander, *Four Arguments for the Elimination of Television*; and Nicholas Johnson, *How to Talk Back to Your TV Set*.

6. After intense lobbying by the National Association of Broadcasters and other media special interests, the Fairness Doctrine was repealed during the Reagan administration. The "equal time" provision, which provided political candidates free air-time access to the voters, came under attack by the same special interests and was repealed in 1979. Today in the United States, we have forgotten that the public owns the airwaves.

7. I am a small investor in HDN because I like to put my money where my mouth and heart are.

8. See, for example, Miracles, P.O. Box 418, Santa Fe, New Mexico 87540; and again "Miracles," a U.S. TV series on the cable channel Arts and Entertainment.

9. Margaret Mead, "Our Open-Ended Future," *The Next Billion Years*, Lecture Series at the University of California, Los Angeles, 1973.

10. Vicki Robins, coauthor of *Your Money or Your Life*, also published a resource guide, *All-Consuming Passion: Waking Up from the American Dream*, available from the New Road Map Foundation, P.O. Box 15981, Seattle, Washington 98115. A nonprescriptive Lifestyle Simplification Lab was developed by The Institute of Cultural Affairs at Greensboro, 5911 Western Trail, Greensboro, N.C. 27410; Fax: 910-605-9640.

11. "Yearning for Balance," The Harwood Group for the Merck Family Fund, 6930 Carroll Ave., Suite 500, Takoma Park, MD 20912; July 1995.

12. "The World Travel and Tourism Council, Brussels," *The Economist*, 12 August 1995.

13. "The Expanding Entertainment Universe," *Business Week*, 14 August 1995, 114.

14. "One More Place You Can't Escape Ads," *Business Week*, 19 June 1995, 6.

15. *Business Week*, 14 August 1995, 30–37.

16. *New York Times*, 21 August 1995.

17. "West's Wasteful Pursuit of Luxury Cited by Tiger Nations in Debate over Global Warming," *Worldpaper* (January 1996): 1; Boston, Mass.

18. "Dematerialization Now!" *Development Alternatives* 5, no. 2 (December 1995): 1.

CHAPTER 6: GRASSROOTS GLOBALISM

1. Margaret Helen, Institute of Cultural Affairs in Chicago, Illinois, offered me "bubble up" as a way to distinguish between the unworkable "trickle up/trickle down" discussed in economic theory and the excitement of what is authentically rising (like fresh spring waters) from the grassroots.

2. The Union of International Organizations and its assistant secretary-general, Anthony J. N. Judge, also edit the *Encyclopedia of World Problems and Human Potential*. The 4th edition, published in 1994, is available from the UIO, Rue Washington, 40, 1050 Brussels, Belgium; email: info@uia.be. Other information sources on NGOs and INGOs include: the *World Directory of Environmental Organizations* compiled by Thaddeus Tryzna and Roberta Childers, 4th ed., 1992, California Institute of Public Affairs, P.O. Box 189040, Sacramento, California 95818; The International Council of Voluntary Organizations, C.P. 216, 1211 Geneva 21, Switzerland; Fax: 41-22-738-9904; and The Independent Sector, 1828 L Street, N.W., Suite 1200, Washington, D.C. 20036; Fax: 202-416-0580.

3. CIVICUS, World Alliance for Citizen Participation, *Citizens: Strengthening Global Civil Society*, 1994, coordinated by Miguel Darcy de Oliveira, Instituto de Açao Cultural in Brazil; and Rajesh Tandon, Society for Participatory Research in India; in the United States: CIVICUS, 919 18th Street, N.W., 3rd Floor, Washington, D.C. 20006.

4. Samuel Huntington, "The Clash of Civilizations," *Foreign Affairs* 72, no. 3 (summer 1993).

5. Reports on corporate performance are available from the Council on Economic Priorities, 30 Irving Place, New York, N. Y. 10003.

6. See, for example, Michael S. Greve and Fred L. Smith, Jr., eds., *Environmental Politics*.

7. See, for example, World Commission on Environment and Development, *Our Common Future*.

8. *Timeline*, July–August 1995, 2–5; contact the Foundation for Global Community, 222 High Street, Palo Alto, California 94301.

9. *The Economist*, 22 July 1994, 35.

10. *Peace Newsletter*, edited by Elise Boulding, is available from International Non-Violent Peace Teams, 624 Pearl Street, #206, Boulder, Colorado 80302.

11. "Copenhagen Alternative Declaration," 8 March 1995. Available from NGO Forum '95, Njalsgade #13C, DK-2300 Copenhagen, S, Denmark; Fax: 45-32-96-8919.

12. Reports of the U.S. Office of Technology Assessment are available from the U.S. Government Printing Office, Washington, D.C. 20515.

13. Rocky Mountain Institute Reports are available from the Rocky Mountain Institute, 1739 Snowmass Creek Road, Snowmass, Colorado 81654.

14. See, for example, Jessica Lipnack and Jeffrey Stamps, *Networking*. Updates are available from the Networking Institute, 505 Waltham Street, West Newton, Massachusetts 02166; Fax: 617-965-2341.

15. See, for example, *The Elmwood Quarterly* 8, no. 3, available from the Center for Eco-Literacy, 2522 San Pablo Avenue, Berkeley, California 94702.

16. Mark Dowie, "American Environmentalism," *World Policy Journal* (winter 1991–92): 67–92.

17. J. Perera, C. Marasinghe, and L. Jayasekera, *A People's Movement Under Siege*, 1992, available from Sarvodya, 41 Lumbini Mawatha, Ratmalana, Sri Lanka ($10).

18. White Paper on the Philippine Economy, 1992, is available from Green Forum, Liberty Building, Pasay Rd., Makati, Metro, Manila, Philippines.

19. The proceedings of this conference, *Agenda 21: The Rio Declaration*, can be obtained from the United Nations, Room S-845, New York, N. Y. 10017; Fax: 212-963-4556.

20. United Nations Department of Public Information. S.G./S.M. 5416, 19 September 1994.

21. *Edges* 5, no. 1; available from the Institute of Cultural Affairs, 577 Kingston Road, Toronto, M4E 1R3 Canada; Fax: 416-691-2491 ($25 per year).

CHAPTER 7: RETHINKING HUMAN DEVELOPMENT AND
THE TIME OF OUR LIVES

1. See Hazel Henderson, chaps. 7 and 8 in *Paradigms in Progress*, which contain fourteen sets of such principles. CERES may be contacted at 711 Atlantic Ave., Boston, MA 02111.

2. See, for example, *Earth Systems Science: A Program for Global Change* (Washington, D.C.: NASA, 1988).

3. Robert Muller, former assistant secretary-general of the UN, now rector of the University for Peace, Escazu, Costa Rica, personal conversation with the author, Santa Barbara, California, 4 May 1994.

4. See, for example, Americans Talk Issues Survey #17, "Perceptions of Globalization" (Nov./Dec. 1991). For information write to: Americans Talk Issues Foundation, 10 Carrera St., St. Augustine, Florida 32084.

5. Americans Talk Issues Foundation, Survey #25: "The United Nations at Fifty: Mandate from the American People" (summer 1994).

6. *System of National Accounts, 1993*, published by the UN and released by the World Bank in February 1994, reflects the official rethinking of its sponsoring organizations: the World Bank, the IMF, the OECD, the European Commission, and the United Nations Statistical Division.

7. *The Economist*, 22 July 1995, 17.

8. Newsletter of the National Center for Children in Poverty 5, no. 2 (summer 1995); available from Columbia University, 154 Haven Avenue, New York, NY 10032.

9. Worldwatch Institute, "What about Male Responsibilities?" *Worldwatch* (March/April 1994).

10. Riane Eisler, David Loye, and Kari Norgaard, "Women, Men, and the Global Quality of Life," Center for Partnership Studies, Pacific Grove, Calif., 1995.

11. Transcripts of these conversations are in the form of a still unpublished manuscript, *The Power of Yin*, available from the authors.

12. Jean Houston, The Foundation for Mind Research, P.O. Box 3300, Pomona, NY 10970.

13. See, for example, Barbara Marx Hubbard's seminar "New Memes for the New Millennium" given at the World Future Society 1995 Annual Meeting in Atlanta, Georgia. Audio tapes are available from the World Future Society, 7910 Woodmont Ave., Suite 450, Bethesda, MD 20814.

14. Hazel Henderson, "The Decline of Jonesism," reprinted from *The Futurist* 8, no. 5 (October 1974); available from the World Future Society, Bethesda, MD 20814. New notes (numbers fifteen through twenty-four below) have been added to the original.

15. You can write to Appropriate Technology International, 1828 L Street, N.W., Washington, D.C. 20036.

16. The Shanghai Branch of the International Economy and Technology Institute concentrates on reinvigorating traditional and local technologies. I have been a senior research professor at this institute since 1986.

17. In 1995, $150 billion was spent.

18. In the 1980s, demand-side management (DSM) became a large consulting industry in itself, helping companies save energy and money as Amory Lovins of the Rocky Mountain Institute and I had predicted. Amory Lovins talked of utilities selling "negawatts" rather than megawatts.

19. In the 1990s, magazines such as *Ad-Busters* in Canada and *Media and Values* in Los Angeles grew, along with the Center for the Study of Commercialism in Washington, D.C., and its publication, *Ad-Vice*.

20. This same Jerry Mander went on to found the Public Media Center of San Francisco and to author several books. See the bibliography.

21. "Steady-state economy" was the term used in the 1970s for what I called a "sustained-yield economy" in *The Politics of the Solar Age*. Sustainable development was the term widely adopted after my colleague Lester Brown at Worldwatch Institute promoted it, as did the 1987 Brundtland Report "Our Common Future."

22. This process of decentralization has been going on since the late 1970s and has culminated in many of today's devolutions and networked businesses.

23. A spate of books on this subject followed in the 1980s, for example: Ken Wilber, *Up From Eden*; William Irwin Thompson, *The Time Falling Bodies Take to Light*; Linda E. Olds, *Fully Human*; Eva Keuls, *Reign of the Phallus*; Mary Daly, *Pure Lust*.

24. See, for example, Juliet B. Schor, *The Overworked American*; and Mario Cogoy, "Market and Non-Market Determinants of Private Consumption and Their Impacts on the Environment," *Ecological Economics* 13, no. 3 (June 1995).

CHAPTER 8: CULTURAL DNA CODES AND BIODIVERSITY:
THE REAL WEALTH OF NATIONS

1. Dirk J. Struik, "Everybody Counts," *Technology Review* (August–September 1995): 36–44.

2. *Human Development Report, 1994* (New York: United Nations Development Programme, 1994), 47.

3. W. Wayt Gibbs, "Lost Science of the Third World," *Scientific American* (August 1995): 92–99.

4. UNESCO, *Mexico City Declaration on Cultural Policies* (Paris: UNESCO, 1982)

5. D. Paul Shafer, "Cultures and Economies," *Futures* 26, no. 8 (October 1994).

6. *Akwesasne Notes*, Mohawk Nation Territory, P.O. Box 196, Rooseveltown, NY 13683-0196; phone: 518-358-9531. *Daybreak*, Chief Oren Lyons, publisher, P.O. Box 315, Williamsville, NY 14231-0315; phone: 716-829-2249.

7. Henry S. Kariel, "Letters to the Editor: Comment on Ziauddin Sardar," *Futures* 25, no. 8 (October 1993).

8. *Futures* 27, no. 4 (May 1995).

9. *World Futures Studies Federation Newsletter* (summer 1995), Melbourne, Australia.

10. Center for Public Integrity, 1910 K Street, N.W., #802, Washington, D.C. 20006; phone: 202-223-0299. Common Cause, 2030 M Street, N.W., Washington, D.C. 20036; phone: 202-736-5741. Public Citizen, 2000 P Street, Suite 200, Washington, D.C. 20036; phone: 202-833-3000.

11. Wouter van Dieren, conversation with the author, 31 May 1995, en route to the Parliament of Europe Conference and on the release of *Taking Nature into Account*, ed. Wouter van Dieren. (Note: As one of the authors, I was misidentified. This will be corrected in future editions.)

12. Americans Talk Issues Foundation, Survey #21 (18 May 1993).

13. Thierry Verhelst, ed., *Cultures and Development* (June 1995): 11; Brussels, Belgium.

14. *The Economist*, 8 July 1995, 100.

15. Rebecca Adamson, "Indigenous Economics and First Nations," paper for First Nations Development Institute, Fredericksburg, Virginia (n.d.).

16. Development Alternatives institute, B-32, Tara Crescent, Qutub Institutional Area, New Delhi, India 110016.

17. From the report on the three-day dialogue on culture and development sponsored by the Kapur Surya Foundation, Bijwasan Najafgarh Road, P.O. Kapas Hera, New Delhi, India 110037; Fax: 91-11-3316331.

18. See Hazel Henderson, chaps. 10, 11, and 12 in *The Politics of the Solar Age*.

19. Proceedings of the UN Symposium on "The Science and Practice of Complexity" (1985) is available from the United Nations University, Tokyo, Japan.

20. "From Complexity to Perplexity," *Scientific American* (June 1993): 104.

21. Hazel Henderson, "The Three Zones of Transition: A Guide to Riding the Tiger of Change," *Futures Research Quarterly* 2, no. 1 (spring 1986).

22. Jean Houston, *The Possible Human* and *Life Force*. At least a dozen titles in print give individuals multiple possibilities for approaching the future quest from the perspective of their current understanding of their own coding.

23. Joao Caraça and Manuel Maria Carrilho, "A New Paradigm in the Organization of Knowledge," *Futures* 26, no. 7.

CHAPTER 9: INFORMATION: THE WORLD'S REAL
CURRENCY ISN'T SCARCE

A version of Chapter 9 appeared in *World Business Academy Perspectives*, September 1994, available from Berrett-Koehler Publishers, San Francisco, Calif.

1. *The Economist*, 9 September 1995, 107.

2. Hazel Henderson, "Social Innovation and Citizen Movements," *Futures* 25, no. 3 (April 1993): 322.

3. "The Software Revolution," *Business Week*, 4 December 1995, 78.

4. John Heielmann, "President 2000," *Wired*, December 1995, 153.

5. "A New Stock Market Arises on the Internet," *Scientific American* (July 1995): 31.

6. "Patrolling the Black Holes of Cyberspace," *Business Week*, 12 June 1995, 78.

7. U.S. Office of Technology Assessment, "Updates on Information, Security and Privacy in Network Environments" (June 1995).

8. *The Economist*, 26 March 1994.

9. "On-Line Investing," *Business Week*, 5 June 1995, 64; and "The Future of Money" 12 June 1995, 66.

10. "Call it the Supernet," *Business Week*, 8 May 1995, 93.

11. Hazel Henderson, "Emerging Change Models," chap. 3 in *Paradigms in Progress*.

12. Hazel Henderson, *The Politics of the Solar Age*, 161–62.

13. "Bill Gates and the Open Road," *The Economist*, 3 June 1995, 30.

14. "Thoroughly Modern Monopoly," *The Economist*, 8 July 1995, 76.

15. "Law and Order in Cyberspace?" *Business Week*, 4 December 1995, 44.

16. *The Economist*, 21 October 1995, 33.

17. "Small Businesses Cashing in on Bartering," *Washington Post*, 7 July 1995.

18. My editorials on this subject for InterPress Service Rome were carried by four hundred newspapers in twenty-seven languages in Asia, Europe, Latin America, and Africa—but were not picked up in the United States.

19. *The Economist*, 8 July 1995, 73.

20. *Business Week*, 15 May 1995, 46.

21. See, for example, William Greider, *The Secrets of the Temple*, and Steven Solomon, *The Confidence Game* .

22. Such data on unpaid work in the United States is tracked by the Independent Sector, Washington, D.C.

23. Hazel Henderson, "A Farewell to the Corporate State," chap. 10 in *Creating Alternative Futures*.

24. *At Work* 2, no. 6 (November–December 1993).

25. See, for example, Lewis Hyde, *The Gift*; Vandana Shiva, *Staying Alive*; Marshall Sahlins, *Stone Age Economics* ; and Karl Polanyi, *The Great Transformation*.

26. Full-page advertisement in *The Economist*, 30 April 1994, 20.

27. Hank Monrobey runs Dynamic Capital Network, an Internet exchange where network members' initiation fees become a "user pool" of capital for the members' own investment and borrowing needs—analogous to the community savings and loan pools used in many developing countries. Dynamic Capital Network can be reached at P.O. Box 15656, Ann Arbor, MI 48106.

28. LETS LINK can be reached at 61 Woodcock Road, Warminster, Wiltshire, BA12 9DH, UK. News of LETS and other barter clubs is covered by *New Economics*, The New Economics Foundation, First Floor, Vine Court, 112–116 Whitechapel Road, London, E1 1JES, UK.

29. Information is available from the National Cooperative Bank and Co-op America, both of Washington, D.C.

30. See, for example, Edgar Cahn, Ph.D., J.D., and Jonathan Rowe, *Time Dollars*.

31. Letters were printed in the June/July 1994 issue of *Ithaca Money*.

32. Nandini Joshi describes this simple solution in *Development without Destruction*. Additional eminently practical advice is contained in *Money and Debt* by Thomas H. Greco, Jr.; *Only Connect* by Sabine Kurjo and Ian McNeill; and *The Money Rebellion* by Andrew Von Sonn.

33. Many other local exchange systems, including those inspired by Robert Swann, Susan Witt, and Terrence Mollner, and many others associated with such organizations as the Community Land Trust and the Schumacher Society are discussed in chap. 5 of *Paradigms in Progress* by Hazel Henderson.

CHAPTER 10: REDEFINING WEALTH AND PROGRESS: THE NEW INDICATORS

1. Questions asked of the author at the National Conference for New Corporate Values, Hilton Head, North Carolina, 7 February 1995.

2. "Fewer Bangs More Bucks," *The Economist*, 15 July 1995, 60.

3. Americans Talk Issues Foundation, Survey #24: "Steps for Democracy" (March 1994).

4. *Business Week*, 22 May 1995, 43.

5. "The Shakeup in Economic Statistics," *Business Week*, 31 July 1995, 98.

6. "Bean Counters Unite," *The Economist*, 10 June 1995, 67.

7. *USA Today*, 10 August 1995.

8. "Putting a Value on People," *The Economist*, 24 June 1995, 69.

9. National Association of Women Business Owners Foundation, Washington, D.C., 1996.

10. David Birch, *Cognetics*, Cambridge, Massachusetts.

11. *The Economist*, 21 October 1995, 32.

12. *Handbook of National Accounting*, 1993.(New York: UN Statistical Division, 1994).

13. Emile van Lennep, conversation with the author, London, April 1991.

14. Hirofumi Uzawa as cited in Hazel Henderson, *Creating Alternative Futures*, 52.

15. John C. O'Connor, "Towards Environmentally Sustainable Development: Measuring Progress." Paper presented at the 19th Session, General Assembly of the IUCN (World Conservation Union), Buenos Aires, Argentina, January 1994.

16. *The Economist*, 15 April 1995, 74.

17. *The Economist*, 25 March 1995, 86.

18. "Integrated Economic and Environmental Satellite Accounts," *Survey of Current Business*, U.S. Dept. of Commerce, April 1994.

19. Dr. Carol S. Carson, personal communication with the author, May 1994. Also quoted in Hazel Henderson, "Feeding on the Numbers," *WorldPaper* (January 1994).

20. See Hazel Henderson, chaps. 4 and 6 of *Paradigms in Progress*; and Marilyn Waring, *If Women Counted*.

21. See, for example, South Commission, *Challenge to the South*.

22. *Business Week*, 22 May 1995, 44.

23. *The Economist*, 8 February 1992, 66.

24. *Redefining Wealth and Progress: The Caracas Report on Alternative Development Indicators* (New York: Bootstrap Press, 1990).

25. "Healthy Cities" indicators are available on the Internet at THF@Healthonline.com offered by the San Francisco-based Healthcare Forum.

26. *The Economist*, 7 January 1994.

27. *The Independent* (London), 7 July 1995.

28. The Council on Economic Priorities, 30 Irving Place, New York, NY.

29. *Coming Clean: Corporate Environmental Reporting* was published in 1993 by Deloitte, Touche, Tomatsu International and distributed by the International Institute for Sustainable Development, London. Rob Gray and Richard Laughlin, eds., "Green Accounting," *Accounting, Auditing and Accountability Journal* 4, no. 3 (Bradford, UK: MCB Press, 1991).

30. *The Economist*, 4 March 1995, 81.

31. Videotape of C-Span national coverage of press briefing, National Press Club, cosponsored by the University of Missouri School of Journalism's New Directions for News. Videotape is available from the Public Affairs Archives, Purdue University, 1000 Liberal Arts and Education Bldg., West Lafayette, Indiana 47907-1000.

32. William M. Alexander, "The Sustainable Development Process: Kerala," *International Journal of Sustainable Development* (May 1992).

33. See, for example, the 1992 volume, *Ecological Economics*, edited by Robert Costanza of the University of Maryland (New York: Elsevier Press).

34. Frances Cairncross, *Costing the Earth* (Boston: Harvard Business School Press, 1992); and *Green, Inc.: A Guide to Business and the Environment 1995* (Washington, D.C.: Island Press, 1995).

35. "Sixth Graders Buy Smog," *Business Ethics* (July–August 1995): 14.

36. *New York Times*, 1 June 1995.

37. Graciela Chichilnisky, "Global Environmental Markets: The Case for an International Bank for Environmental Settlements," presented at the World Bank, 4 October 1995.

38. Personal discussions by the author with Costa Rican officials, San Jose, Costa Rica, July 1995.

39. *Development Alternatives* is published by the nonprofit Development Alternatives institute, B-32, Tara Crescent, Qutub Institutional Area, New Delhi, India 110016. Subscription: $50 per year or $25 for civil society organizations.

40. Domini Clean Yield Index, Kinder, Lydenberg, Domini and Co., Cambridge, Mass. (a performance index covering four hundred progressive companies).

41. The Social Investment Forum, located in Boston, Massachusetts, in the United States and in London in the United Kingdom, offers directories of such funds, trade associations, portfolio managers, and investment advisors, and can be reached at P.O. Box 2234, Boston, MA 02107; phone: 617-451-3369. Also, Business for Social Responsibility can be reached at 1683 Folsom Street, San Francisco, CA 94103; phone: 415-865-2500.

CHAPTER 11: PERFECTING DEMOCRACY'S TOOLS

1. *The Economist*, 20 May 1995, 55.

2. Alberto Alesini and Enrico Spolaore, "The Number and Size of Nations," Working Paper #5050, National Bureau of Economic Research, Cambridge, Mass., 1995.

3. "The Orwellian State of Sudan," *The Economist*, 24 June 1995, 21.

4. "Can Anyone Fix This Country?" *Business Week*, 8 May 1995, 56.

5. Jacques Attali, *Verbatim II, 1986–1988* (Paris: Fayard, 1995).

6. Warren G. Bennis and Philip E. Slater, "Democracy Is Inevitable," *Harvard Business Review* (April 1964).

7. Hazel Henderson, "Computers: Hardware of Democracy," *forum 70* 2, no. 2 (February 1970). *forum 70* was an early and now defunct computer magazine formerly based in New York.

8. See, for example, *Business Week*, "Populism: A Diverse Movement Is Shaking America and May Imperil Its Role in the Global Economy," 13 March 1995, 73; and "Who Speaks for America?" 8 May 1995, 90.

9. "Green Swingers," *The Economist*, 20 May 1995, 49.

10. *The Economist*, 15 July 1995, 41.

11. Americans Talk Issues Foundation, *"Interviews with the Public Guide Us . . . on the Road to Consensus"* (April 1994). For copies of all surveys write to Americans Talk Issues Foundation, 10 Carrera St., St. Augustine, Florida 32084.

12. Alan F. Kay, "Revealed in ATIF Survey #28: Important Stories Leaders Won't Mention and the Press Ignores." Unpublished paper, Americans Talk Issues Foundation, Washington, D.C., 12 September 1995, 6.

13. Conducted by the Survey Research Center, School of Social Sciences and Public Affairs, Boise State University, 1990. Sponsored by and available from the Idaho Centennial Commission, 217 West State Street, Boise, Idaho 83702.

14. Ross Perot, *United We Stand* (New York: Hyperion, 1992), 2–4.

15. Hazel Henderson, "Toward Managing Social Conflict," *Harvard Business Review* (May–June 1971).

16. "If You're So Smart, You Cut the Deficit," *Business Week*, 19 June 1995, 6.

17. "Democracy and Technology," *The Economist*, 17 June 1995, 22.

18. Ibid.

19. See, for example, "Full-Flavored, Unfiltered State House Shenanigans," *Business Week*, 22 May 1995.

20. Samuel Dunn, "The Challenge of the '90s in Higher Education," *Futures Research Quarterly* (fall 1994): 35–55.

21. Henderson, "Computers: Hardware of Democracy."

22. "Cities: Many Splendored Things," special section of *The Economist*, 29 July 1995.

23. "The Papers That Ate America," *The Economist* 10 October 1992, 21.

24. Joseph Tainter, "Sustainability of Complex Societies," *Futures* 27, no. 4 (May 1995).

25. "NAFTA's Bubble Bursts," *New York Times*, 11 September 1995, A11.

26. *Business Week*, 29 May 1995, 26; and 14 August 1995.

CHAPTER 12: NEW MARKETS AND NEW COMMONS: THE COOPERATIVE ADVANTAGE

1. "A World of Greased Palms: Inside the Dirty War for Global Business," *Business Week*, 6 November 1995, 36.

2. See, for example, *The Economist*, 8 October 1994, 85–86; and Jeffrey Sachs, "Beyond Bretton Woods," *The Economist*, 1 October 1994, 23–27.

3. *Business Week*, 21 August 1995, 42.

4. Sachs, "Beyond Bretton Woods."

5. *New York Times*, 22 November 1993.

6. *The Economist*, 5 August 1995, 72.

7. *The Economist*, 1 October 1994, 96.

8. Gary S. Becker, "Forget Monetary Union," *Business Week*, 13 November 1995, 34.

9. "Are Regulations Bleeding the Economy?" *Business Week*, 17 July 1995.

10. Michael Porter and Claes van der Linde, "Green and Competitive," *Harvard Business Review* (September–October 1995): 120.

11. "Voodoo Regulation," *Business Week*, 13 March 1995.

12. "Guess Who's Gunning for the SEC," *Business Week*, 14 August 1995, 40–41.

13. Martin Feldstein, "Too Little, Not Too Much," *The Economist*, 24 June 1995, 72–73.

14. *The Economist*, 10 June 1995, 70.

15. "Orange County's Artful Dodger," *New York Times*, 4 August 1995.

16. "What If Uncle Sam Defaults?" *Business Week*, 13 November 1995, 44.

17. "The Big Sleaze in MUNI Bonds," *Fortune*, 7 August 1995, 113–120.

18. *Business Week*, 14 August 1995, 52.

19. Garrett Hardin, "The Tragedy of the Commons," *Science* 13 (December 1968): 1243.

20. See, for example, Frederico Aguilera-Klink "Some Notes on the Misuse of Classical Writings in Economics on the Subject of Common Property," *Ecological Economics* (April 1994): 221–228.

21. Hazel Henderson, "From Economism to Earth Ethics and Systems Theory," chap. 3 in *Paradigms in Progress*.

22. Richard N. Cooper, Stephany Griffith-Jones, Peter B. Kenen, John Williamson, et al., *The Pursuit of Reform*, ed. Jan Joost Teunissen (The Hague: Forum on Debt and Development [FONDAD], November 1993); Fax: 31-70-346-3939.

23. Brett D. Fromson, "Regulators Adopt Crisis Measures," *The Washington Post*, 18 May 1995.

24. Hazel Henderson, "Riding the Tiger of Change," *Futures Research Quarterly* (1986).

25. See also Hazel Henderson, "Beyond GNP," chap. 5 in *Paradigms in Progress*.

26. *Human Development Report, 1994* (New York: United Nations Development Programme, 1994), 70.

27. James Tobin, "On the Efficiency of the Financial System," *Lloyds Bank Review* (July 1984) is an update of his 1978 proposal.

28. V. Summers and L. Summers, "When Financial Markets Work Too Well: A Cautious Case for a Financial Transactions Tax," *Journal of Financial Services*, no. 3 (1989).

29. Rudi Dornbusch, "Cross-Border Payments, Taxes and Alternative Capital Account Regimes," unpublished draft report to The Group of Twenty-Four, September 1995.

30. Americans Talk Issues Foundation, Survey #17: "Perceptions of Globalization" (March 1992); Alan F. Kay and Hazel Henderson with Fred Steeper and Stanley Greenberg, conducted by Greenberg-Lake, Inc., and Market Strategies. Available from Americans Talk Issues Foundation, 10 Carrera St., St. Augustine, FL 32084; Fax: 904-826-4194.

CHAPTER 13: AGREEING ON RULES AND SOCIAL INNOVATIONS FOR OUR COMMON FUTURE

1. Economists Allied for Arms Reduction (ECAAR), 25 West 45th Street, New York, NY 10036. ECAAR publishes the journal *Peace Economics, Peace Science and Public Policy*.

2. The best account of all this is from diplomat Giandominico Picco in "The UN and the Use of Force," *Foreign Affairs* (September/October 1994).

3. Americans Talk Issues Foundation, Survey #28, August 1995.

4. Alan F. Kay and Hazel Henderson, "Financing UN Functions in the Post-Cold-War Era: A Proposal for a United Nations Security Insurance Agency" *Futures* 27, no. 1 (January/February 1995): 3–10.

5. "What the World Wants and How to Pay for It," Plate 8-39 in *Paradigms in Progress*, 230; originally created by The World Game founded by Buckminster Fuller in Philadelphia, Pennsylvania.

6. *Bulletin* of the United Nations Department of Peacekeeping Operations, New York, February 1994.

7. See, for example, *The United Nations in Its Second Half-Century* (New York: The Ford Foundation, 1995); and the 1995 Report of the American Assembly, Columbia University, New York, N.Y.

8. Americans Talk Issues Foundation, Survey #25, 25 July 1994.

9. *Parliamentarians for Global Action*, Annual Report, 1994; 211 E. 43rd St., Suite 1604, New York, NY 10017.

10. European Parliament proceedings are available from Kairios Europa, 3 Avenue du Parc Royal, 1020 Brussels, Belgium.

11. *Update on Trade-Related Issues* is available from the International Coalition for Development Action, rue Stevin #115, B-1040 Brussels, Belgium.

12. Christian Azar and John Holmberg, "Defining the Generational Environmental Debt," *Ecological Economics* 14, no. 1 (July 1995).

13. Brian Bacon, "The WBA and the ILO: Partners in Social Development," *World Business Academy Perspectives* 9, no. 2 (1995).

14. "Money Matters: Financing Social Development in the Twenty-First Century," a World Times White Paper published by *WorldPaper* (summer 1995); 210 World Trade Center, Boston, MA.

15. *The Economist*, 8 April 1995, 57.

16. For further information, see *Business Ethics* magazine, Minneapolis, Minnesota, or contact the Ethics Resource Center, Washington, D.C.

17. "Money Matters," *WorldPaper*.

18. *Wall Street Journal*, 3 July 1995.

19. Mohan Munasinge, "Economywide Policies and the Environment," World Bank, 1818 H Street, N.W., Washington, D.C. 20433.

20. See, for example, Morris Miller, *Coping Is Not Enough* and *Debt and Environment*.

21. "A Stunning Debut," *USA Today*, 10 August 1995.

22. For information on Soka Gakkai, contact the Boston Research Center for the Twenty-First Century, 396 Harvard Street, Cambridge, MA 02138.

23. U.S. Department of State, Bureau of Public Affairs, Washington, D.C., 24 March 1995.

24. *South Letter* (summer 1995): 2; South Centre, South Commission, Case Postale 228, 1211 Geneva 19, Switzerland.

25. Hazel Henderson and Alan F. Kay, "Introducing Competition into Global Financial Markets," in *Futures* (London: Elsevier Scientific Ltd., May 1996).

26. Ruben Mendez, "A Proposal for a Foreign Exchange Facility: Harnessing the Global Currency Markets for the Global Common Good," report to the UN Social Summit, March 1995, UNDP, New York.

27. David Felix, "The Tobin Tax Proposal: Background, Issues and Prospects," policy paper commissioned by UNDP for the World Summit on Social Development, Copenhagen, March 1995. Published by the Division of Public Affairs, UNDP, New York.

28. UNDP Office of Development Studies, "New and Innovative Financing for Development Cooperation," 10 October 1995; 1 UN Plaza, New York, NY 10017.

29. "McLaren Rejects Tobin Tax" *Toronto Globe and Mail*, 4 April 1995.

30. International Monetary Fund, G-7 Canada Summit Background Document: *Review of International Institutions* (June 1995): 2, 6.

31. GCFUN, 1511 K Street N.W., Washington, D.C. 20005.

32. *Rethinking Bretton Woods* can be ordered from the Center of Concern, 3700 13th Street, N.E., Washington, D.C. 20017.

33. Rudi Dornbusch, "Studies on International and Monetary Issues for the Group of Twenty-Four: Cross-Border Payments, Taxes and Alternative Capital Account Regimes," UNCTAD, Geneva, September 1995 (unpublished draft).

34. *The Financial Times* (London), 30 July 1992.

35. "Using a Global Lottery to Protect the Earth," *Toronto Globe and Mail*, 30 March 1995.

36. Alan F. Kay and Hazel Henderson, *UNSIA Progress Report—From Concept to Organization and Test Cases* (August 1995) and *The Flexibility of UNSIA* (30 December 1995); available from the Global Commission to Fund the United Nations, 1511 K Street, N.W., Suite 1120, Washington, D.C. 20005.

37. UN Department of Public Information, New York, July 1995.

38. The Harwood Group for the Merck Family Fund, 6930 Carroll Ave., Suite 500, Takoma Park, MD 20912.

39. Dragoljub Najman and Hans d'Orville, "Towards a New Multilateralism: Funding Global Priorities"; available from the Independent Commission on Population and Quality of Life, 1255 Fifth Avenue, 7 K, New York, NY 10029.

40. *Washington Post*, 25 January 1996.

GLOSSARY OF ACRONYMS

"Win-Win"	Cooperative games and decisions (see also "win-lose," i.e. competitive games, Axelrod 1984)
APC	Association for Progressive Communications
APEC	Asia Pacific Economic Cooperation
ATIF	Americans Talk Issues Foundation
BBC	British Broadcasting Corporation
BEA	Bureau of Economic Analysis
BUSCO	Business Council for the Social Summit
BIS	Bank for International Settlements
CAFE	Corporate Automobile Fuel Efficiency
CAPM	Capital Asset Pricing Model
CBOT	Chicago Board of Trade
CEDS	Community Economic Development Scrip
CEN	Currency Exchange Network
CEO	Chief Executive Officer
CERES	Coalition for Environmentally Responsible Economies
CFCs	Chlorofluorocarbons
CFI	Country Futures Indicators
CFTC	Commodity Futures Trading Commission
CIS	Commonwealth of Independent States
CO_2	Carbon Dioxide
COPORA	(United States) Congressional Office of Public Opinion Research and Assessment
CPI	Consumer Price Index
CSO	Civil Society Organization
DNA	Deoxyribonucleic Acid—in cell nuclei, the molecular basis of heredity in many organisms (chief constituent of chromosomes, responsible for transmitting genetic information)
DSM	Demand-Side Management
ECAAR	Economists Allied for Arms Reduction
ECOSOC	(United Nations) Economic and Social Council
EDP	Environmentally Adjusted Net Domestic Product
EFTS	Electronic Funds Transfer System
EITC	Earned Income Tax Credit
EMS	European Monetary System
EMU	European Monetary Union
ENI	Environmentally Adjusted National Income
ERM	Exchange Rate Mechanism
ESI	Electronic Share Information, Ltd.
ESOP	Employee Stock Ownership Plan

ETM	Electronic Town Meeting
EU	European Union
FCC	Federal Communications Commission
FISD	Framework of Indicators for Sustainable Development
FONDAD	Forum on Debt and Development
FSLIC	Federal Savings and Loan Insurance Corporation
FXE	Foreign Exchange Facility
G-7	Economic Summit countries: United States, Britain, Germany, Italy, Canada, France, and Japan
GACD	General Agreement on Culture and Development
GATT	General Agreement on Tariffs and Trade
GCFUN	Global Commission to Fund the United Nations
GDP	Gross Domestic Product
GED	Generational Environmental Debt
GEF	Global Environment Facility
GNP	Gross National Product
GPI	(United States) 'Genuine' Progress Indicator
GRB	(United States) Global Resource Bank
HDI	Human Development Index
HDN	Human Development Network
IAEA	International Atomic Energy Agency
IATA	International Air Traffic Association
ICDA	International Coalition for Development Action
IEESA	Integrated Economic and Environmental Satellite Accounts
ILO	International Labor Organization (Agency of the UN)
IMF	International Monetary Fund
INGO	International Nongovernmental Organization
INTELSAT	International Telecommunications Satellite
IOSCO	International Organization of Securities Commissions
IPAT	I=PAT; I (Impact) is the product of P (Population size) times A (per capita Affluence) times T (damage done by Technology used to supply each unit of consumption)
IPCC	Intergovernmental Panel on Climate Change
IPU	International Postal Union
ISEW	Index of Sustainable Economic Welfare (Herman Daly and John and Clifford Cobb)
ISP	Index of Social Progress
ITO	International Trade Organization
LETS	Local Exchange Trading System
MEW	Measure of Economic Wealth
NAFTA	North American Free Trade Agreement
NAIRU	Non-Accelerating Inflation Rate of Unemployment
NATO	North Atlantic Treaty Organization
NCO	Noncivil Organization

NGO	Nongovernmental Organization
NIEO	New International Economic Order
NIMBY	Not-in-My-Backyard
ODA	Official Development Assistance
OECD	Organization for Economic Cooperation and Development
OPEC	Organization of Petroleum Exporting Countries
OTA	United States Office of Technology Assessment
PAC	Political Action Committee
PC	Personal Computer
PIN	Personal Identification Number
PPP	Purchasing Power Parity
PQLI	Physical Quality of Life Index
PVO	Private Voluntary Organizations
R&D	Research and Development
S&L	Savings and Loan
SCI	Science Citation Index
SDR	Special Drawing Right
SEC	Securities and Exchange Commission
SEWA	Self-Employed Women's Association
SNA	System of National Accounts
SNI	Sustainable National Income
TNC	Transnational Corporations
TOES	The Other Economic Summit
TRAFTA	Trans-Atlantic Free Trade Agreement
UIO	Union of International Organizations
UN	United Nations
UNA	United Nations Association
UNCTAD	United Nations Commission on Trade and Development
UNDP	United Nations Development Programme
UNEP	United Nations Environment Program
UNESCO	United Nations Economic, Scientific, and Cultural Organization
UNSIA	United Nations Security Insurance Agency
UNSNA	United Nations System of National Accounts
USSR	Union of Soviet Socialist Republics
UWSA	United We Stand America
VAT	Value Added Tax
vBNS	Very High-Speed Backbone Network Service
VET	Value Extracted Tax
WCCD	World Commission on Culture and Development
WEDO	Women's Environment and Development Organization
WHO	World Health Organization
WMO	World Meteorological Organization
WTO	World Trade Organization

BIBLIOGRAPHY

Adamson, Rebecca. n.d. "Indigenous Economics and First Nations," paper for First Nations Development Institute, Fredericksburg, Va.

Arthur, W. Brian. 1994. *Increasing Returns: Path Dependence in the Economy.* Ann Arbor: University of Michigan Press.

Asbell, Bernard. 1995. *The Pill: A Biography of the Drug That Changed the World.* New York: Random House.

Ascher, Marcia. 1991. *Ethnomathematics: A Multicultural View of Mathematical Ideas.* Pacific Grove, Calif.: Brooks/Cole Publishing.

Ascher, Marcia, and Robert Ascher. 1981. *The Code of the Quipu: A Study in Media, Mathematics and Culture.* Ann Arbor: University of Michigan Press.

Axelrod, Robert. 1984. *The Evolution of Cooperation.* New York: Basic Books.

Barber, Benjamin R. 1992. *An Aristocracy of Everyone.* New York: Oxford University Press.

Barnet, Richard, and John Cavanaugh. 1994. *Global Dreams: Imperial Corporations and the New World Order.* New York: Simon & Schuster.

Barney, Gerald O., Jane Blewett, and Kristen R. Barney. 1993. *Global 2000 Revisited: What Shall We Do?* Arlington, Va.: Millennium Institute. Available from the Millennium Institute, 1117 North 19th Street, Suite 900, Arlington, VA 22209.

Bateson, Gregory. 1973. *Steps to an Ecology of Mind.* New York: Ballantine.

Becker, Ernest. 1973. *The Denial of Death.* New York: Free Press.

Bell, Daniel. 1973. *The Coming of Post-Industrial Society.* New York: Basic Books.

Berry, Thomas. 1988. *Dream of the Earth.* San Francisco: Sierra Club Books.

———. 1995. "Fourfold Wisdom," from a work in progress, *Teilhard Perspective,* vol. 28, no. 1 (February).

Bezold, Clement. 1978. *Anticipatory Democracy.* New York: Random House.

Bogdanov, A. 1984. *Essays in Tektology,* trans. G. Gorelik and M. Zeleny of Fordham University. New York: Intersystems Publications.

Borman, F. H., D. Balmore, and G. T. Geballe. 1993. *Redesigning the American Lawn.* New Haven: Yale University Press.

Boston Research Center for the 21st Century. 1995. "The United Nations and the World's Religions: Prospects for a Global Ethic." Proceedings of a conference at Columbia University (October 7). Boston Research Center for the 21st Century, 396 Harvard Street, Cambridge, MA 02138.

Boulding, Elise. 1976. *The Underside of History.* Boulder, Colo.: Westview.

———. 1988. *Building a Global Civic Culture.* New York: Columbia University Press.

Boulding, Kenneth E. 1956. *The Image.* Ann Arbor: University of Michigan Press.

———. 1968. *Beyond Economics.* Ann Arbor: University of Michigan Press.

Boutros-Ghali, Boutros. 1992. *Agenda for Peace: Preventive Diplomacy, Peacemaking and Peacekeeping: Report of the secretary-general pursuant to the statement adopted by the summit meetings of the Security Council on 31 January 1992.* New York: United Nations Publications. 1995 with a new supplement and related UN documents. New York: United Nations Publications.

———. 1995. *An Agenda for Development 1995: With Related UN Documents.* New York: UN Department of Public Information (United Nations Publications Sales E.95.I.16).

Bracho, Frank. 1992. *Toward a New Human Development Paradigm.* Caracas: Better Living Publications.

———. 1992. *Indo-Asiatic Encounters with Ibiro-Americans.* New Delhi: Embassies of Venezuela and New Delhi.

Brandt, Barbara. 1995. *Whole Life Economics.* Philadelphia: New Society.

Braudel, Fernand. 1980. *On History.* Chicago: University of Chicago Press.

———. 1984. *Civilization and Capitalism.* London: William Collins & Sons.

Brook, James, and Iain A. Boal, eds. 1995. *Resisting the Virtual Life: The Culture and Politics of Information.* San Francisco: City Lights.

Brown, Lester, Nicholas Lenssen, and Hal Kane. 1995. *Vital Signs 1995.* New York: W. W. Norton.

Brown, Norman O. 1959. *Life against Death.* Middletown, Conn.: Wesleyan University Press.

Cahn, Edgar, Ph.D., J.D., and Jonathan Rowe. 1992. *Time Dollars.* Emmaus, Pa.: Rodale Press.

Callenbach, Ernest. 1972. *Living Poor with Style.* New York: Bantam.

Callenbach, Ernest, and Michael Phillips. 1985. *A Citizen Legislature.* Berkeley: Banyan Tree Books.

Capra, Fritjof. 1975. *The Tao of Physics.* Berkeley, Calif.: Shambala.

———. 1981. *The Turning Point.* New York: Simon & Schuster.

Carey, Ken. 1988. *Return of the Bird Tribes.* New York: A Uri-Sun Book, distributed by the Talman Company.

Childers, Erskine, and Brian Urquhart. 1990. "A World in Need of Leadership." *Development Dialogue,* vols. 1 and 2. Dag Hammarskjold Foundation, Uppsala, Sweden or the Ford Foundation, 320 E. 43rd St., New York, NY 10017.

———. 1991. "Toward a More Effective United Nations." *Development Dialogue,* vols. 1 and 2. Dag Hammarskjold Foundation, Uppsala, Sweden or the Ford Foundation, 320 E. 43rd St., New York, NY 10017.

Chinese Academy of Sciences, The. 1983. *Ancient China's Technology and Science.* Beijing: The Chinese Academy.

Clark, John. 1990. *Democratizing Development: The Role of Voluntary Organizations.* West Hartford, Conn.: Kumarian Press.

Clark, Mary E. 1989. *Ariadne's Thread: The Search for New Modes of Thinking*. New York: St. Martin's.

Cleveland, Harlan. 1993. *Birth of a New World*. New York: Jossey Bass.

Cleveland, Harlan, Hazel Henderson, and Inge Kaul, eds. 1995. *The United Nations at Fifty: Policy and Financing Alternatives*. Special issue of *FUTURES*, vol. 27, no. 2 (March). Oxford: Elsevier Scientific. Available from the Global Commission to Fund the United Nations, 1511 K Street, N.W., Washington, D.C. 20005 or from The Apex Press, P.O. Box 337, Croton-on-Hudson, NY 10520, 1-800-316-2739; $12.95.

Commission on Global Governance. 1995. *Our Global Neighborhood*. London: Oxford University Press.

Commoner, Barry. 1971. *The Closing Circle*. New York: Knopf.

Cronin, Thomas E. 1989. *Direct Democracy: The Politics of Initiative, Referendum and Recall*. Cambridge: Harvard University Press.

Daly, Herman, and John B. Cobb, Jr. 1989. *For the Common Good*. Boston: Beacon.

Daly, Mary. 1984. *Pure Lust*. Boston: Beacon.

Dean, Jonathan. 1994. *Ending Europe's Wars: The Continuing Search for Place and Security*. New York: Twentieth Century Fund Press.

Deane, Marjorie, and Robert Pringle. 1994. *The Central Banks*. New York: Viking.

Dickson, David. 1974. *Alternative Technology*. Glasgow: Fontana.

Dieren, Wouter van, ed. 1995. *Taking Nature into Account*. New York: Springer-Verlag.

Dominguez, Joe, and Vicki Robins. 1992. *Your Money or Your Life*. New York: Viking.

Douthwaite, Richard. 1993. *The Growth Illusion: How Economic Growth Has Enriched the Few, Impoverished the Many and Endangered the Planet*. Tulsa, Okla.: Council Oak Books.

Durning, Alan T. 1992. *How Much Is Enough?* New York: W. W. Norton.

Easterbrook, Gregg. 1995. *A Moment on Earth: The Coming Age of Environmental Optimism*. New York: Viking.

Eisler, Riane. 1988. *The Chalice and the Blade*. New York: Harper & Row.

———. 1995. *Sacred Pleasure: Sex, Myth and the Politics of the Body*. San Francisco: Harper.

Elgin, Duane. 1981. *Voluntary Simplicity: Toward a Way of Life That Is Outwardly Simple, Inwardly Rich*. New York: Morrow.

———. 1993. *Awakening Earth: Exploring the Dimensions of Human Evolution*. New York: Morrow.

Elmanjdra, Mahdi. 1992. *Premiere Tuerre Civilisationnelle*. Casablanca, Morocco: Les Editions Toubkal.

Environment and Urbanization. 1995. "Urban Poverty: Characteristics, Causes and Consequences," vol. 7, no. 1 (April).

Erickson, Eric H. 1969. *Gandhi's Truth*. New York: W. W. Norton.

Estes, Richard J. 1988. *Trends in World Social Development: The Social Progress of Nations, 1970–1987.* New York: Praeger.

Everett, Melissa. 1995. *Making a Living While Making a Difference: A Guide to Creating Careers with a Conscience.* New York: Bantam.

Fisher, Roger, and William Ury. 1991. *Getting to Yes.* New York: Penguin.

French, Hilary. 1995. *Partnership for the Planet: An Environmental Agenda for the UN.* Washington, D.C.: Worldwatch Institute.

Fuller, R. Buckminster. 1981. *Critical Path.* New York: St. Martin's.

Galbraith, John Kenneth. 1958. *The Affluent Society.* Boston: Houghton Mifflin.

Giarini, Orio, and Henri Louberge. 1979. *The Diminishing Returns to Technology.* London: Pergamon.

Gimbutas, Marija. 1989. *The Language of the Goddess.* San Francisco: Harper & Row.

Goldsmith, Edward. 1988. *The Great U-Turn: De-Centralizing Society.* New York: Published in North America by Bootstrap Press, an imprint of the Intermediate Technology Development Group of North America.

Goldsmith, Edward, ed. 1972. *Blueprint for Survival.* Boston: Houghton Mifflin.

Goswami, Amit. 1995. *The Self-Aware Universe: How Consciousness Creates the Material World.* New York: Tarcher Putnam.

Gray, Rob, Jan Bebbington, and Diane Walters. 1993. *Accounting for the Environment: The Greening of Accountancy.* London: Paul Chapman.

Greco, Thomas H., Jr. 1990. *Money and Debt.* Tucson, Ariz.: Thomas H. Greco, Jr., Publisher. Available from Thomas H. Greco, Jr., P.O. Box 42663, Tucson, AZ 85733.

———. 1994. *New Money for Healthy Communities.* Tucson: Thomas H. Greco.

Greenberg, Jonathan, and William Kistler, eds. 1992. *Buying America Back: Economic Choices for the 1990s.* Tulsa, Okla.: Council Oak Books.

Greider, William. 1987. *The Secrets of the Temple.* New York: Simon & Schuster.

Greve, Michael S., and Fred L. Smith, Jr., eds. 1992. *Environmental Politics: Public Costs, Private Rewards.* New York: Praeger.

Griesgraber, Jo Marie, ed. 1994. *Rethinking Bretton Woods.* Washington, D.C.: Center of Concern. 1995. London: Pluto Press.

Gross, Ronald. 1982. *The Independent Scholar's Handbook: How to Turn Your Interest in Any Subject into Expertise.* Reading, Mass.: Addison Wesley.

Haq, Mahbub ul. 1995. *Reflections on Human Development.* London: Oxford University Press.

Harcourt, Wendy, ed. 1994. *Feminist Perspectives on Sustainable Development.* London: Zed Books.

Heilbroner, Robert. 1974. *An Inquiry into the Human Prospect.* New York: W. W. Norton.

Heinberg, Richard. 1989. *Memories and Visions of Paradise: Exploring the Universal Myth of a Lost Golden Age*. Los Angeles: Tarcher.

Heisenberg, Werner. 1971. *Physics and Beyond*. New York: Harper Torchbook.

Henderson, Hazel. 1978. *Creating Alternative Futures: The End of Economics*. New York: Putnam's. 1996. West Hartford, Conn.: Kumarian Press.

―――. 1981. *The Politics of the Solar Age: Alternatives to Economics*. Garden City, N.Y.: Anchor/Doubleday. 1988. Indianapolis: Knowledge Systems. Available from The Apex Press, P.O. Box 337, Croton-on-Hudson, NY 10520, 1-800-316-2739.

―――. 1991. *Paradigms in Progress: Life Beyond Economics*. Indianapolis: Knowledge Systems. 1995. San Francisco: Berrett-Koehler.

Horney, Karen. 1937. *The Neurotic Personality of Our Time*. New York: W. W. Norton.

Houston, Jean. 1980. *Life Force: The Psycho-Historical Recovery of the Self*. New York: Dell Publishing Co. 1993. Wheaton, Ill.: Quest.

―――. 1982. *The Possible Human*. Los Angeles: Tarcher.

Hubbard, Barbara Marx. 1982. *The Evolutionary Journey*. San Francisco: Evolutionary Press.

―――. 1993. *The Revelation: Our Crisis Is a Birth*. The Foundation for Conscious Evolution, P.O. Box 1491, Sonoma, CA 95476.

Hussein, Aziza. 1994. "The ICPD: Another Triumph for NGOs," *Ru' ya*, newsletter published by the Institute of Cultural Affairs―Middle East and North Africa, no. 5 (autumn).

Hyde, Lewis. 1979. *The Gift*. New York: Vintage.

Illich, Ivan. 1974. *Energy and Equity*. New York: Harper & Row.

Inglehart, Ronald. 1977. *The Silent Revolution*. Princeton: Princeton University Press.

Innes, Harold. 1950. *The Bias of Communication*. Toronto: University of Toronto.

Institute for Advanced Study. 1990. *Redefining Wealth and Progress: The Caracas Report on Alternative Development Indicators*. New York: Bootstrap Press. Available from The Apex Press, P.O. Box 337, Croton-on-Hudson, NY 10520, 1-800-316-2739.

Institute of Cultural Affairs―Middle East and North Africa. 1995. "Politics and Development." Thematic issue of *Ru' ya*, newsletter published by the Institute, no. 6 (winter).

Interfaith Center on Corporate Responsibility. 1995. *Principles for Global Corporate Responsibility: Benchmarks for Measuring Business Performance*. Special issue of *The Corporate Examiner*, vol. 24, nos. 2–4 (September). Interfaith Center on Corporate Responsibility, 475 Riverside Drive, Room 566, New York, NY 10015.

Johnson, Huey D., foreword by David R. Brower. 1995. *Green Plans: Greenprint for Sustainability*. Lincoln, Neb.: University of Nebraska Press.

Johnson, Nicholas. 1970. *How to Talk Back to Your TV Set*. Boston: Little Brown.

Joshi, Nandini. 1992. *Development without Destruction*. Ahmedabad, India: Navajiran Publishing House.

Kelso, Louis O., and Patricia Hetter. 1967. *Two-Factor Theory: The Economics of Reality*. N.Y.: Vintage.

———. 1991. *Democracy and Economic Power*. Lanham, N.Y. and London: University Press of America.

Kennard, Byron. 1982. *Nothing Can Be Done: Everything Is Possible*. Andover, Mass.: Brickhouse Publishers.

Keuls, Eva. 1985. *Reign of the Phallus*. New York: Harper & Row.

Keynes, John Maynard. 1934. *The General Theory of Employment, Interest and Money*. New York: Harcourt Brace.

Kohn, Alfie. 1986. *No Contest*. New York: Houghton Mifflin.

Korten, David. 1995. *When Corporations Rule the World*. San Francisco: Berrett-Koehler.

Krugman, Paul. 1994. *Peddling Prosperity*. New York: W. W. Norton.

Kuhn, Thomas. 1962. *The Structure of Scientific Revolutions*. Chicago: University of Chicago Press.

Kurjo, Sabine, and Ian McNeill. 1988. *Only Connect*. London: Turning Points.

Lappé, Frances Moore. 1971. *Diet for a Small Planet*. New York: Ballantine.

Lasch, Christopher. 1995. *The Revolt of the Elite*. New York: W. W. Norton.

Laszlo, Ervin. 1991. *The New Evolutionary Paradigm*. New York: Gordon and Breach Science Publishers.

———. 1994. *The Choice: Evolution or Extinction?* New York: Tarcher Putnam.

Lemkow, Anna F. 1990. *The Wholeness Principle: Dynamics of Unity within Science, Religion and Society*. Wheaton, Ill.: Quest.

Lewin, Kurt. 1948. *Resolving Social Conflicts*. New York: Harper & Row.

Lewin, Roger. 1992. *Complexity: Life at the Edge of Chaos*. New York: Macmillan.

Lind, Michael. 1995. *The Next American Nation: A New Nationalism and the Fourth American Revolution*. New York: Free Press.

Linder, Staffan. 1970. *The Harried Leisure Class*. New York: Columbia University Press.

Lipnack, Jessica, and Jeffrey Stamps. 1982. *Networking*. New York: Doubleday.

Loye, David. 1971. *The Healing of a Nation*. New York: W. W. Norton.

Lux, Kenneth. 1990. *Adam Smith's Mistake*. New York: Random House.

Mander, Jerry. 1978. *Four Arguments for the Elimination of Television*. New York: Morrow.

———. 1991. *In the Absence of the Sacred*. San Francisco: Sierra Club Books.

Maslow, Abraham. 1962. *Toward a Psychology of Being*. Princeton: Van Nostrand.

McLuhan, Marshall. 1951. *The Mechanical Bride*. New York: Vanguard Press.

———. 1966. *Understanding Media*. New York: McGraw-Hill.

Meeker-Lowry, Susan. 1995. *Invested for the Common Good*. Philadelphia: New Society Publishers.

Mele, Andrew. 1993. *Polluting for Pleasure*. New York: W. W. Norton.

Mellor, Mary. 1992. *Breaking the Boundaries*. London: Virago.

Mendez, Ruben. 1992. *International Public Finance: A New Perspective on Global Relations*. New York: Oxford University Press.

Miller, Morris. 1986. *Coping Is Not Enough*. Homewood, Ill.: Dow Jones-Irwin.

———. 1991. *Debt and Environment: Converging Crises*. New York: United Nations Press.

Millman, Gregory. 1995. *The Vandals' Crown: How the World's Currency Traders Beat the Central Banks*. New York: Viking.

Mills, Stephanie. 1995. *Ecological Restoration: In Service of the Wild*. Boston: Beacon Press.

Mitchell, Ralph A., and Neil Shafer. 1984. *Depression Scrip of the United States*. Iola, Wis.: Krause Publications.

Møller, J. Ørstrøm. 1995. *The Future European Model: Economic Internationalization and Cultural Decentralization*. Westport, Conn.: Praeger/Greenwood.

Mumford, Lewis. 1966. *The Myth of the Machine*. New York: Harcourt Brace Jovanovich.

Nabhan, Gary Paul. 1982. *The Desert Smells Like Rain: A Naturalist in Papago Indian Country*. San Francisco: North Point.

Naisbitt, John. 1994. *Global Paradox: The Bigger the World Economy, the More Powerful Its Smallest Players*. New York: Morrow.

Norberg-Hodge, Helena. 1991. *Ancient Futures: Learning from Ladakh*. San Francisco: Sierra Club Books.

Norris, Russel B. 1995. *Creation, Cosmology, and the Cosmic Christ: Teleological Implications of the Anthropic Cosmological Principle*. Teilhard Studies, no. 31, published by the American Teilhard Association (spring).

Norwood, Janet L. 1995. "Organizing to Count: Change in the Federal Statistical System." The Urban Institute Press, 2100 M Street N.W., Washington, D.C. 20037.

Olds, Linda E. 1981. *Fully Human*. New York: Spectrum Books, Prentice Hall.

Olsen, Mancur. 1965. *The Logic of Collective Action*. Cambridge: Harvard University Press.

Oliveira, Miguel Darcy de, and Rajesh Tandon, coordinators. 1994. *Citizens: Strengthening Global Civil Society*. Washington, D.C.: CIVICUS.

Owen, Dave, ed. 1992. *Green Reporting: Accounting and the Challenge of the 90's*. London: Chapman and Hall.

Packard, Vance. 1957. *The Hidden Persuaders*. New York: D. McKay Co.

———. 1959. *The Status Seekers*. New York: D. McKay Co.

———. 1960. *The Wastemakers*. New York: D. McKay Co.

Peterson, Peter G. 1994. *Facing Up: Paying Our Nation's Debt and Saving Our Children's Future*. New York: Simon & Schuster.

Phillips, Kevin. 1994. *Arrogant Capital: Washington, Wall Street and the Frustrations of American Politics*. Boston: Little Brown.

Pierson, Paul. 1995. *Dismantling the Welfare State*. Cambridge: Cambridge University Press.

Pietila, Hilkka, and Jeanne Vickers. 1990. *Making Women Matter: The Role of the United Nations*. London: Zed Books.

Polanyi, Karl. 1944. *The Great Transformation*. Boston: Beacon.

Postman, Neil. 1985. *Amusing Ourselves to Death*. New York: Viking.

———. 1992. *Technopoly*. New York: Knopf.

Potter, David M. 1954. *People of Plenty*. Chicago: University of Chicago Press.

Reder, Alan. 1995. *Seventy-Five Best Practices for Socially Responsible Companies*. New York: Tarcher Putnam.

Renner, Michael. 1994. *Budgeting for Disarmament: The Costs of War and Peace*. Washington, D.C.: Worldwatch Institute.

Rich, Bruce. 1994. *Mortgaging the Future*. Boston: Beacon.

Riesman, David. 1950. *The Lonely Crowd: A Study of the Changing American Character*. New Haven: Yale University Press.

Rifkin, Jeremy. 1989. *Entropy: Into the Greenhouse World*. Rev. ed. New York: Bantam.

———. 1995. *The End of Work: The Decline of the Global Labor Force and the Dawn of the Post-Market Era*. New York: Putnam.

Rifkin, Jeremy, and Ted Howard. 1977. *Who Shall Play God?: The Artificial Creation of Life and What It Means for the Future of the Human Race*. New York: Delacorte.

Rifkin, Jeremy, in collaboration with Nicnor Perlas. 1984. *Algeny*. New York: Penguin.

Rinpoche, Sogyal. 1992. *The Tibetan Book of Living and Dying*. San Francisco: Harper.

Robertson, James. 1976. *Power, Money and Sex: Toward a New Social Balance*. London: M. Boyars.

Robins, Vicki. *All-Consuming Passion: Waking Up from the American Dream*. New Road Map Foundation, P.O. Box 15981, Seattle, WA 98115.

Rostow, Walt W. [1960] 1991. *Stages of Economic Growth: A Non-Communist Manifesto*. Reprint. Cambridge: Cambridge University Press.

Roszak, Theodore. 1972. *Where the Wasteland Ends: Politics and Transcendence in Post-Industrial Society*. Garden City, N.J.: Doubleday.

———. 1994. *The Cult of Information: A Neo-Luddite Treatise on High-Tech, Artificial Intelligence and the True Art of Thinking*. Berkeley: University of California Press.

Rothschild, Michael. 1990. *Bionomics: The Inevitability of Capitalism*. New York: Henry Holt.

Roxas, Sixto. 1987. *Community-Based Organization and Management Technology*. Manila: SKR Managers and Advisors, Inc.

Sahlins, Marshall. 1972. *Stone Age Economics.* Hawthorne, N.Y.: Aldine de Gruyter.

Sale, Kirkpatrick. 1990. *The Conquest of Paradise.* New York: Knopf.

Sardar, Ziauddin. 1977. *Science, Technology and Development in the Muslim World.* London: Croom Helm.

———. 1988. *The Revenge of Athena: Science, Exploitation and the Third World.* London and New York: Mansell Publishing Limited.

Schafer, D. Paul. 1994. "Cultures and Economies: Irresistible Forces Encounter Immovable Objects," *Futures,* vol. 26, no. 8.

Schor, Juliet B. 1991. *The Overworked American: The Unexpected Decline of Leisure.* New York: Basic Books.

Schumacher, E. F. 1973. *Small Is Beautiful.* New York: Harper & Row.

Schwartz, James D. 1993. *Enough: A Guide to Reclaiming Your American Dream.* Englewood, Colo.: Labrador.

Sheldrake, Rupert. 1995. *Seven Experiments That Could Change the World: A Do-It-Yourself Guide to Revolutionary Science.* New York: River Head Books, Putnam.

Sherraden, Michael. 1989. "The Policy: Making the Case for an Asset Base," *Entrepreneurial Economic Review* (Nov./Dec.).

Shiva, Vandana. 1989. *Staying Alive.* London and Atlantic Highlands, N.J.: Zed Books.

Sivard, Ruth Leger. 1991. *World Military and Social Expenditures.* 14th ed. Washington, D.C.: World Priorities Inc.

Skidelsky, Robert. 1994. *John Maynard Keynes. Volume Two: The Economist as Savior, 1920–1937.* Bergenfield, N.J.: Viking/Penguin.

———. 1995. *The World after Communism.* London: Macmillan.

Skinner, B. F. 1971. *Beyond Freedom and Dignity.* New York: Bantam.

Slayton, Christa Daryl. 1992. *Televote: Expanding Citizen Participation in the Quantum Age.* New York: Praeger.

Smith, Adam. [1776] 1976. *An Inquiry into the Nature and Causes of the Wealth of Nations.* Edited by Edwin Cannan, two volumes in one. Chicago: University of Chicago Press.

Solomon, Steven. 1995. *The Confidence Game: How Unelected Central Bankers Are Governing the Changed World Economy.* New York: Simon & Schuster.

Soros, George. 1995. *Soros on Soros: Staying Ahead of the Curve.* New York: John Wiley.

South Commission. 1990. *Challenge to the South.* London and New York: Oxford University Press.

Steinem, Gloria. 1994. *Moving Beyond Words.* New York: Simon & Schuster.

Stoll, Clifford. 1995. *Silicon Snake Oil: Second Thoughts on the Information Highway.* New York: Doubleday.

Tainter, Joseph. 1988. *The Collapse of Complex Societies.* New York: Cambridge University Press.

Tapscott, Don, and Art Caston. 1992. *Paradigm Shift*. New York: McGraw Hill.

Terry, Roger. 1995. *Economic Insanity*. San Francisco: Berrett-Koehler.

Thayer, Fred. [1973] 1981. *An End to Hierarchy: An End to Competition*. Franklin Watts, N.Y.: New Viewpoints.

Theobald, Robert. 1968. *Committed Spending*. New York: Anchor Doubleday.

Thompson, William Irwin. 1973. *Passages about Earth*. New York: Harper & Row.

———. 1981. *The Time Falling Bodies Take to Light*. New York: St. Martin's.

———. 1991. *The American Replacement of Nature*. New York: Doubleday-Currency.

———. ed. 1987. *GAIA: A Way of Knowing*. Great Barrington, Mass.: Lindisfarne Press.

Tocqueville, Alexis de. [1835] 1969. *Democracy in America*. Garden City, N.Y.: Doubleday.

Toffler, Alvin. 1970. *Future Shock*. New York: Random House.

———. 1980. *The Third Wave*. New York: Morrow.

Toffler, Alvin, and Heidi Toffler. 1993. *War and Anti-War*, Boston: Little, Brown & Co.

———. 1995. *Creating a New Civilization: The Politics of the Third Wave*. Atlanta: Turner.

Tryzna, Thaddeus, and Roberta Childers, comps. 1992. *World Directory of Environmental Organizations*. Sacramento: California Institute of Public Affairs.

Union of International Organizations. 1994. *Encyclopedia of World Problems and Human Potential*. 4th ed. A two volume series. Munich, New York: K. G. Saur.

United Nations High Commissioner for Refugees. 1995. *Refugees II: Focus, Refugee Women*. Geneva: United Nations High Commissioner for Refugees (UNHCR).

United Nations University, The. 1985. *The Science and Praxis of Complexity*. Contributions to the symposium held at Montpellier, France (May 9–11, 1984).

Vernon, Raymond, and Debora Spar. 1989. *Beyond Globalism: Remaking American Foreign Policy*. New York: Macmillan Free Press.

Von Sonn, Andrew. 1984. *The Money Rebellion*. P.O. Box 1136, Venice, California 90291.

Wachtel, Howard M. 1990. *The Money Mandarins*. New York: M. E. Sharp.

Wallerstein, Emmanuel. 1991. *Un-Thinking Social Science: The Limits of Nineteenth Century Paradigms*. Cambridge, U.K.: Polity Press.

Ward, Barbara. 1966. *Spaceship Earth*. New York: Columbia University Press.

Waring, Marilyn. 1988. *If Women Counted*. San Francisco: Harper Collins.

Weisbord, Marvin R., and Sandra Janoff. 1995. *Future Search: An Action Guide to Finding Common Ground in Organizations and Communities*. San Francisco: Berrett-Koehler.

Weisskopf, Walter A. 1971. *Alienation and Economics*. New York: Dutton.

Weizsäcker, Ernst Ulrich von, and Jochen Jesinghaus. 1992. *Ecological Tax Reform*. London: Zed Books.

Wilber, Ken. 1981. *Up from Eden: A Transpersonal View of Human Evolution*. Garden City, N.Y.: Anchor/Doubleday.

———. 1985. *The Spectrum of Consciousness*. Wheaton, Ill.: Quest.

World Business Council for Sustainable Development. 1992. *Changing Course: A Global Business Perspective on Development and the Environment*. Cambridge: MIT Press.

———. 1996. *Financing Change*. Cambridge: MIT Press.

World Commission on Environment and Development. 1987. *Our Common Future*. New York and London: Oxford University Press.

Wub-E-Ke-Niew. 1995. *We Have the Right to Exist*. New York: Black Thistle.

Zachariah, Mathew, and R. Sooryemoorthy. 1994. *Science in Participatory Development*. London and Atlantic Highlands, N.J.: Zed Books.

Zaslavsky, Claudia. 1973. *Africa Counts*. Boston: Prindle, Webber and Schmidt.

Zohar, Danah, and Ian Marshall. 1994. *The Quantum Society: Mind, Physics and a New Social Vision*. New York: Morrow.

ABOUT THE AUTHOR

HAZEL HENDERSON is an independent futurist, syndicated columnist, and consultant on sustainable development in over thirty countries. Her editorial columns are syndicated by InterPress Service worldwide. She has published articles in over 250 journals, magazines, and newspapers including *The Harvard Business Review, The New York Times, Newsweek, U.S. News and World Report, The Christian Science Monitor, Mainichi* (Japan), *El Diario* (Venezuela), *Australian Financial Review,* and *World Economic Herald* (China). Her books have been translated into German, Spanish, Japanese, Dutch, Portuguese, Korean, Swedish, and Chinese. The first version of her Country Futures Indicators™ (an alternative to gross national product) launched in 1996 as a coventure with the Calvert Group, Inc., as the Calvert-Henderson Quality-of-Life Indicators.

Henderson serves on the boards of many organizations, including the Calvert Social Investment Fund, the Cousteau Society, the Council on Economic Priorities, and the Worldwatch Institute. She also serves on several editorial boards, including *WorldPaper* (an insert in twenty-five newspapers distributed in Asia, Latin America, China, Japan, Russia, Africa, and the Middle East), *Futures Research Quarterly,* and *Futures* (U.K.). She served on the World Business Council for Sustainable Development Task Force on Eco-Efficiency in Global Capital Markets (Geneva) and is a fellow of the World Business Academy. Henderson also serves on the Global Commission to Fund the United Nations and coedited its first report (with Harlan Cleveland and Inge Kaul) as a special issue of *Futures,* "The United Nations at Fifty: Policy and Financing Alternatives" (Elsevier Scientific Ltd., U.K., March 1995). She has been a Regent's Lecturer at the University of California (Santa Barbara), held the Horace

Albright Chair in Conservation at the University of California (Berkeley), and served on the U.S. Congressional Office of Technology Assessment Advisory Council from 1974 to 1980. She is a member of the Social Venture Network, the National Press Club, the World Future Society, and the World Futures Studies Federation.

Other books by Hazel Henderson are *Creating Alternative Futures* (1978, 1996), *The Politics of the Solar Age* (1981, 1988), and *Paradigms in Progress* (1991, 1995), and co-edited volumes, *Redefining Wealth and Progress* (1990) and *The United Nations: Policy and Financing Alternatives* (1995, 1996).